HISTORIC PHOTOS OF MINNEAPOLIS

TEXT AND CAPTIONS BY
HEATHER BLOCK LAWTON

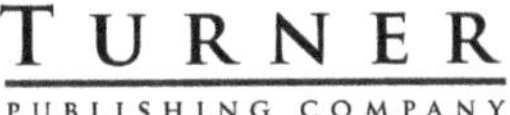
TURNER
PUBLISHING COMPANY

The Stone Arch Bridge, depicted here around 1900, spans the Mississippi just below St. Anthony Falls. The bridge provided the means for trains to reach the mill district. Built in 1882–1883 and financed by railroad magnate James J. Hill, the bridge stands 82 feet above the water below.

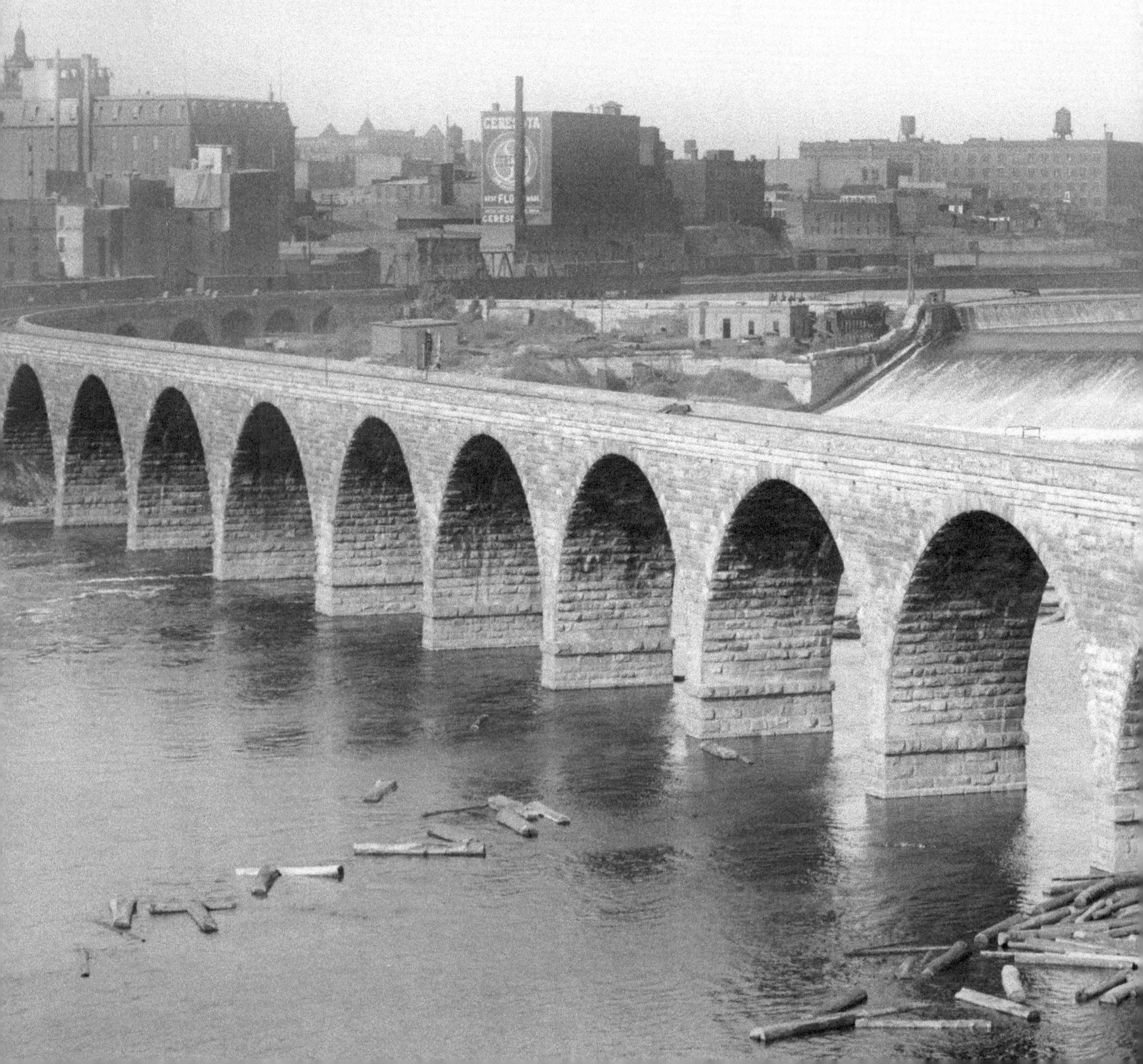

HISTORIC PHOTOS OF MINNEAPOLIS

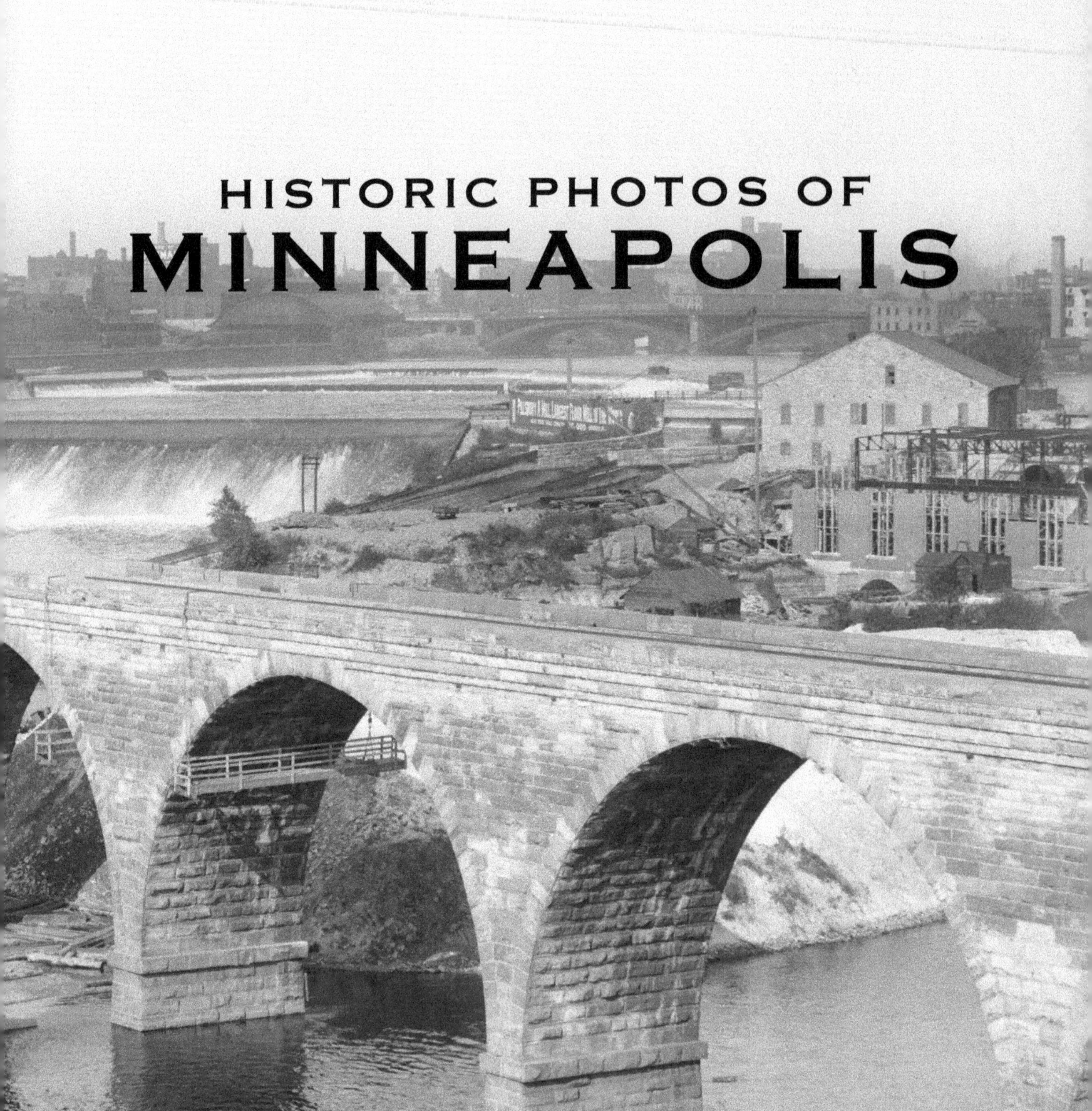

Turner Publishing Company
www.turnerpublishing.com

Historic Photos of Minneapolis

Library of Congress Control Number: 2006937080

ISBN-13: 978-1-59652-328-9
ISBN: 1-59652-328-X

Printed in the United States of America

ISBN 978-1-68336-942-4 (hc)

Contents

The Hotel Leamington, founded in 1912 and seen here in 1962, specialized in housing convention attendees. For decades the Minnesota Democratic-Farmer-Labor Party used the hotel as a home base while awaiting results on election nights. In 1990 the hotel was razed and the lot rebuilt as a parking ramp.

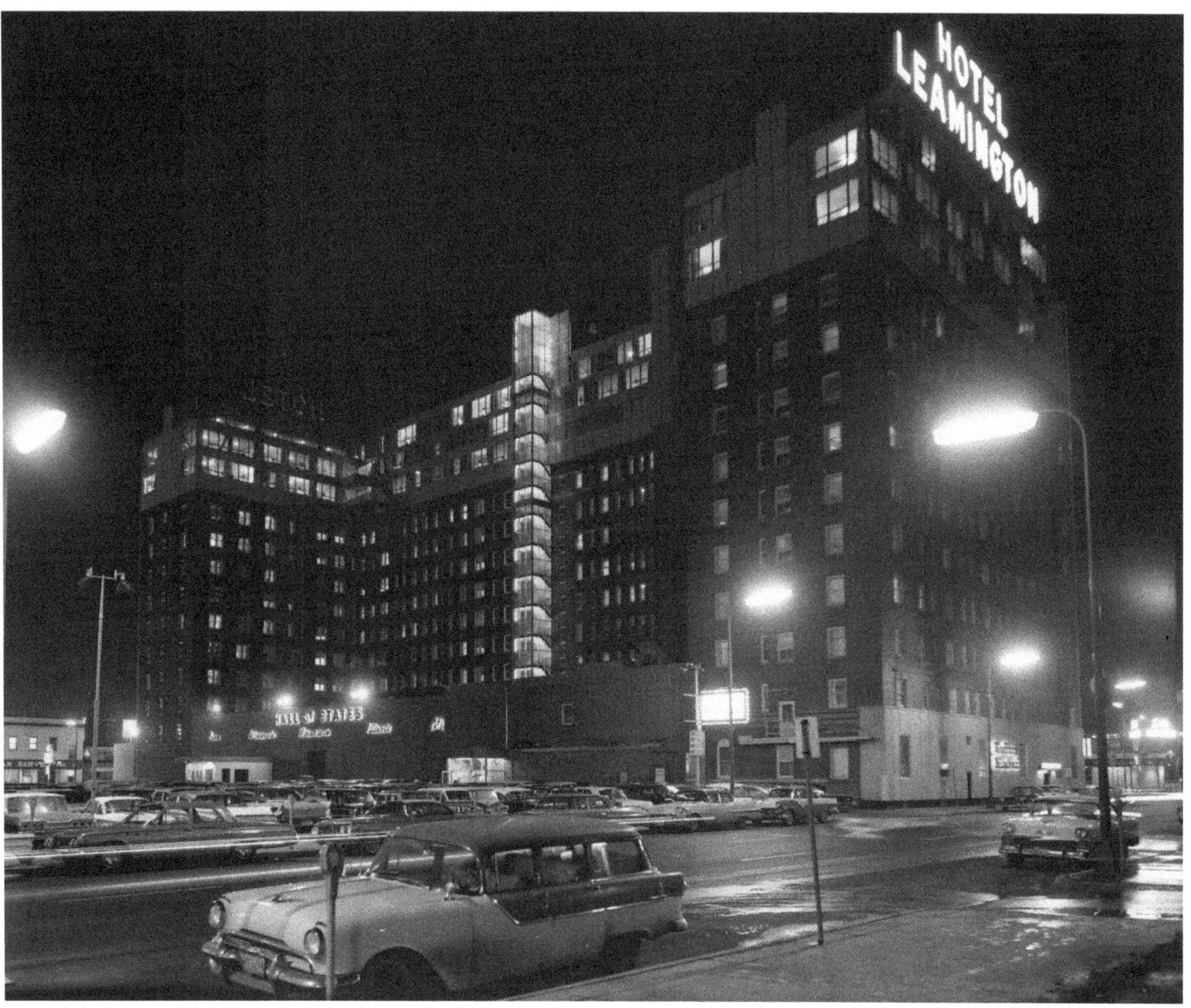

Acknowledgments

Heather Block Lawton wishes to thank photographer Rachel McFarland for providing her headshot and John Lawton for countless hours spent proofreading and offering editorial advice. She also thanks Renee Willkom, Katie Weiblen, Marla Siegler, and Wendy Adamson.

This volume, *Historic Photos of Minneapolis,* is the result of the cooperation and efforts of many individuals and organizations. It is with great thanks that we acknowledge the valuable contribution of the Minneapolis Public Library and the Minnesota Historical Society for their generous support. We would also like to thank Heather Block Lawton, our writer, for valuable contributions and assistance in making this work possible.

The goal in publishing this work is to provide broader access to a set of extraordinary photographs. The aim is to inspire, provide perspective, and evoke insight that might assist officials and citizens, who together are responsible for determining Minneapolis's future. In addition, the book seeks to preserve the past with respect and reverence.

With the exception of touching up imperfections caused by the vicissitudes of time and cropping where necessary, no other changes have been made. The focus and clarity of many images is limited to the technology of the day and the skill of the photographer who captured them.

We encourage readers to reflect as they explore Minneapolis, stroll along its streets, or wander its neighborhoods. It is the publisher's hope that in making use of this work, longtime residents will learn something new and that new residents will gain a perspective on where Minneapolis has been, so that each can contribute to its future.

—Todd Bottorff, Publisher

Preface

How does one tell the story of a city? Is it possible to say anything definitive about a place that is characterized by impermanence? Buildings rise and fall, the landscape is altered, and residents move on or pass away. The story itself is impossibly fragmented, scattered among dusty documents and residing in the individual memories of each person who has maintained a connection to the place. The act of weaving a coherent narrative from such a disjointed jumble of facts and impressions and recollections presents a daunting task.

Photographs are a valuable tool in the quest to understand the past. They permit us to visualize history, if only for one second in time, so that it might be studied. They are a tangible way to gain access to distant moments in time, and they possess a unique power to jog our collective memory. When grouped together, photographic images acquire a special potency and they allow the city to speak for itself. The information they transmit about the reality of place and time goes well beyond the scope of information that mere language can convey.

The photographs in this book are grouped into four chronological divisions. The first section, which covers the years 1850 to 1899, examines the explosive growth that characterized Minneapolis in the last half of the nineteenth century. The milling industry and the jobs it spawned drew both adventuresome spirits and workers desperate for a decent wage from the East Coast and from abroad. These settlers built the city in a startlingly short time. By the beginning of the twentieth century, Minneapolis had undergone a remarkable transformation from backwater military outpost and mission territory to leading American city.

The second section, spanning the years 1900 to 1920, chronicles the city's continued growth and dizzying rate of expansion. All the familiar trappings of modern urban life—streets and sidewalks, public transportation and department stores, parks and theaters—gained a firm foothold in Minneapolis during these two hectic decades.

During the third period of Minneapolis's history represented in this book's photographs, the years 1921 to 1946, the city lurched wildly between extremes. Like all American cities, Minneapolis found itself caught in the wake of economic

and political forces far beyond local control. Minneapolis basked in the optimism and opulence of the 1920s, endured the depression and scarcity that characterized the 1930s, and finally benefited from the economic upswing ushered in by the Second World War.

The familiar theme of change played a major role in the final period addressed by this work. Between the close of World War II and the dawn of the 1970s, Minneapolis radically restructured its downtown and connected itself to the rest of the country via a complex network of highways and interstates. These changes altered both the physical and the social landscape of the city and set the stage for the city's continued development into the next century.

The first Hennepin Avenue suspension bridge, designed by the engineer Thomas M. Griffith and completed in 1855, connected Minneapolis to Nicollet Island.

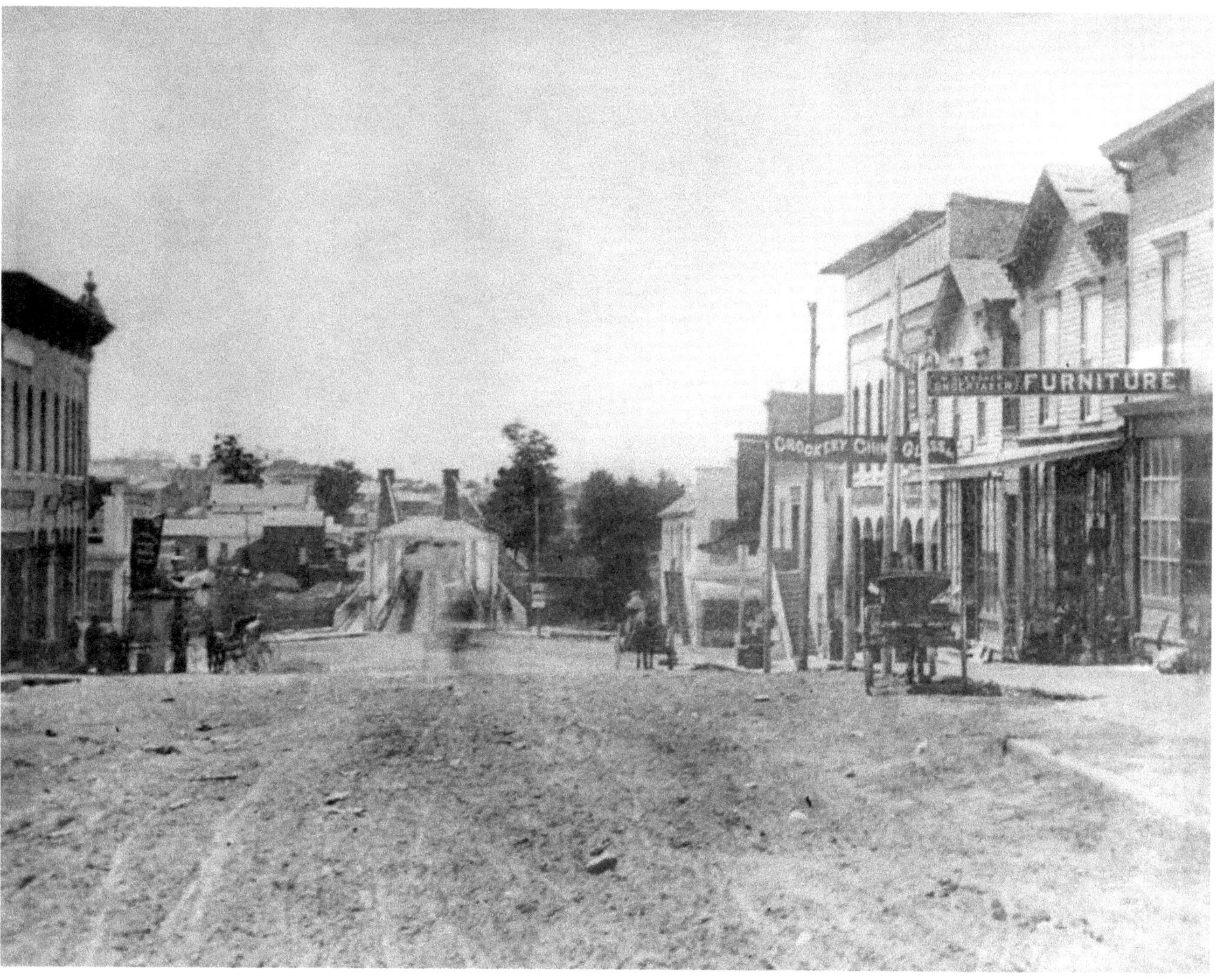

Rise of the Mill City

(1850–1899)

In 1850 Colonel John H. Stevens built the first permanent settlement on the west bank of the Mississippi River where Minneapolis would soon emerge. By 1856 the newly incorporated Town of Minneapolis had witnessed the beginning of a dramatic era of growth. The population ballooned to nearly 2,000 at the end of 1857 and these new residents erected a total of almost five hundred new houses and businesses. In 1868 the town was formally upgraded to a city, and in 1872 Minneapolis subsumed its neighbor across the river, the City of St. Anthony. At the close of the nineteenth century Minneapolis claimed more than 200,000 residents and its population eclipsed that of its twin, the capital city of St. Paul. Within the space of five decades the once quiet frontier outpost became the nineteenth-largest city in the United States.

The word *Minneapolis* derives from the Dakota name for water, "mine," and the Greek word for city, "polis." It is an appropriate moniker for a city that owes its existence to the Mississippi River. Minneapolis rises at the site of the only significant waterfall to be found along the Mississippi's 2,200-mile course. This waterfall, St. Anthony Falls, powered the sawmilling industry that economically sustained Minneapolis during its early history. Millions of felled pine trees were floated down the river from the state's northern forests to Minneapolis, where they were cut into boards and subsequently sent by a rapidly expanding network of railroads throughout the Midwest. The mills provided employment for the thousands of new residents who flocked to the city during this period.

When Minnesota's northern forests were depleted, Minneapolis turned its attention from lumber to flour milling. Beginning in 1880 the power produced at St. Anthony Falls propelled the growth of companies such as Minneapolis Milling Company (later General Mills) and Pillsbury. Minneapolis was dubbed the "Mill City" and soon led the nation in flour production.

Minneapolis's growing population spurred the development of the city's infrastructure and social institutions. In 1857 five churches and a school were built to accommodate the city's residents. That same year Edward Murphy donated land for the city's first park. In 1871 Minneapolis's first hospital opened in a rented house, and in 1875 a horse-drawn streetcar system commenced operations along the ungraded and unpaved streets of Minneapolis.

First National Bank, which grew from a private bank that opened in 1857, became in 1864 the first bank in Minneapolis to receive a national charter. It occupied many locations throughout its long history including this site at the corner of Nicollet and Washington.

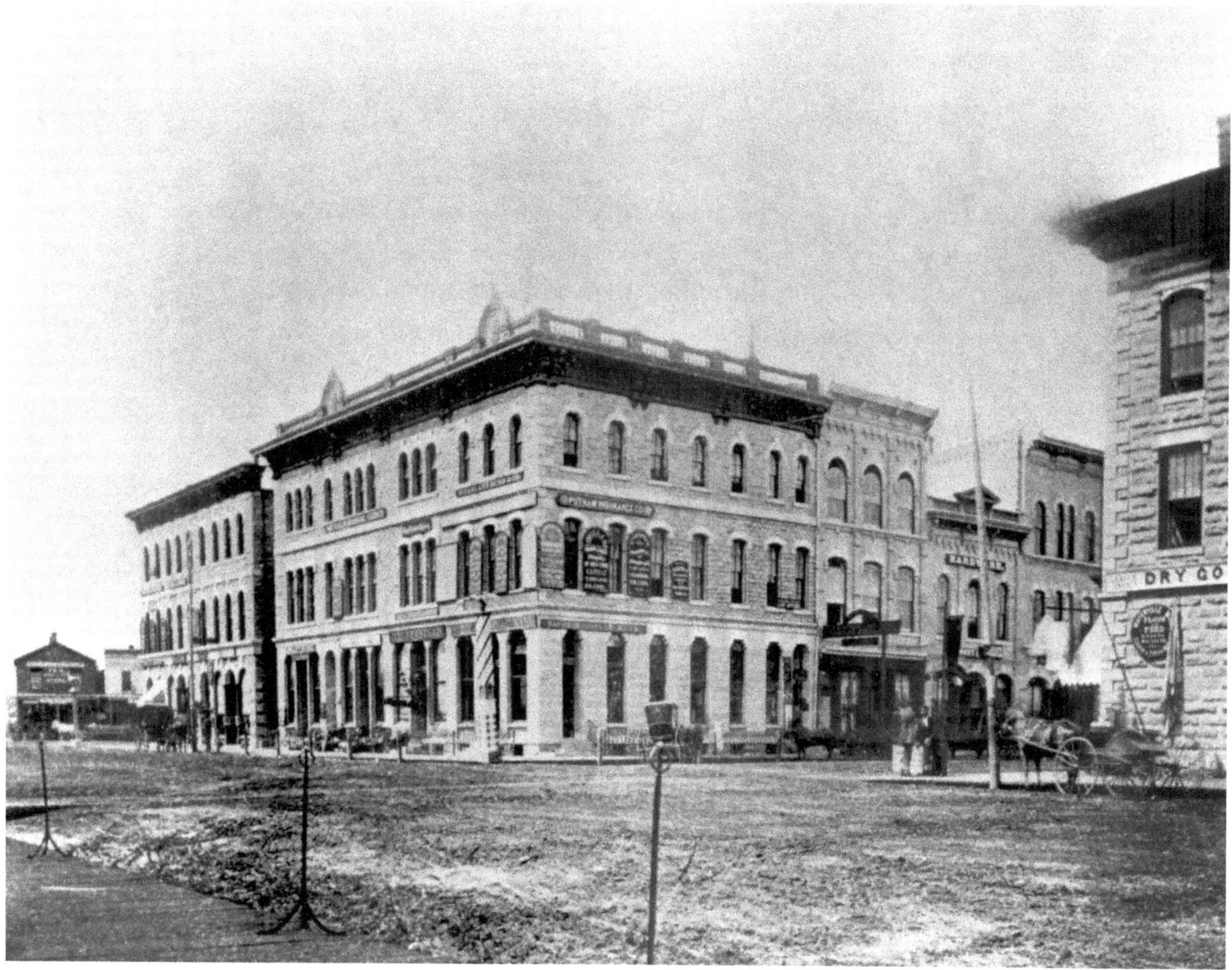

The first Hennepin County courthouse was erected in 1856 and occupied the corner of Fourth Street and Eighth Avenue South.

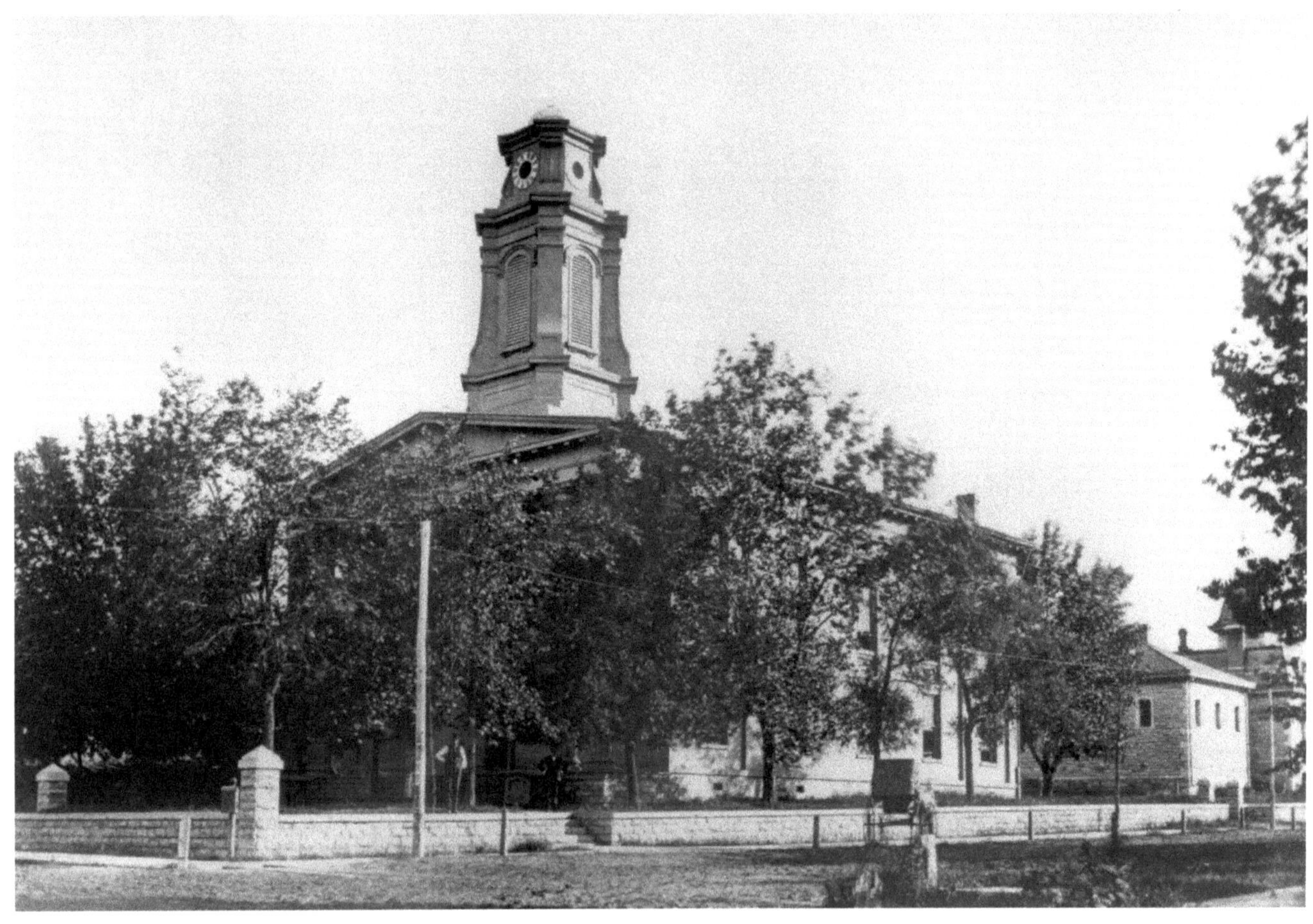

Thomas Lowry, founder of the Twin Cities Rapid Transit Company, persuaded the Minneapolis city council in 1875 to allow him to implement a street railroad. The earliest streetcars were ten feet long, served twelve passengers, and were pulled by horses or mules.

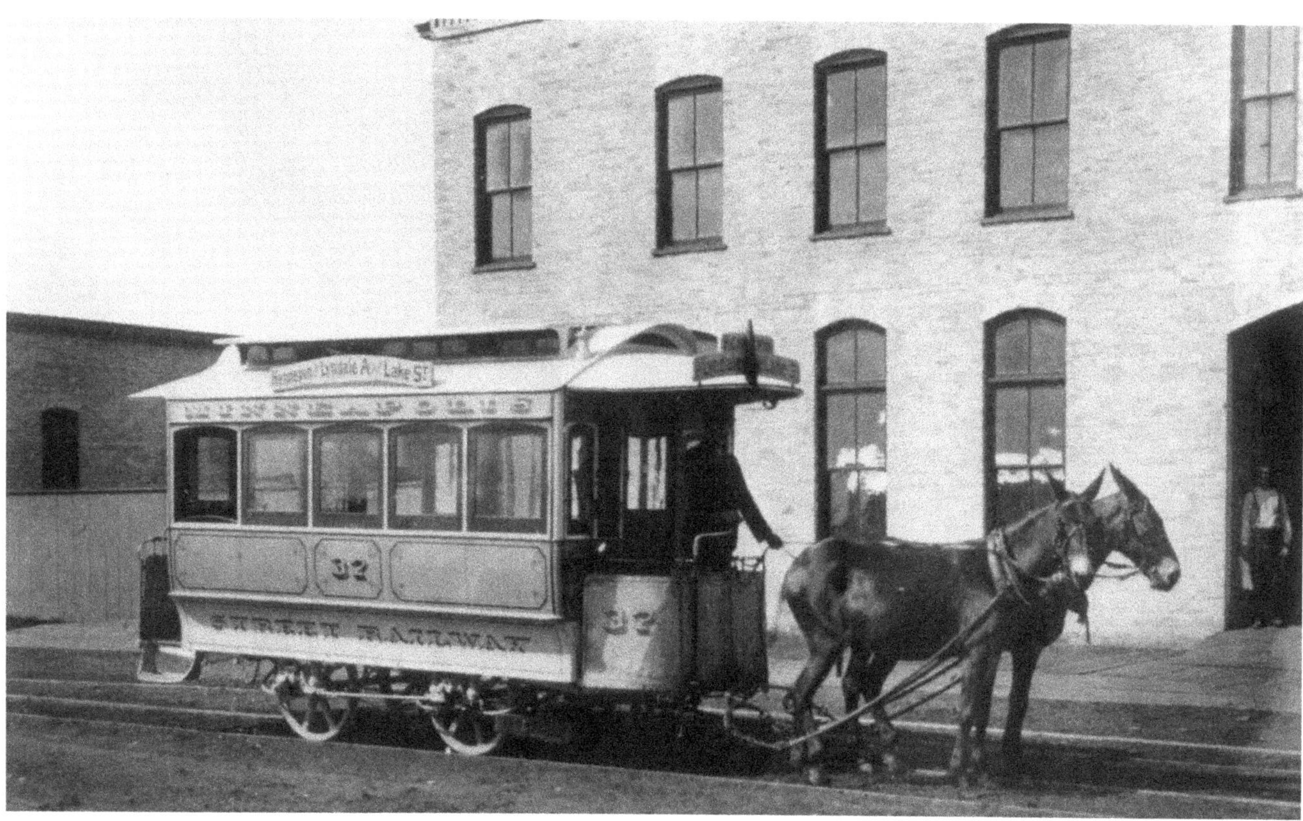

The Academy of Music opened on the third floor of this hall, located at the corner of Washington and Hennepin avenues, in 1872. Its first concert featured performances by two beloved local groups, the St. Paul Musical Society and the Harmonia Singing Society.

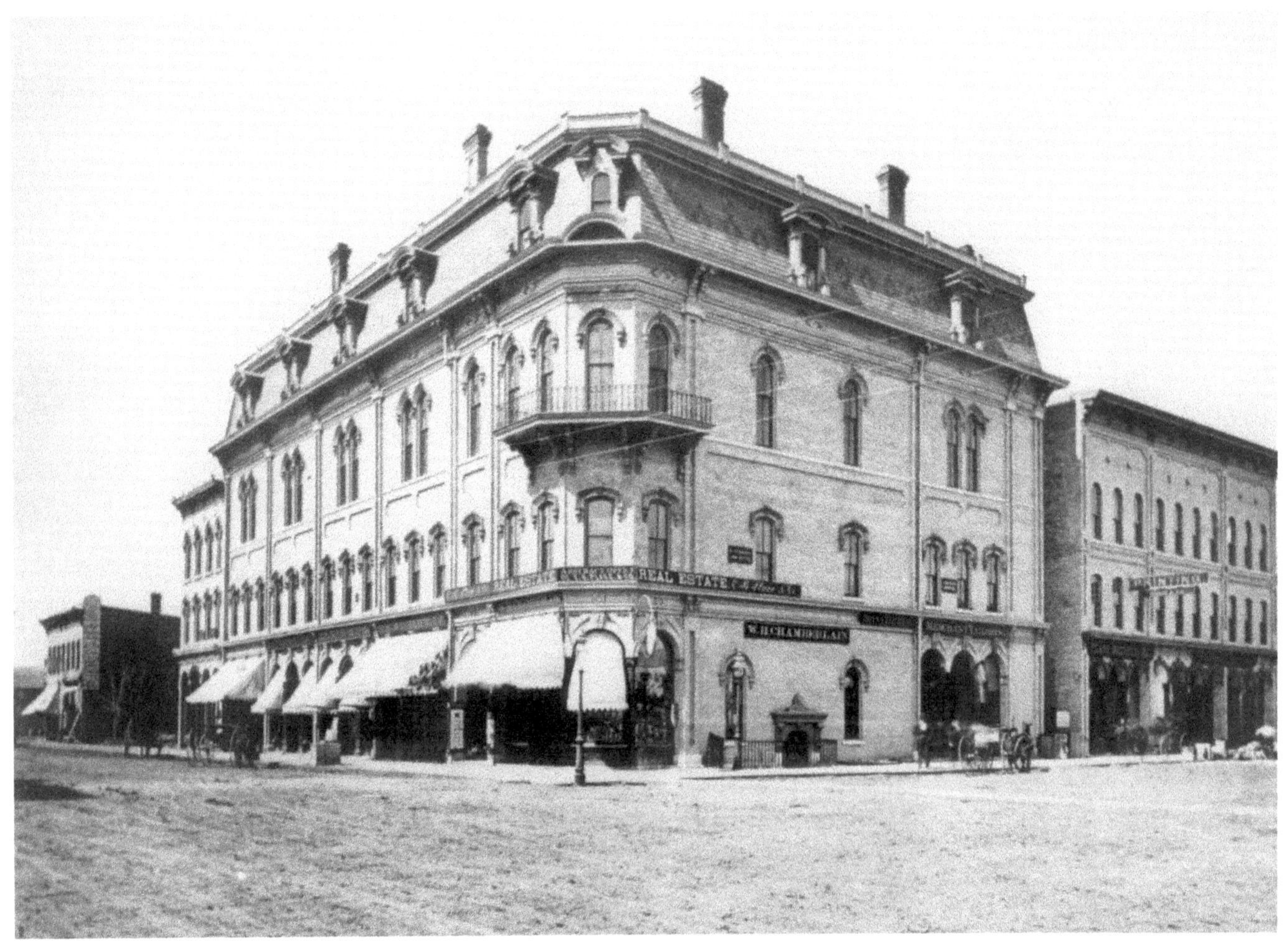

In 1878 Colonel Bill King, former president of the Minnesota State Fair, started a rival fair at Minnehaha Avenue and Thirty-eighth Avenue South. Here fairgoers at King's Fair gather around a hot-air balloon.

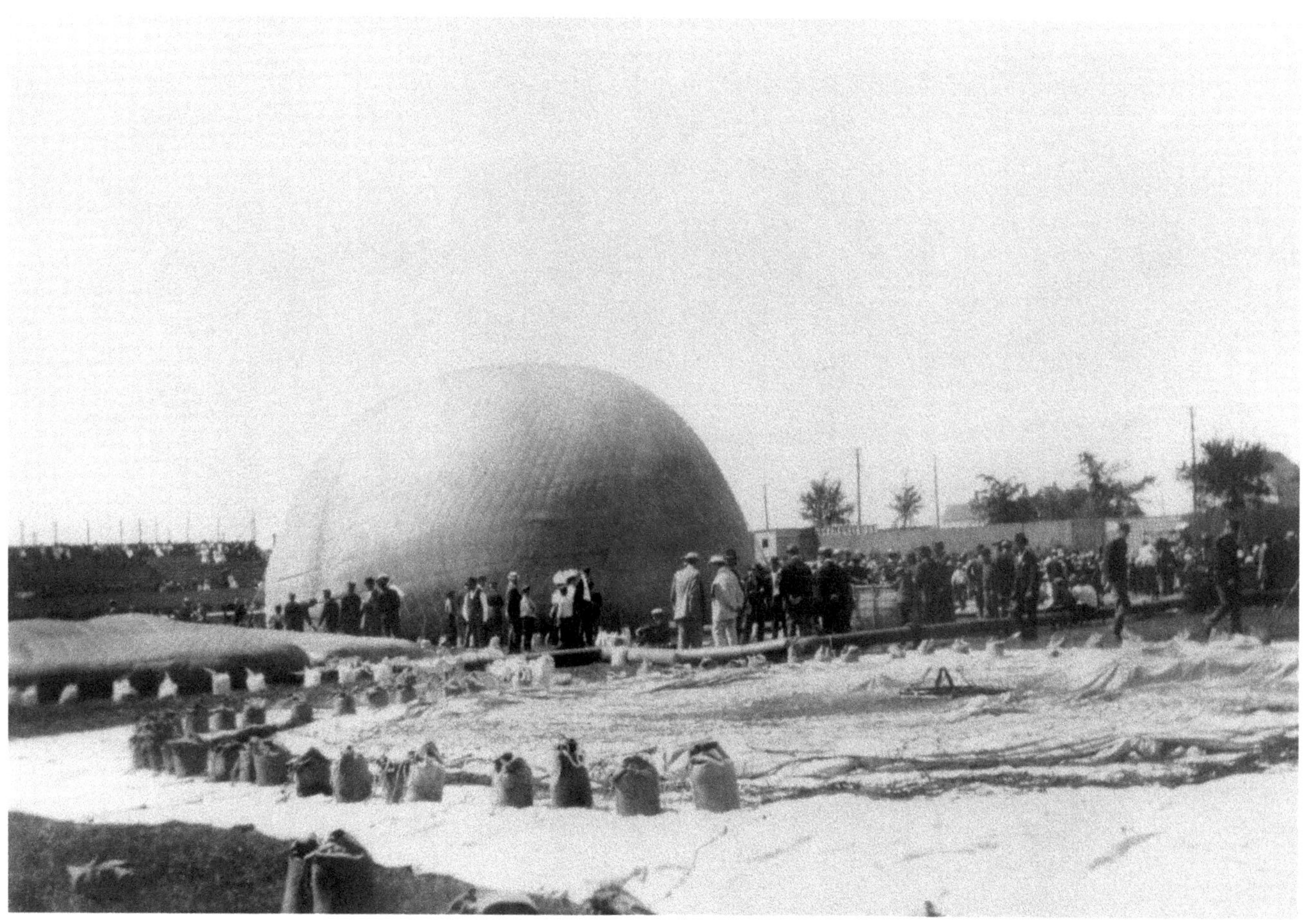

More than 338,000 people visited the Exposition Building when it opened in 1886. The building was intended to house exhibitions of Minneapolis's industrial products, but it was often used for other meetings, including the 1892 Republican National Convention.

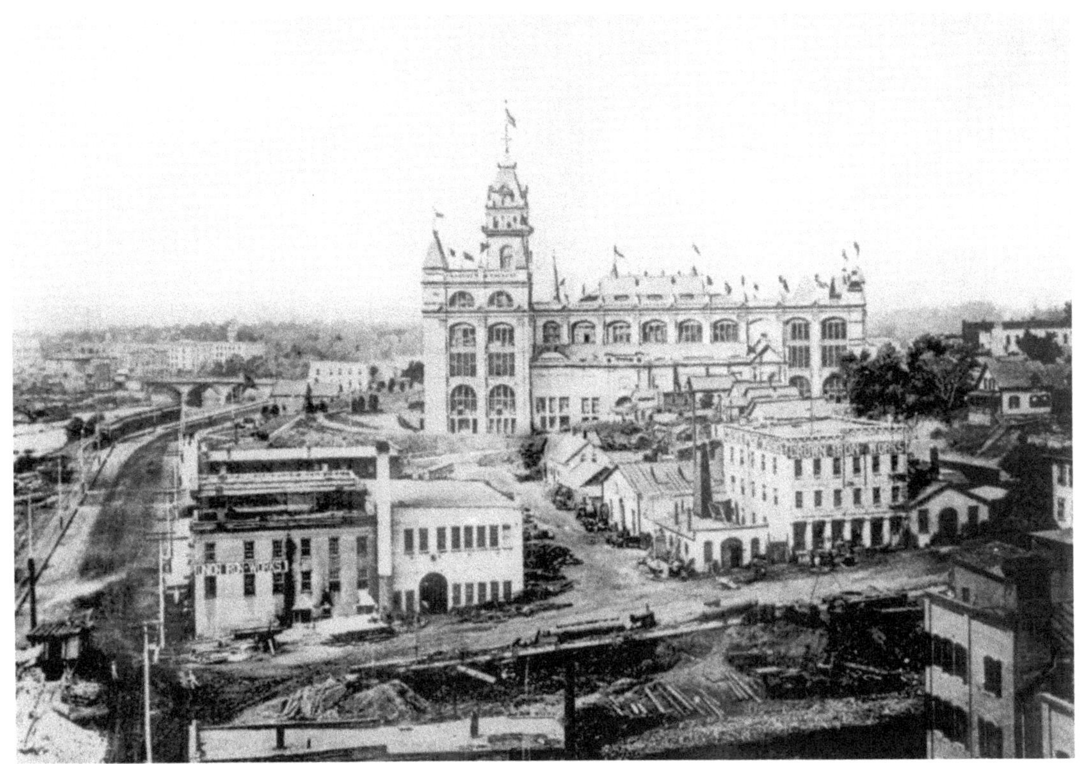

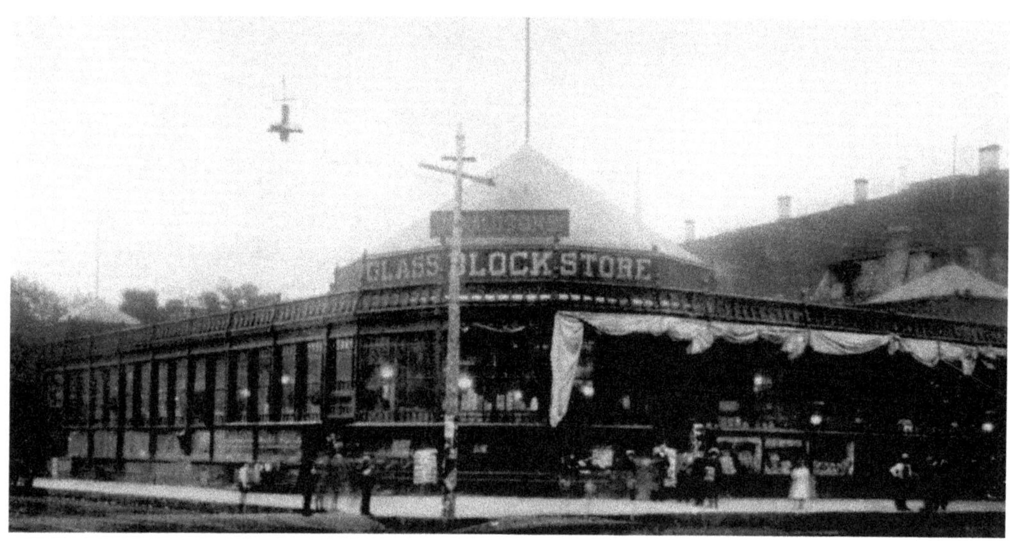

Donaldson's Department Store, located between Sixth and Seventh streets on Nicollet Avenue, first opened in 1881. In 1882 local architects Long and Kees redesigned the store, which was subsequently dubbed Donaldson's Glass Block because of its unique appearance.

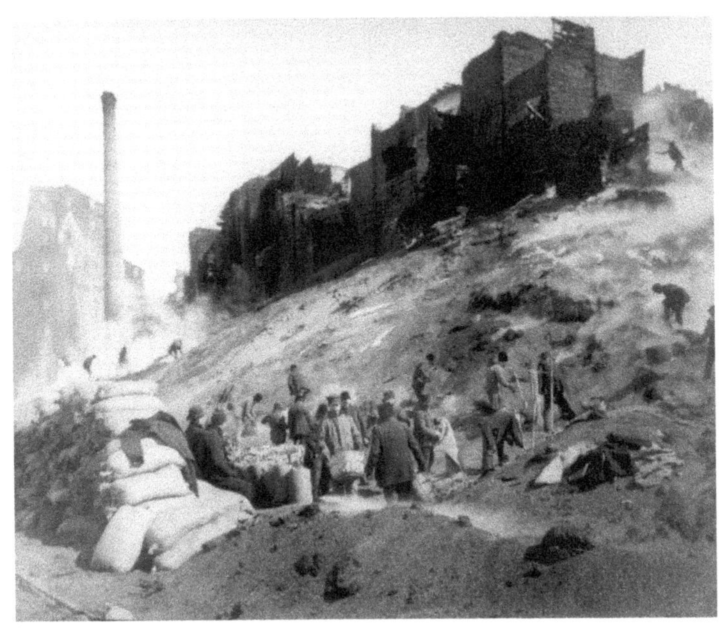

Fires were a common occurrence in the Mill District, where hot metal machinery was operated close to highly volatile flour dust. Here a group of men watch a fire at Elevator B on the Great Northern Railroad tracks near Western Avenue, probably in the 1880s.

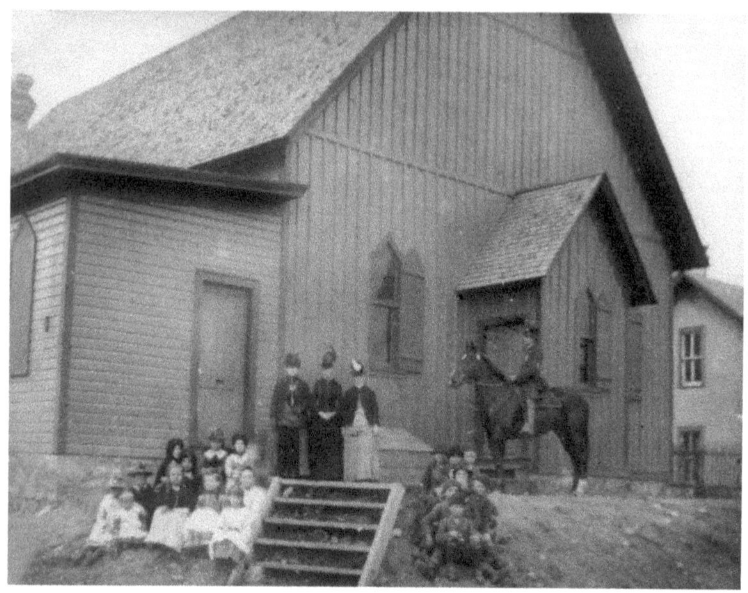

In 1883 the city's Congregational churches formed the Minneapolis City Missionary Society to "promote religion and morality" in Minneapolis. This mission, located at 2533 Riverside Avenue, served the city's Scandinavian immigrant community.

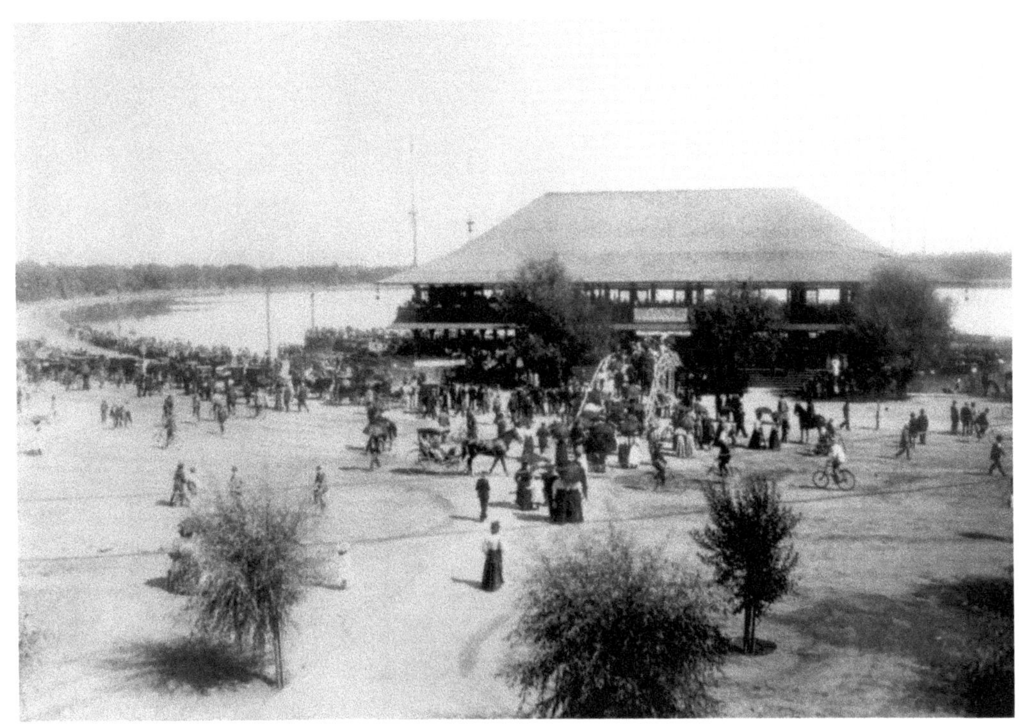

After the first pavilion at Lake Harriet in southwest Minneapolis burned to the ground in 1891, architect and future Park Board Commissioner Harry Wild Jones was commissioned to build a second pavilion, shown here.

The Minneapolis City Market relocated from Bridge Square on First Street and Hennepin Avenue to this spot on Second and Third avenues north and North Sixth and Seventh streets in 1892. Farmers congregated at the market to sell their produce to wholesalers.

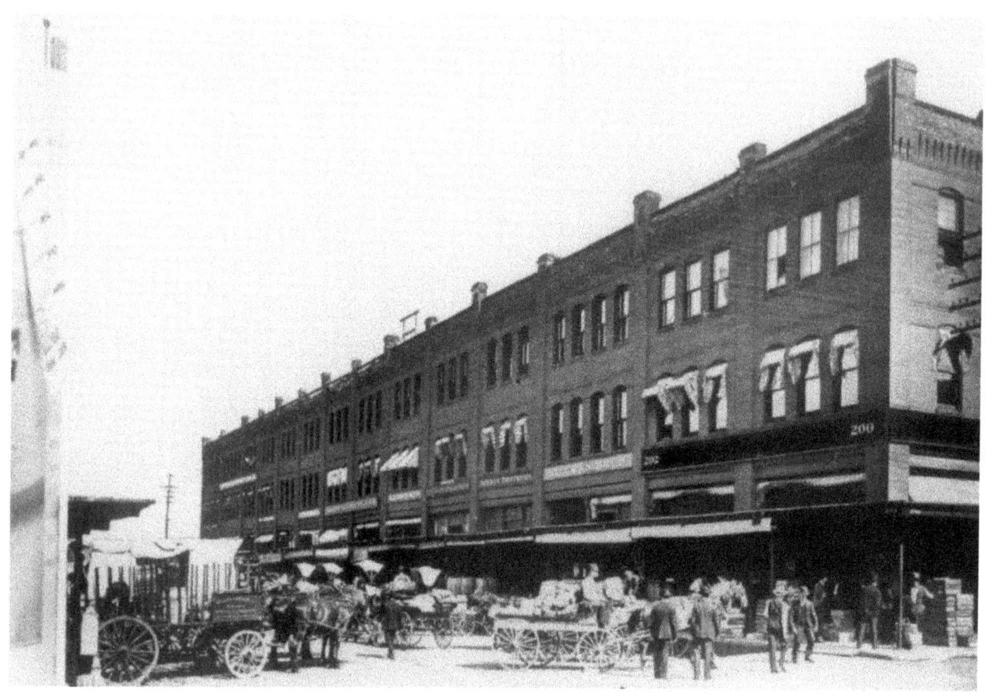

The first Minneapolis city hall, which opened in 1873, sat between Hennepin and Nicollet avenues on the site that would later be occupied by Gateway Park. City officials abandoned this building for larger quarters in 1906.

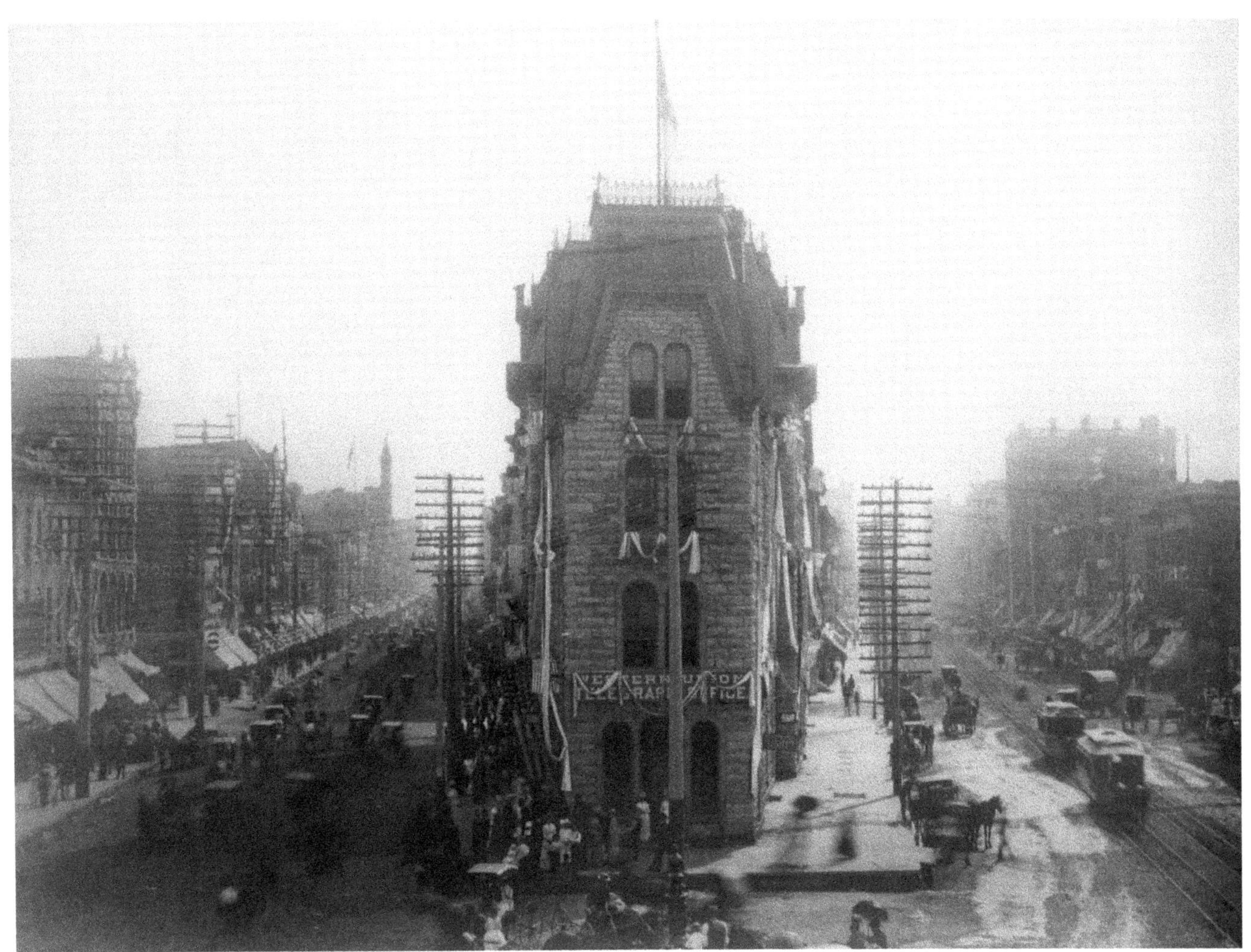

Children and adults alike delighted in pony rides along the shores of Lake Harriet in southwest Minneapolis. The park also offered restaurants and band concerts and was a favorite spot for picnickers, cyclists, and boaters.

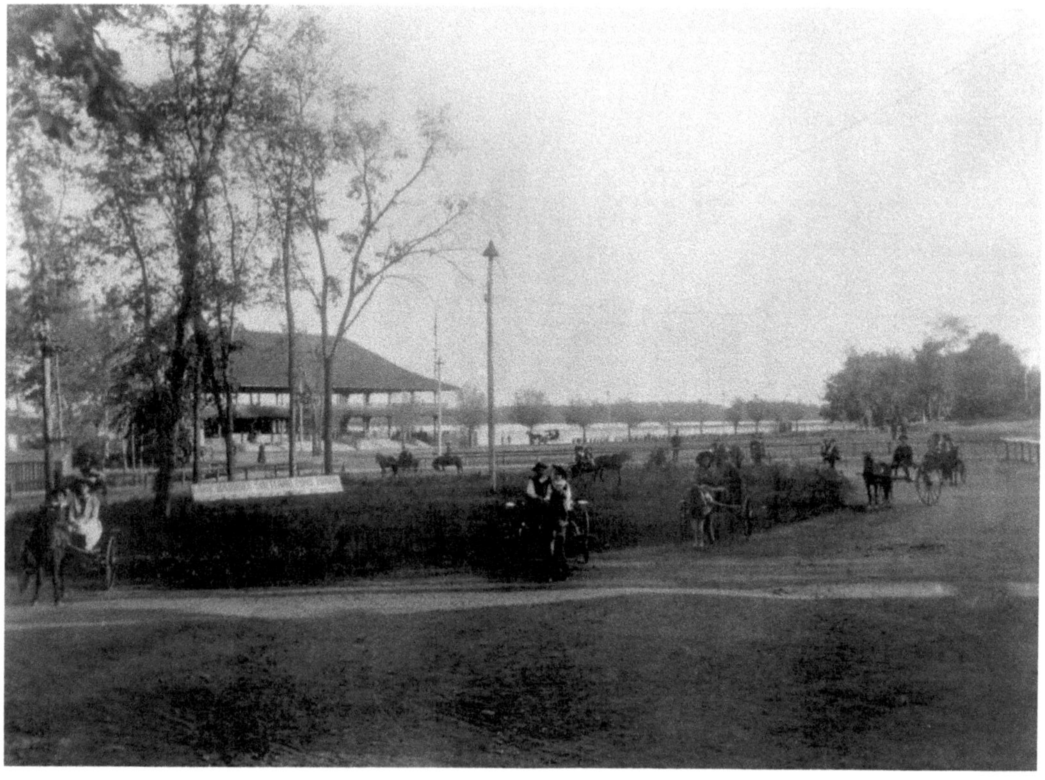

Modest row houses lined Vine Place (La Salle Avenue) in Minneapolis in the 1880s. These houses were razed as the city's commercial district grew and streetcars made it possible for workers to live outside city limits and easily commute to their jobs downtown.

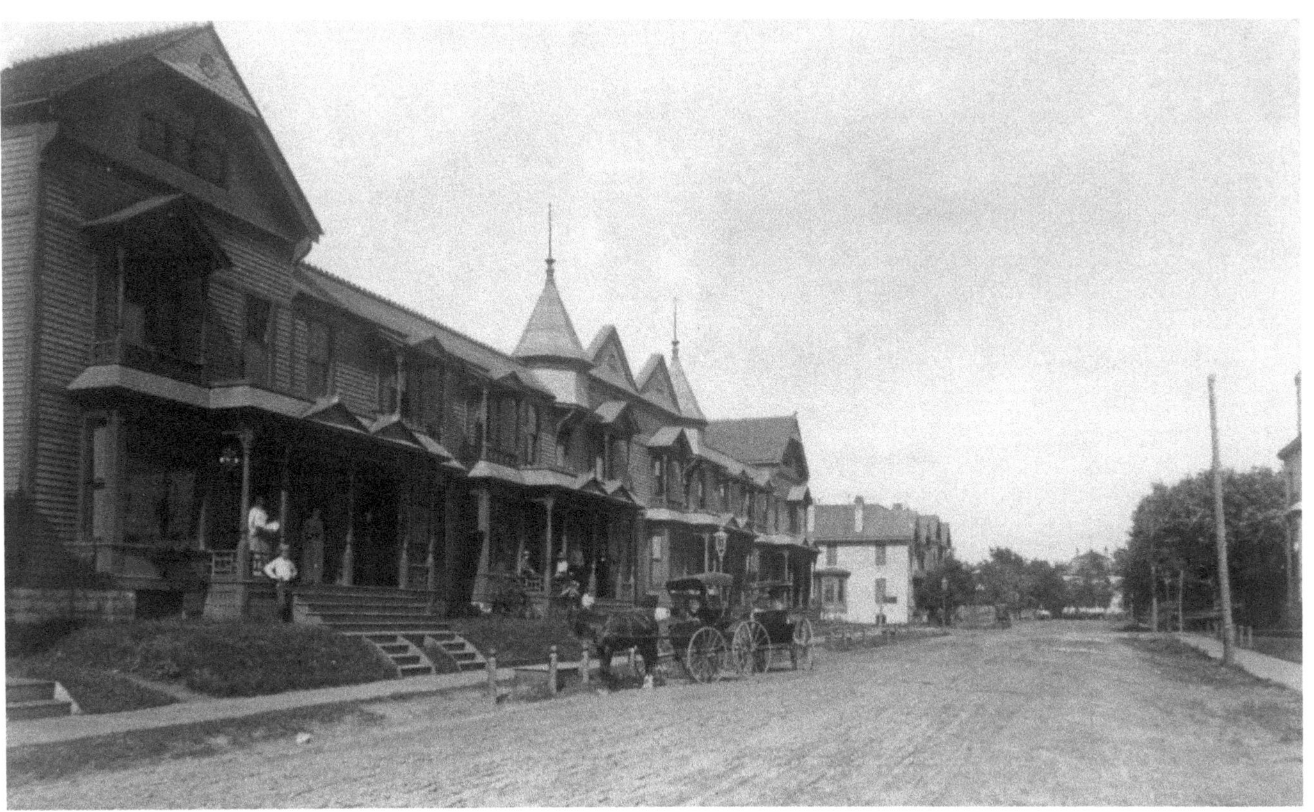

The bustling Nicollet Avenue shopping district between Third Street and Bridge Square as it appeared in the late nineteenth century. Hudson's *Dictionary of Minneapolis* called Nicollet "the most prominent street in the city."

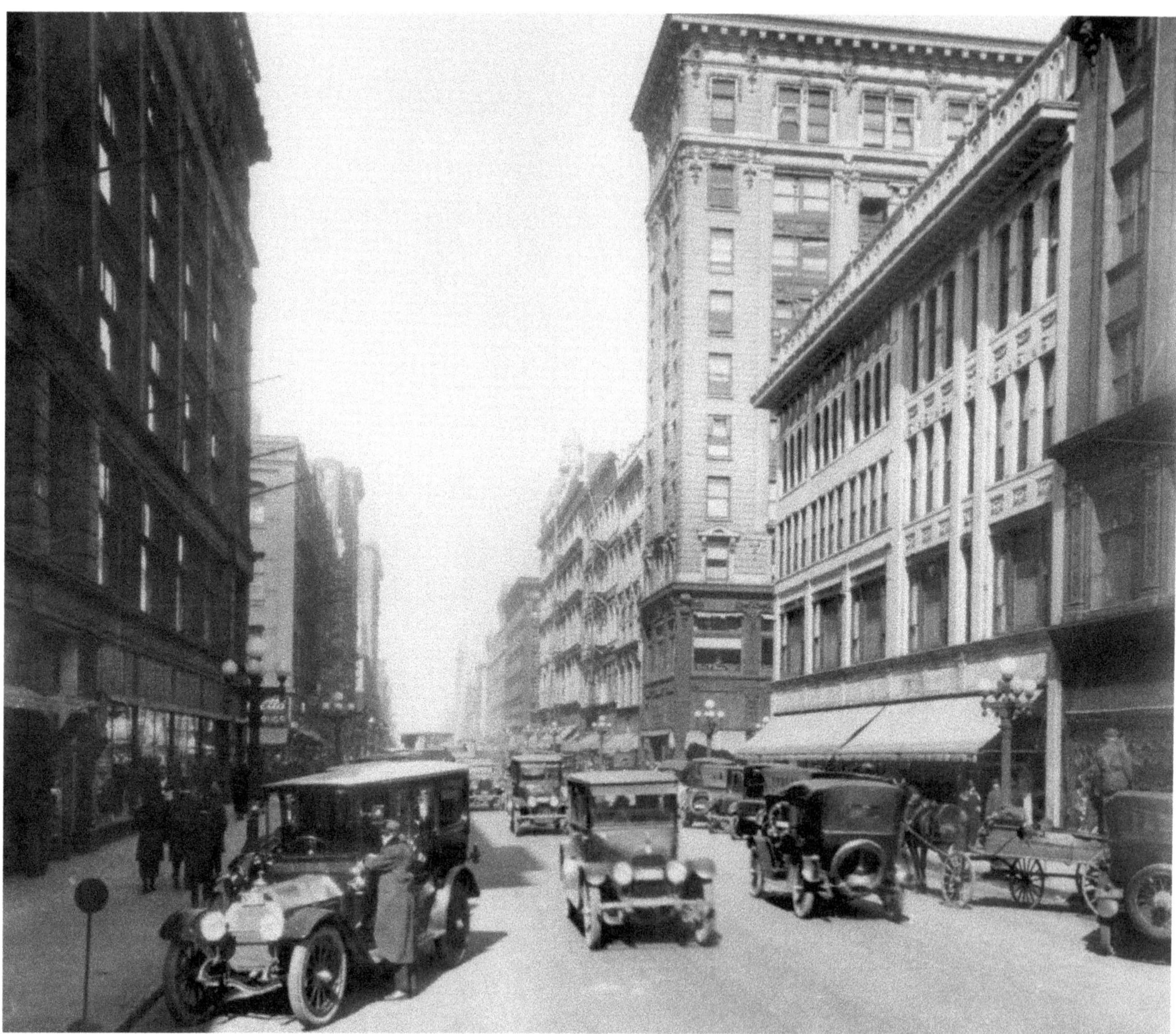

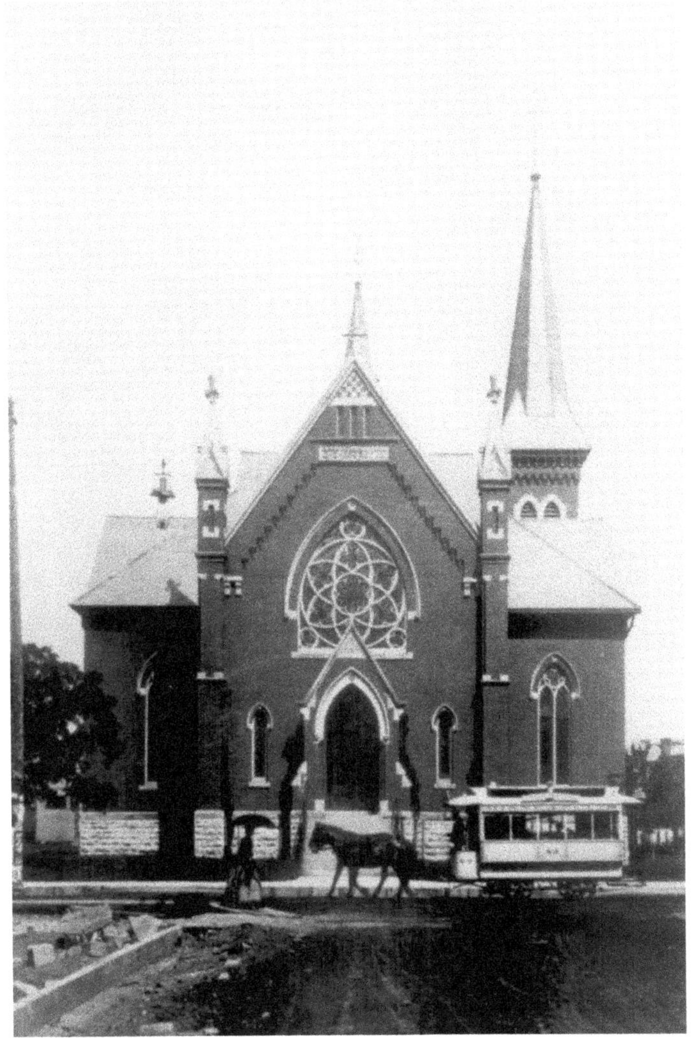

In 1878 one hundred and thirty optimistic Methodists endeavored to raise $65,000 for a new building. Hennepin Avenue Methodist Episcopal Church opened its doors just three years later. Locals affectionately dubbed the building the Red Brick Church.

The Hennepin County Savings Bank was organized in 1870. The 1888–1889 Minneapolis City Directory lists the bank's address as 230 Hennepin Avenue. The beehive sculpture above the door is often mentioned in historical accounts of the building.

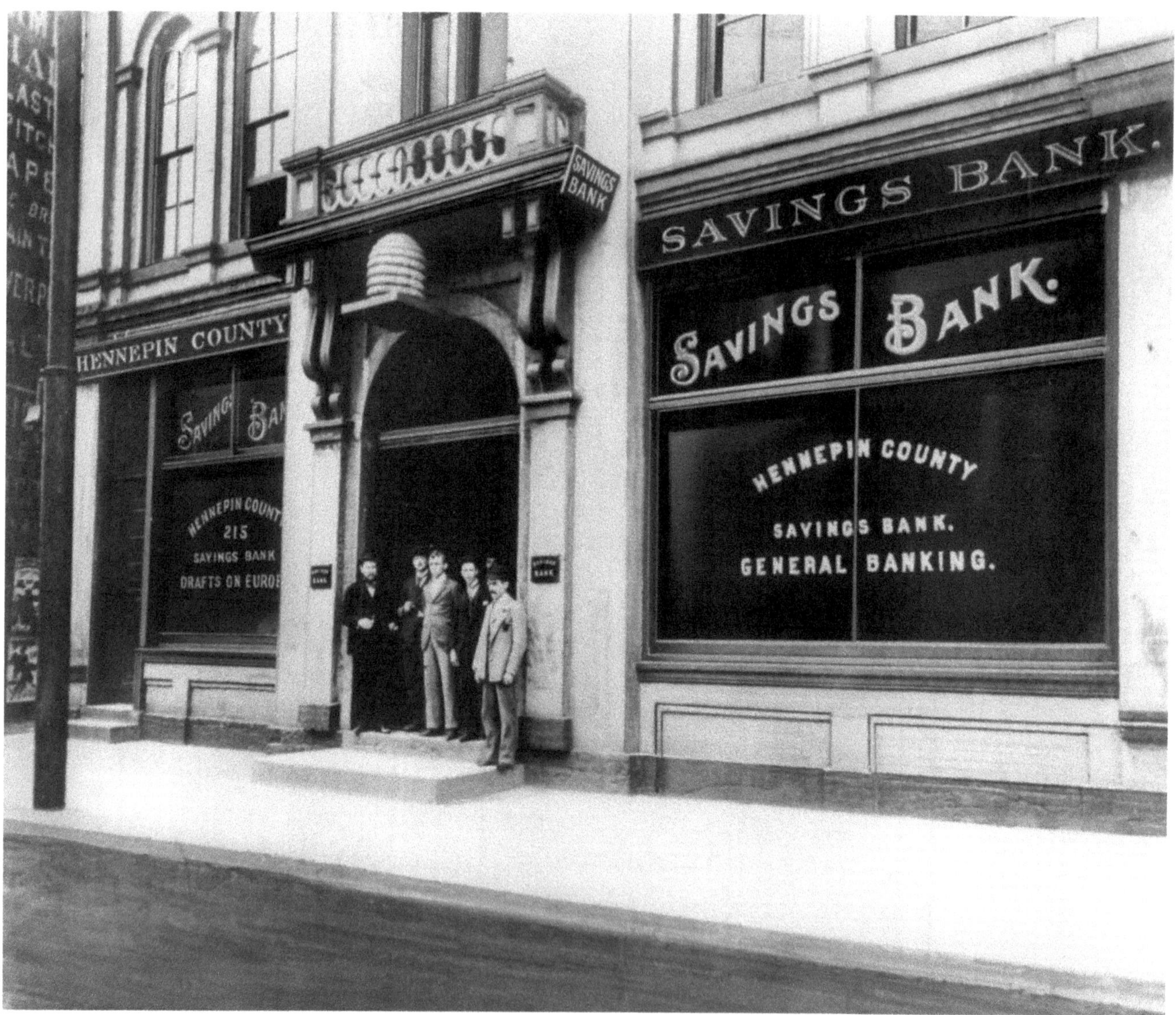

A horse-drawn streetcar travels through the Longfellow neighborhood along Riverside Avenue.

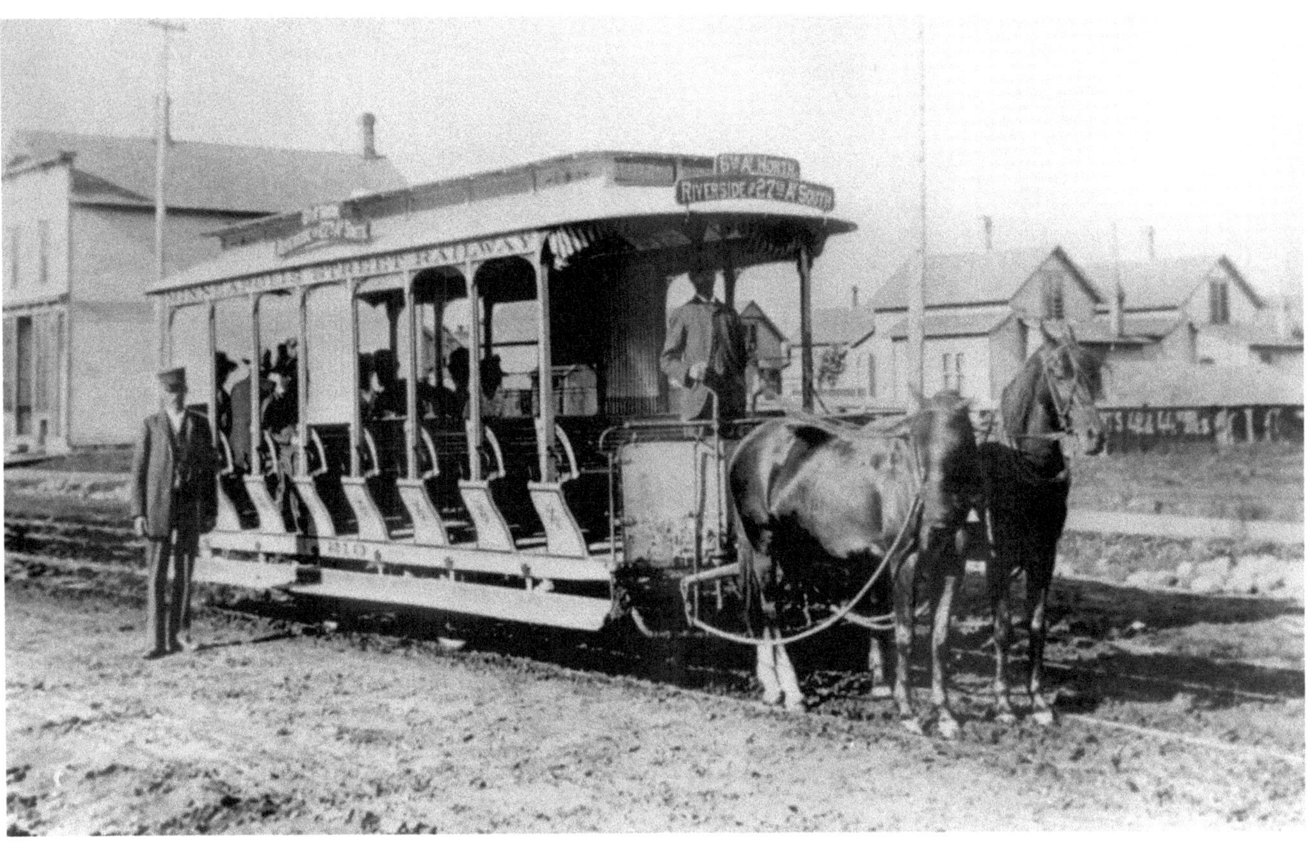

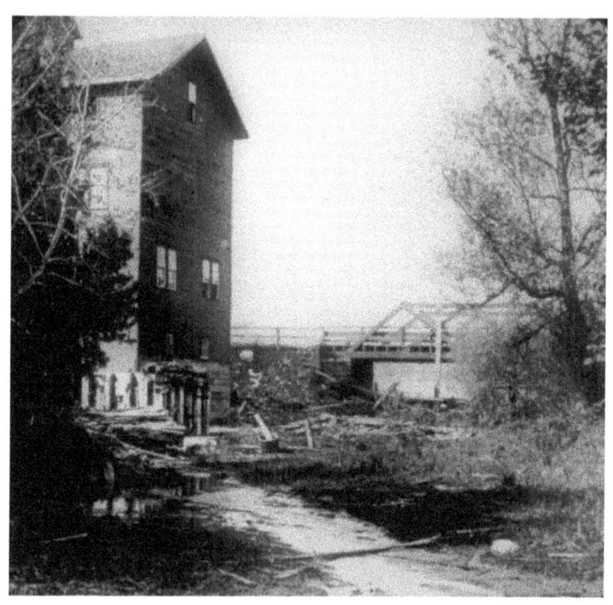

Although the milling district in Minneapolis was always centered on St. Anthony Falls, six small mills operated along the banks of Minnehaha Creek. The Edina Mill, a gristmill built in 1857, stood beside a fifteen-foot drop in the creek and produced flour and oatmeal.

In 1883 the Minnesota Brush Electric Company erected a 257-foot-high electrified mast in Bridge Square. The light mast, said to be the tallest of its kind, represented an attempt by the electric company to persuade Minneapolitans to replace dim gas street-lamps.

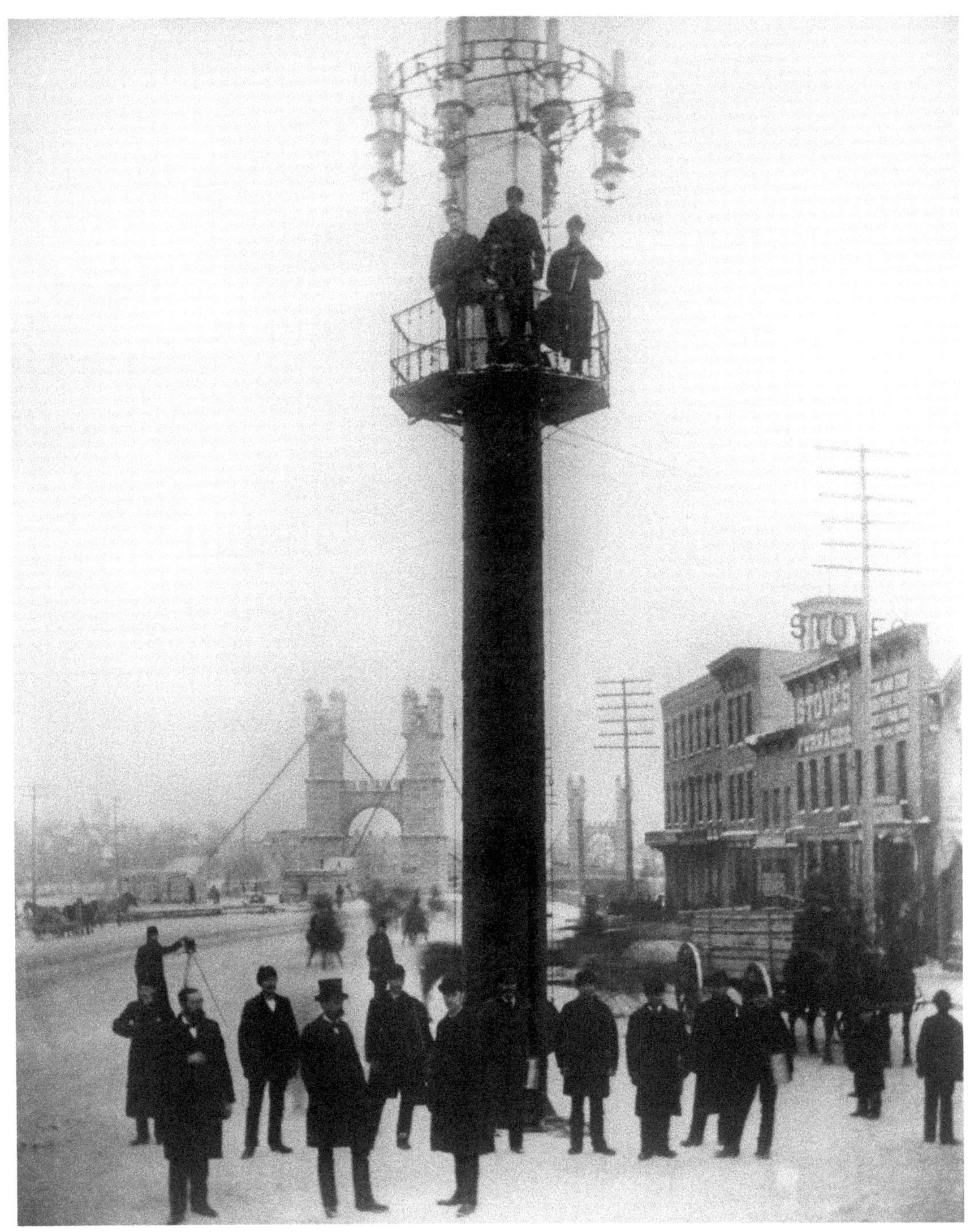

The streets surrounding Bridge Square were studded with three-story and four-story brick buildings known as blocks. Brackett Block was built in 1871 by George Brackett, the man who organized the Minneapolis fire department. Ironically, fire leveled the building in 1880.

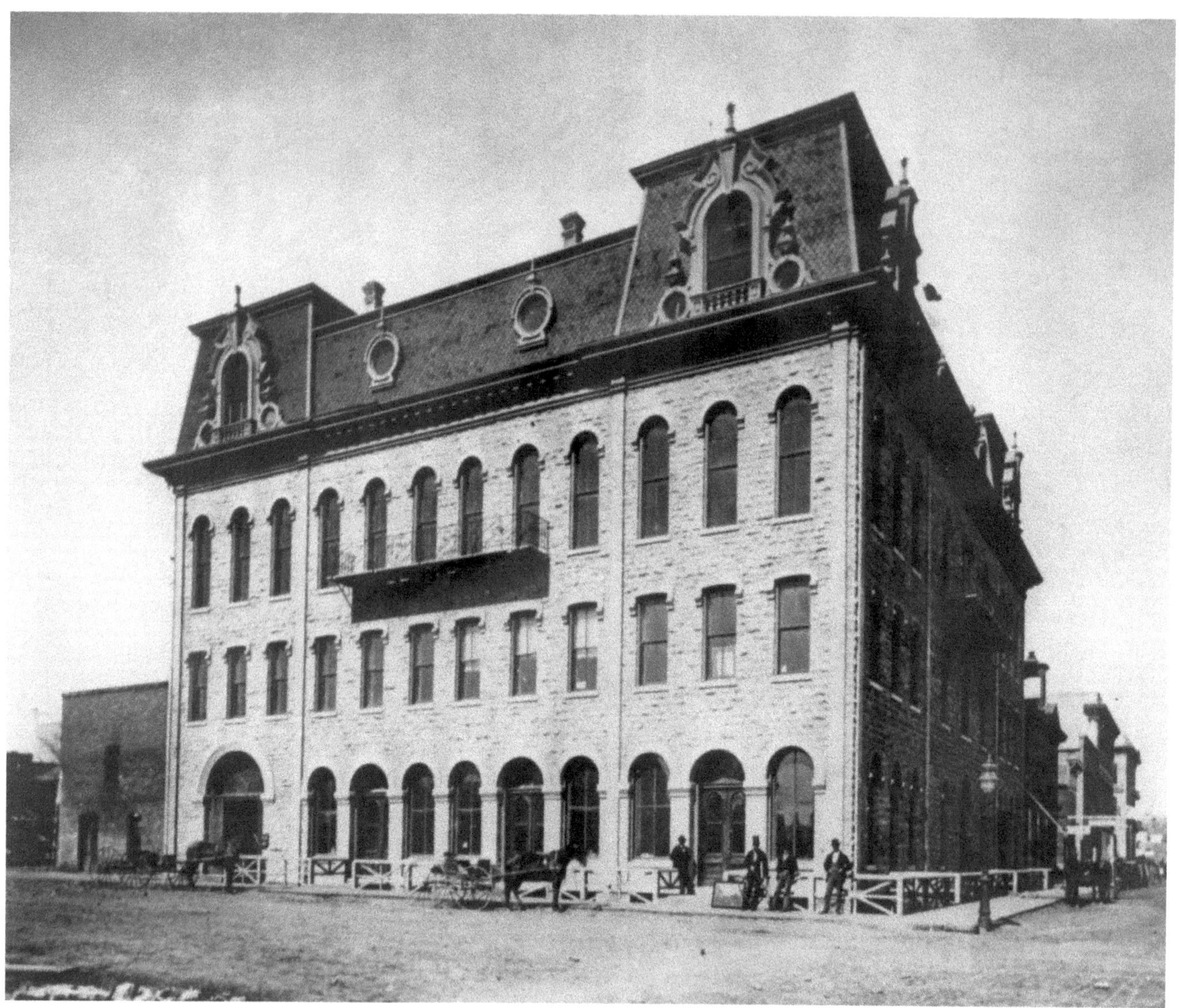

Large crowds gather around 1889 to watch a parade of circus performers marching down Hennepin Avenue as they round the corner from Sixth Street.

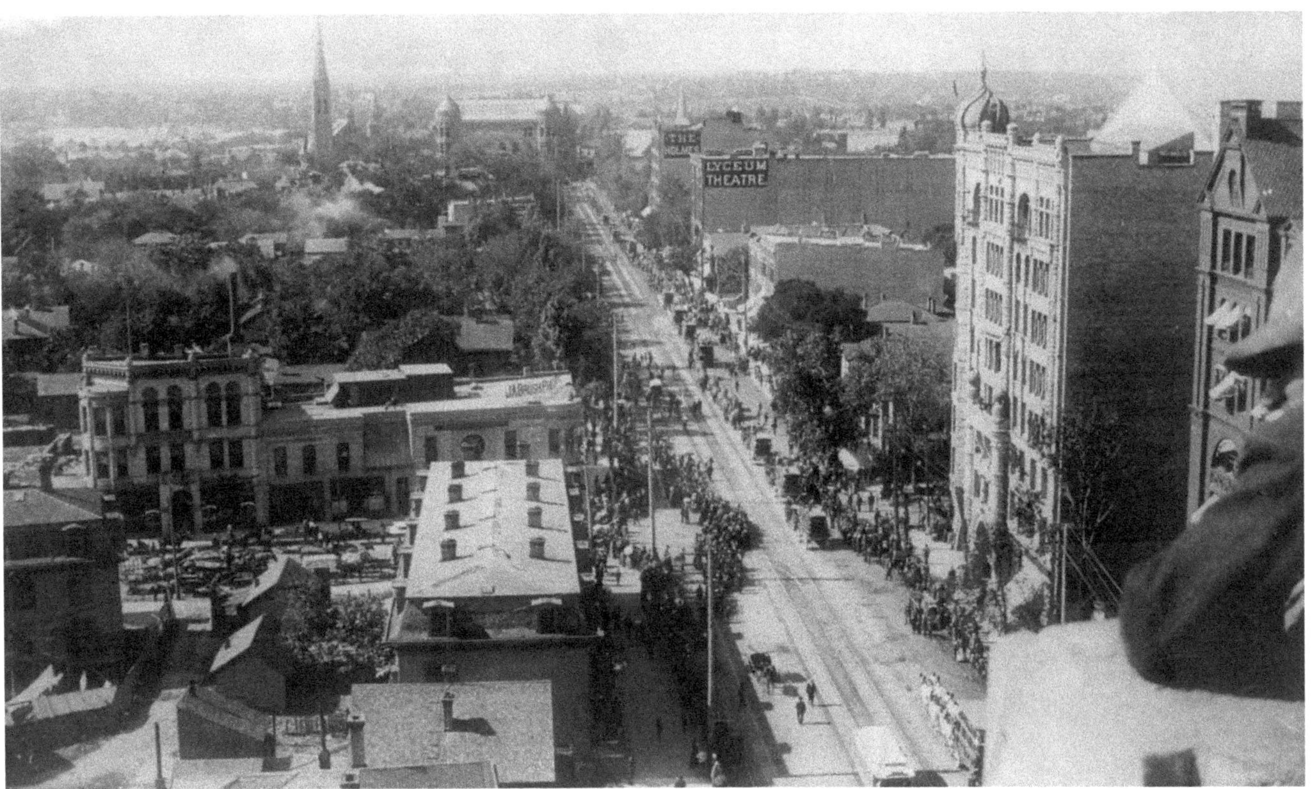

On Christmas Day 1884, the four-story Academy of Music caught fire. Frigid temperatures caused water sprayed from fire hoses to freeze instantly as it reached the structure, resulting in the odd forms visible in this photograph.

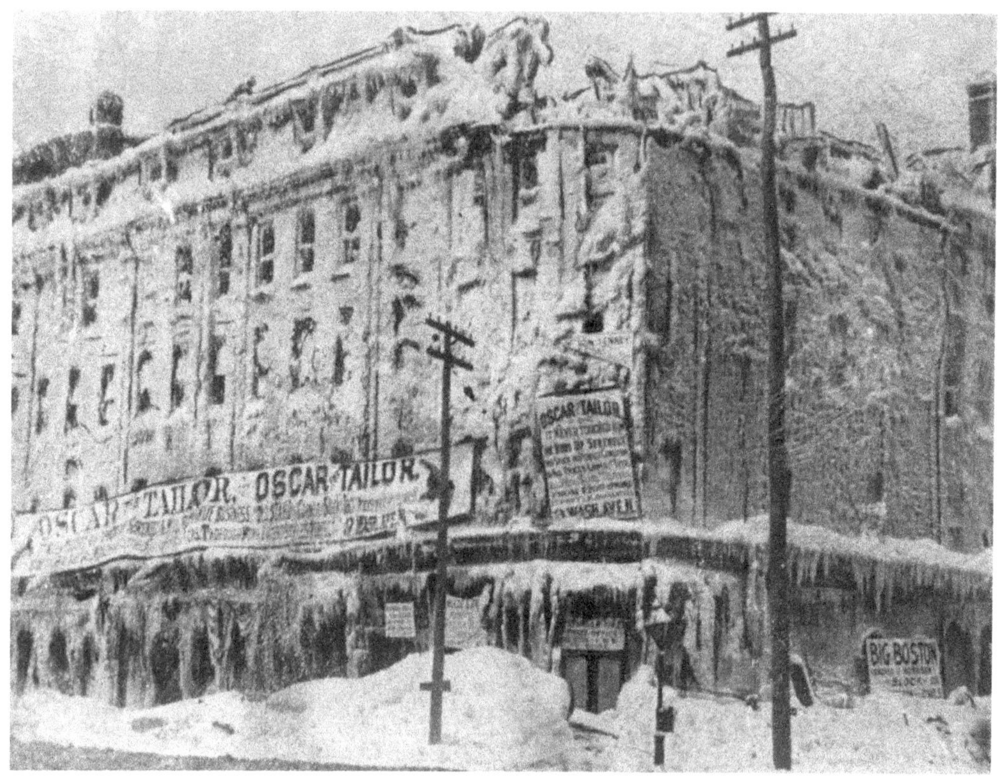

This image shows the busy milling district as it appeared around 1890. The railroad yards, where trains delivered wheat and hauled away milled flour, are visible at center.

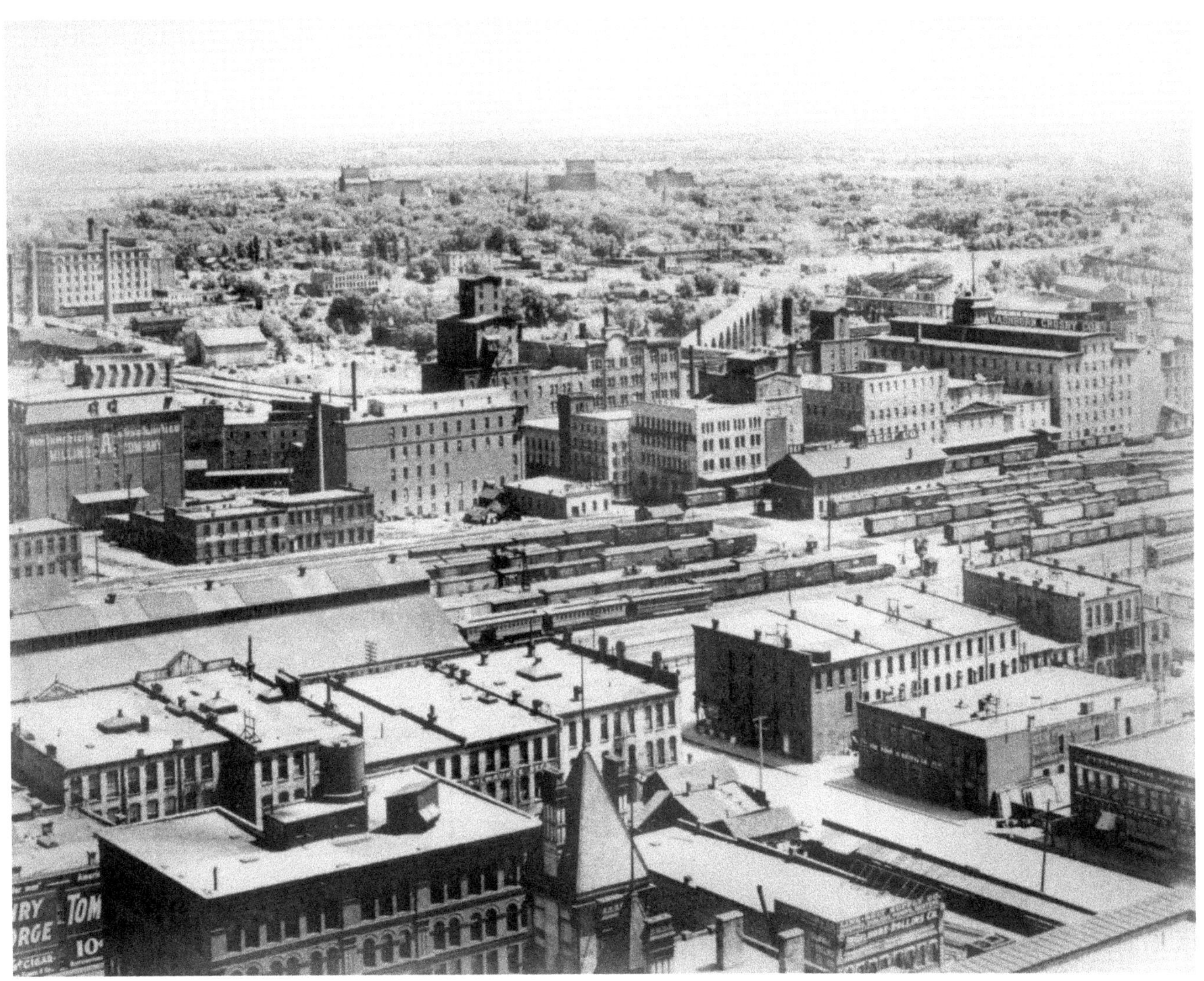

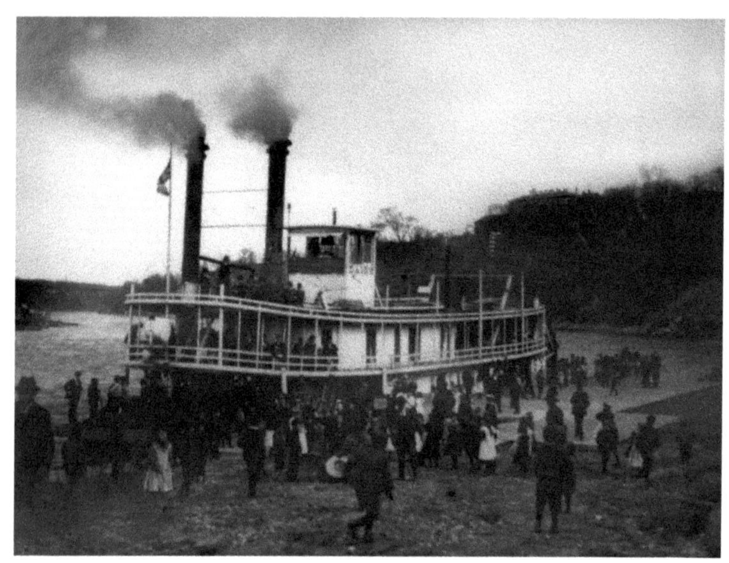

Steamers were popular on the state's lakes, particularly Lake Minnetonka. Steamers were also common on the Mississippi River below Minneapolis. Here passengers debark the steamship *Daisy* around 1890.

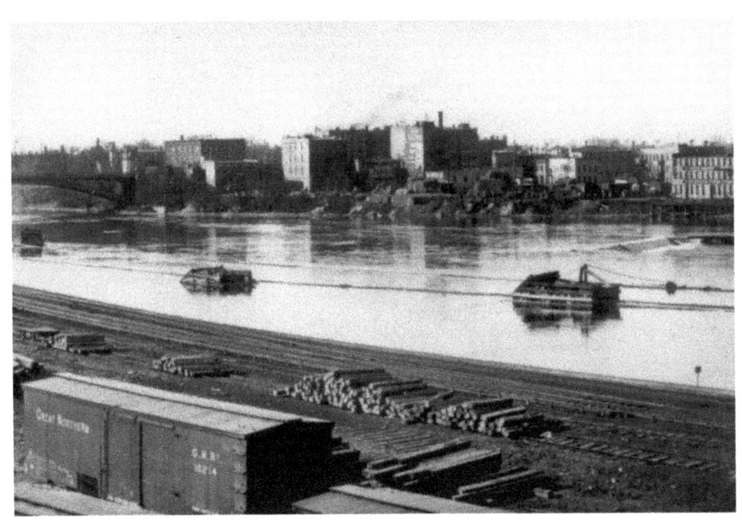

This photograph, looking at Minneapolis across the Mississippi from Nicollet Island, clearly shows the city's gritty industrial nature of earlier days.

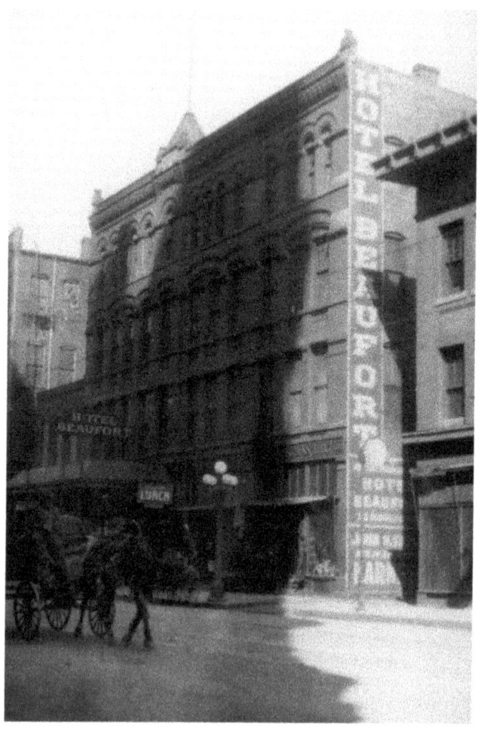

The Metropolitan Life Building casts a long shadow on the Hotel Beaufort, located at 112 South Third Street, around 1900.

The always lively Nicollet Avenue shopping district is shown here between Fourth and Fifth streets around 1890. Doctor Sutherland's dentistry advertises conspicuously to passersby below.

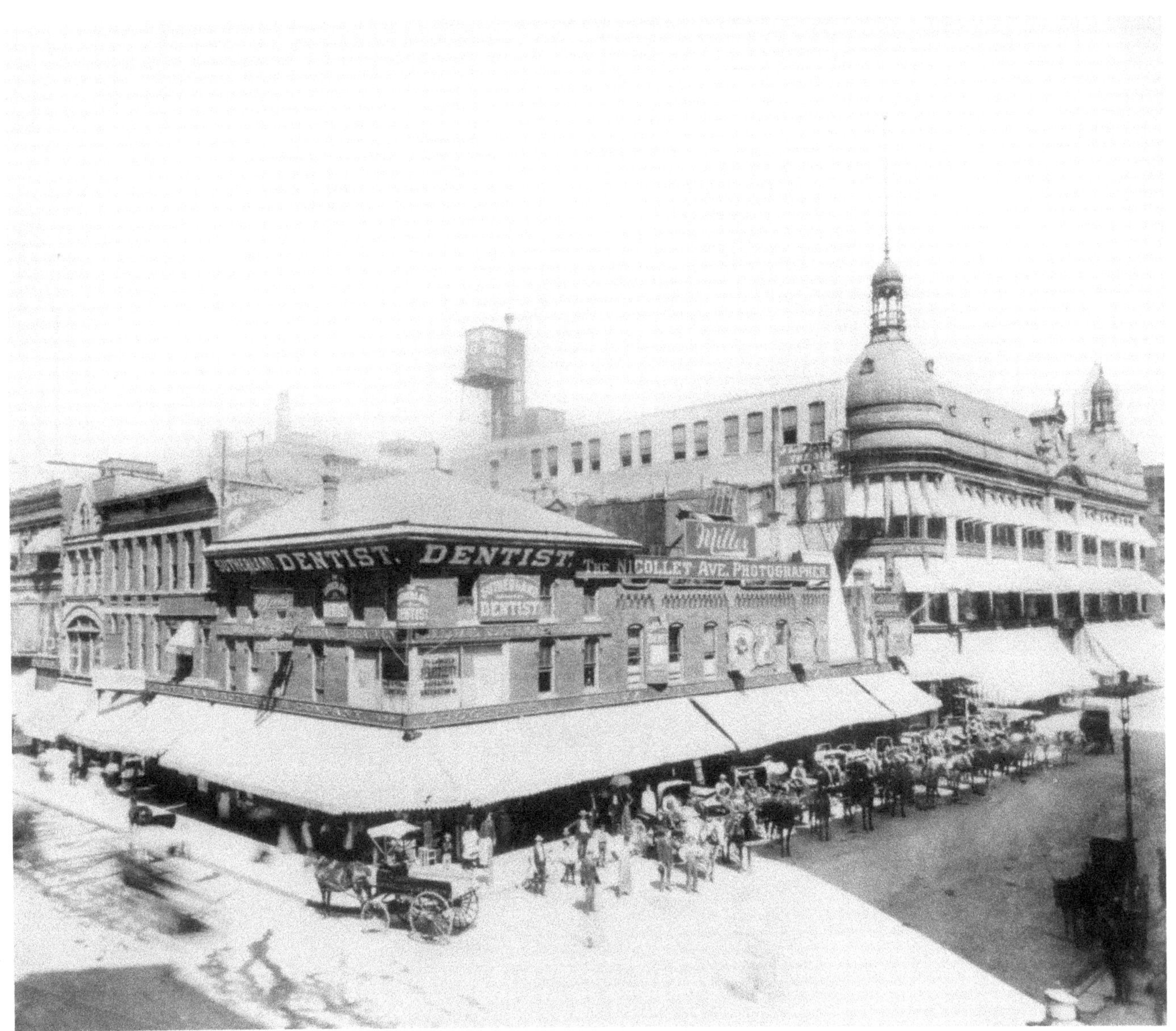

This imposing building, designed by architects Long & Kees, was the first home of the Minneapolis Public Library. The building stood at the corner of Tenth Street and Hennepin Avenue and first opened its doors to the public in 1889.

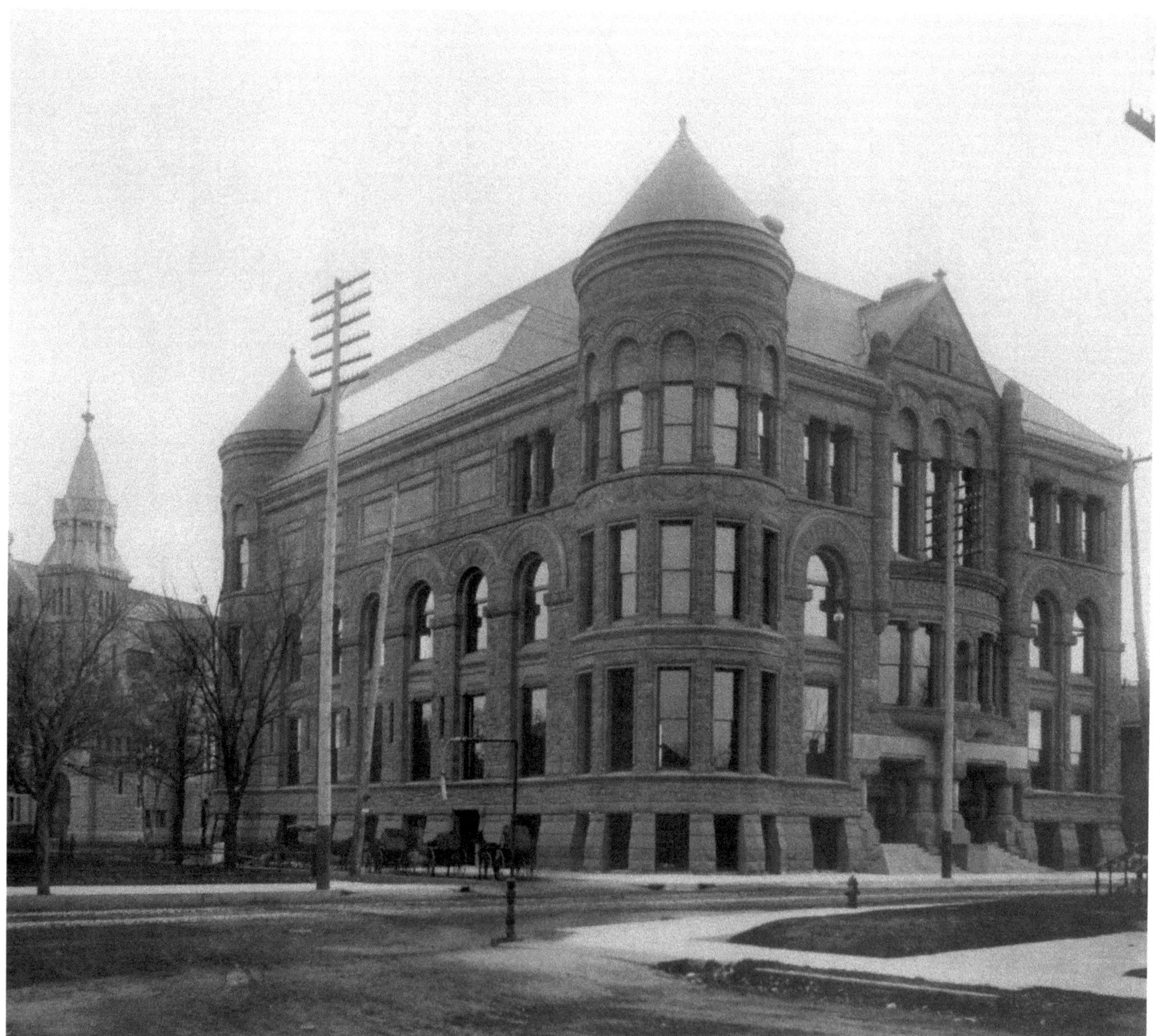

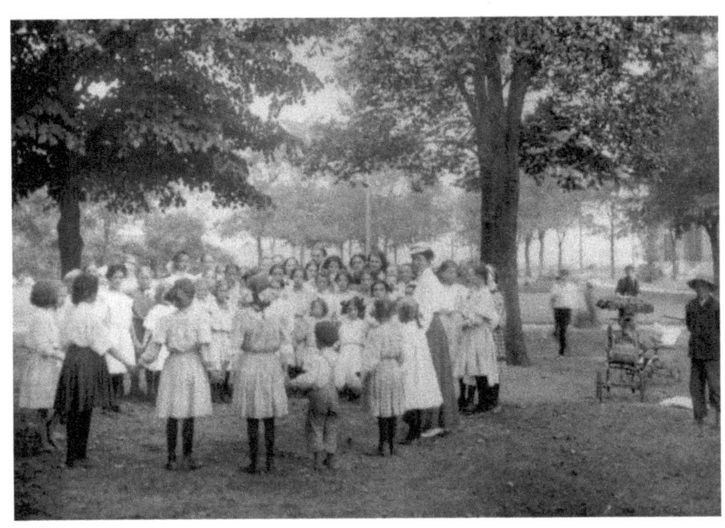

In 1890 the city of Minneapolis established Powderhorn Park, named for the distinctive shape of its lake, on a 25-acre lot located three miles south of downtown. Here a woman leads a group of children in a game at the park, probably in the 1890s.

This image of Nicollet Avenue at Fifth Street was likely captured in the last years of the nineteenth century. The buildings are festooned in festive bunting and several American flags are visible, suggesting an Independence Day or other momentous celebration.

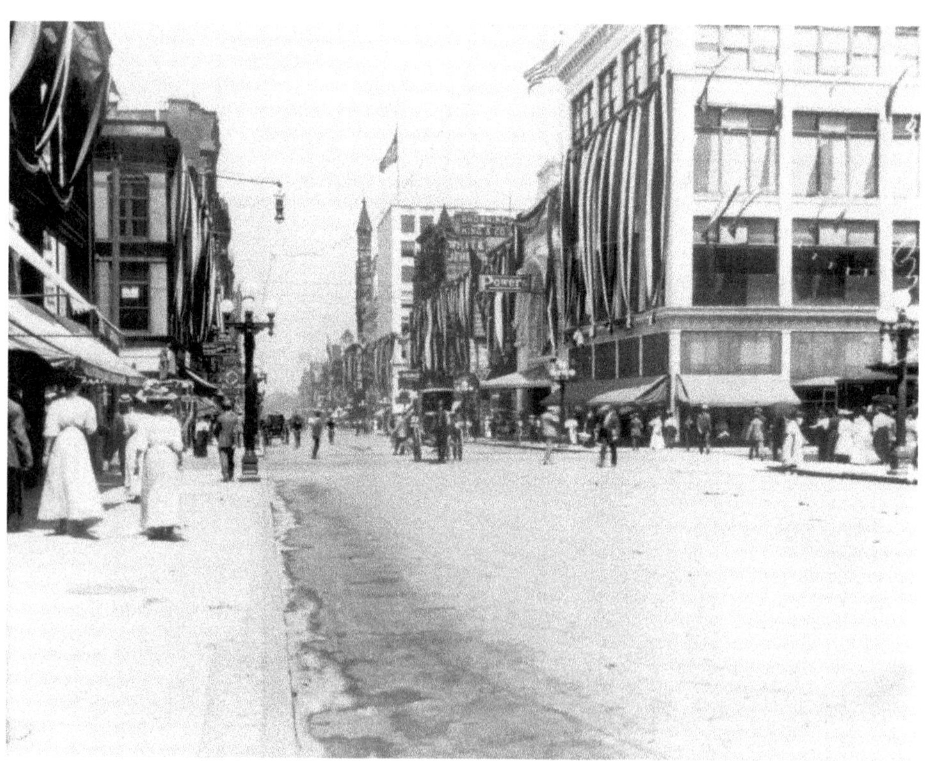

A series of bathhouses appeared at Lake Calhoun starting in 1890, but all were too small to accommodate the masses of swimmers the lake attracted. To meet public demand, the city constructed this elaborate building on the lake's north shore.

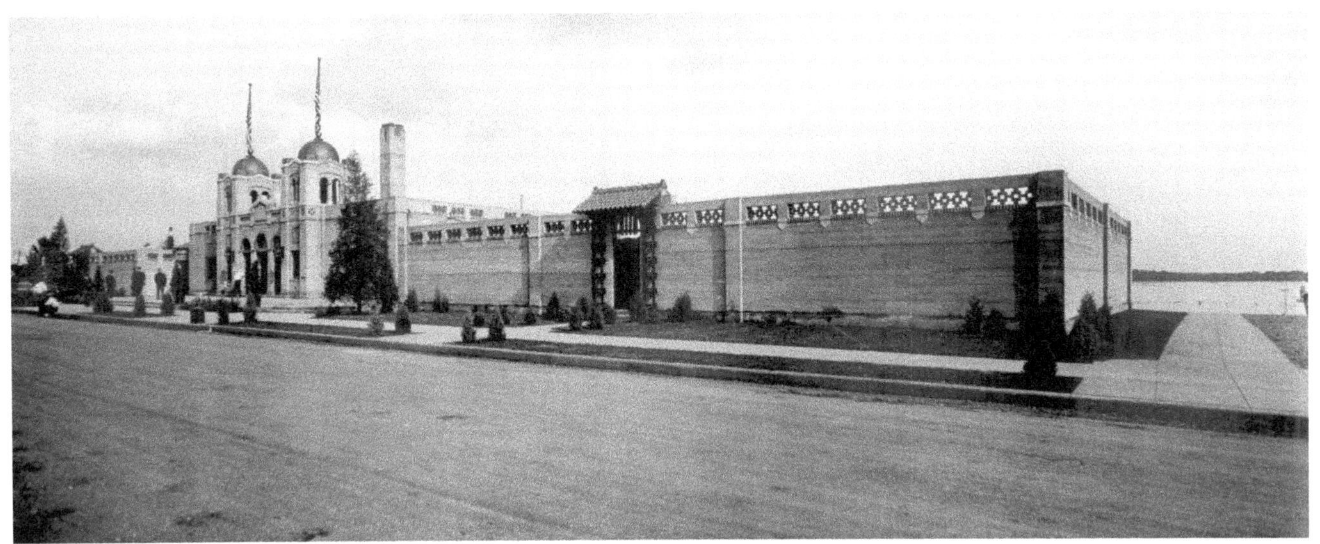

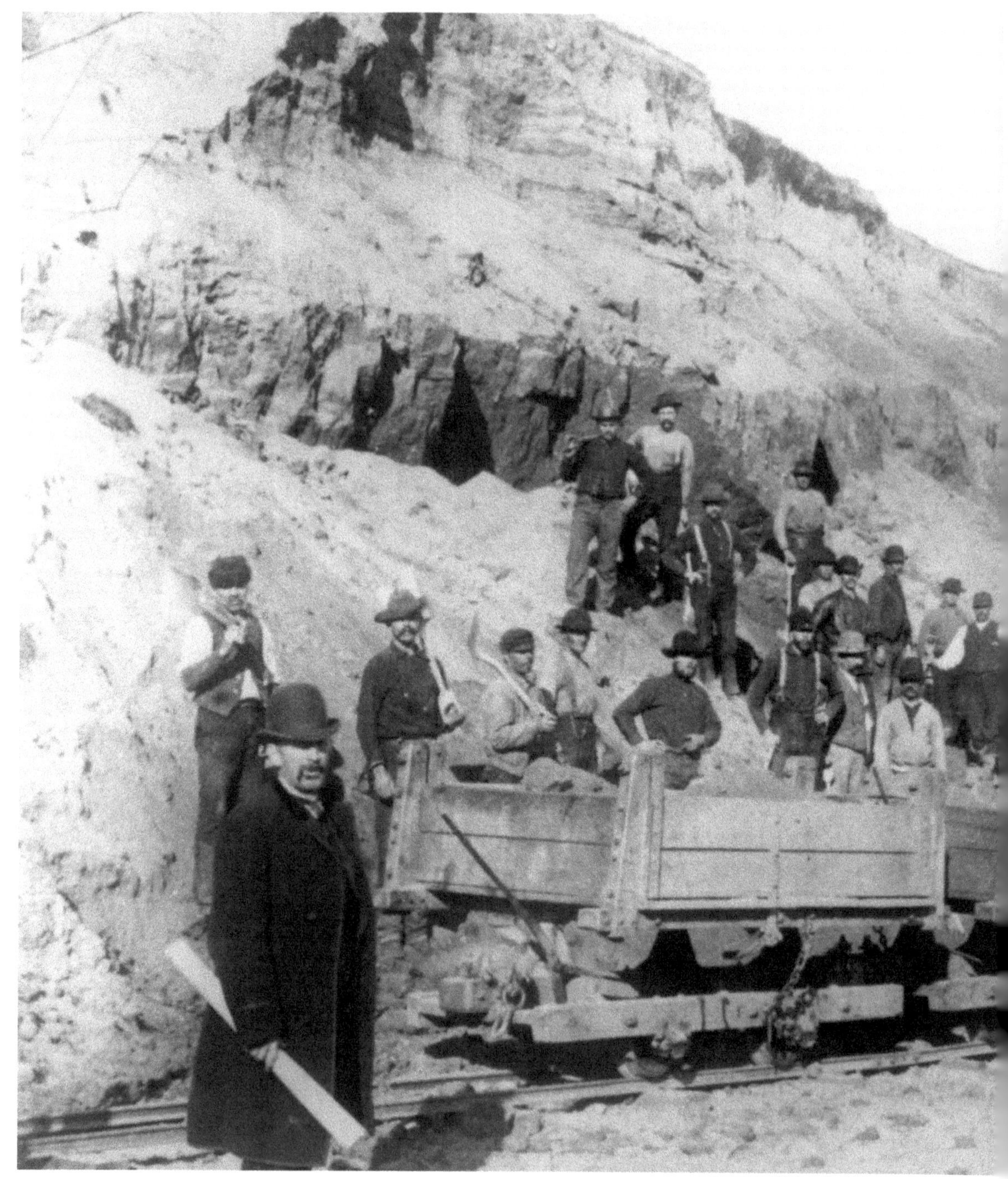

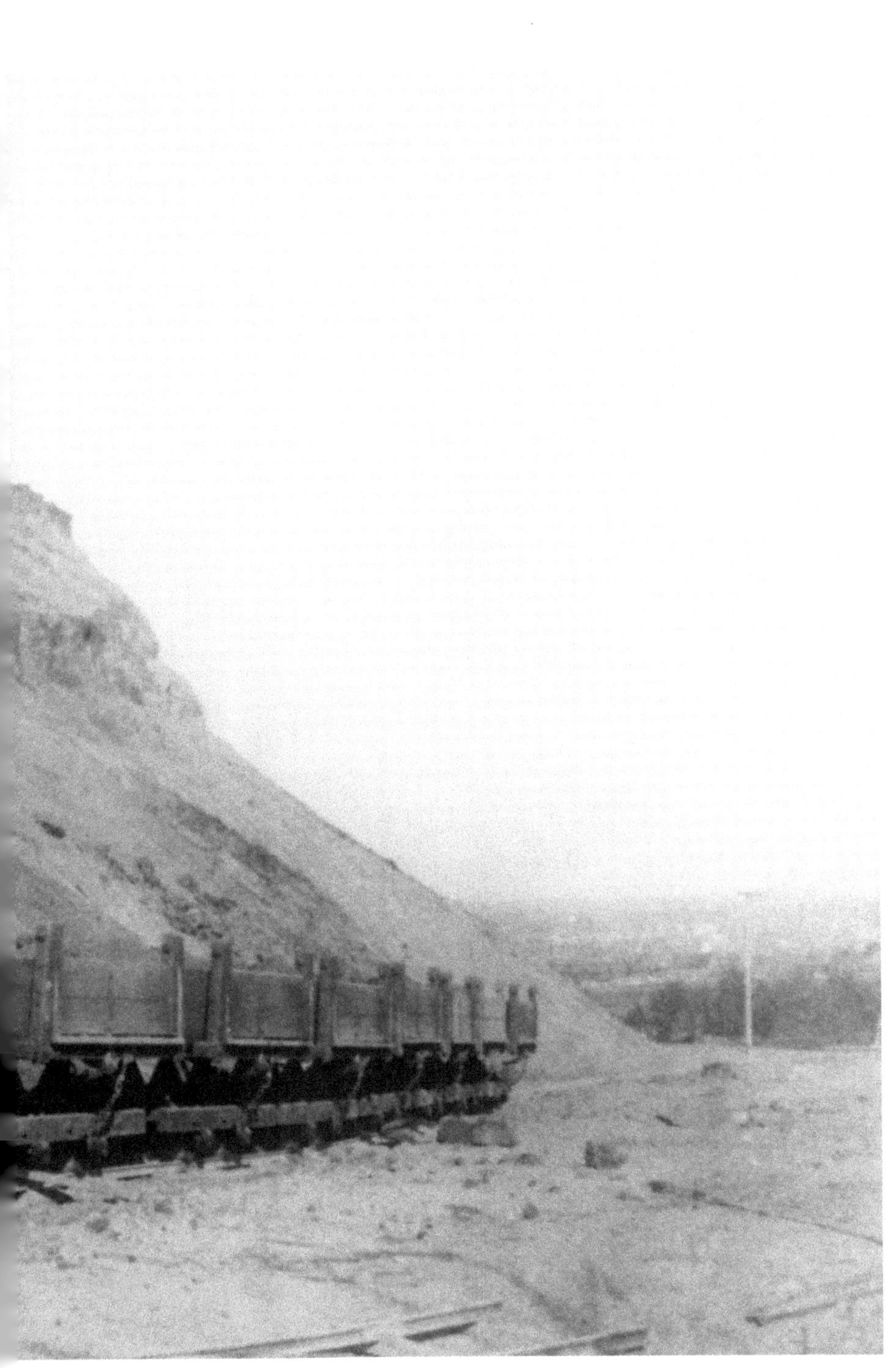

In 1886 the city of Minneapolis removed 270,000 cubic yards of dirt from Lowry's Bluff (also called Lowry Hill) and used it to fill in a marsh. The marsh became a 46-acre park, called the Parade Grounds, near Loring Park.

Minneapolis business mogul William Washburn founded a flour milling empire and later served Minnesota as a U.S. senator. In 1883 he built this lavish estate, Fair Oaks, at Third Avenue South between Twenty-second and Twenty-fourth streets.

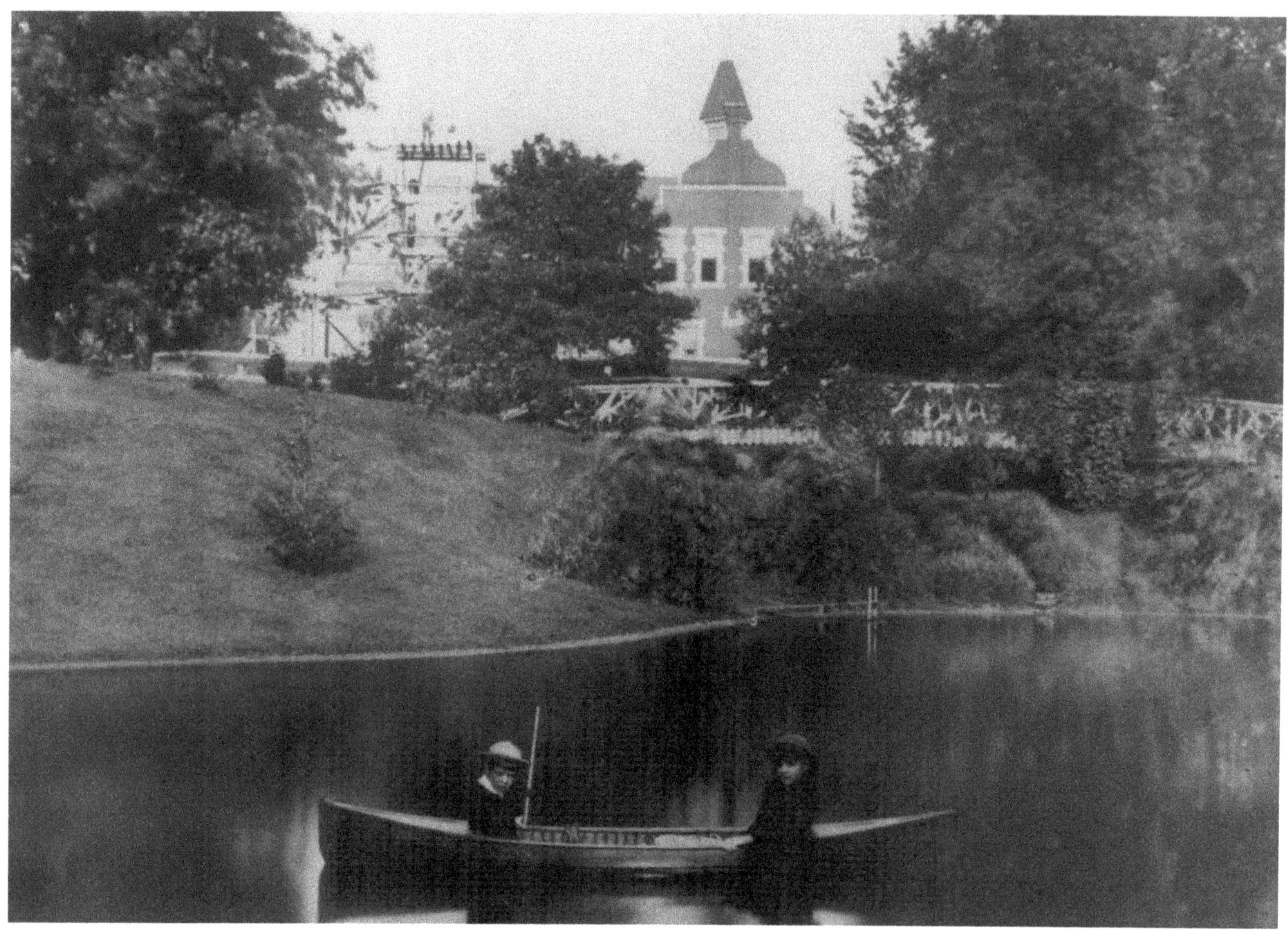

In the 1894-95 Minneapolis City Directory, the Boutell Brothers advertised their furniture company as the "Largest House Furnishing Dealer in the West." Apart from typical house and office furnishings, the brothers also sold goods as varied as stoves, hammocks, and baby carriages.

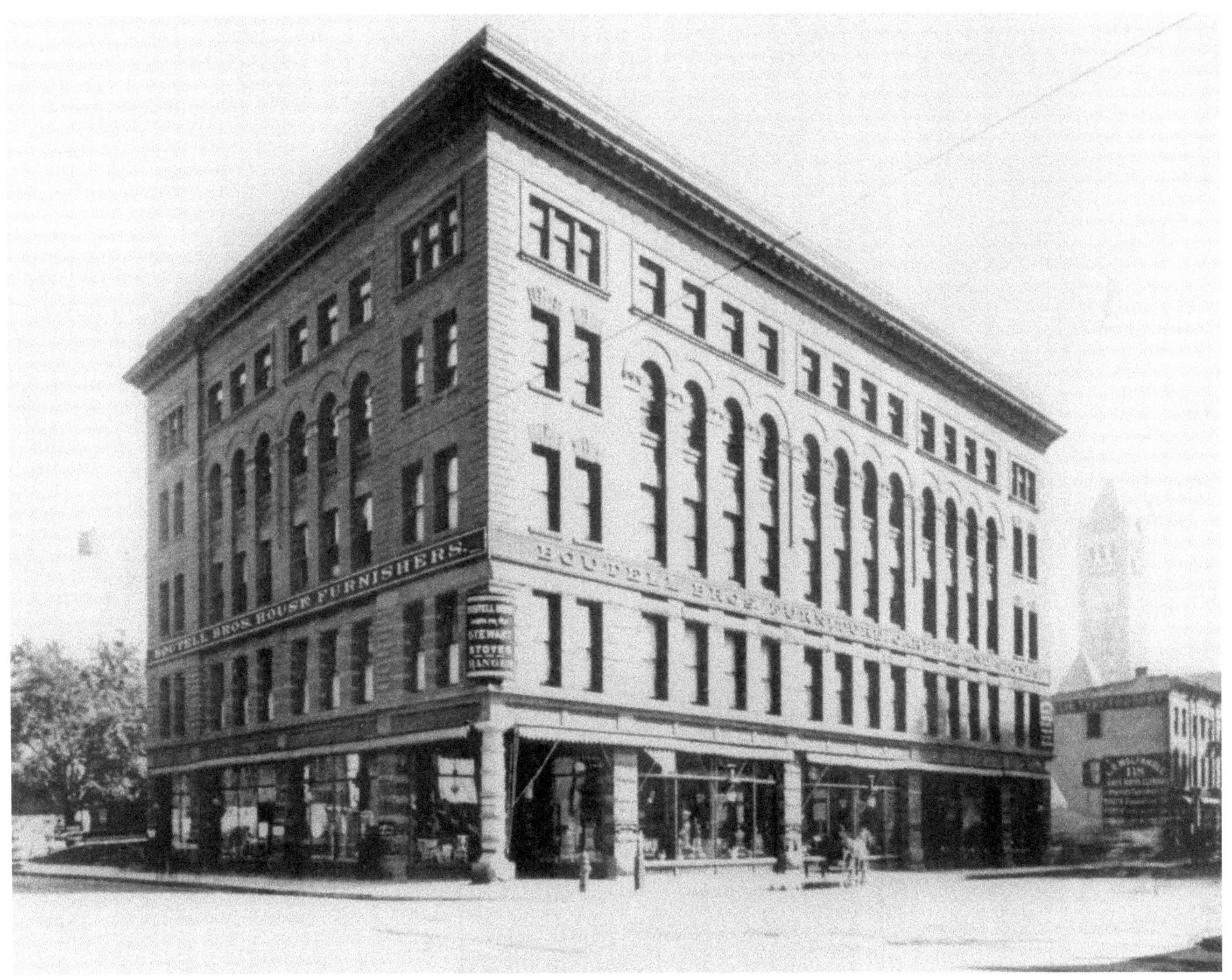

Spurred by the concern that veterans have a pleasant place to live during their later years, the Minnesota legislature voted in 1887 to build a soldiers' home in Minneapolis. Admiral Winfield Scott Schley, a hero of the Spanish-American War, is pictured here visiting the Old Soldiers' Home.

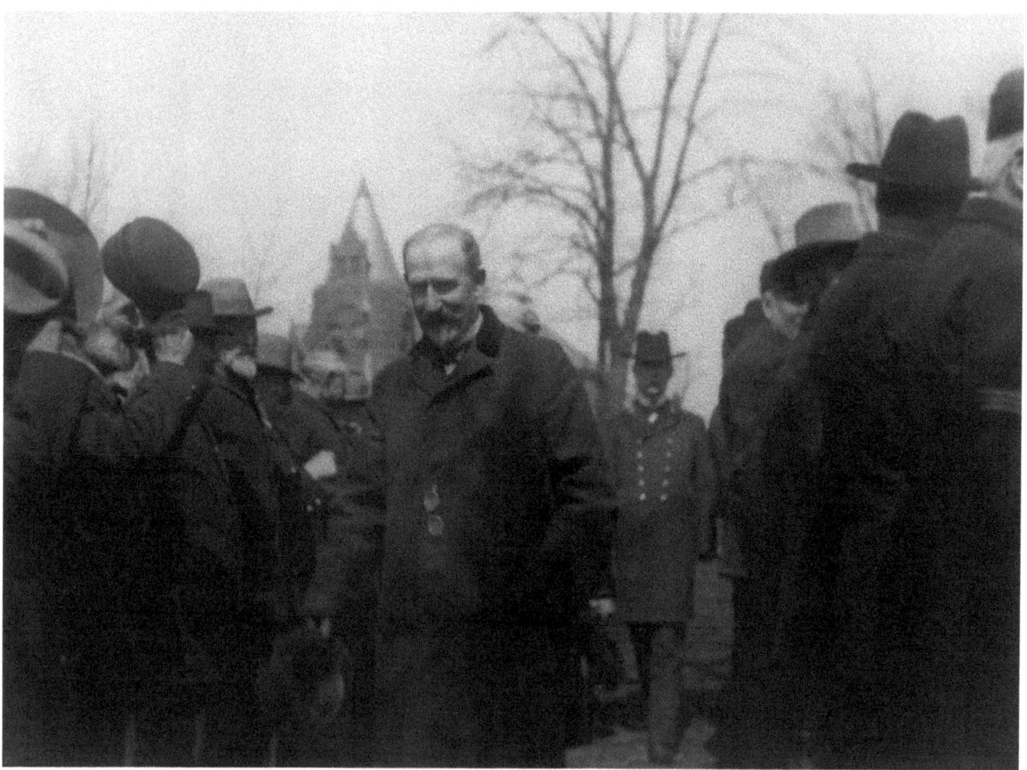

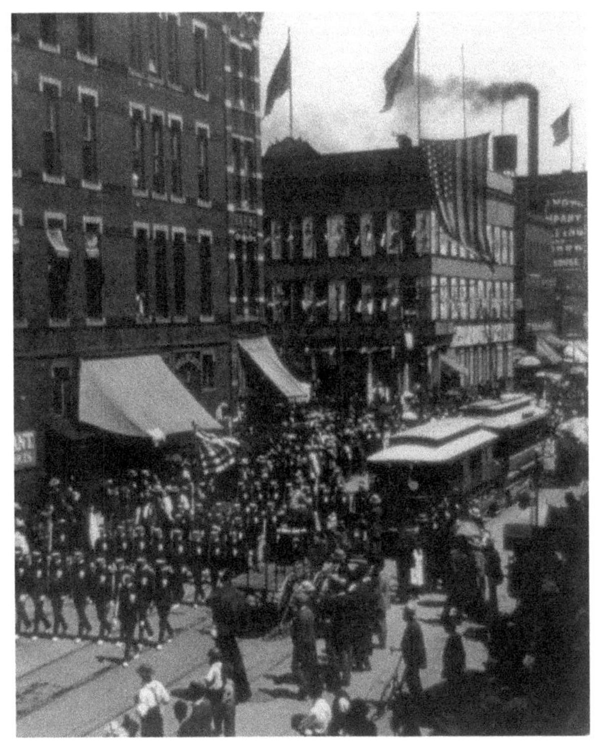

In 1886 fifty-two charter members of the Minneapolis Elks Lodge No. 44 attended their first meeting. The group is shown here parading in Minneapolis in 1897.

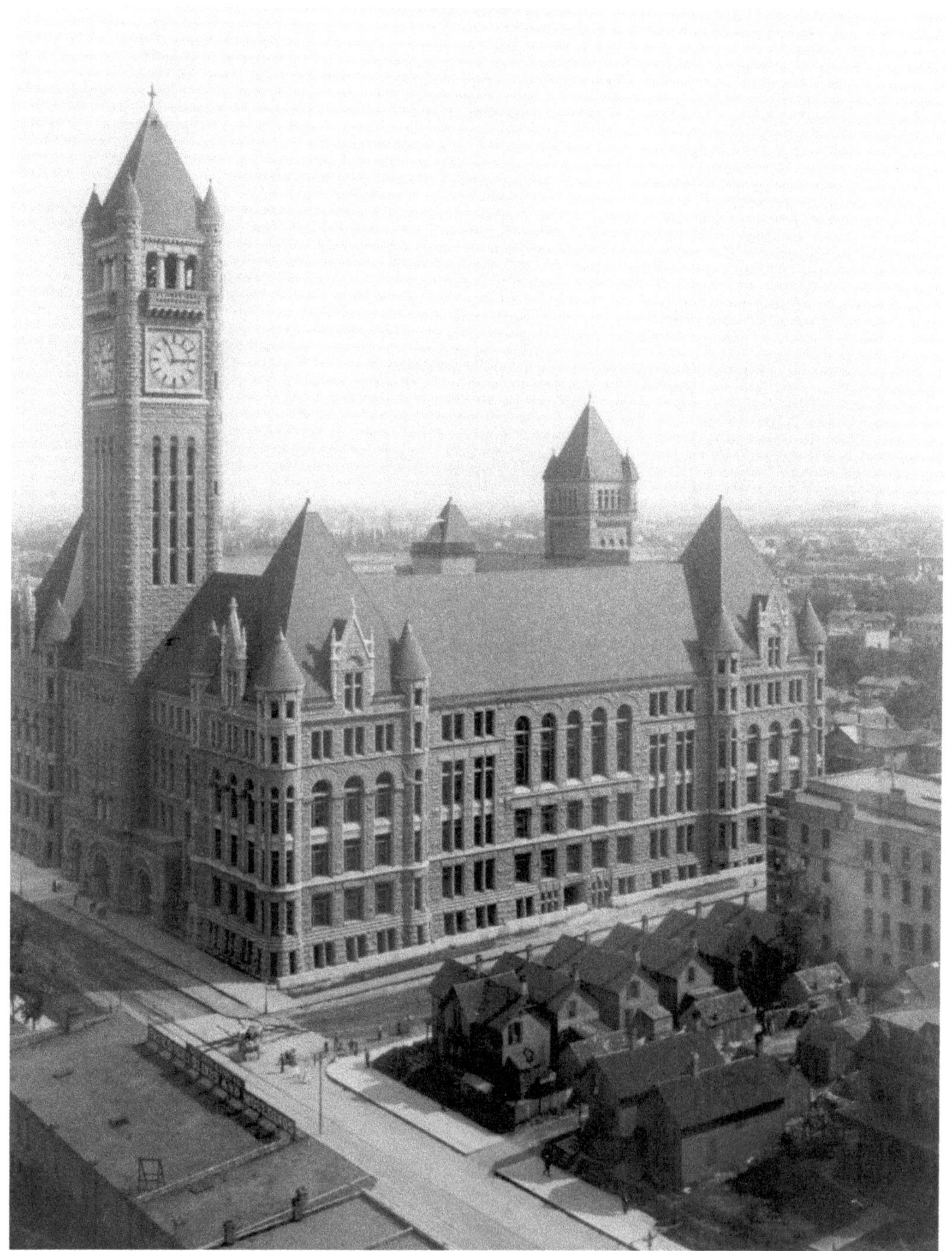

This massive Romanesque structure, officially named the Municipal Building, was built between 1888 and 1909 to house both the Hennepin County courthouse and Minneapolis city hall. The building consumed an entire block of downtown property.

This shot portrays Nicollet Avenue at Sixth Street around 1890. Heffelfinger Brothers Fine Footwear and the Grand Opera House are both visible.

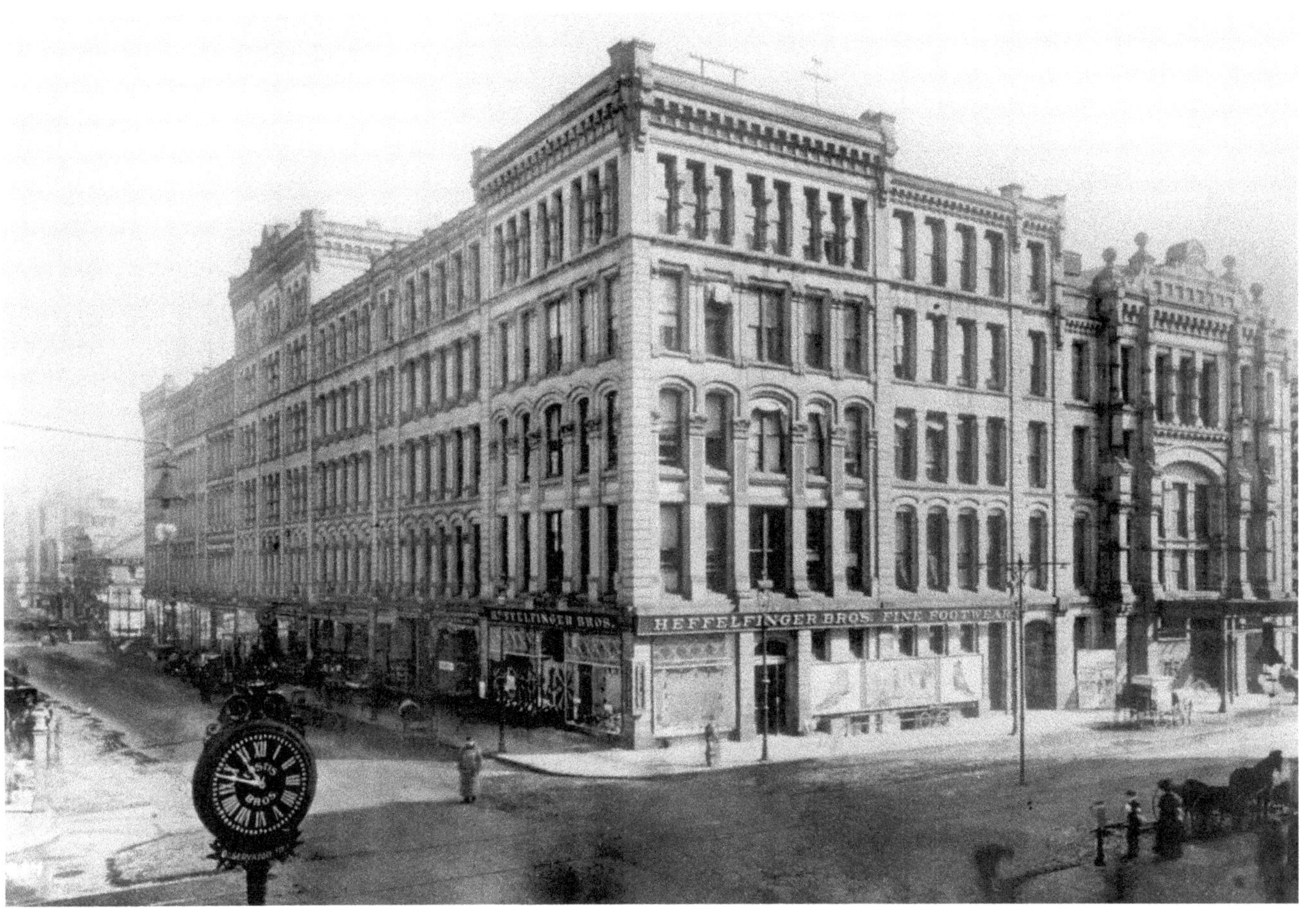

Police Captain Qualey and Harlow Gale stand in front of Gale's Market in Bridge Square, located at Hennepin Avenue and First Street, around 1890.

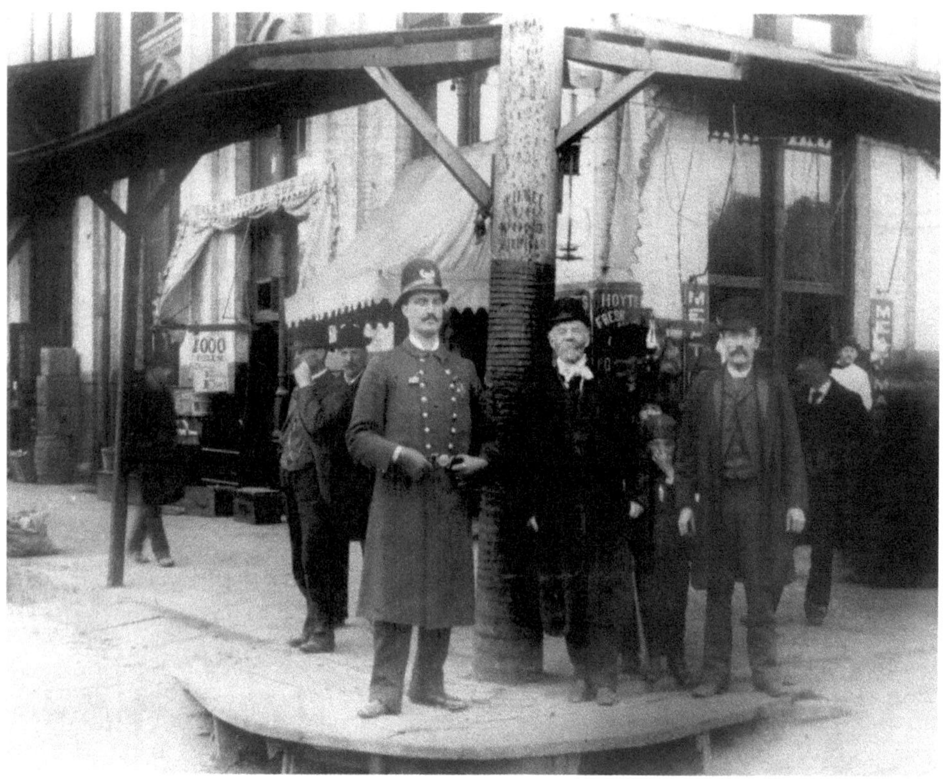

Minneapolitans dubbed Fourth Street between Nicollet and Marquette "newspaper row." Leading papers with a presence on newspaper row included the Tribune, the Minneapolis Journal, and the Daily Star. Here a group of men congregate along newspaper row around the turn of the century.

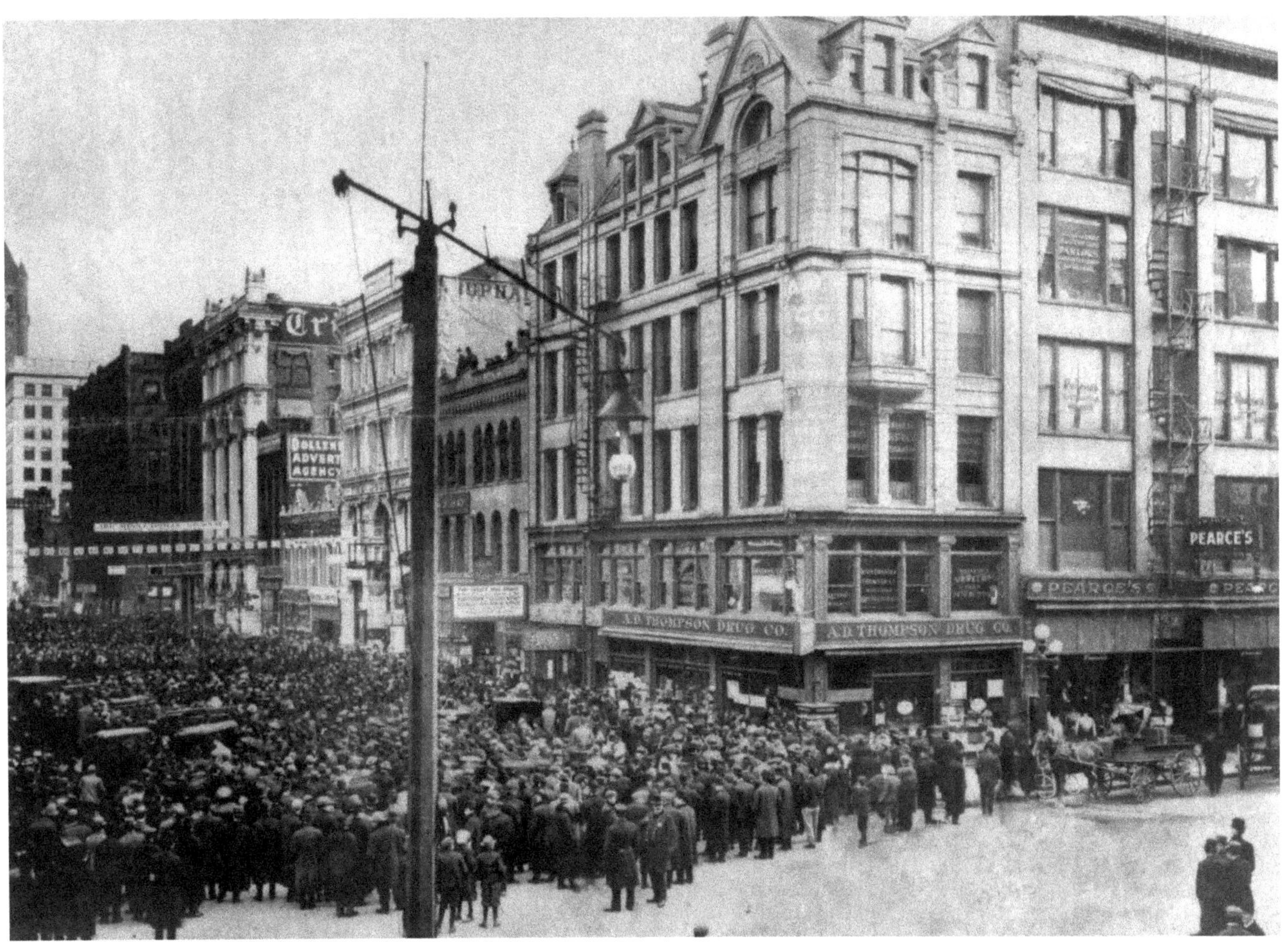

After Minnesota produced a bumper crop in 1891, farmers and merchants celebrated with a harvest festival. Enthusiasm for the festival swept through Minneapolis, and nearly every building in the city bore decorations. Here citizens line the streets to enjoy a three-hour parade.

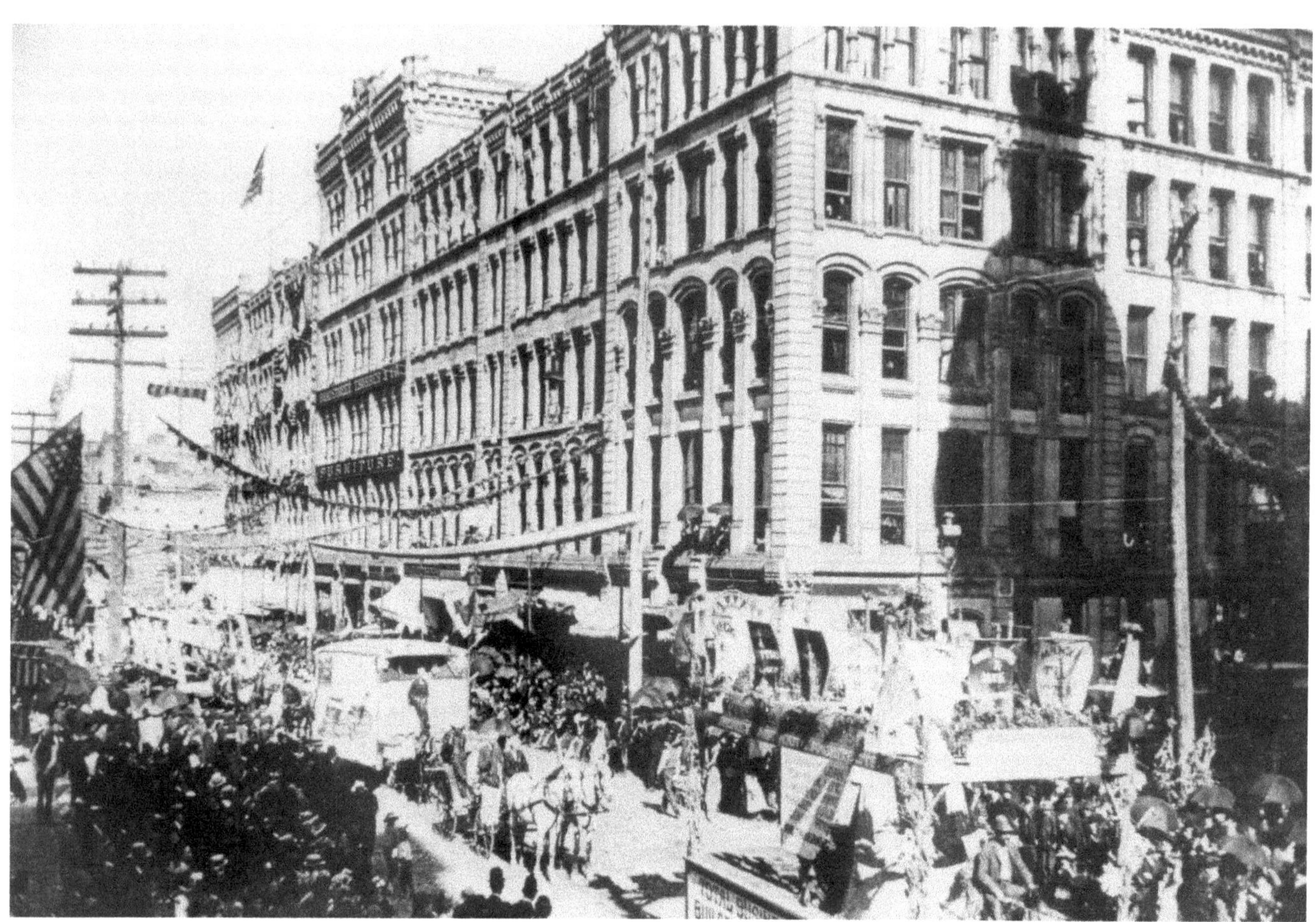

The Bohemian Flats neighborhood in Minneapolis attracted poor immigrant families. Housing was cheap in the Flats because the area sat on a floodplain within feet of the Mississippi River. Here neighborhood children play in the shadow of the Washington Avenue Bridge in the late nineteenth century.

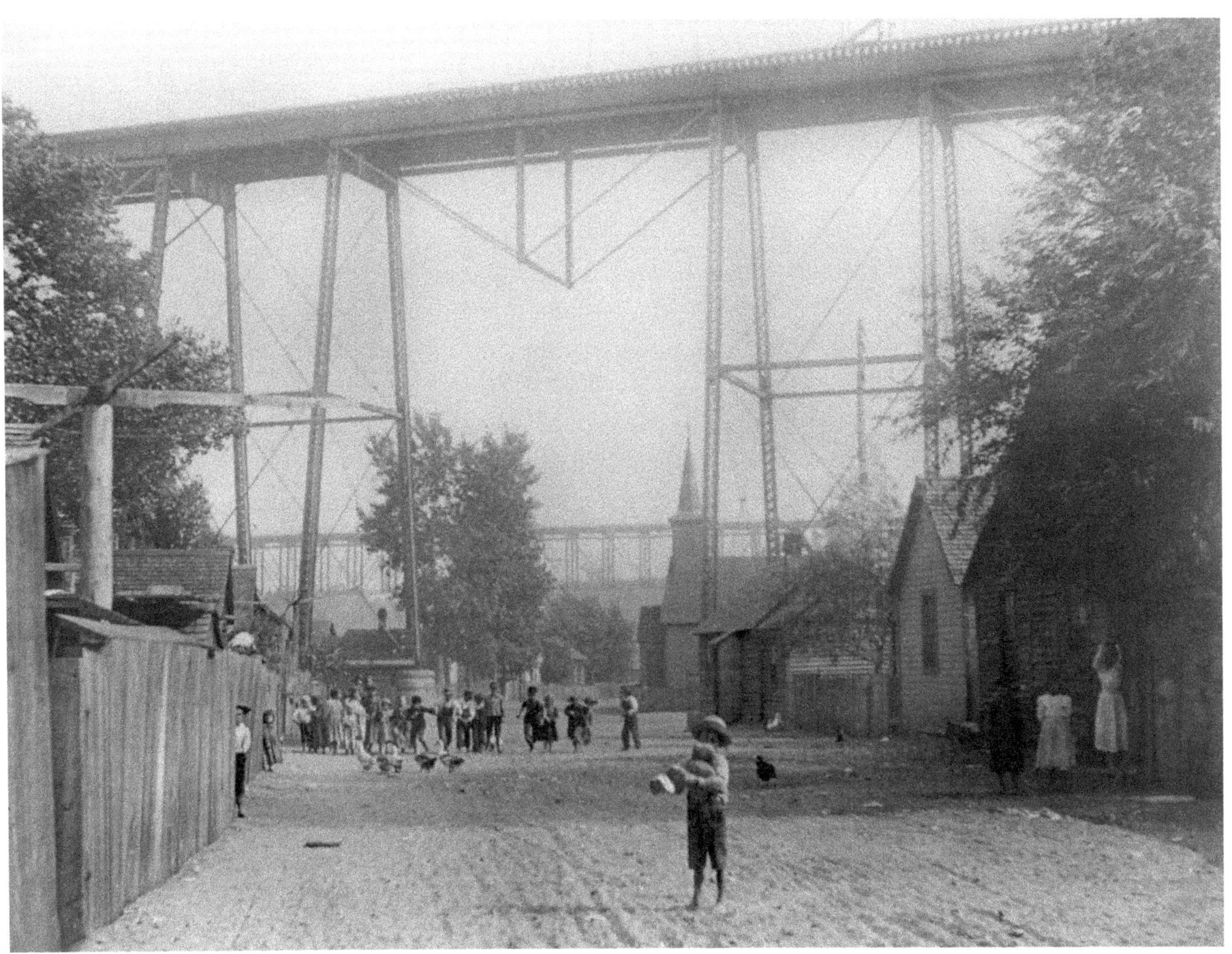

In the early 1880s a bridge was built to carry First Street over the railroad tracks below. This single-span bridge was only 85 feet in length and served pedestrians, horse-drawn wagons, and, eventually, automobiles. This view of the bridge was captured in 1891.

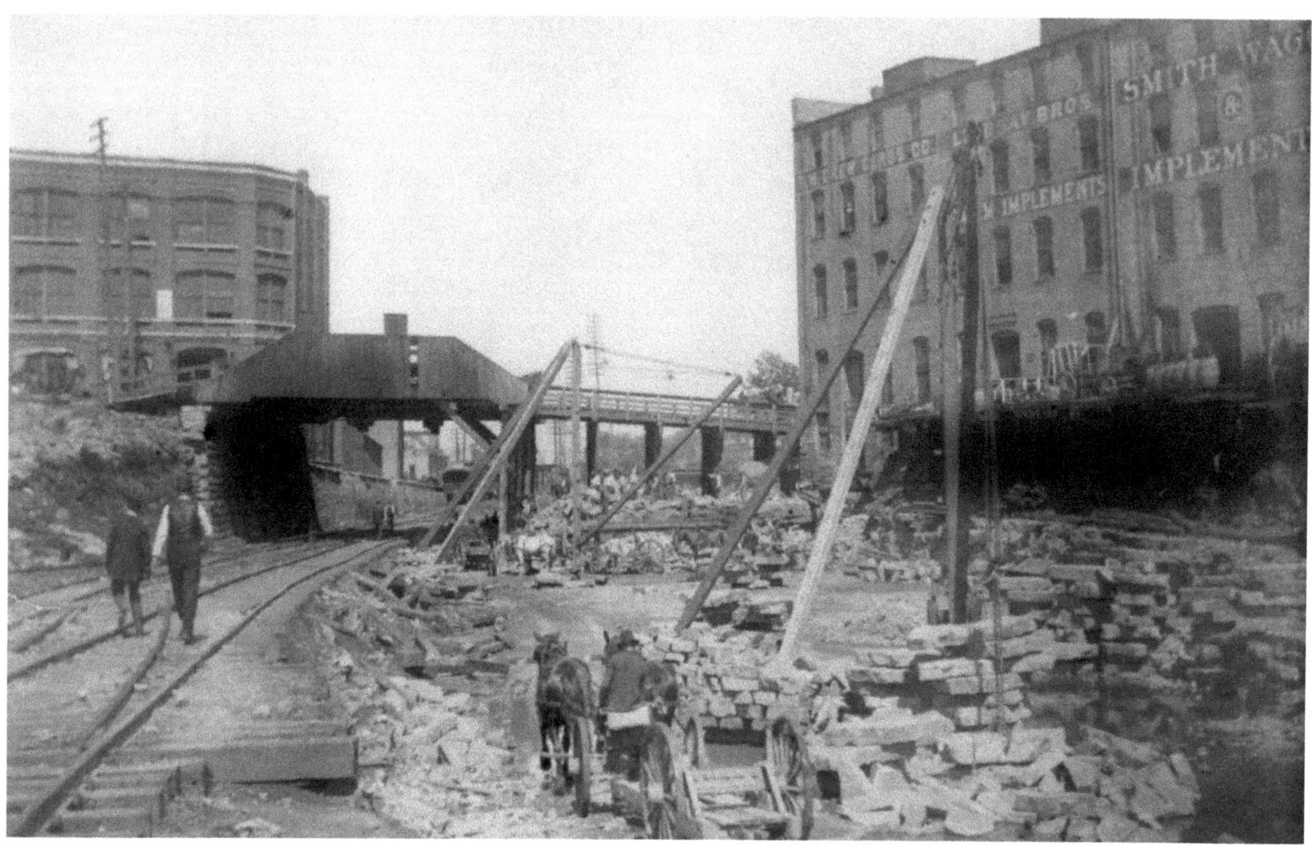

Christmas Lake, located in a western suburb of Minneapolis, often attracted artists because of the water's exceptional clarity. Here a woman paints on the shores of the lake in 1898.

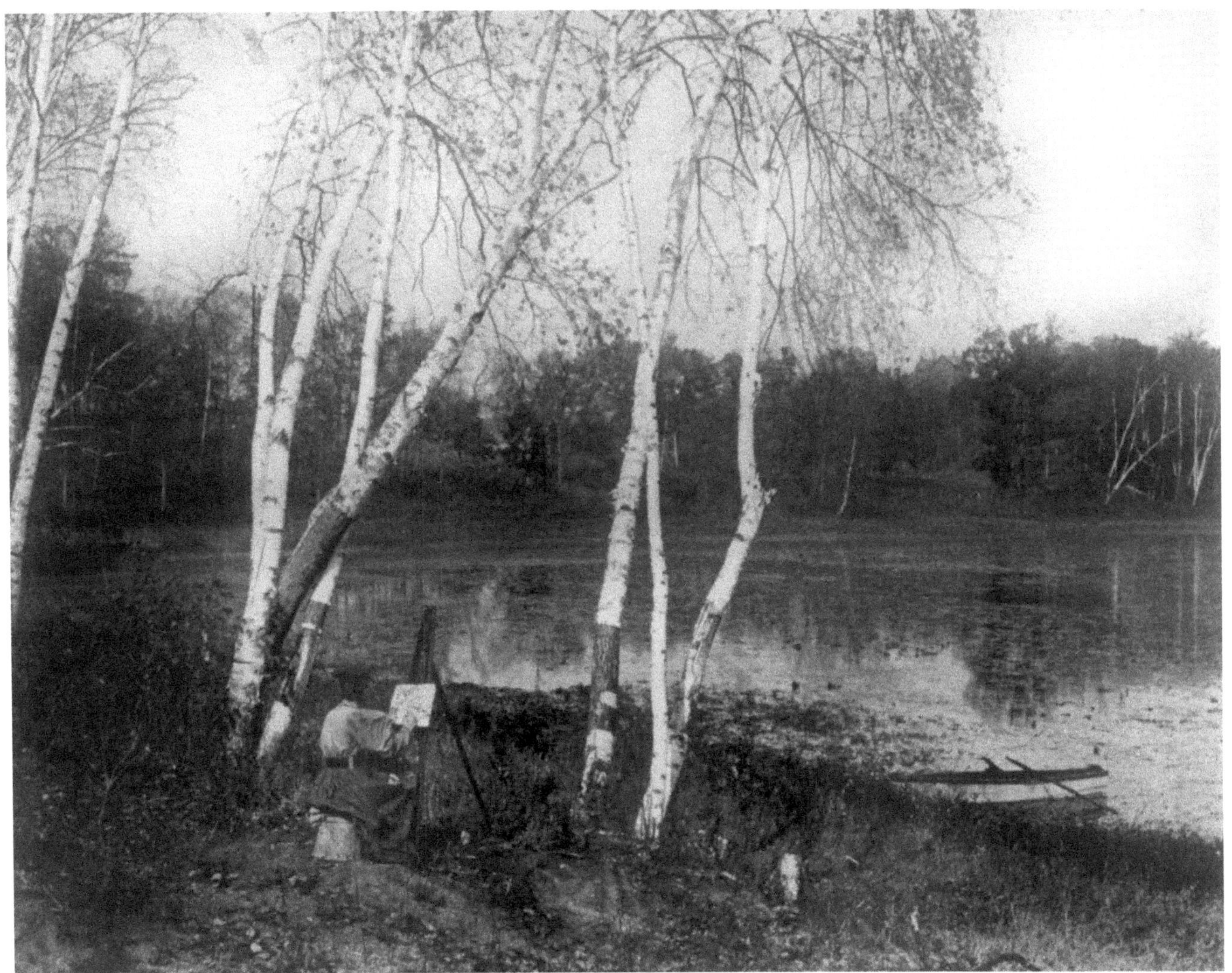

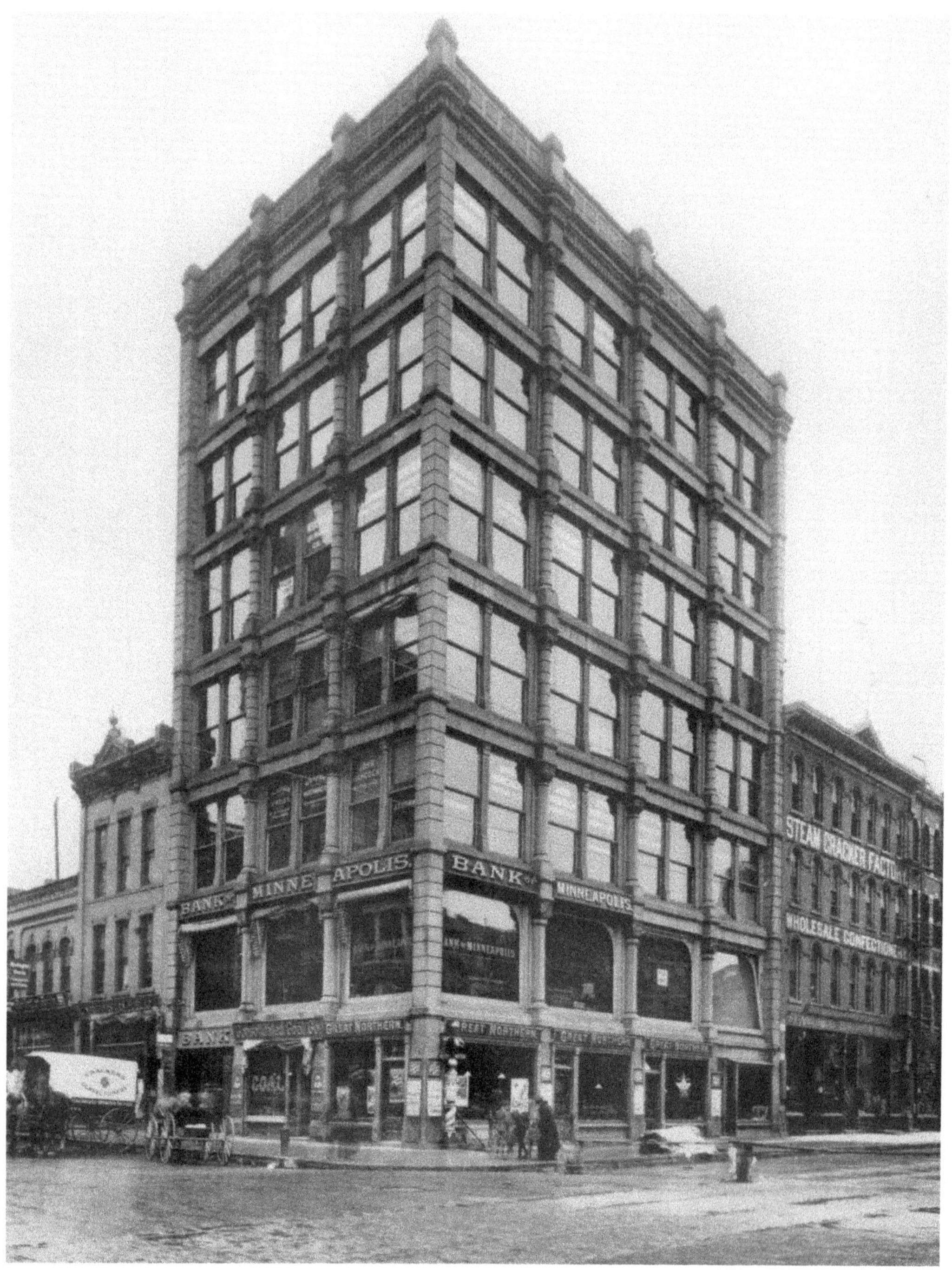

The Bank of Minneapolis, designed by the Hodgson and Son architectural firm in 1896, stood at the corner of Third Street and Nicollet Avenue. The seven-story building awed residents with its unique metal structure and airy plate-glass windows.

Minnesota sent three regiments of volunteers to serve in the Spanish-American War. The Thirteenth Minnesota Infantry lost more than forty men, mostly to disease, in 1899. Here Minneapolitans welcome returning soldiers home with a parade in October of that year.

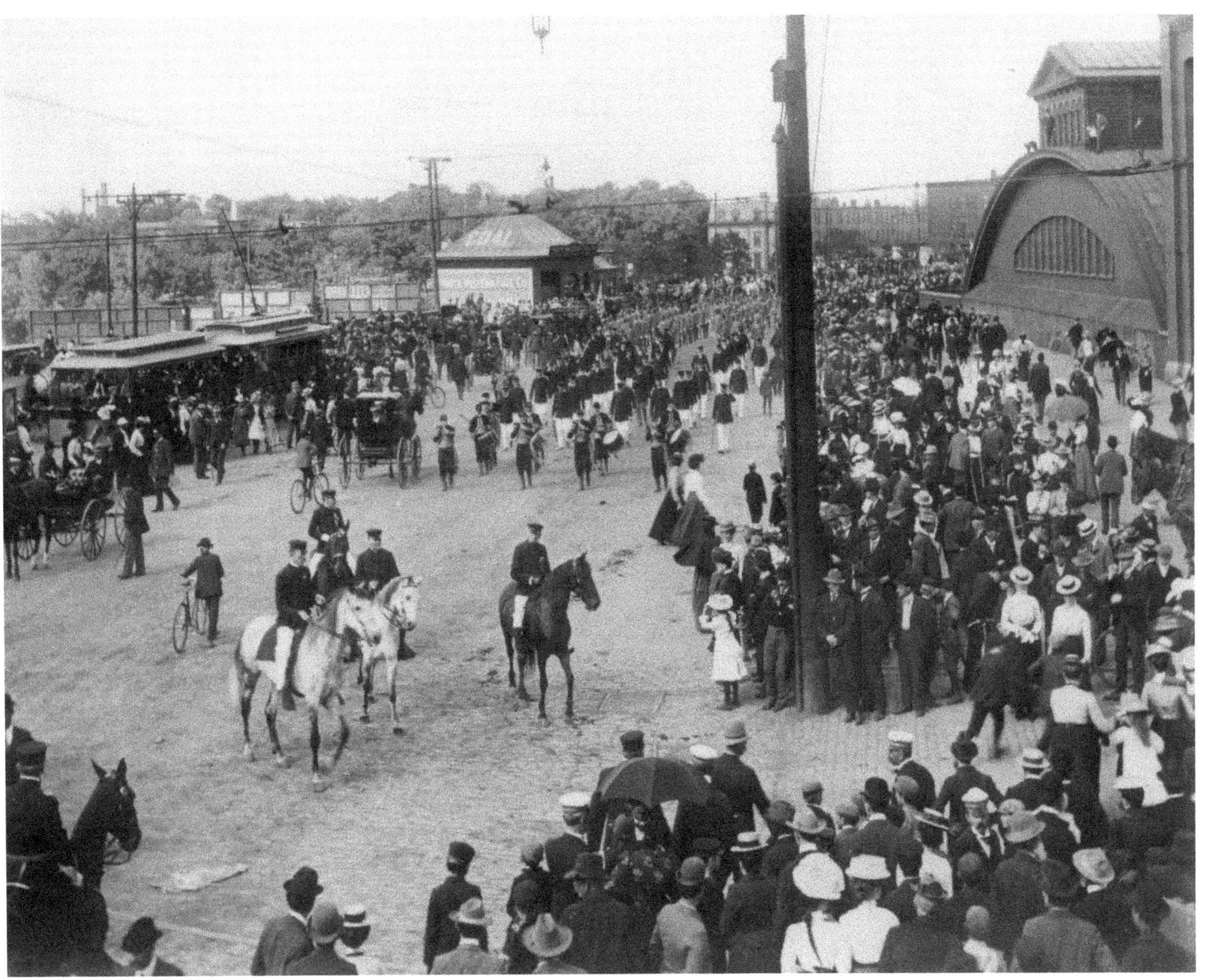

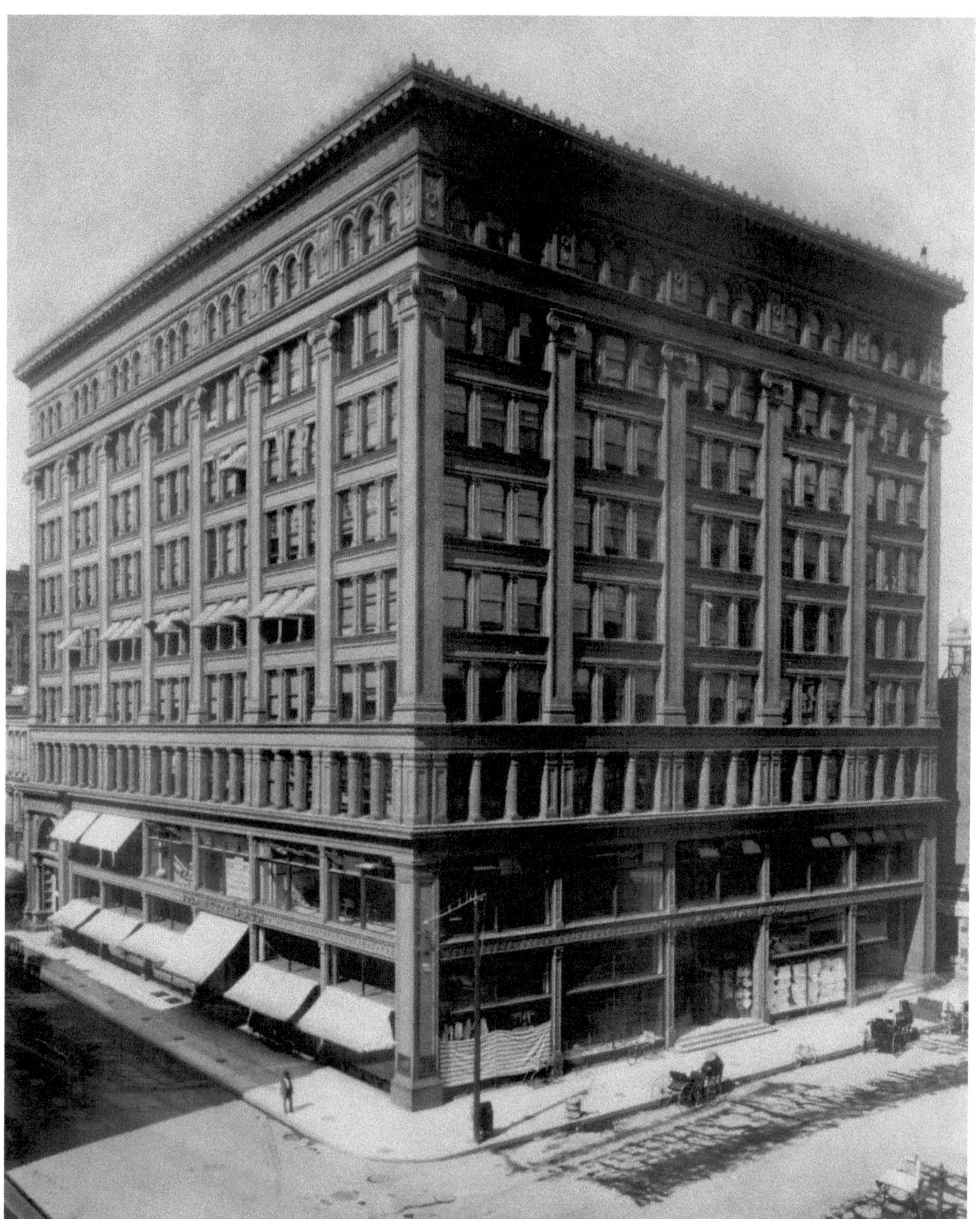

The Andrus Building, seen here around 1899 and located at 512 Nicollet Avenue, served for many years as home to the J. C. Penney Company. Throughout its history it also housed the U.S. Post Office and a regional office of the U.S. Department of Agriculture.

This rooftop view depicts downtown Minneapolis in 1896, as seen looking west from the Northwestern Guaranty Loan Building (later renamed the Metropolitan Building) on the corner of Third Street and Second Avenue South.

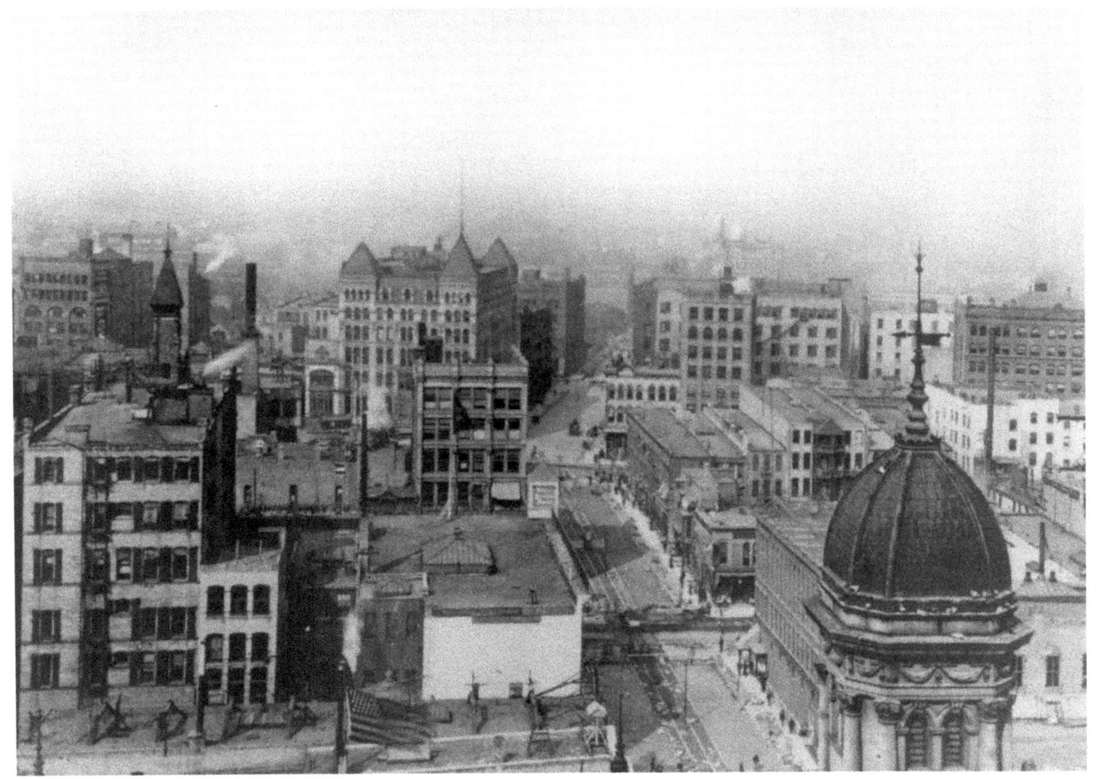

Schoolchildren and their teachers sit for a picture during a field trip to the Old Soldiers' Home (later the Minnesota Veterans Home). The children sang songs to brighten the spirits of veterans at the home.

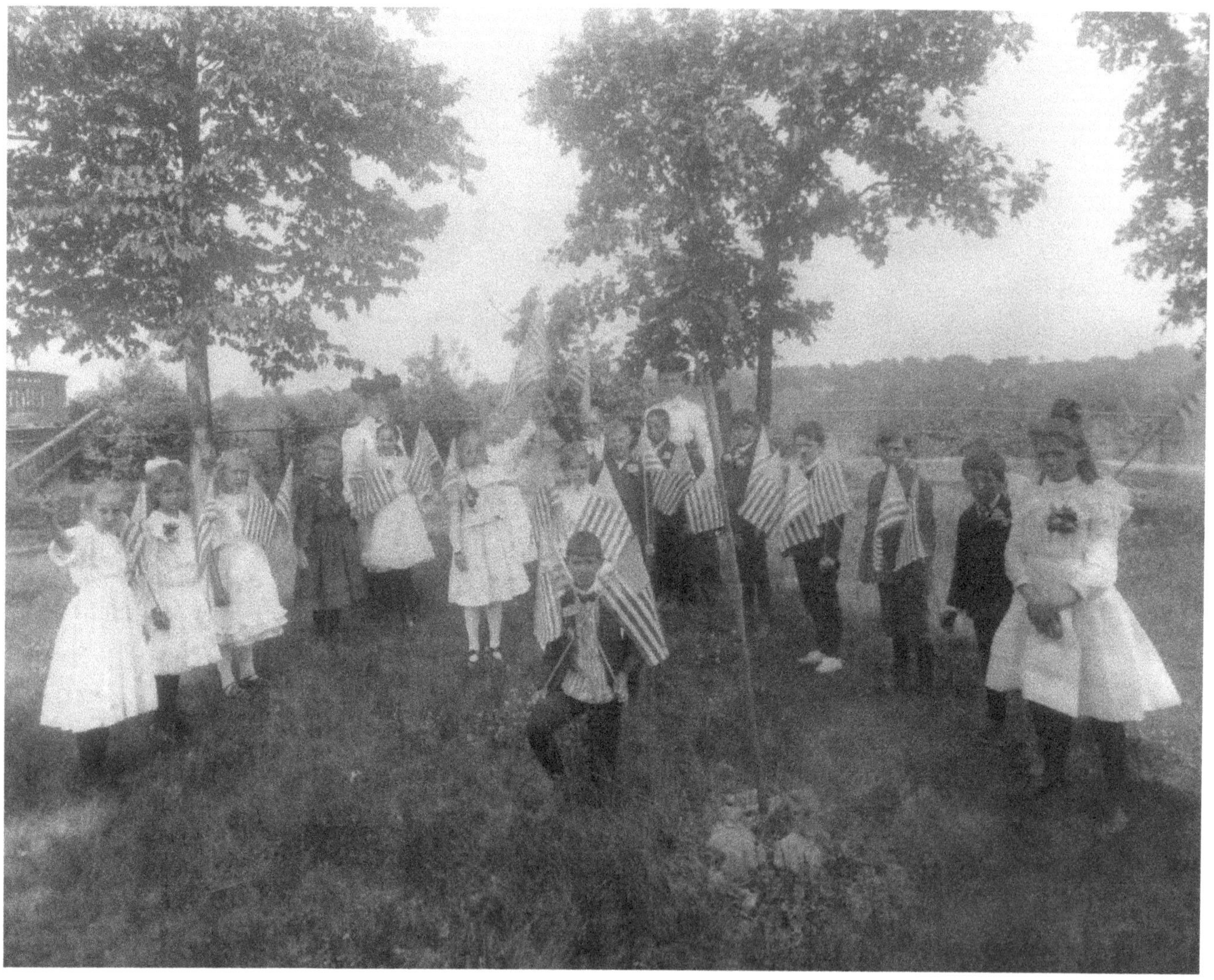

Minneapolis Enters a New Century

(1900–1920)

Minneapolis's frantic rate of growth continued into the early years of the twentieth century. By 1910 the city's population had topped 300,000 and its borders stretched for fifty square miles.

This expansion necessitated massive investment in infrastructure. At the turn of the century Minneapolis had paved 100 miles of streets and by 1911 residents could stroll along nearly 600 miles of sidewalks. Electric streetcars replaced the earlier horse-drawn models and construction of new lines connecting Minneapolis with outlying areas reached a furious pace. During this "golden age" of streetcars Minneapolitans could easily hop a streetcar to reach the extensive new shopping districts in St. Paul or to visit family and friends in the suburbs. During the hot summer months many Minneapolitans gladly paid the 25-cent fare to make the trip from Minneapolis to Big Island Park at Lake Minnetonka, where visitors reveled in live band music, picturesque swimming beaches, and extensive picnic grounds.

Those who chose to stay closer to home found numerous shopping and entertainment venues in the heart of Minneapolis. Businesses and specialty shops lined Nicollet Avenue, the city's premier shopping district, which was anchored by two rival department stores: Donaldson's and Dayton's. Numerous downtown theaters provided regular opportunities for residents to enjoy vaudeville shows and other live entertainment.

The parks system in Minneapolis also continued to expand at a dizzying pace. During this time the park board turned its attention to four large lakes just south of downtown, which had once been described by Park Superintendent Theodore Wirth as "mosquito-infested . . . swamplands." Through a massive dredging project the lakes' swampy shores were filled in and beautified. The Lake District immediately became the recreational hub of Minneapolis.

Not all residents shared in the city's prosperity. In southeast Minneapolis, just across from the University of Minnesota, the Bohemian Flats neighborhood provided cheap, crude housing to recent immigrants. Bohemian Flats was located beneath the Washington Avenue Bridge on the banks of the Mississippi and residents endured regular flooding of their homes. The settlers who lived there formed a tight-knit community that was both physically and economically separated from the bustling city on the banks above.

The band entertains fans at a University of Minnesota football game about 1900. The Armory Building, visible at left, dates from 1896.

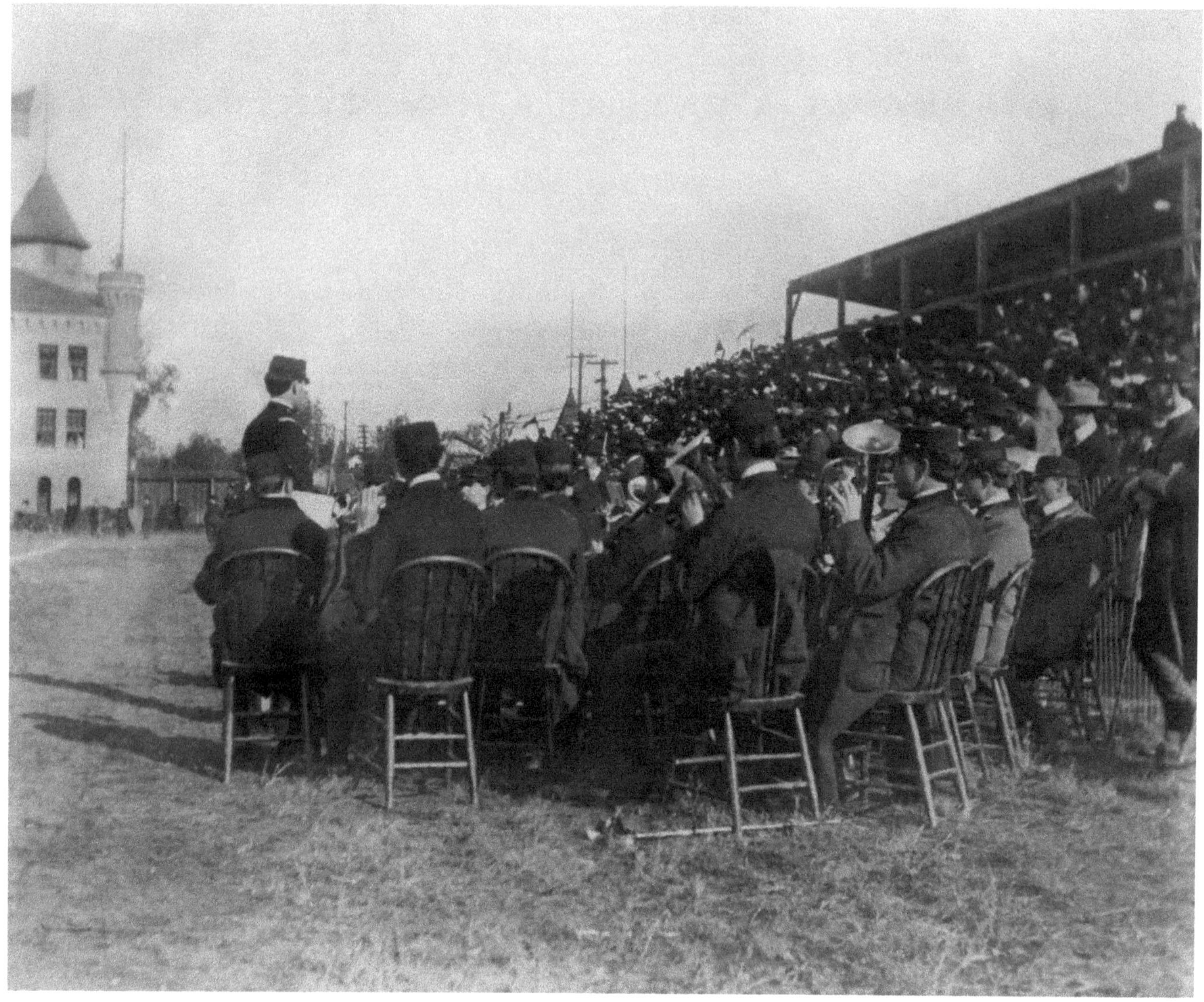

Parishioners of the Thirty-eighth Street Congregational Church ride in a parade float about 1900.

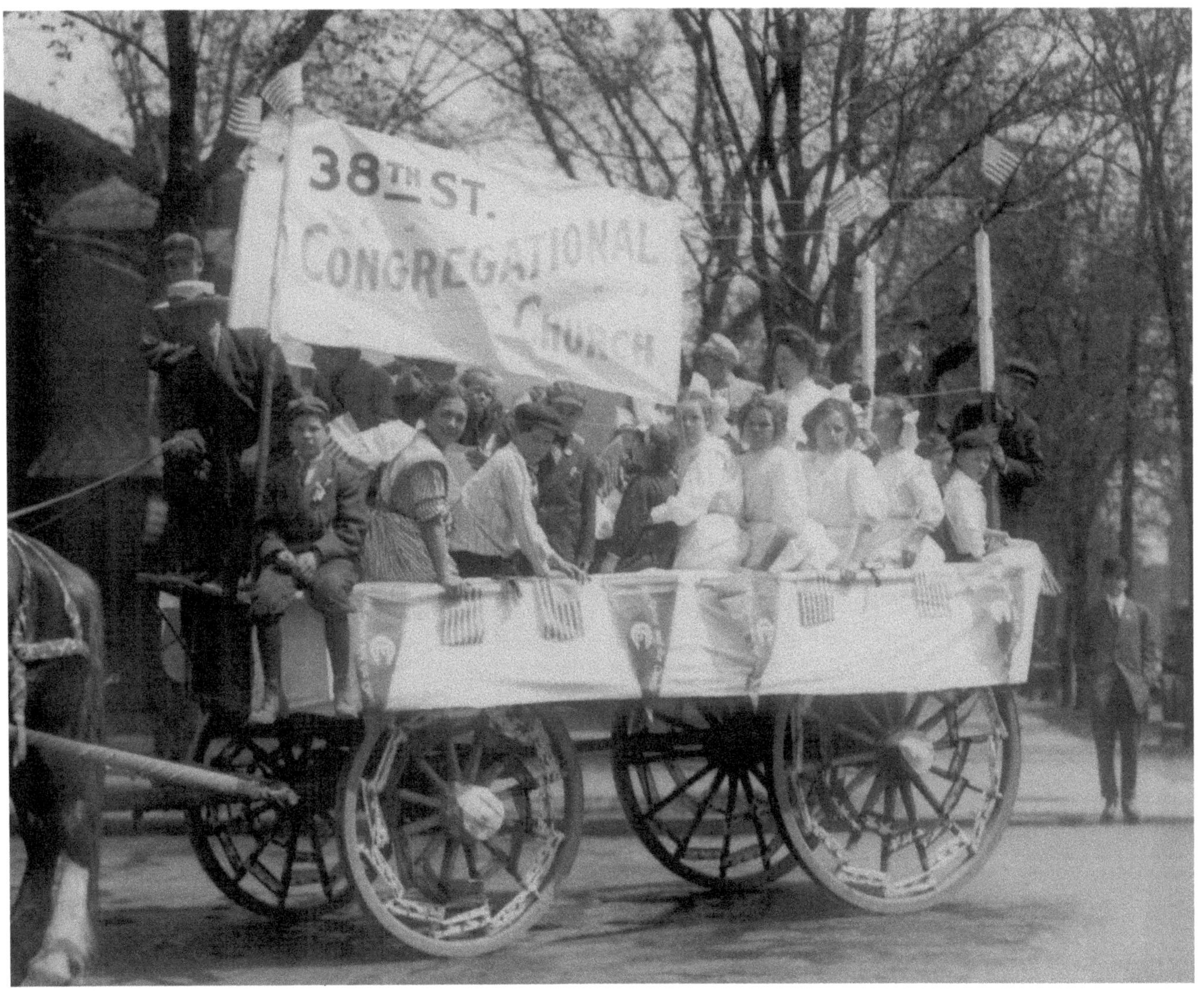

Pedestrians and streetcars navigate snowy streets in the winter of 1902. The marquee of the Metropolitan Opera House, located at 320 First Avenue South, is visible partway down the block at left.

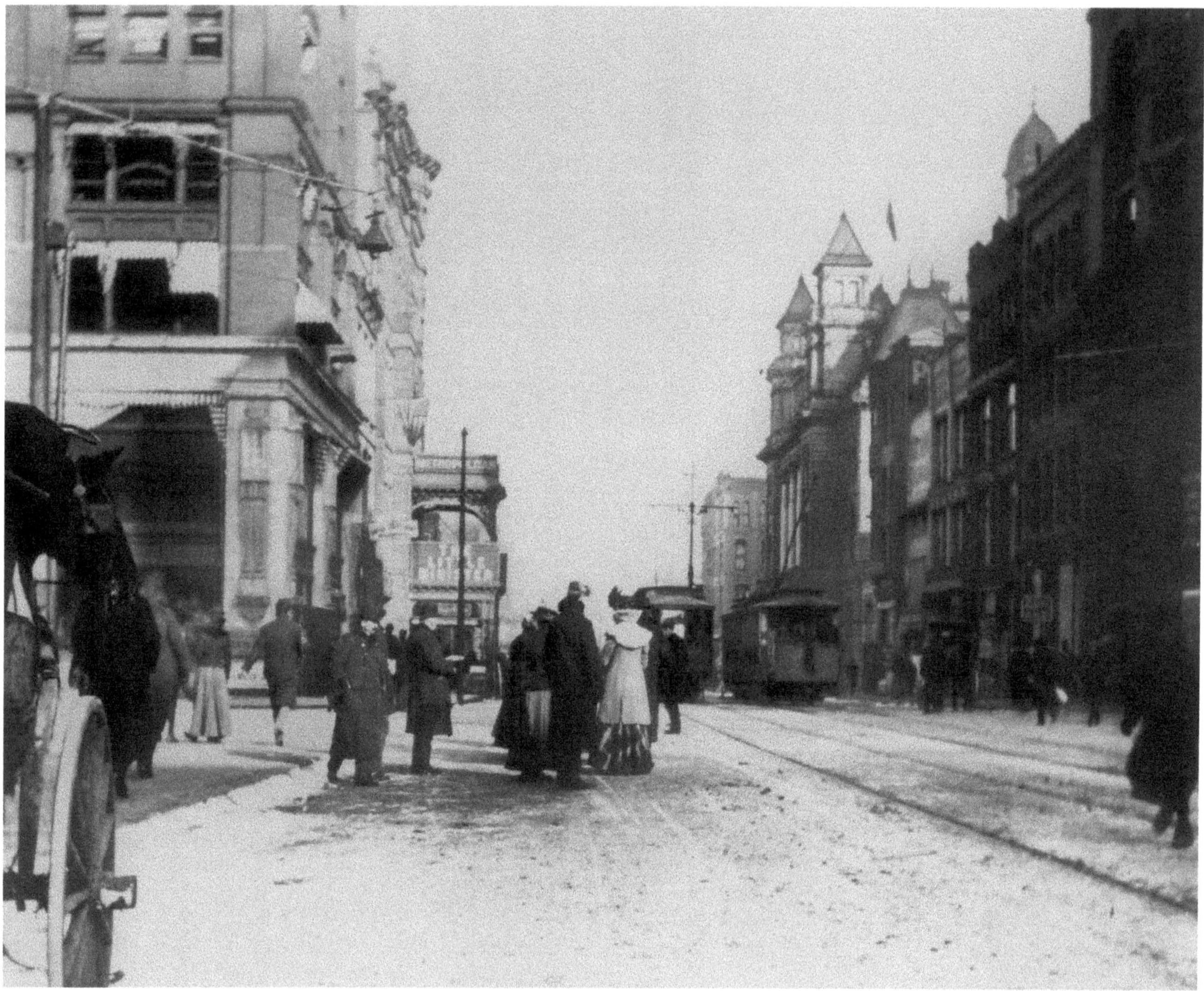

Men gather to celebrate the completion of a streetcar line from Minneapolis to Fort Snelling on August 21, 1905.

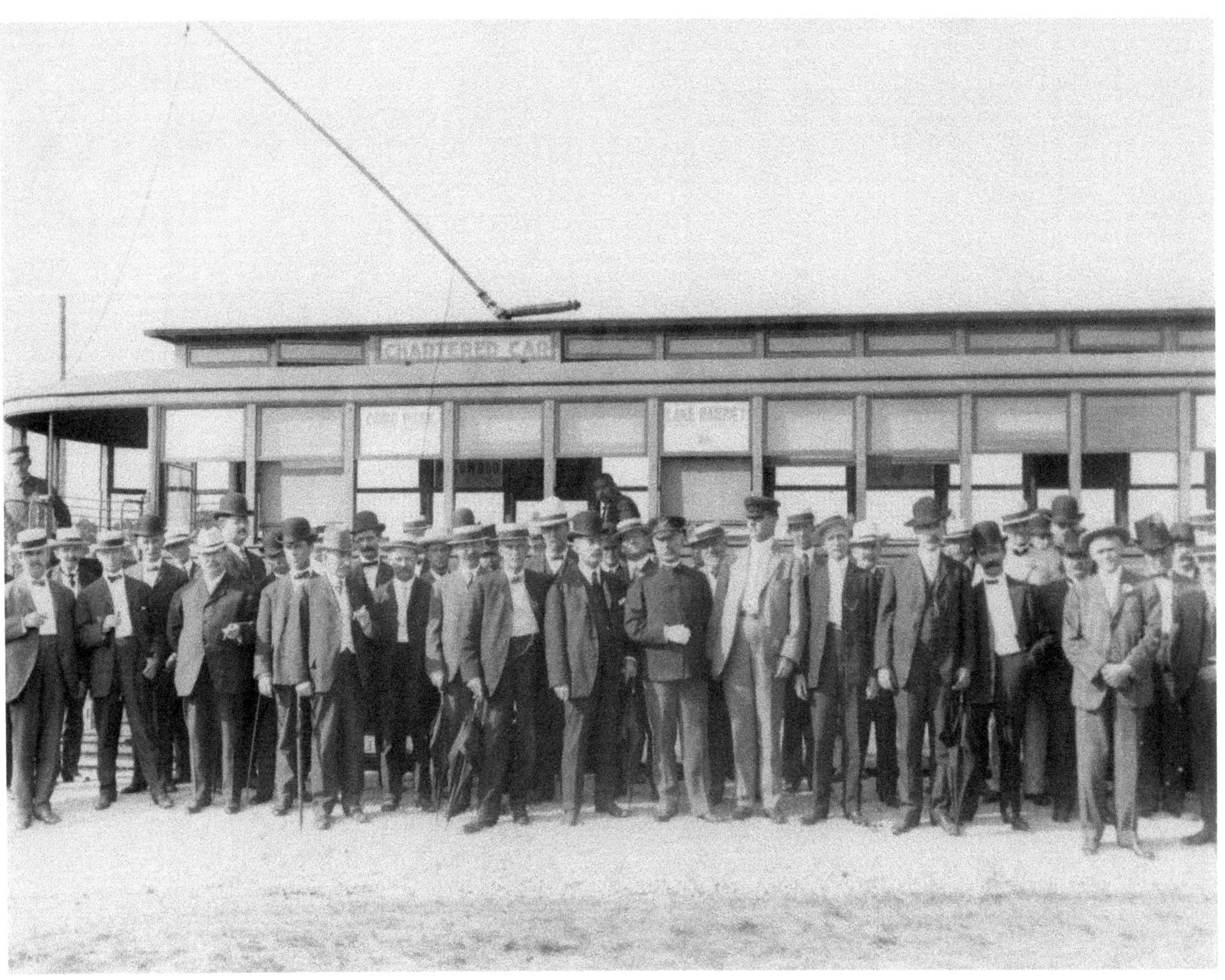

Shown here around 1910 is an interior view of the home at 2200 Sheridan Avenue, in the affluent Calhoun-Isles neighborhood of south Minneapolis.

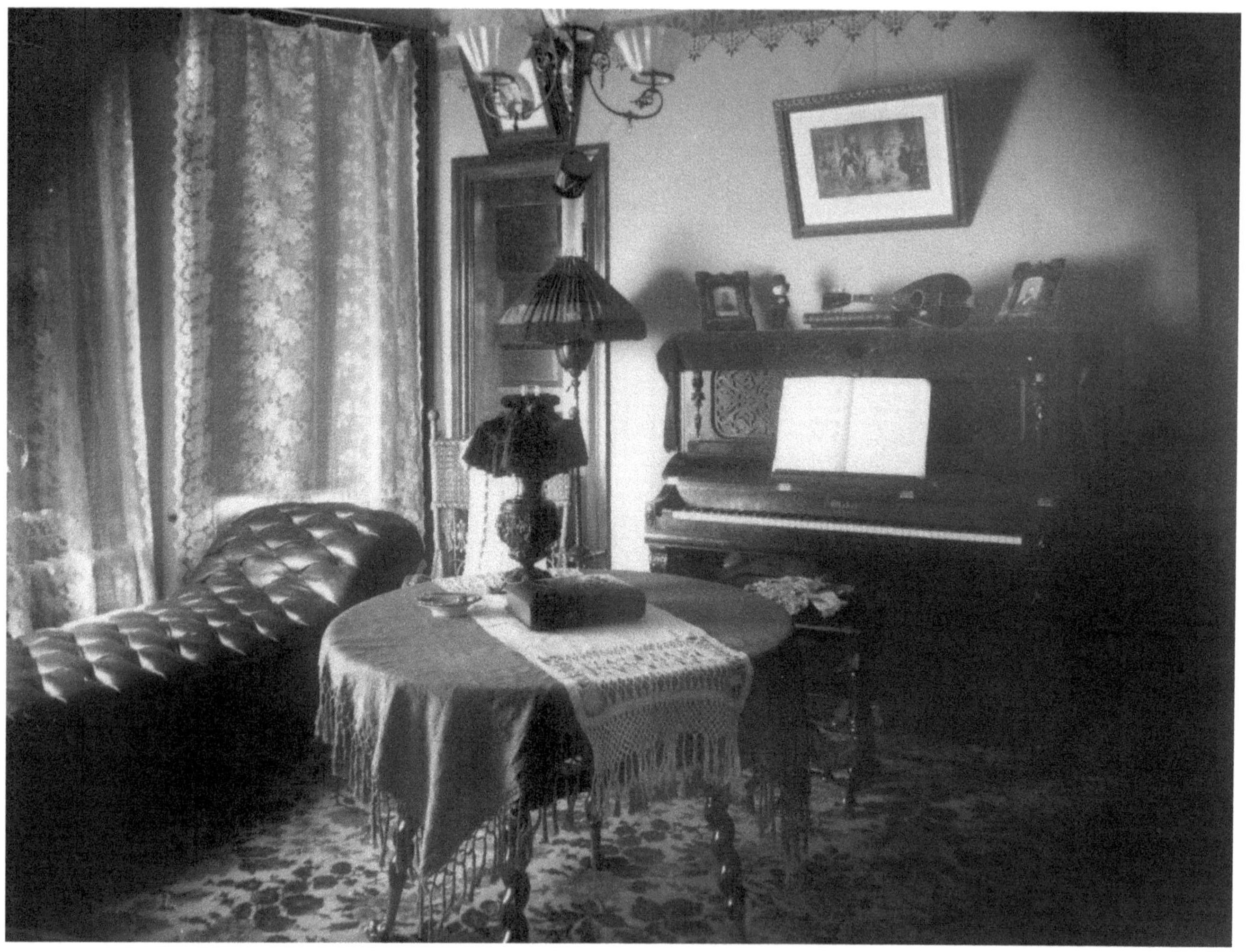

A quiet residential street, probably Second or Third Avenue South, as it appeared around 1910.

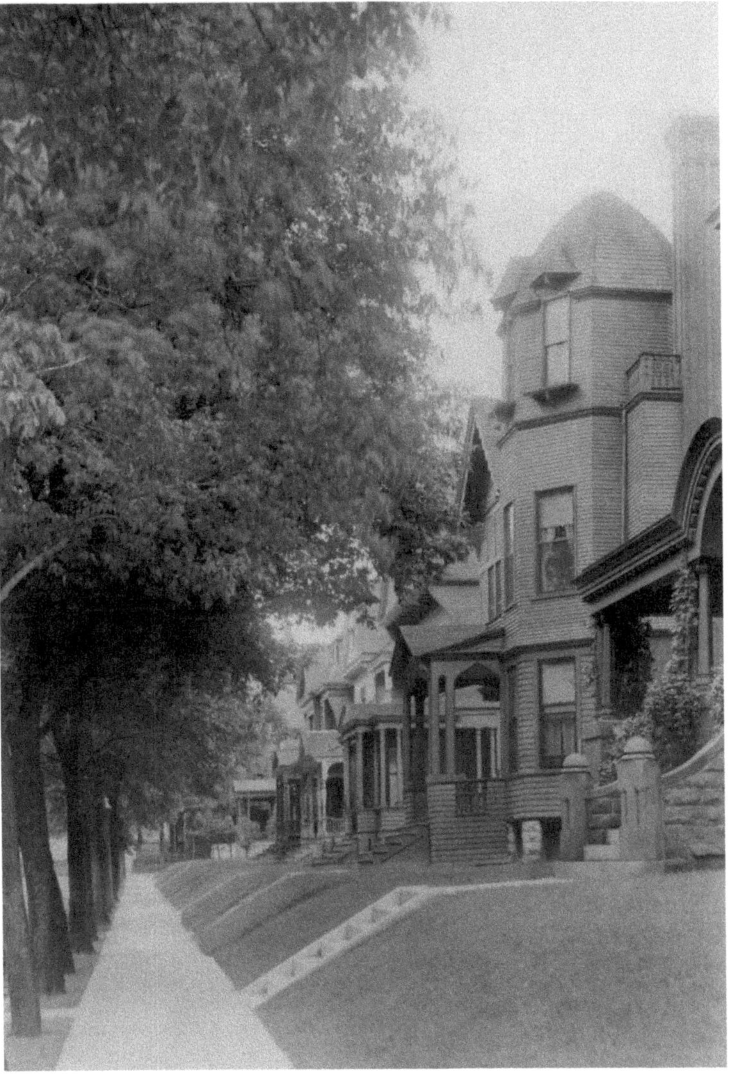

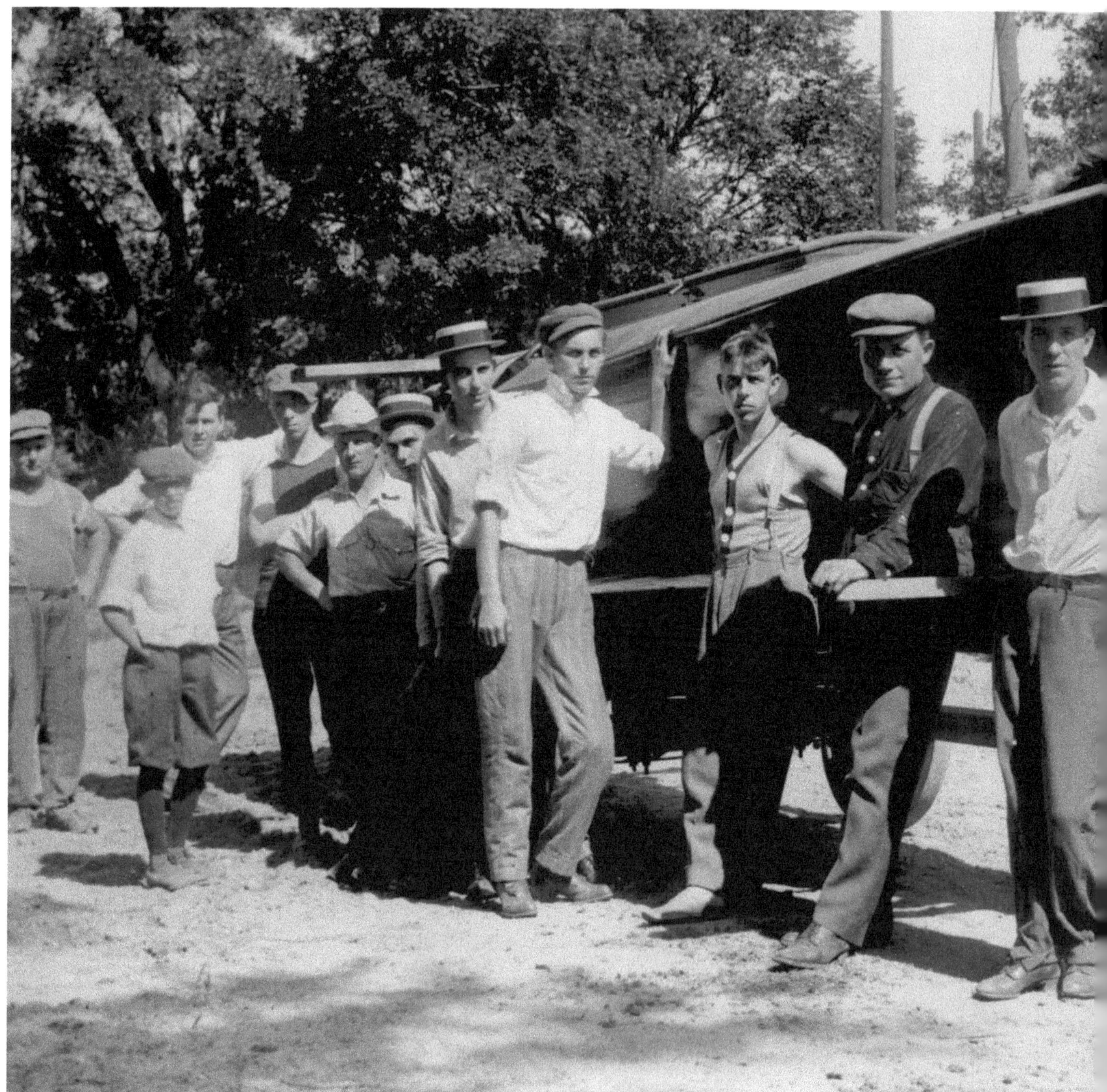

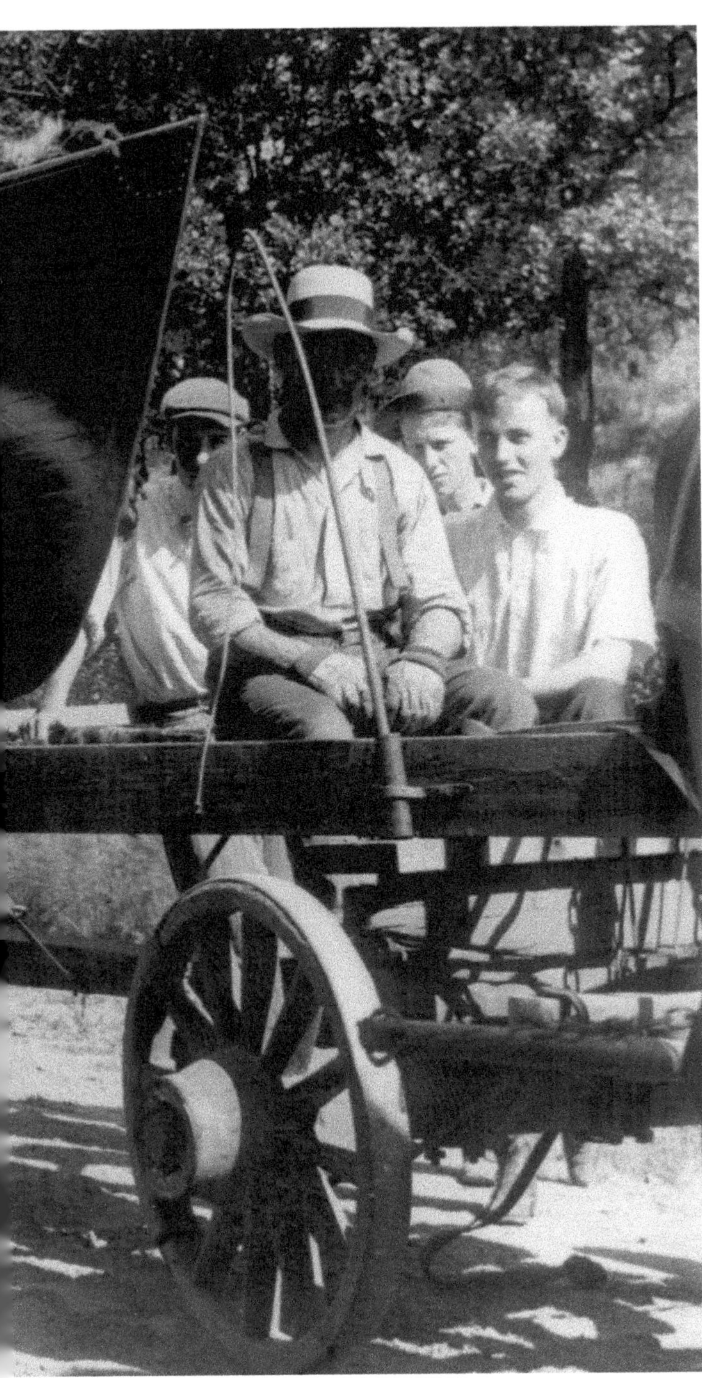

A group poses with a boat attached to a horse-drawn trailer in south Minneapolis's Kenwood neighborhood, not far from Cedar Lake, around 1910.

Camels rumble through downtown Minneapolis in 1901 as part of the perennially popular Circus Parade.

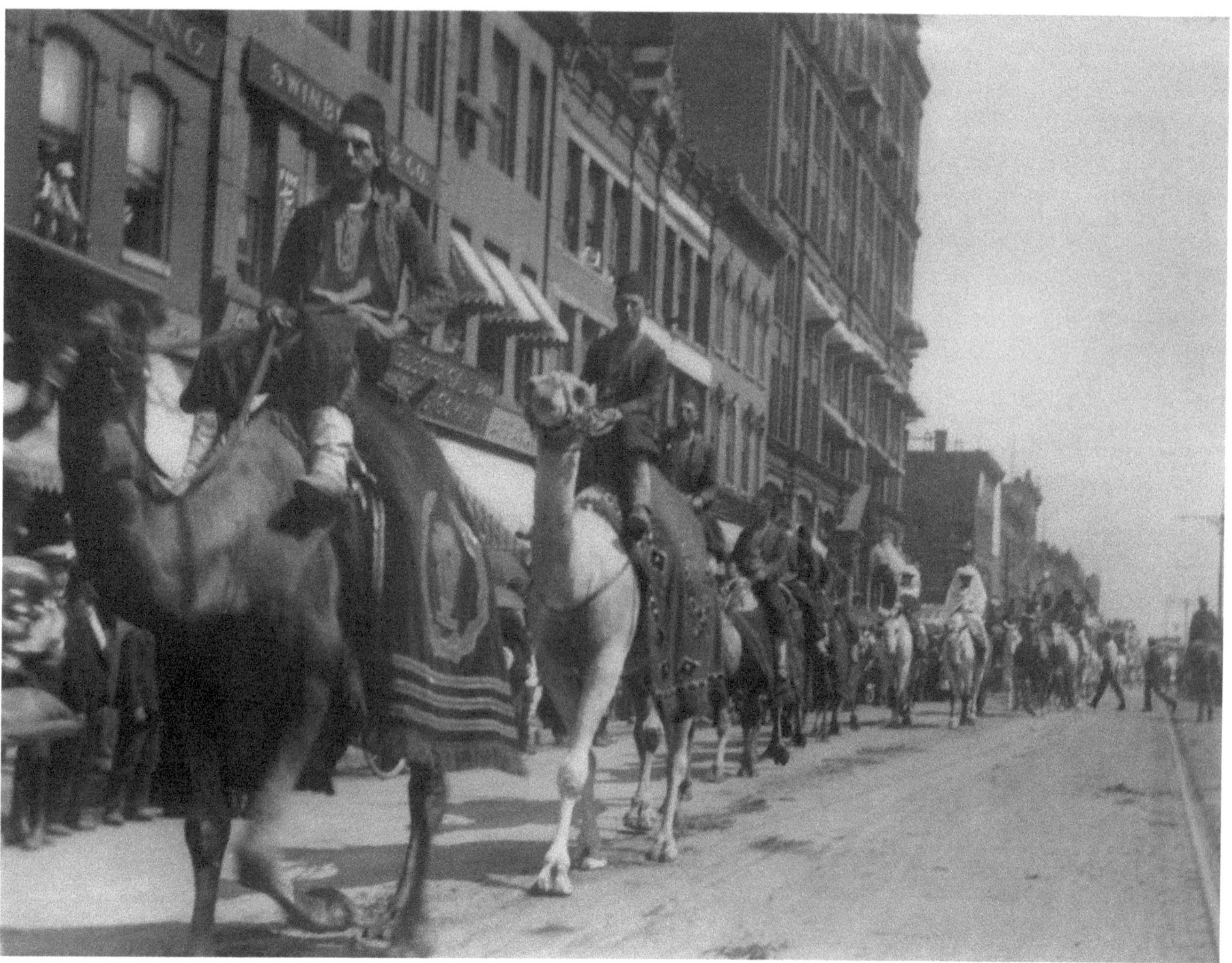

This photograph captures the construction of St. Mark's Cathedral, located at the corner of Hennepin Avenue and Oak Grove Street, in 1910.

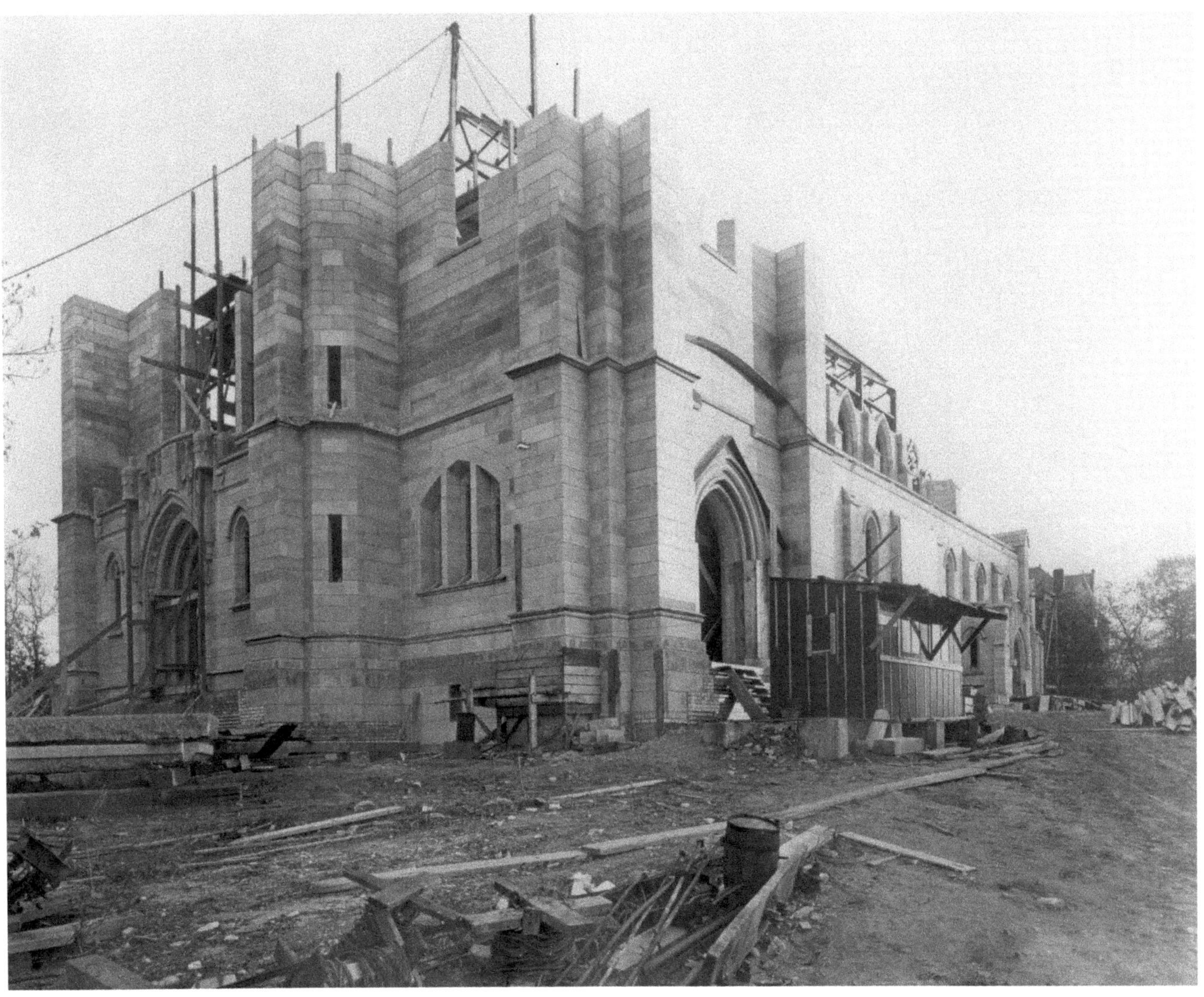

This photo of Bohemian Flats as it appeared around 1902 illustrates the proximity of the flood-prone neighborhood to the Mississippi River. The University of Minnesota campus perches on the bluffs above.

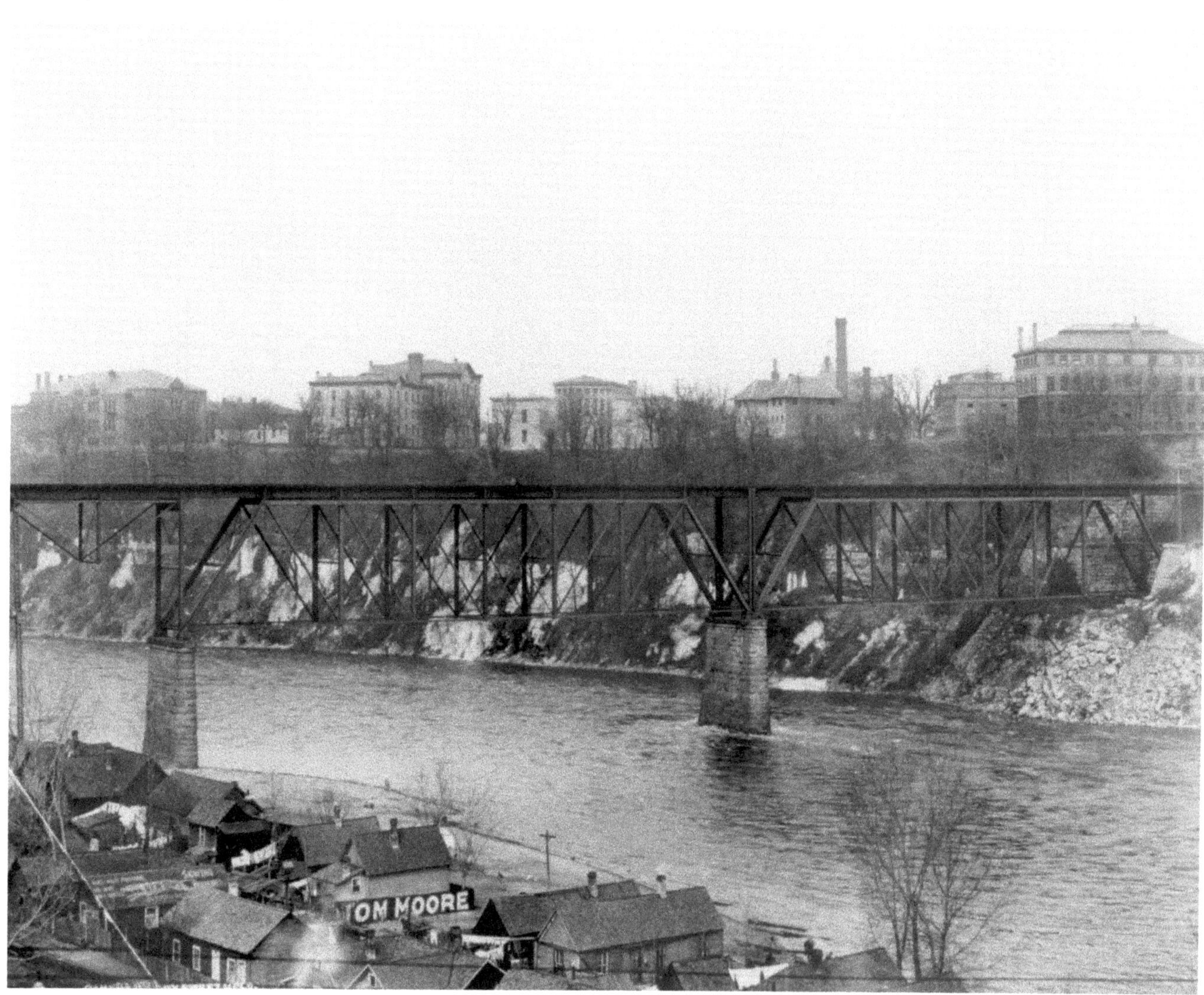

This view of Sixth Street looking west from Marquette Avenue, around 1910, features two newsboys who seem to be posing for the camera. A streetcar passes in front of the New England Furniture Company.

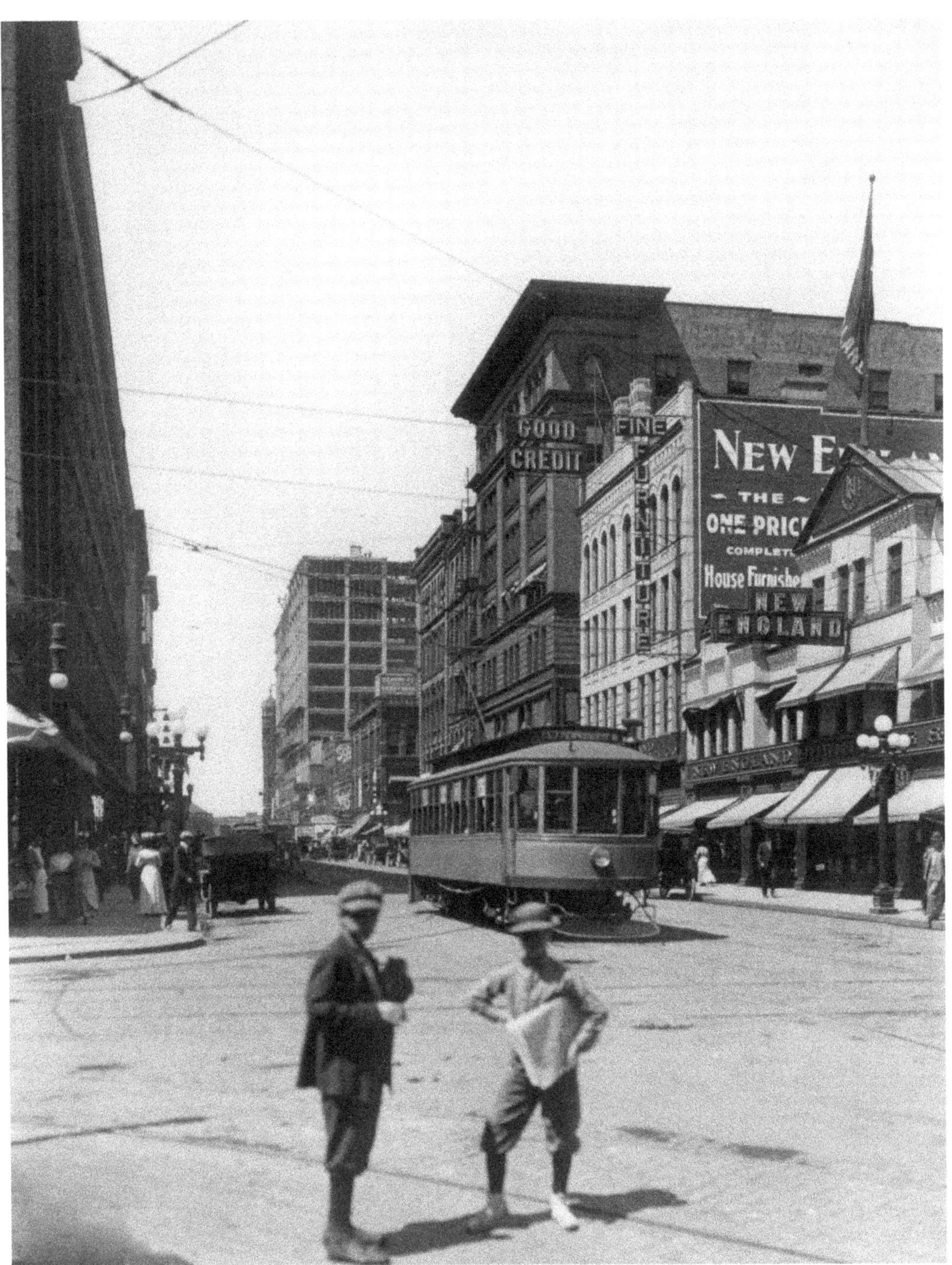

Minnesota held its first state fair in 1859, just one year after achieving statehood. This view, taken in the early years of the twentieth century, features a parade winding its way through the fairgrounds.

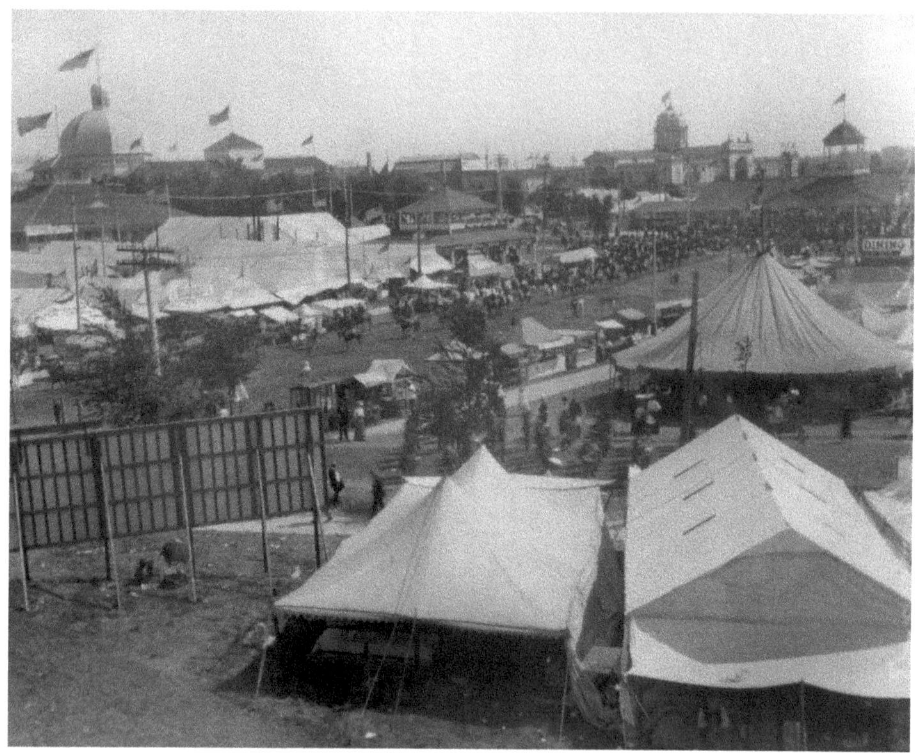

The Nicollet House building, located on Washington Avenue between Hennepin and Nicollet avenues, lodged the throngs of tourists who flocked to see St. Anthony Falls in the late nineteenth century. Nicollet House opened in 1858 and is seen here around 1900.

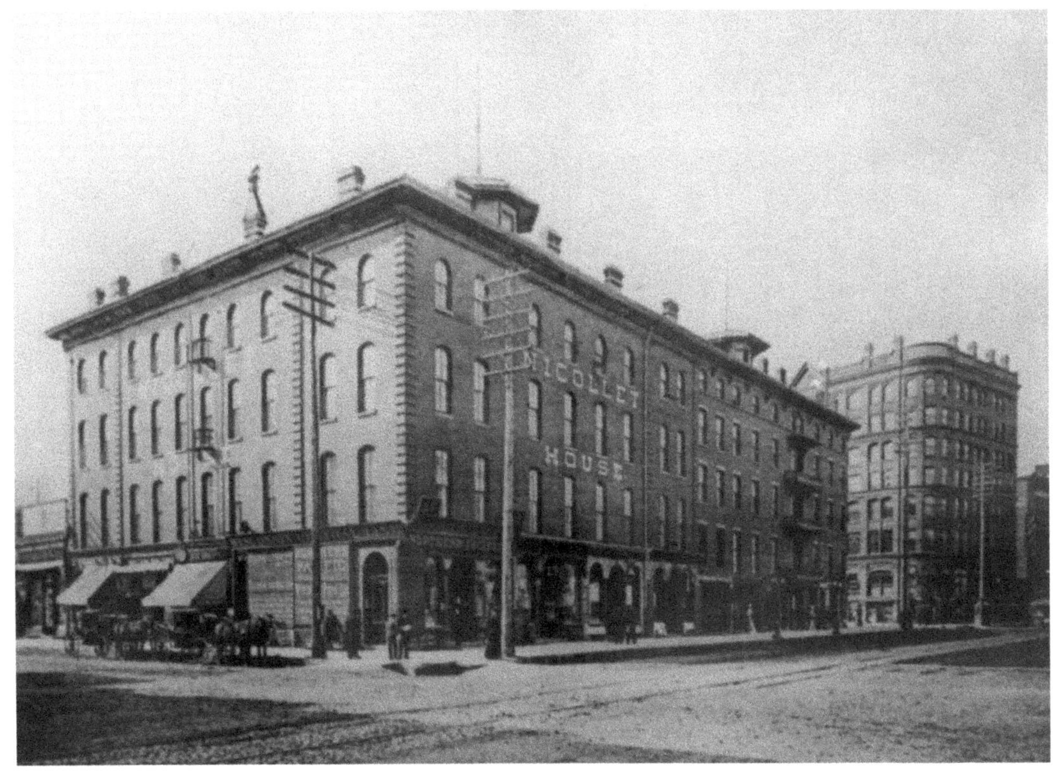

The Bismarck Bar on Washington Avenue North proudly displays three signs advertising Gluek's Beer. Gluek's traced its origins to 1857 when German immigrant Gottlieb Gluek began brewing beer in Minneapolis.

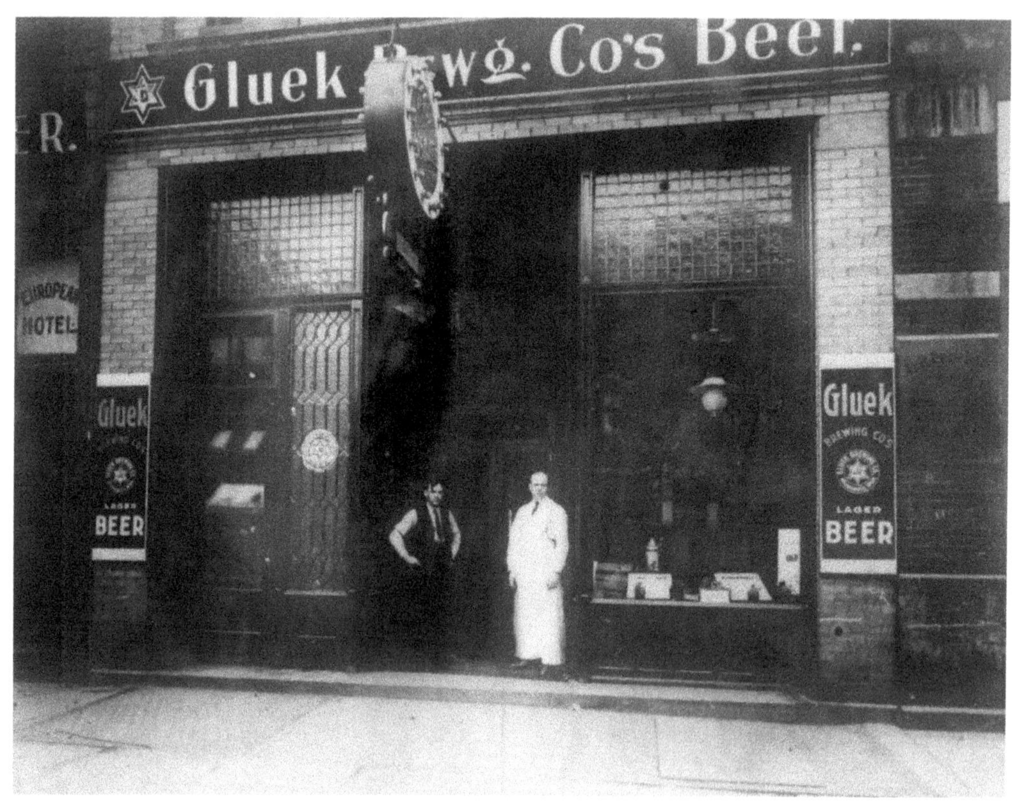

The growing city of Minneapolis erected a Romanesque-style Federal Courts building and Post Office at the corner of Third Street and Marquette Avenue in 1889. The complex is pictured here around 1908.

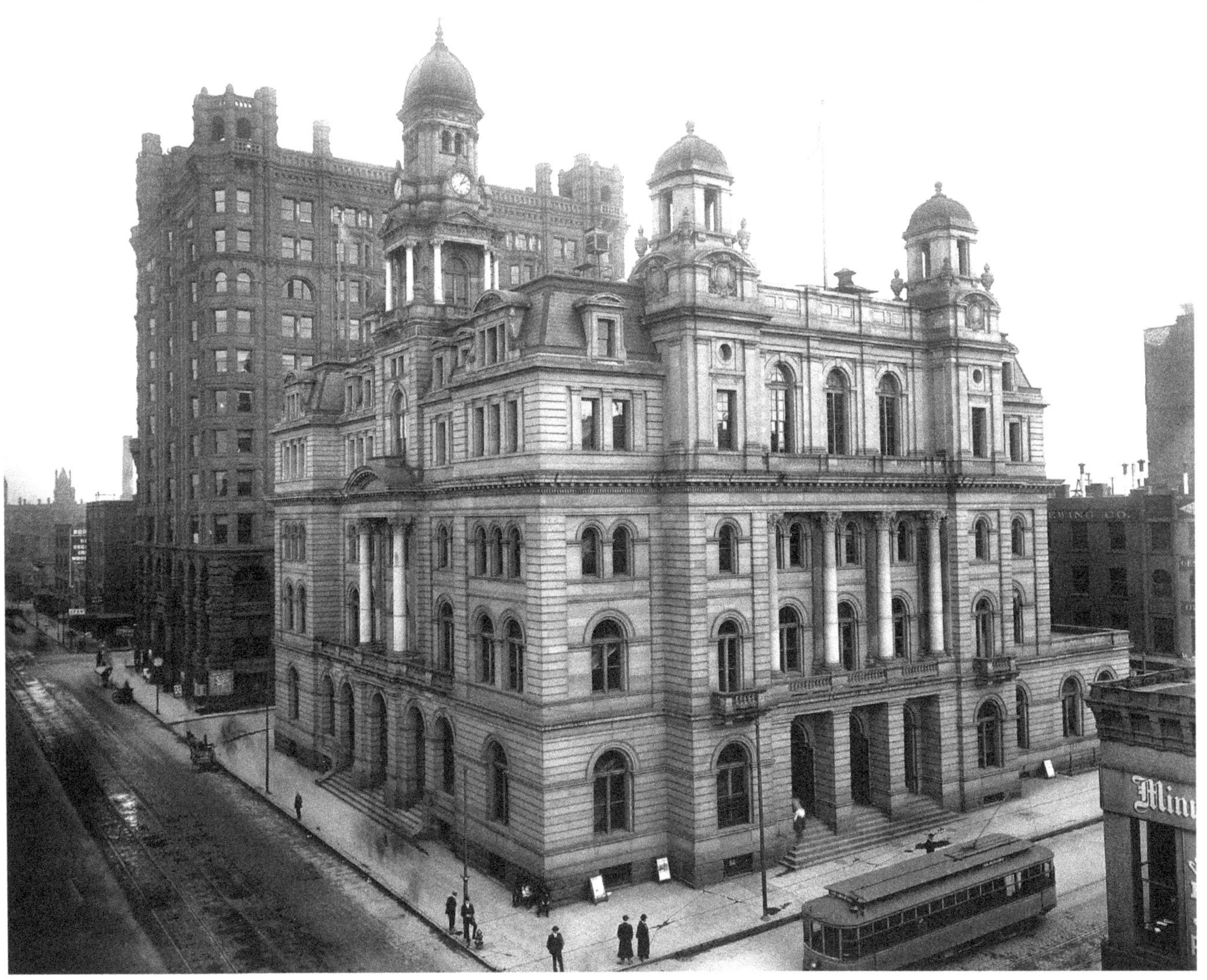

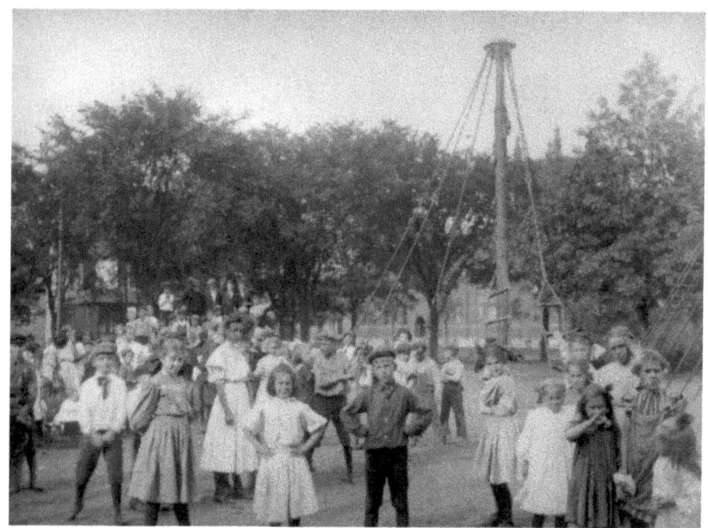

Children at Powderhorn Park around 1900 pose in front of a Giant Stride, a piece of playground equipment popular in England that featured swings secured from the top of a tall pole.

In 1900 Hudson's *Dictionary of Minneapolis* noted that "a continually increasing mileage of bicycle paths, together with the absence of . . . steep gradients, make Minneapolis the ideal place for the bicyclist." Here cyclists peddle along Second Avenue South around 1900.

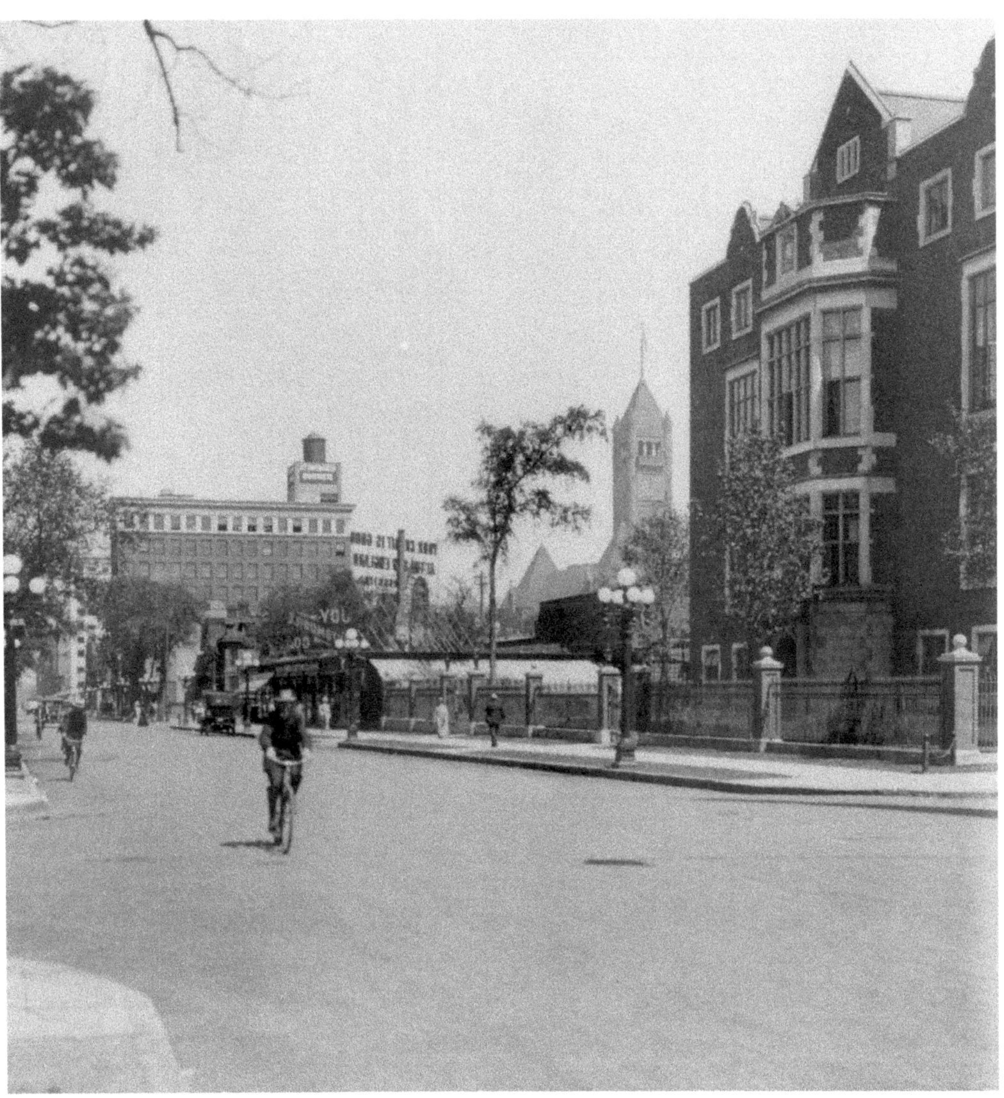

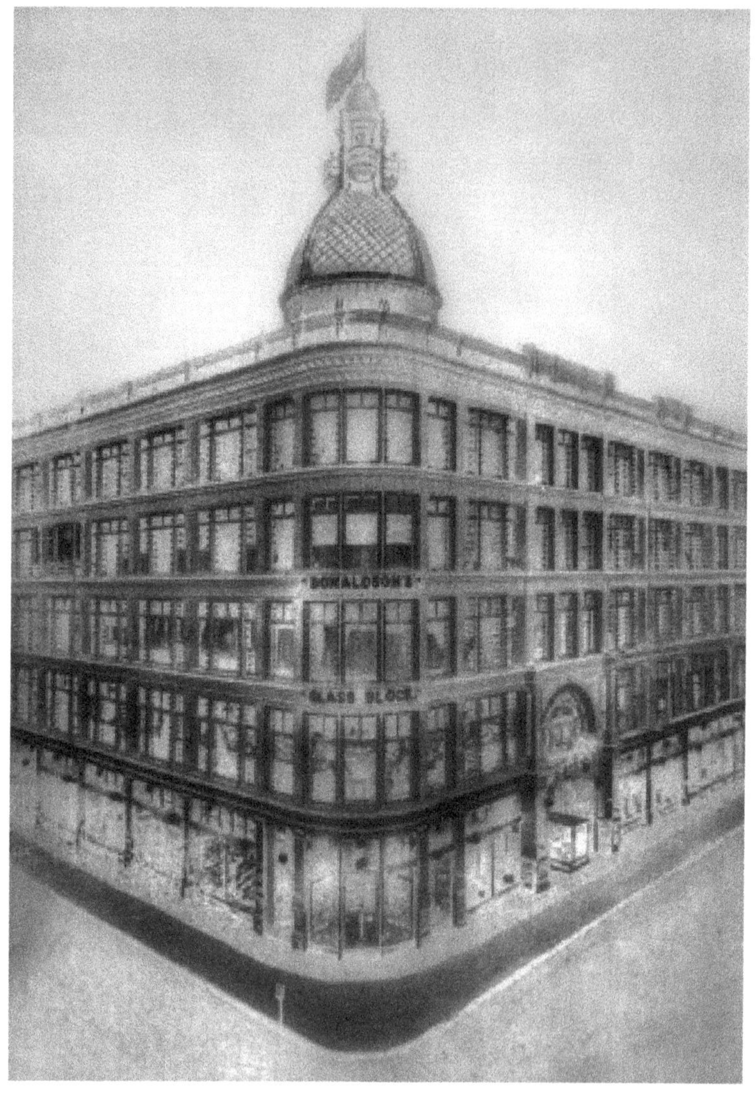

Donaldson's "Glass Block" Department Store at Sixth Street and Nicollet Avenue lit up downtown Minneapolis with thousands of lights that reflected off the building's white exterior.

Milk delivery wagons line up in front of the Crescent Creamery Company around 1902. This thriving business, which eventually became part of the Kemps Dairy Company, occupied numerous locations in Minneapolis including this one at Sixth Street and Hennepin Avenue.

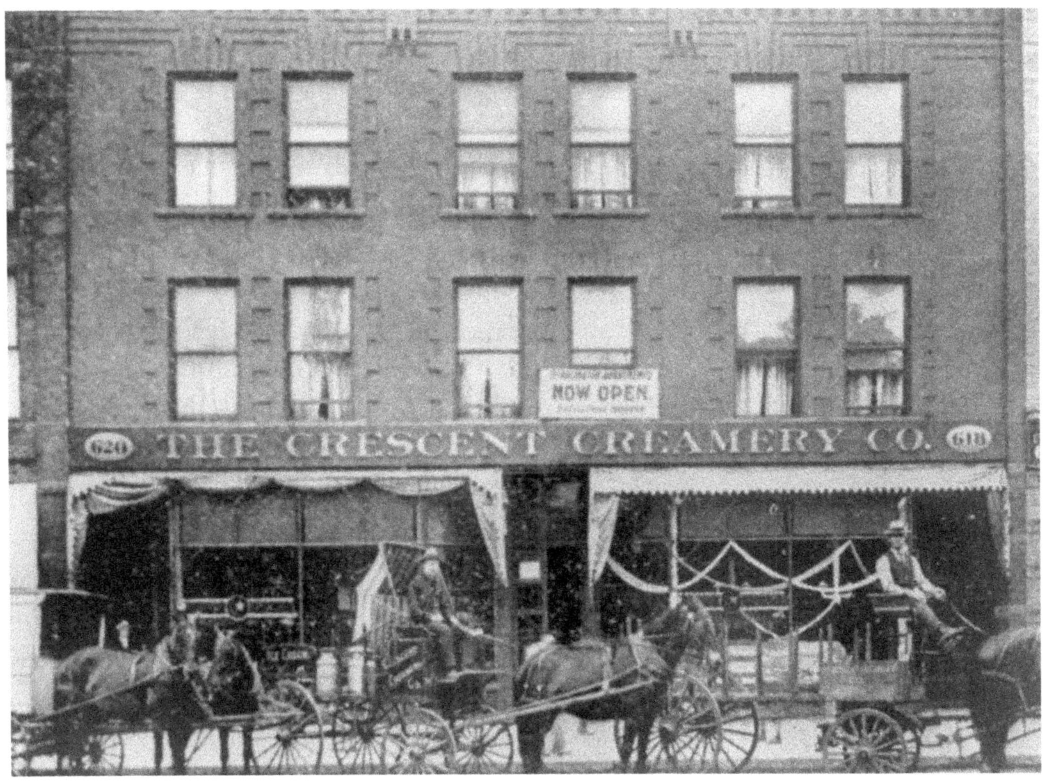

Lake Minnetonka's Tonka Bay featured one of the resort community's premier hotels. Among its many amenities was this casino building that served visitors as a roller rink, dance hall, and meeting room. The casino is pictured here in 1904.

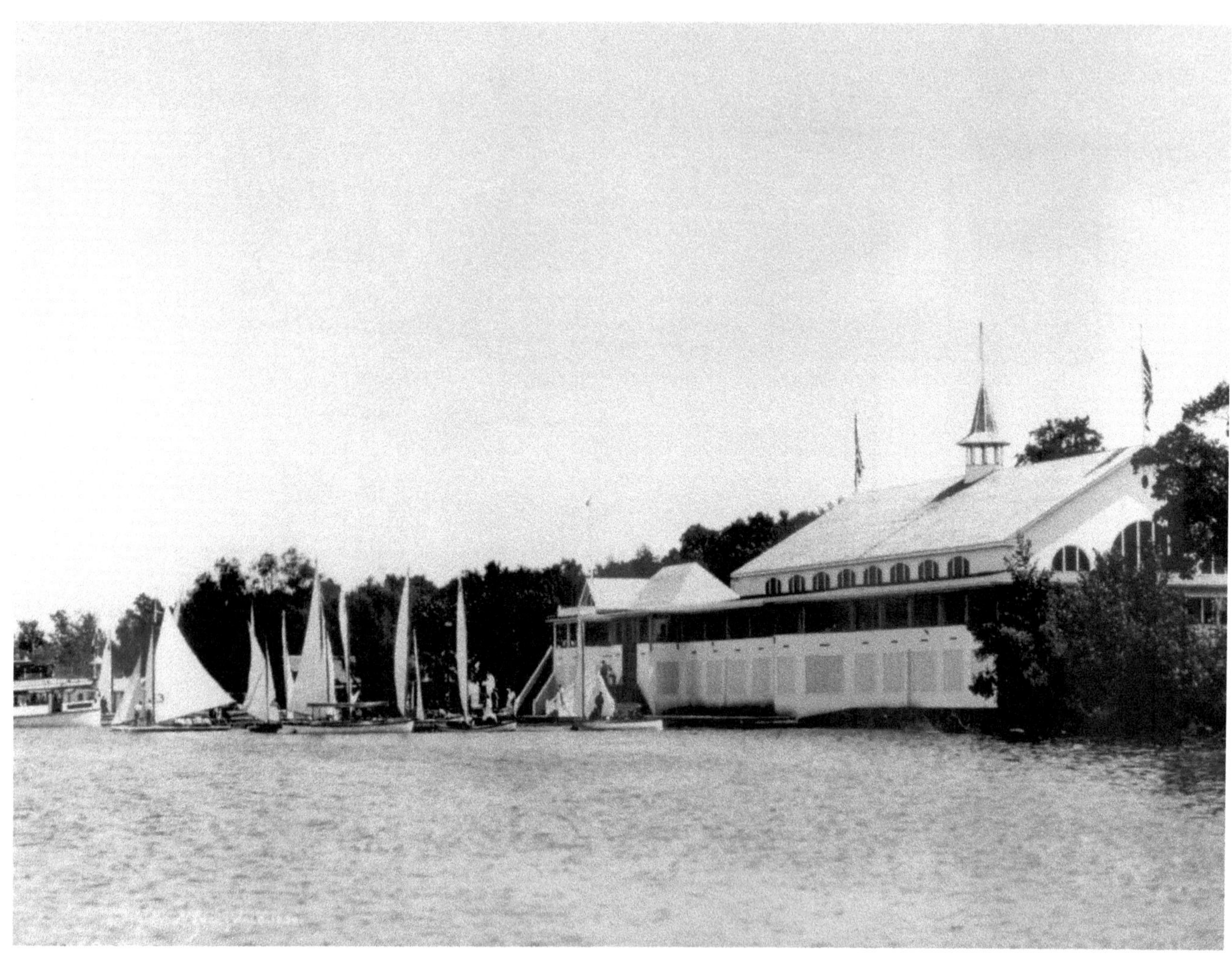

Draft horses hitched to wagons line up in front of Benson Bottling Company around the turn of the century.

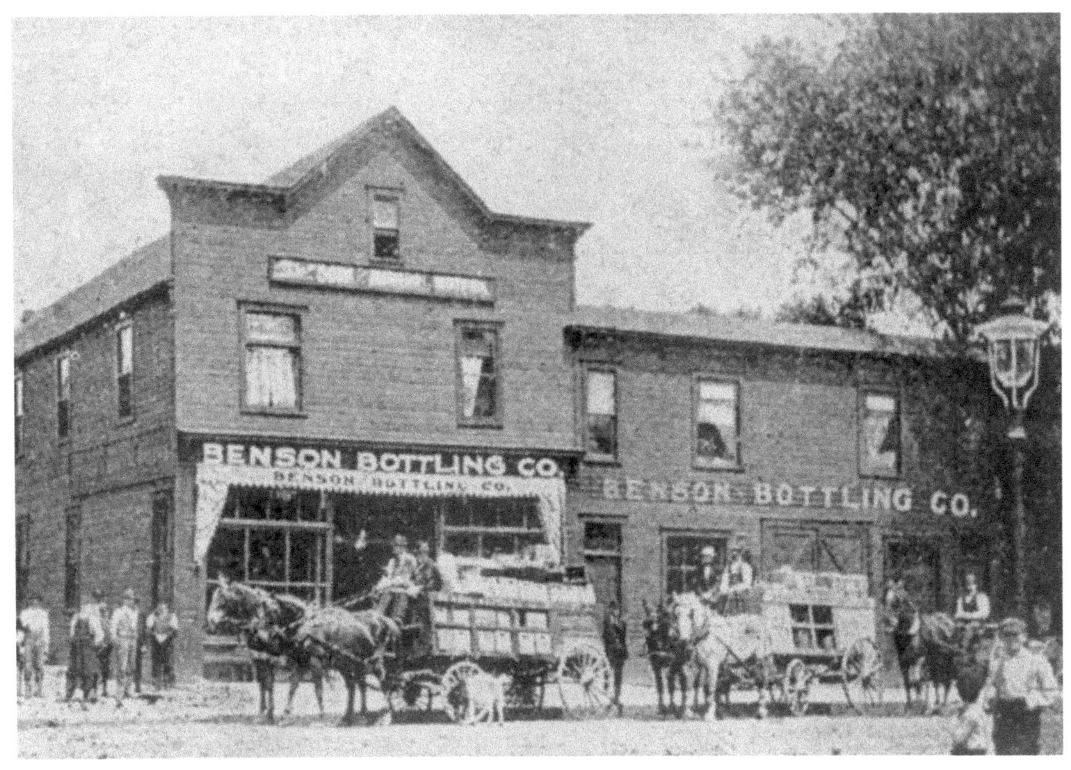

Minneapolitans enthusiastically joined the bicycle craze that swept the nation in the late nineteenth century. Frederic Roach, whose family had resided in Minneapolis as early as 1850, opened this bicycle shop on Fifth Street and Hennepin Avenue around 1898.

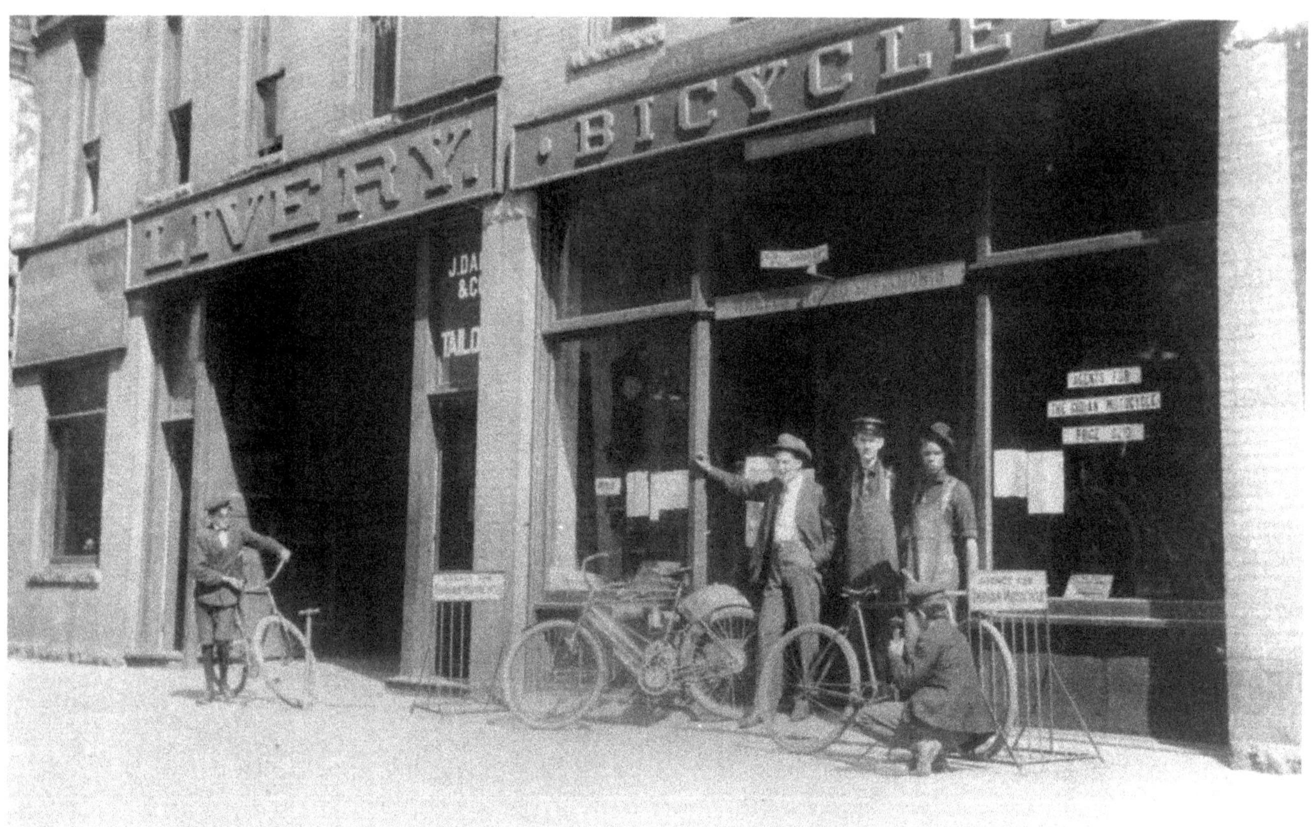

Harry Wild Jones, often considered to be the city's finest architect, designed the classical Cream of Wheat building in 1904. The Cream of Wheat Company occupied this building at the corner of Fifth Street and First Avenue North until it moved to larger quarters in 1927.

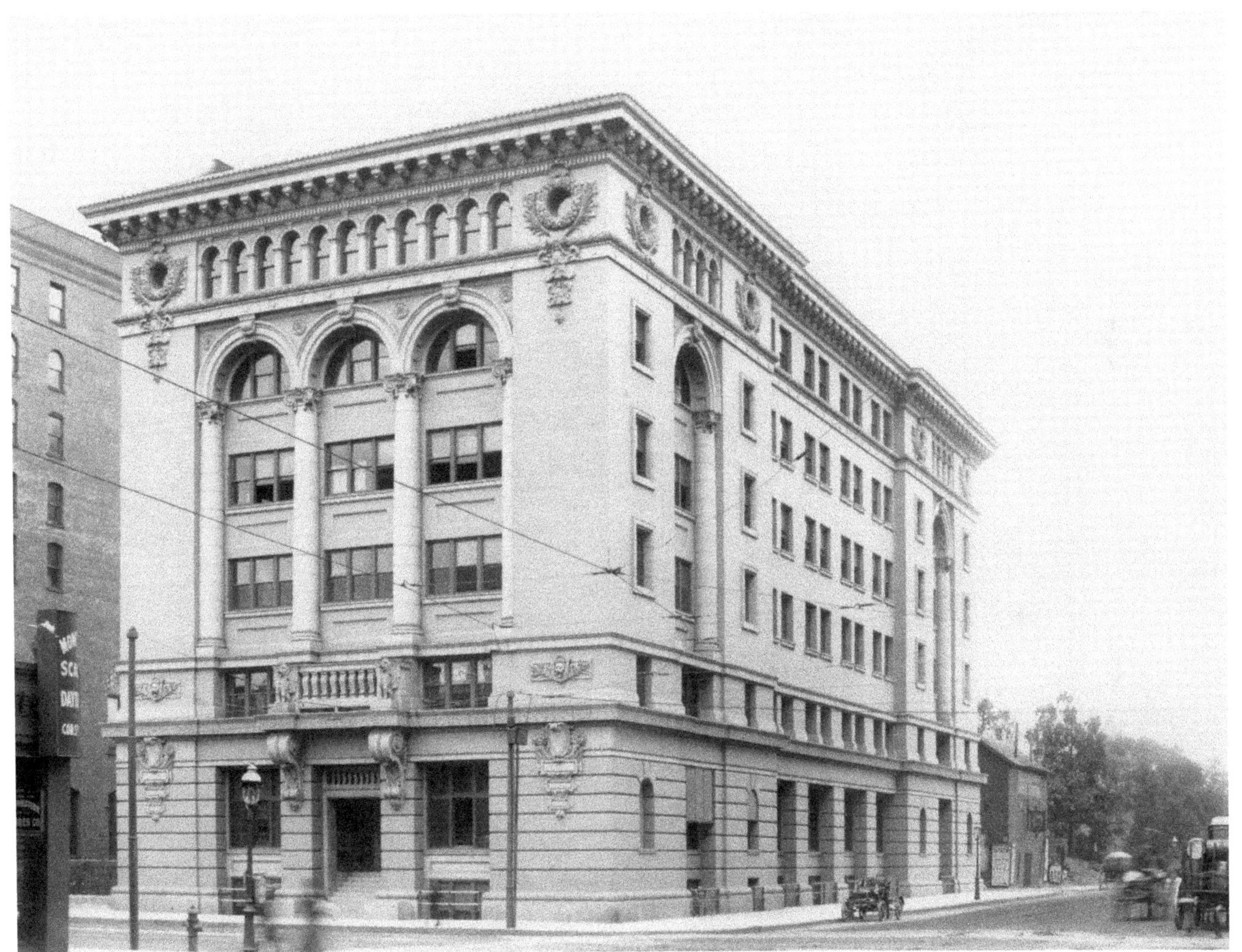

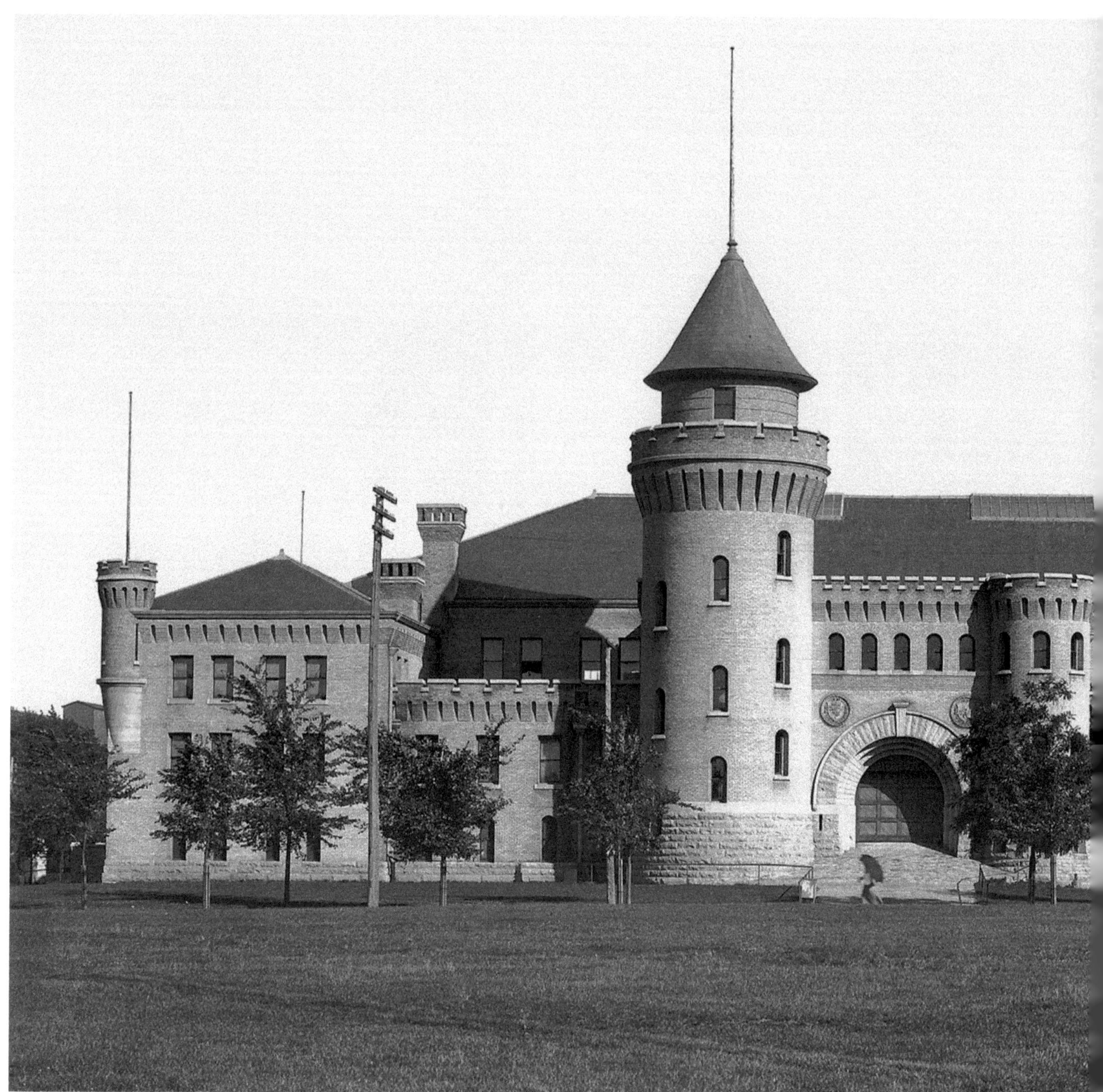

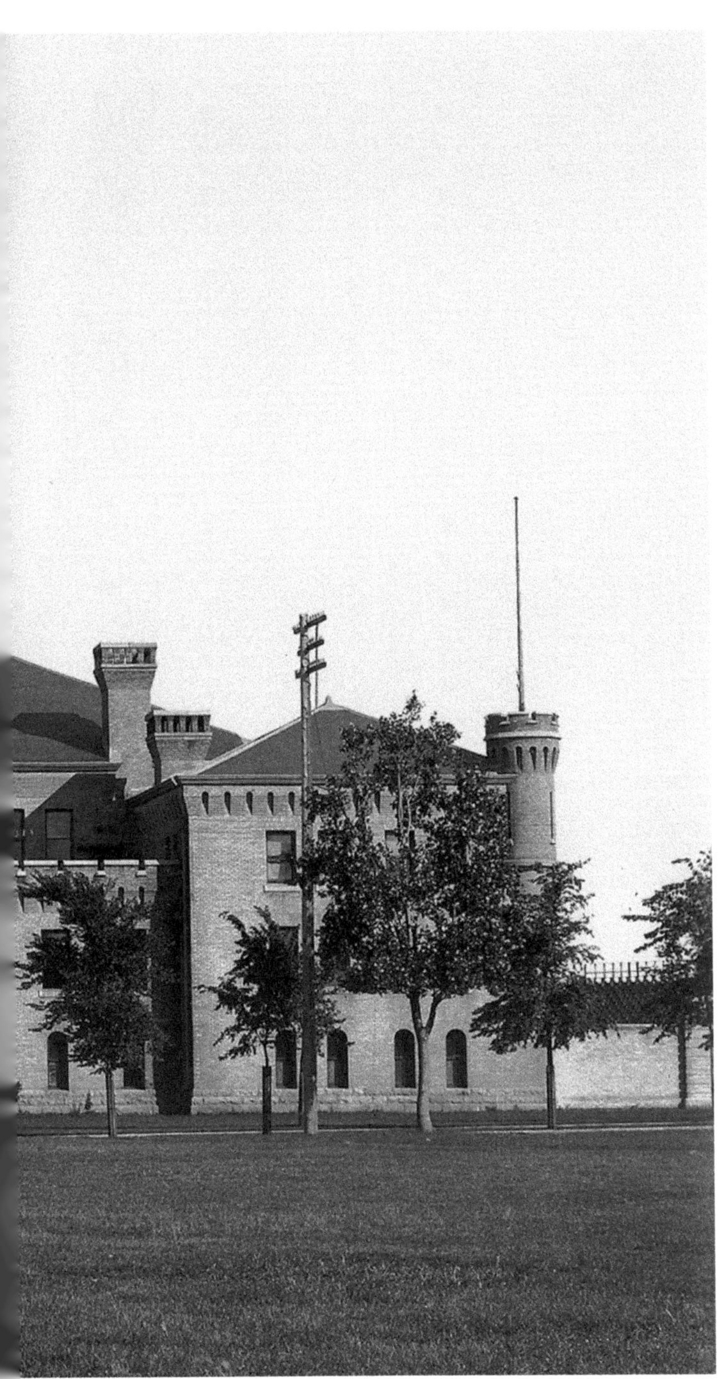

After fire destroyed the University of Minnesota's Coliseum, architecture professor Charles Aldrich designed this new building, the Armory, to resemble a Norman castle. The building, seen here around 1905, housed an assembly hall, locker rooms, and a track.

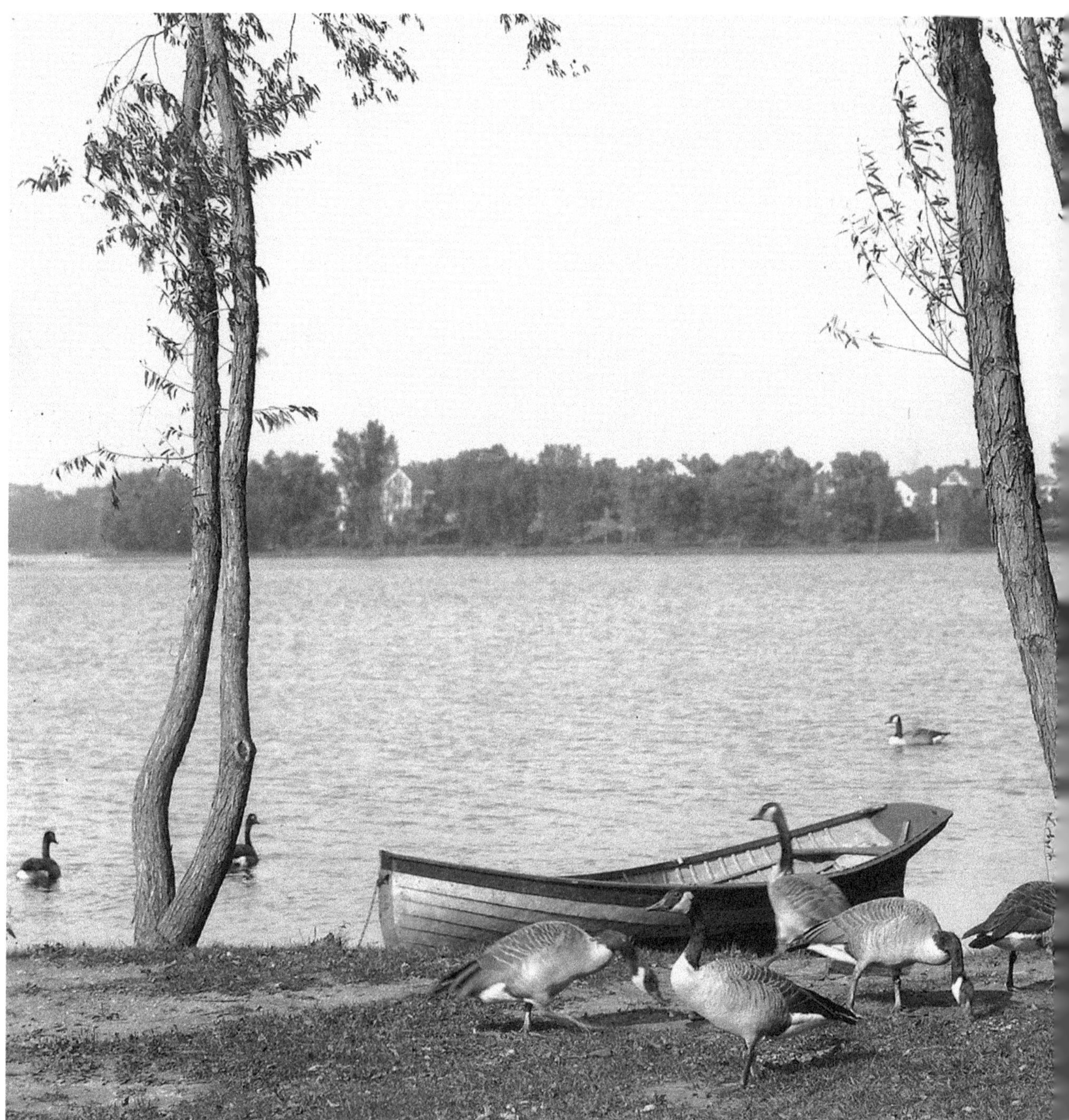

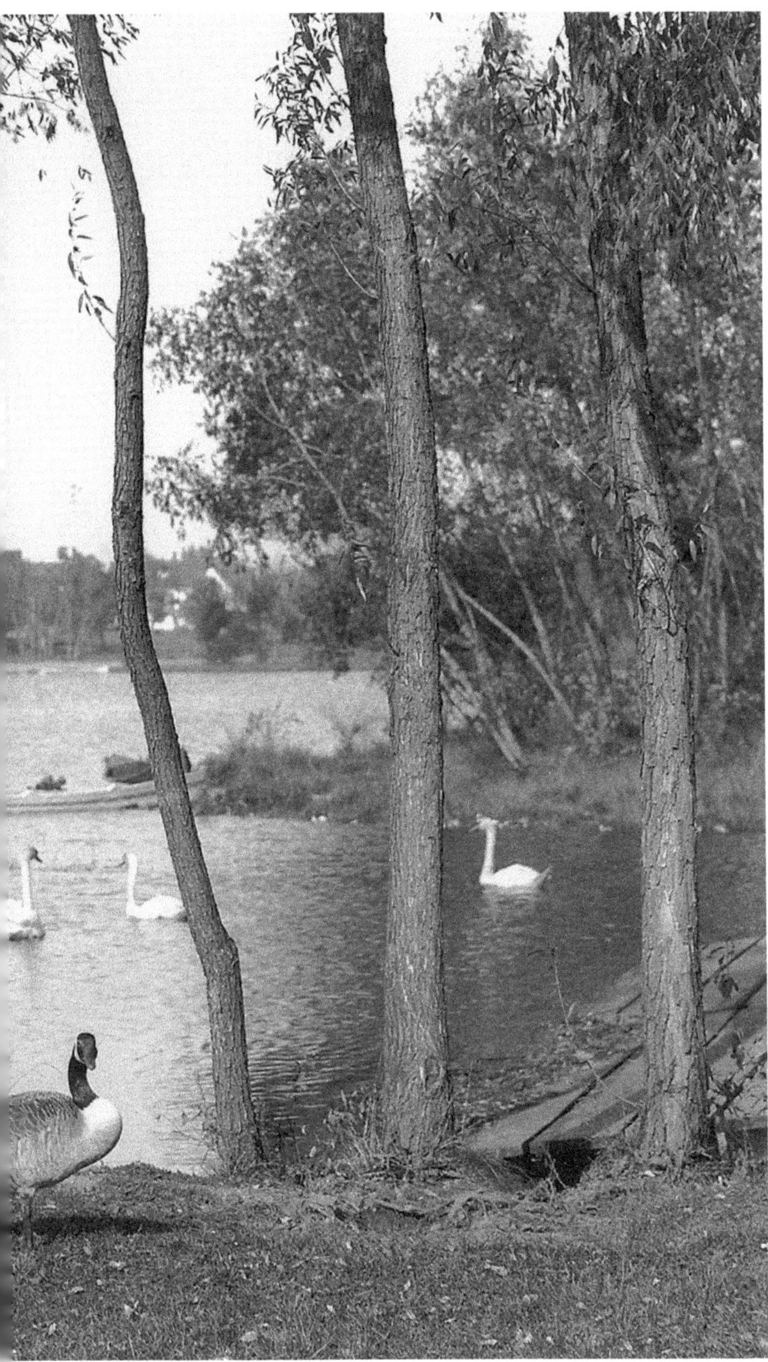

In 1889 the city of Minneapolis commenced dredging at Lake of the Isles, seen here around 1900, to fill in the marshy swampland around its perimeter. When the project ended in 1911, eighty new acres of manicured parkland surrounded the lake.

In the early 1880s the Minneapolis park board hired prominent landscape architect Horace Cleveland to design and build a network of parks and parkways throughout the city. Here in 1905 a couple enjoys a carriage ride along a parkway bordering Lake Harriet.

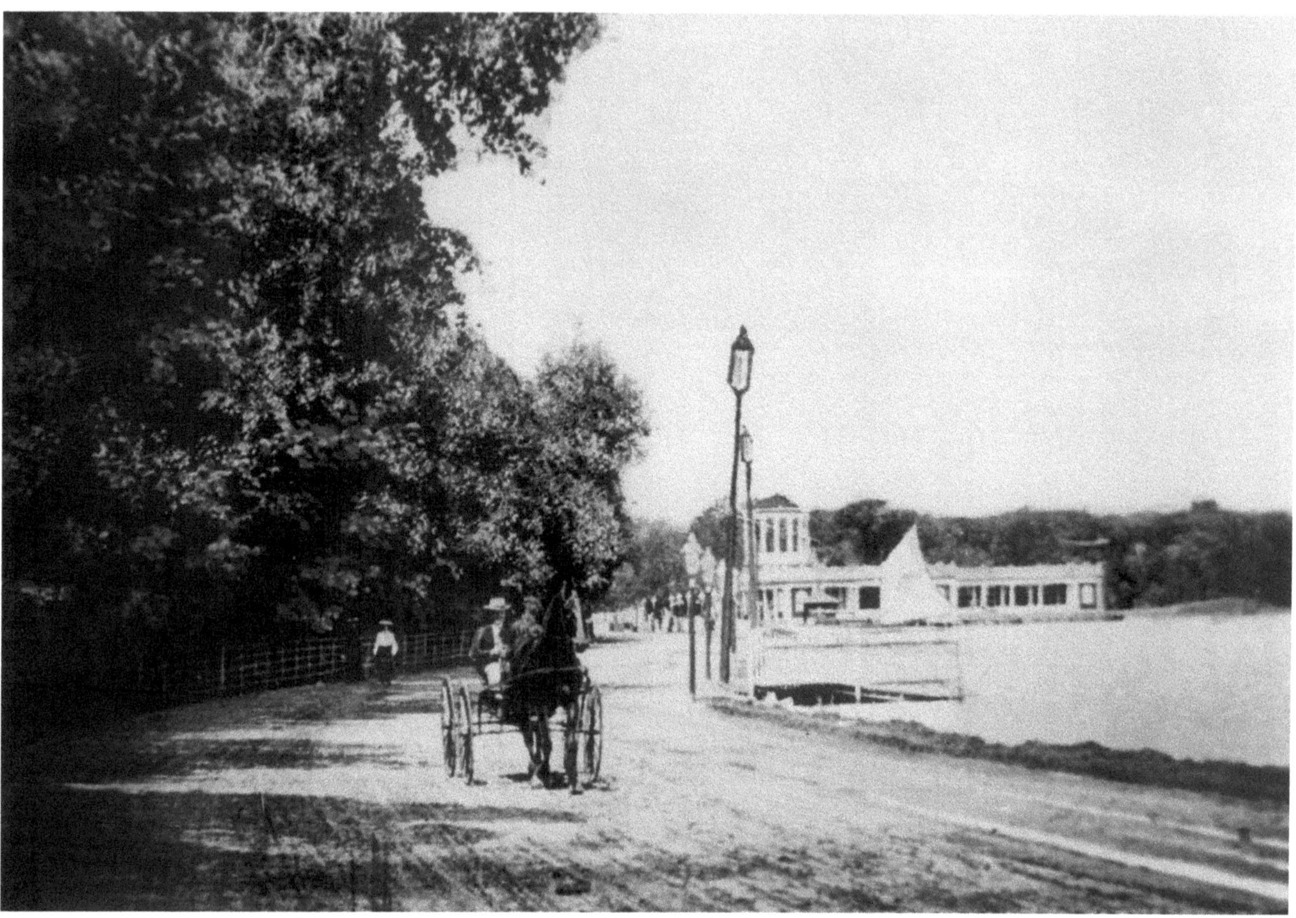

Architect LeRoy Buffington designed the West Hotel, which loomed large on the corner of Fifth Street and Hennepin Avenue from 1884 to 1940. The hotel, pictured here around 1905, served as the unofficial headquarters of notorious Minneapolis mobster Kid Cann.

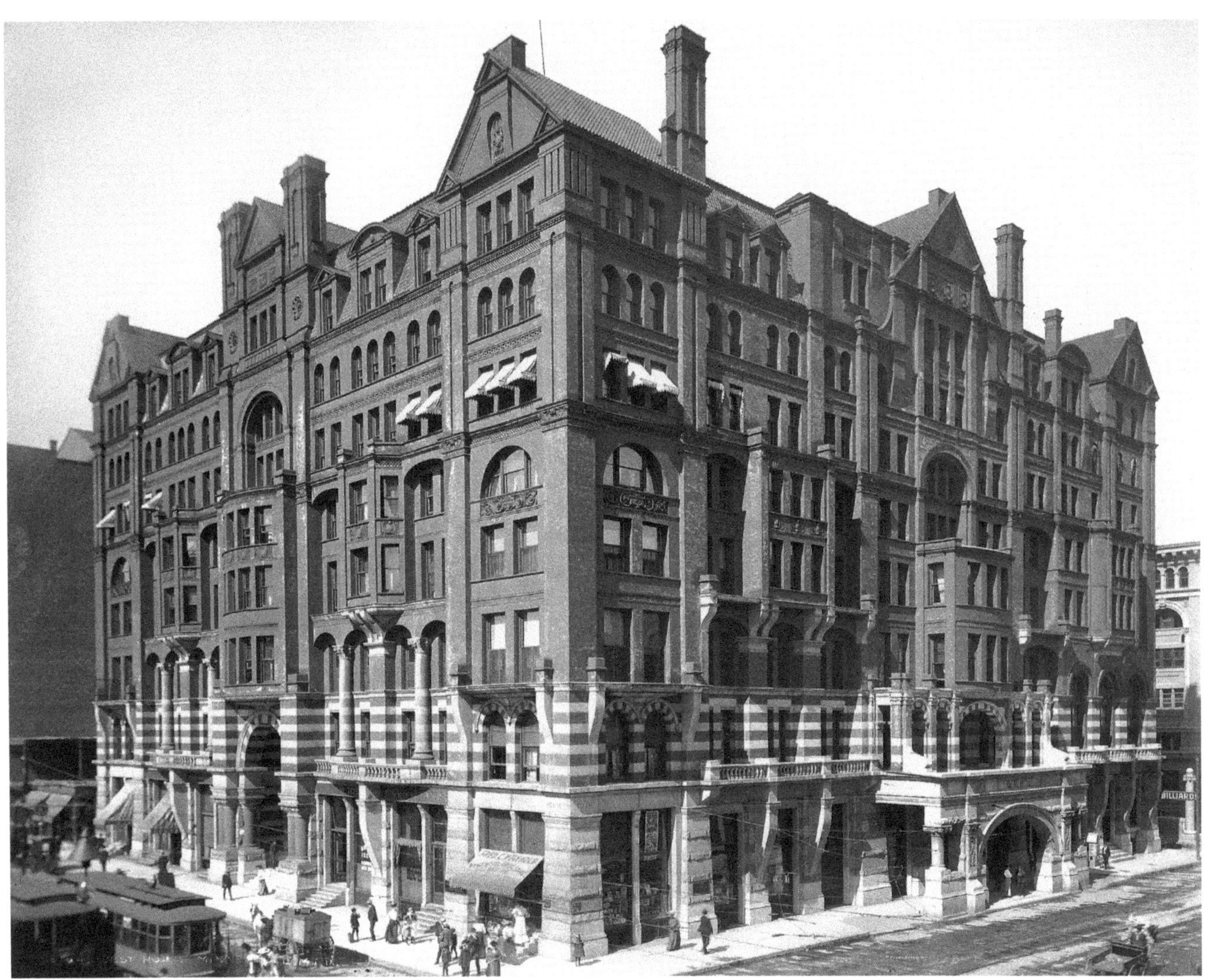

In 1905 the Wonderland Amusement Park opened on Lake Street and Thirty-fourth Avenue South. The park featured a roller coaster, merry-go-round, fun house, and daredevil stunt men. Several unprofitable seasons doomed the park and it was dismantled in 1912.

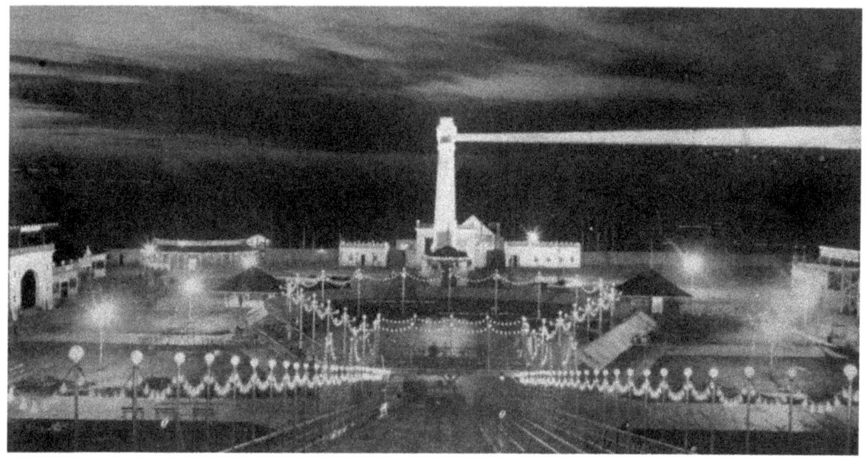

Citizens and officials gather in 1906 to dedicate the Father of Waters statue in the new Municipal Building. The statue symbolically depicts the spirit of the Mississippi River from its origins in northern Minnesota to its delta in Louisiana.

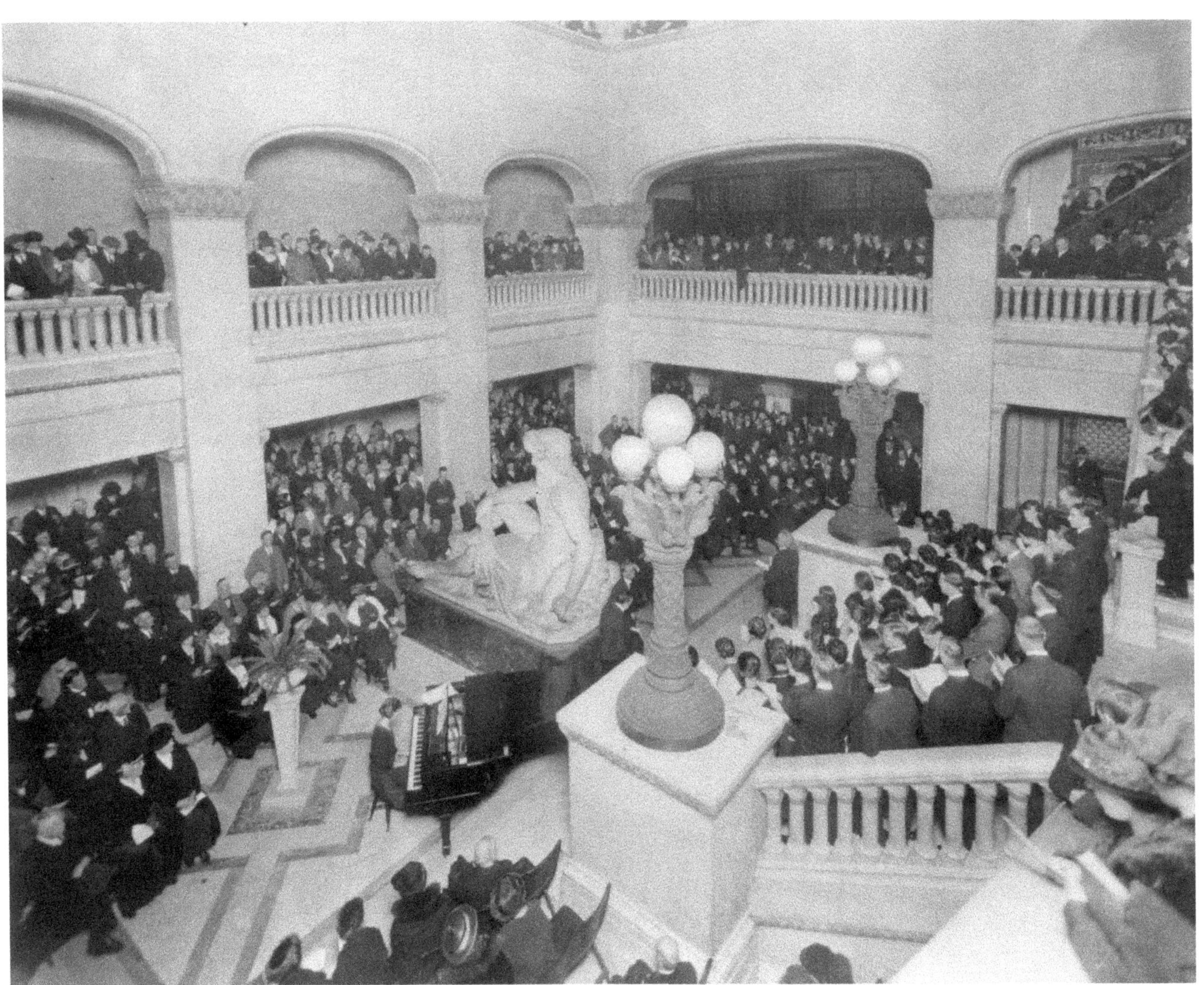

Classical architecture came to dominate the Minneapolis landscape in the early years of the twentieth century. The First National Bank building, erected on the corner of Fifth Street and Marquette Avenue in 1906 and depicted here around 1910, exemplifies this style.

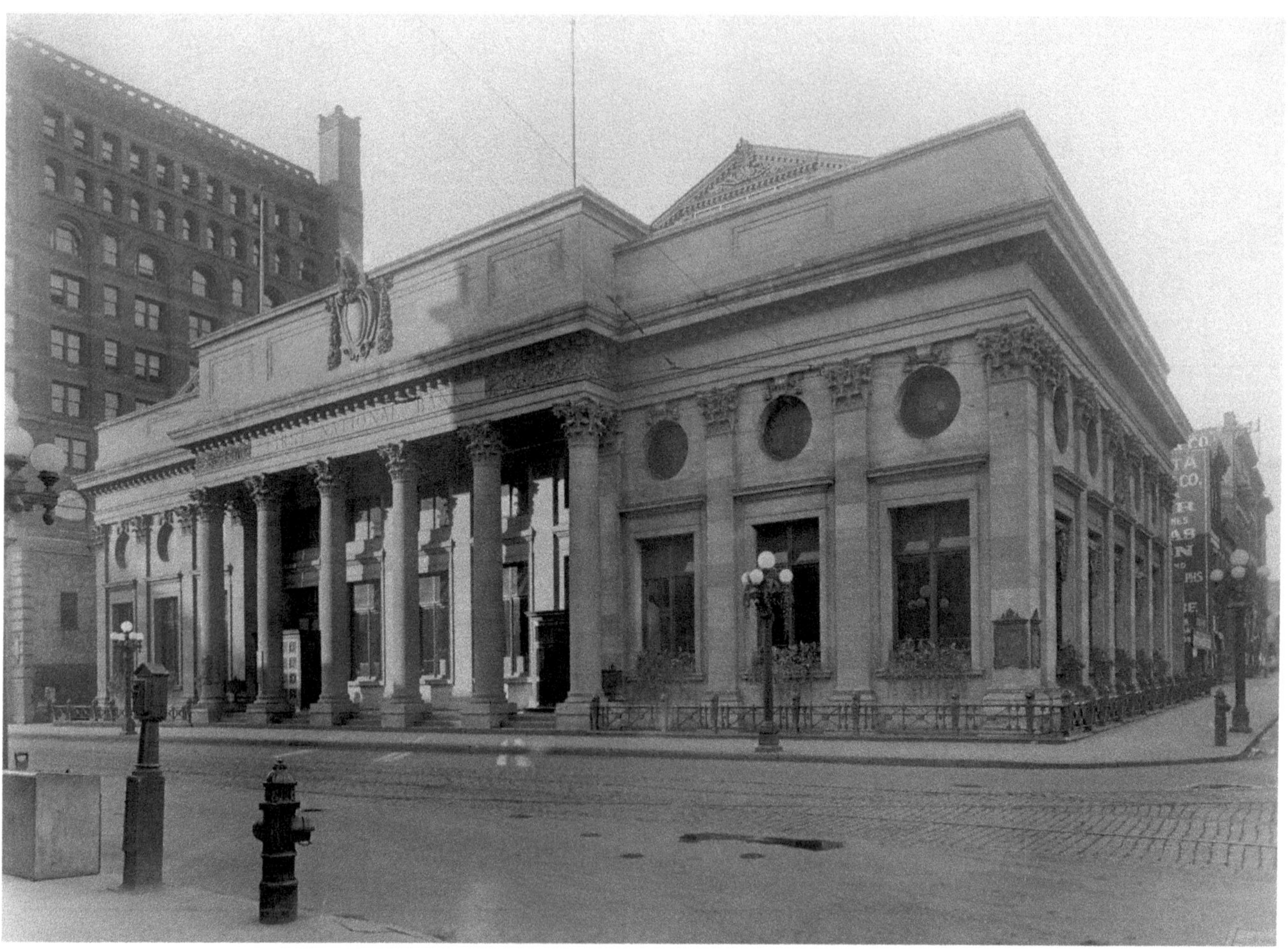

This photo of Lake Calhoun Parkway around 1905 was taken on the east side of the lake at Thirty-sixth Street. A watering trough appears in the middle of the parkway. The Parks Department paved the parkways in later years as automobiles became ubiquitous.

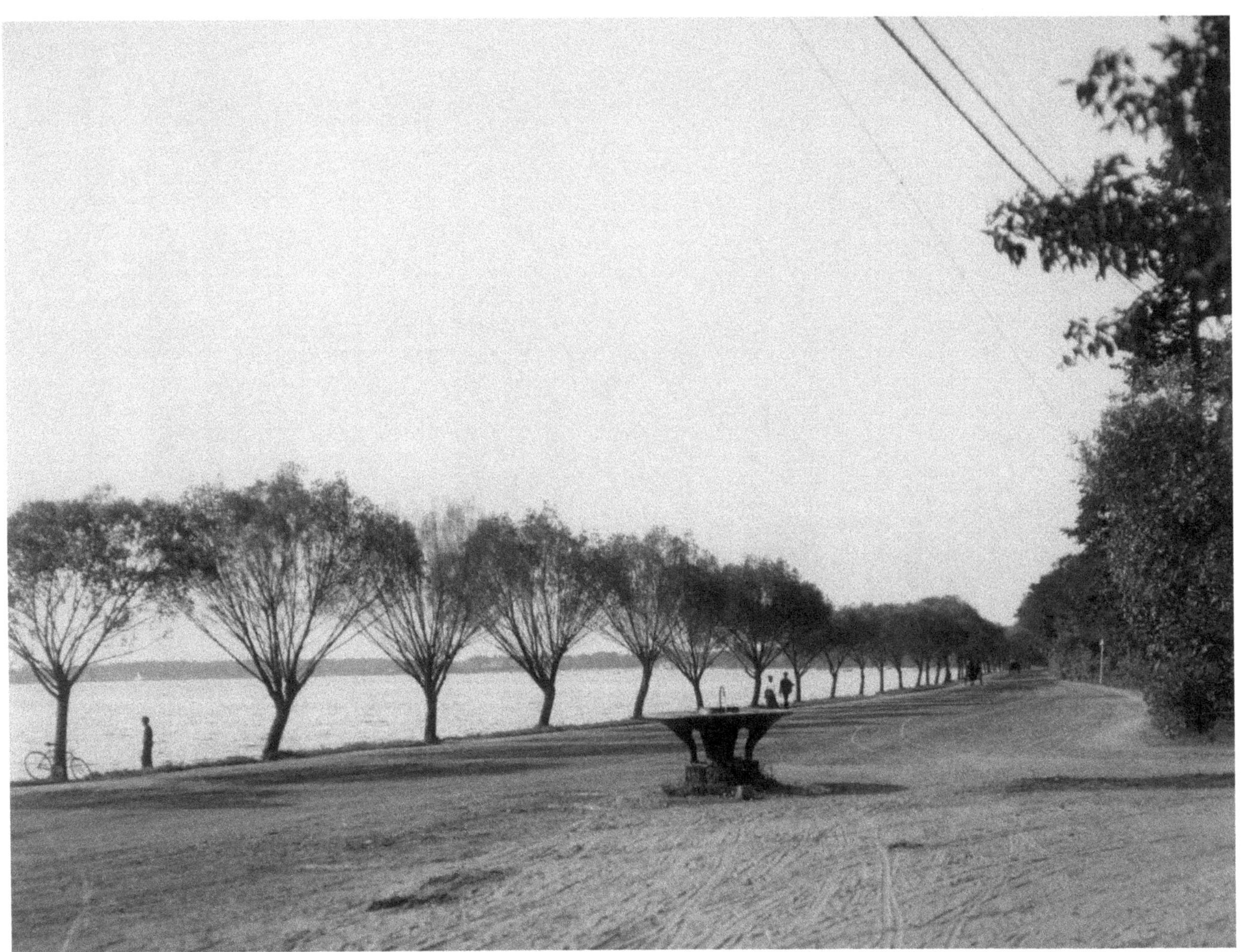

The Flour Exchange building, erected at the corner of Fourth Avenue South and Third and seen here about 1907, began as a four-story building. Seven additional stories were added in 1909. In 1977 the building earned a spot on the National Register of Historic Places.

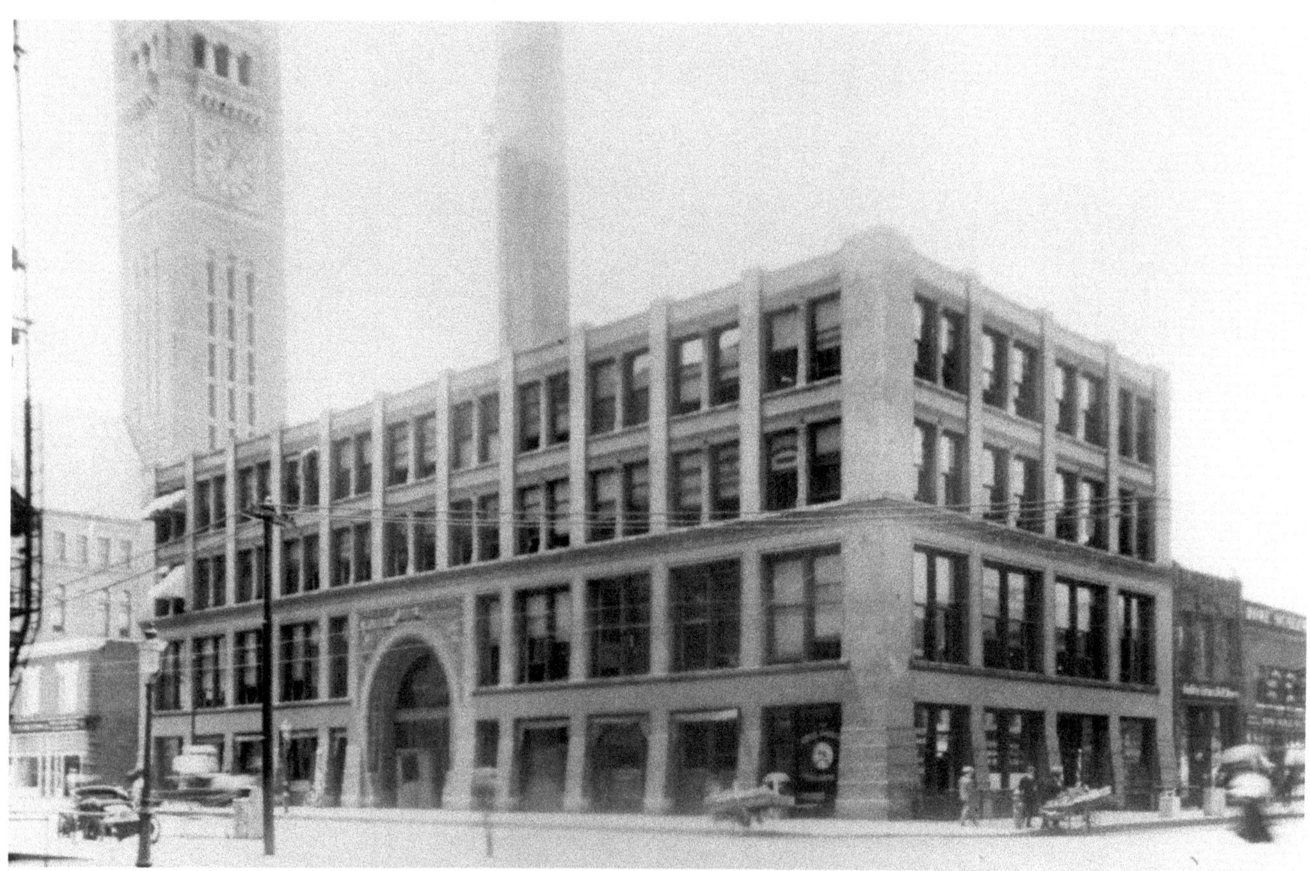

A horse-drawn fire engine races along Cedar Avenue on its way to a fire in 1907. In 1911 a new chief engineer of the Minneapolis fire department, Charles W. Ringer, began the conversion to use of motorized vehicles.

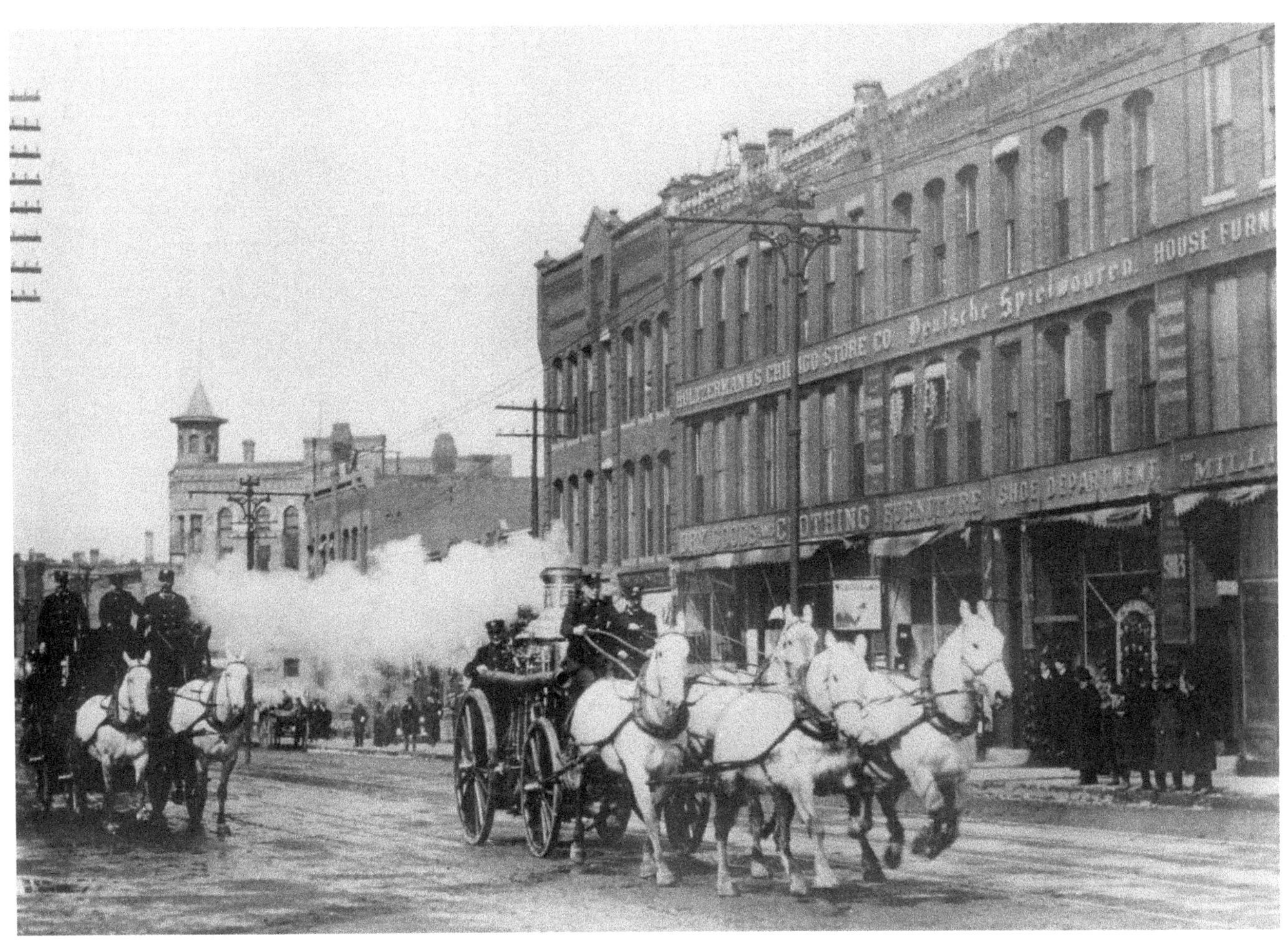

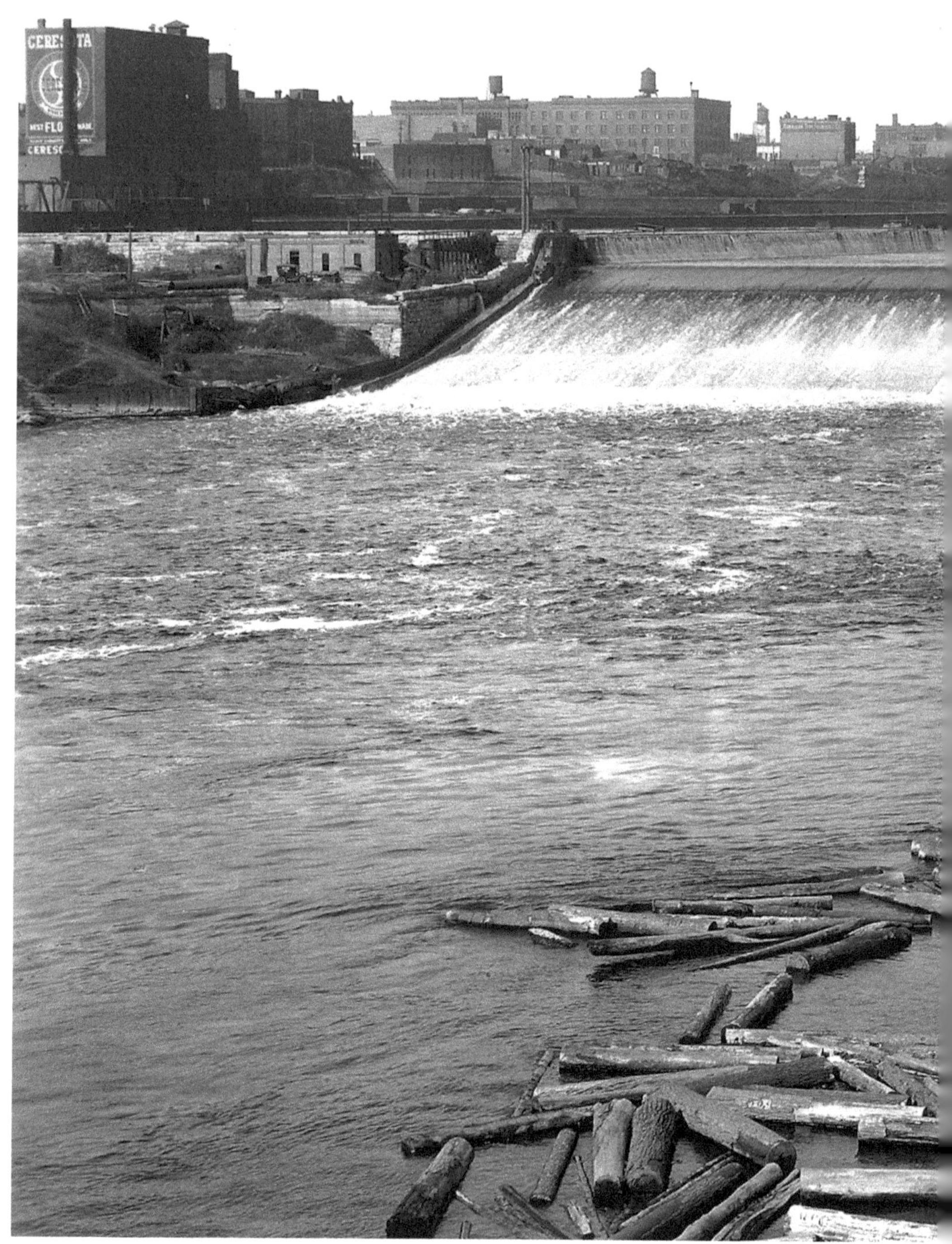

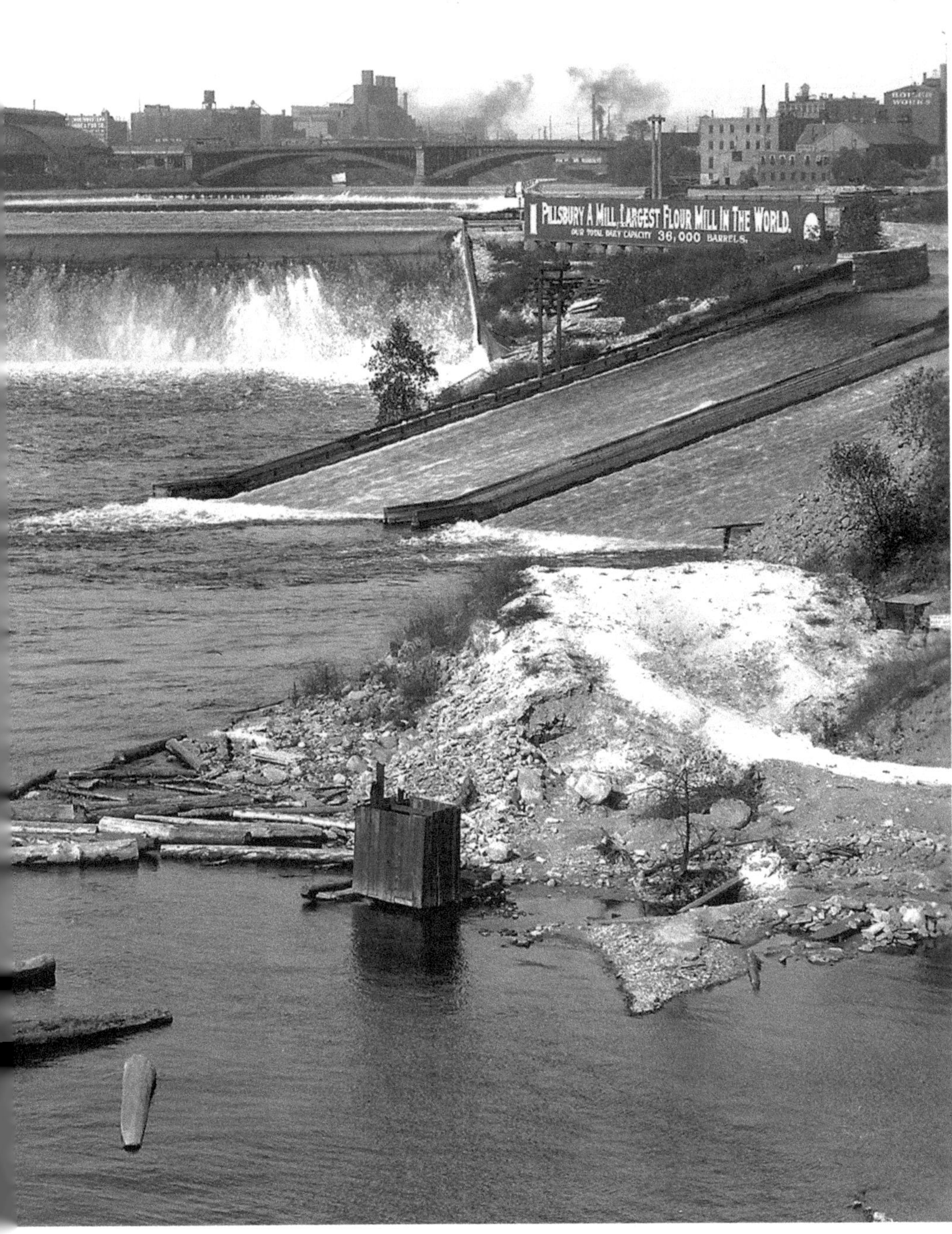

This image depicts St. Anthony Falls as it appeared in 1908. Industrial waste washing downriver from the Minneapolis mills often created a navigation hazard for mariners below the falls.

Students walk past the oldest extant building on the University of Minnesota campus, Eddy Hall, around 1908. Designed by LeRoy Buffington in 1886, the building was named in honor of professor and graduate school dean Henry Turner Eddy.

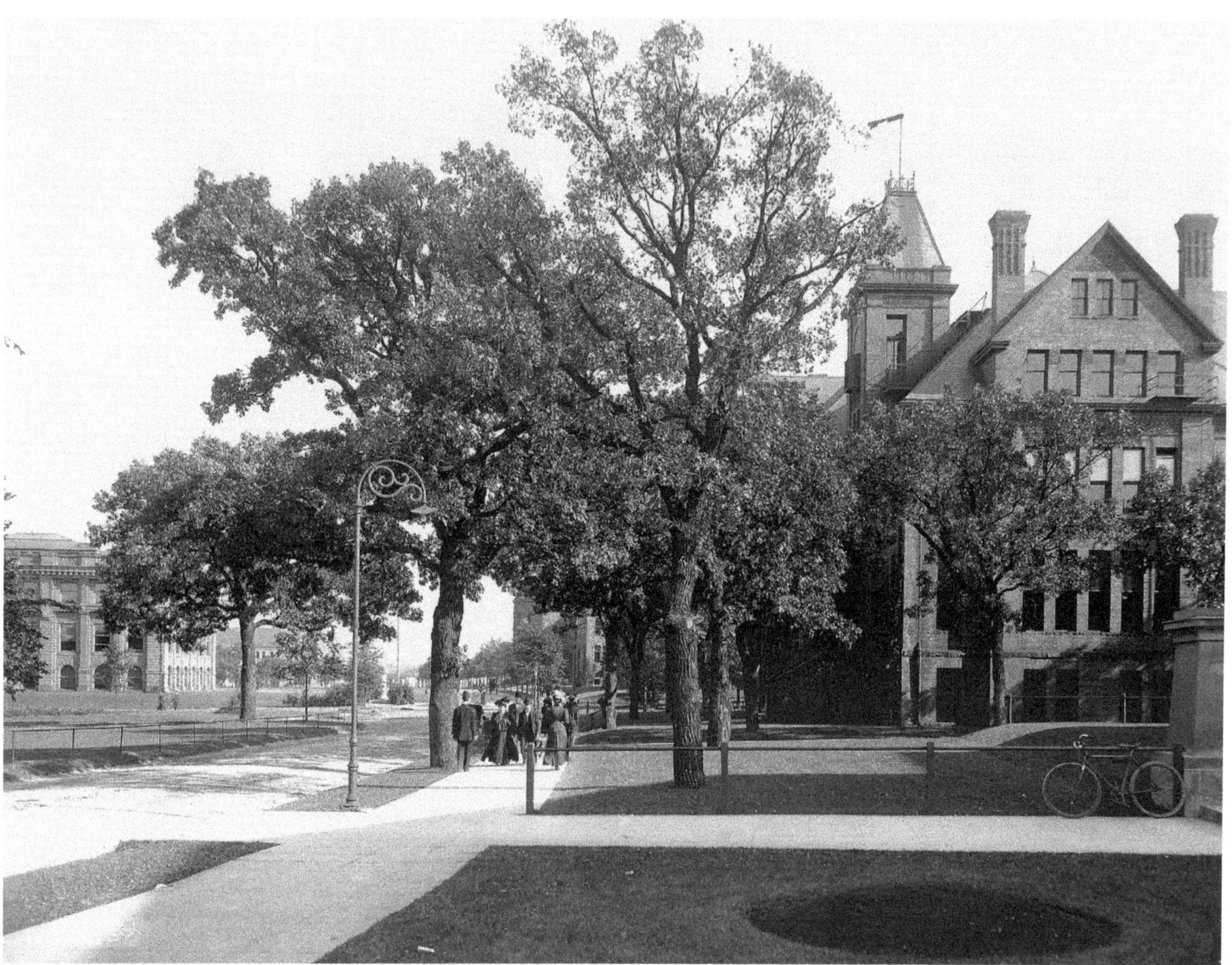

In 1896 Minneapolis's minor league baseball team, the Millers, relocated to the newly constructed Nicollet Park at Thirty-first Street and Nicollet Avenue. The Millers occupied this location, depicted here around 1910, until their move to Metropolitan Stadium in 1956.

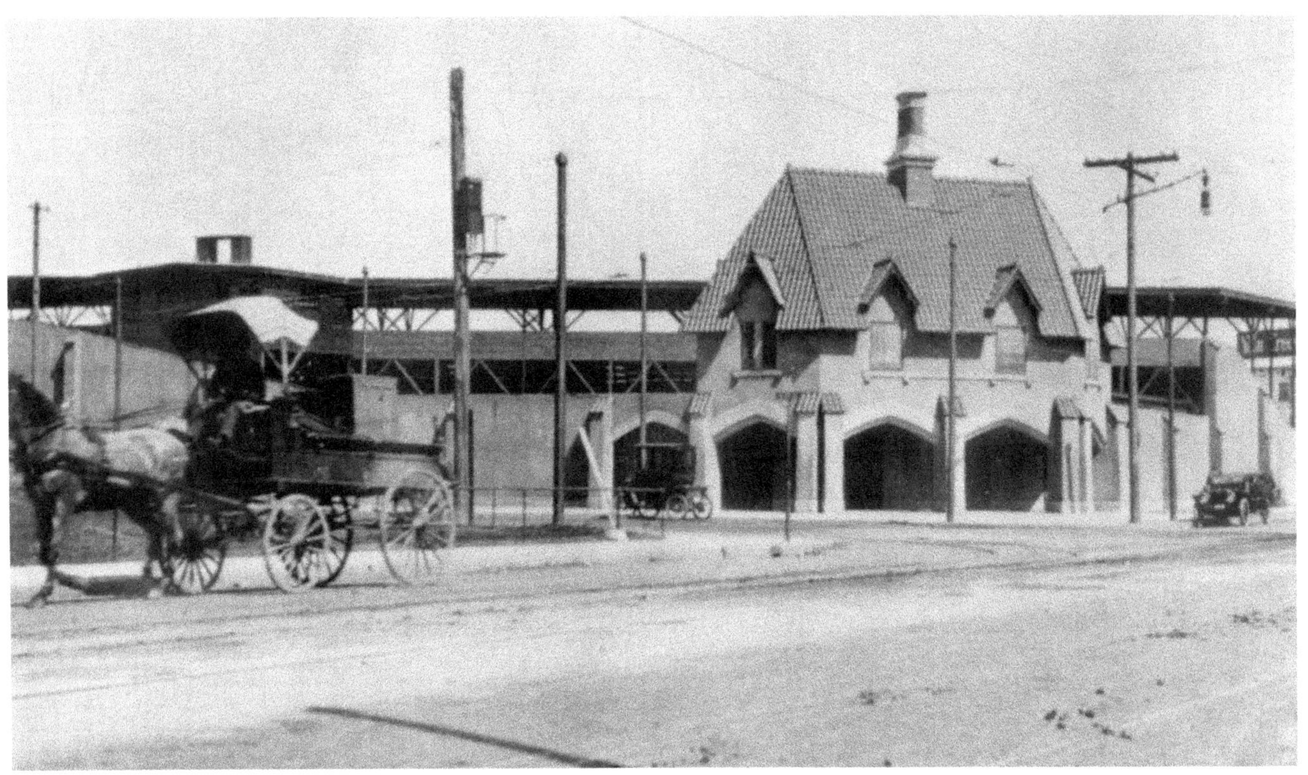

Hennepin Avenue on a quiet day around 1908. Minneapolitans traverse the city by horse, by streetcar, and by foot.

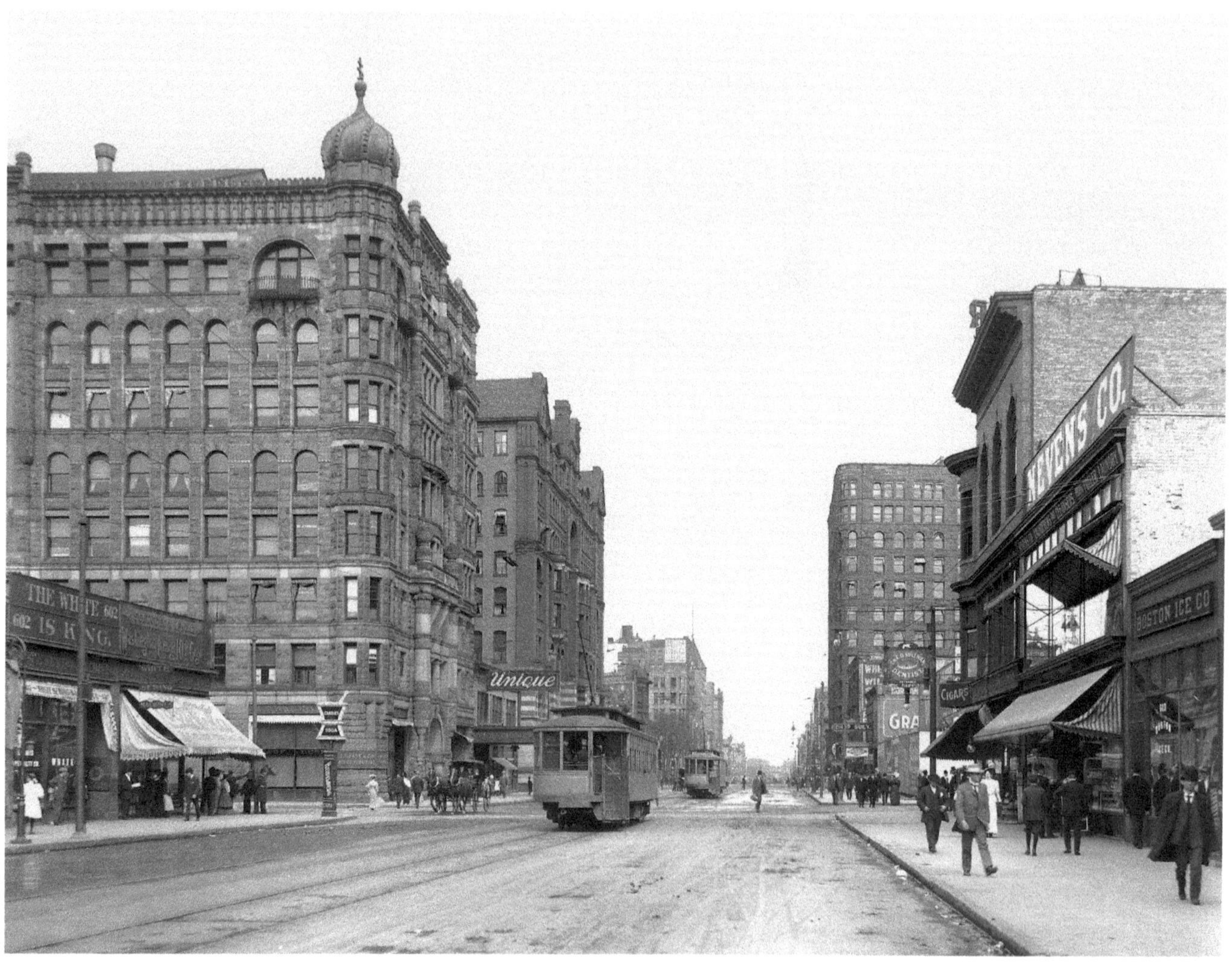

An employee of the Central Provision Company makes a delivery in a residential neighborhood around 1910.

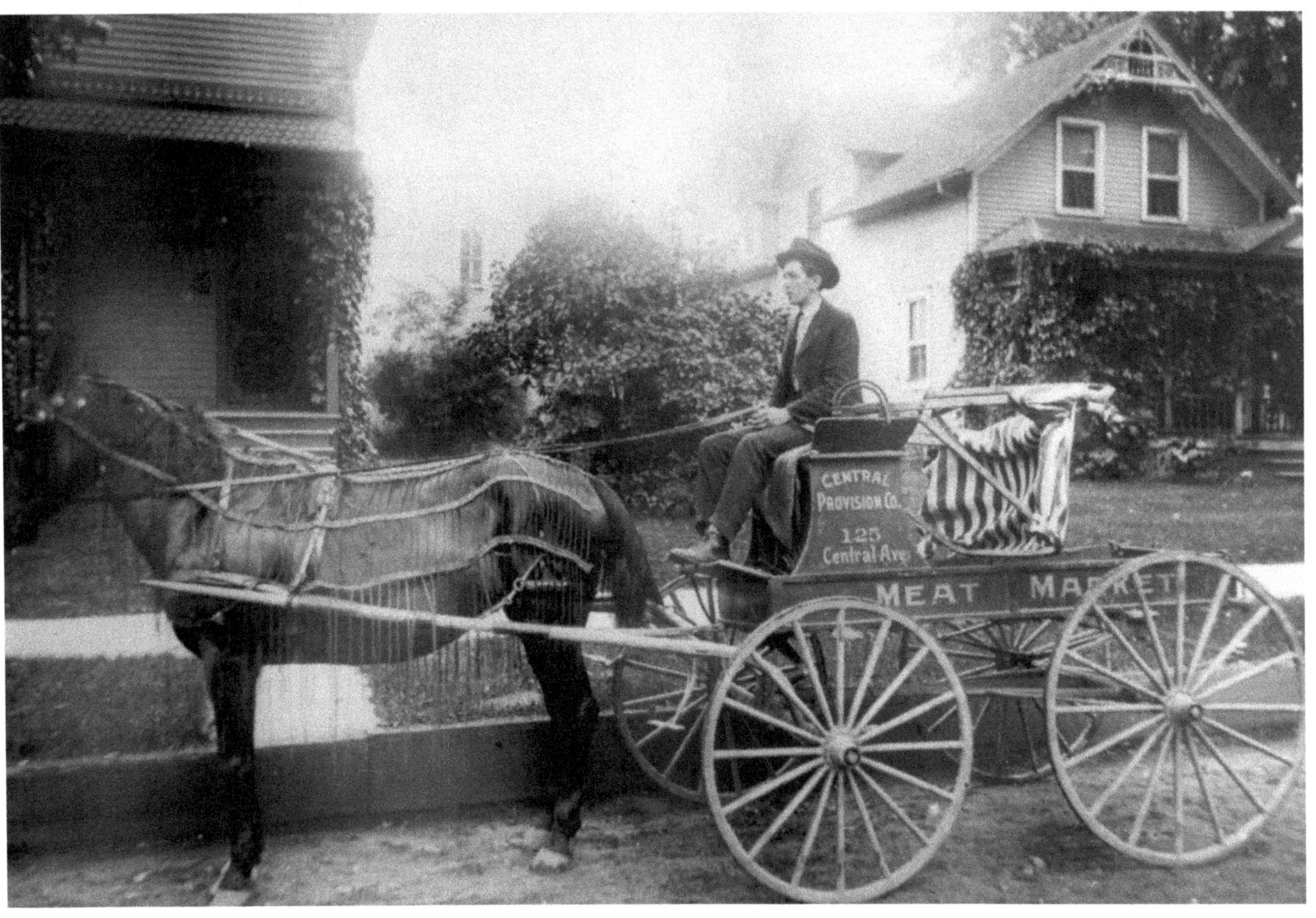

The Milwaukee Road Depot, seen here around 1910, occupies the corner of Third Street and Washington Avenue in the milling district. Smoke emanating from the train shed at rear indicates the presence of steam locomotives arriving at or leaving the station. The last train departed from the depot in 1971. In 1978 the structure was added to the National Register of Historic Places.

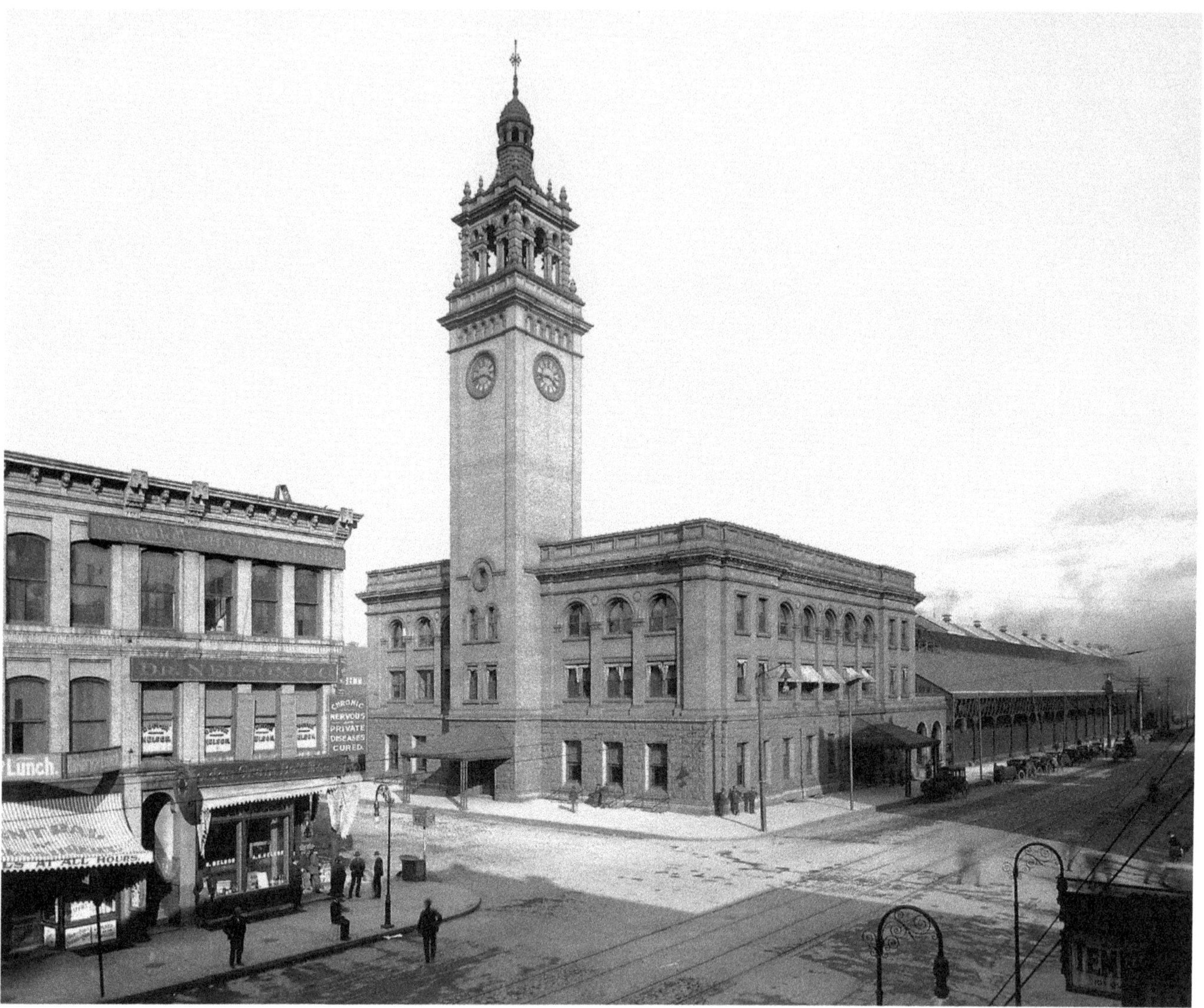

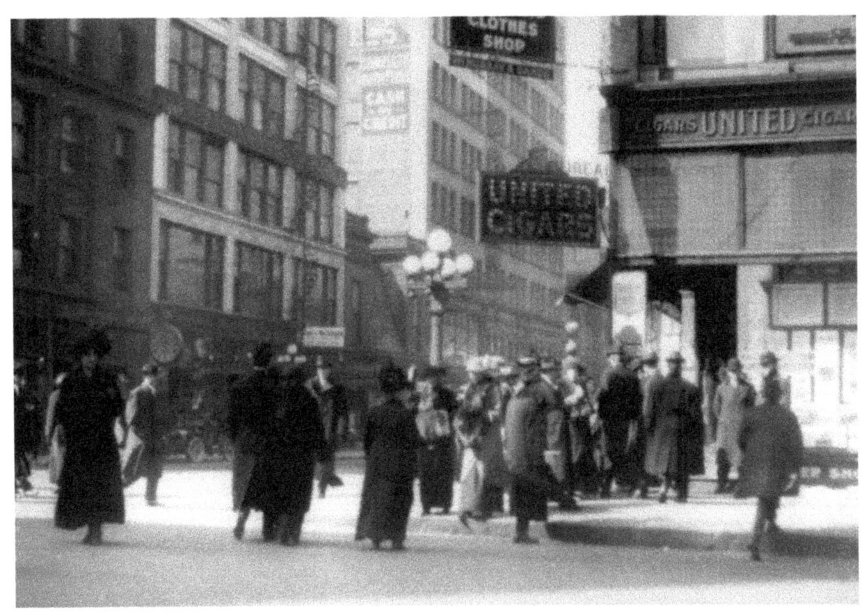

Busy pedestrians hurry along Sixth Street between Hennepin and Nicollet avenues in the early years of the twentieth century. The United Cigars Shop and the Up Stairs Clothes Shop occupied the corner store.

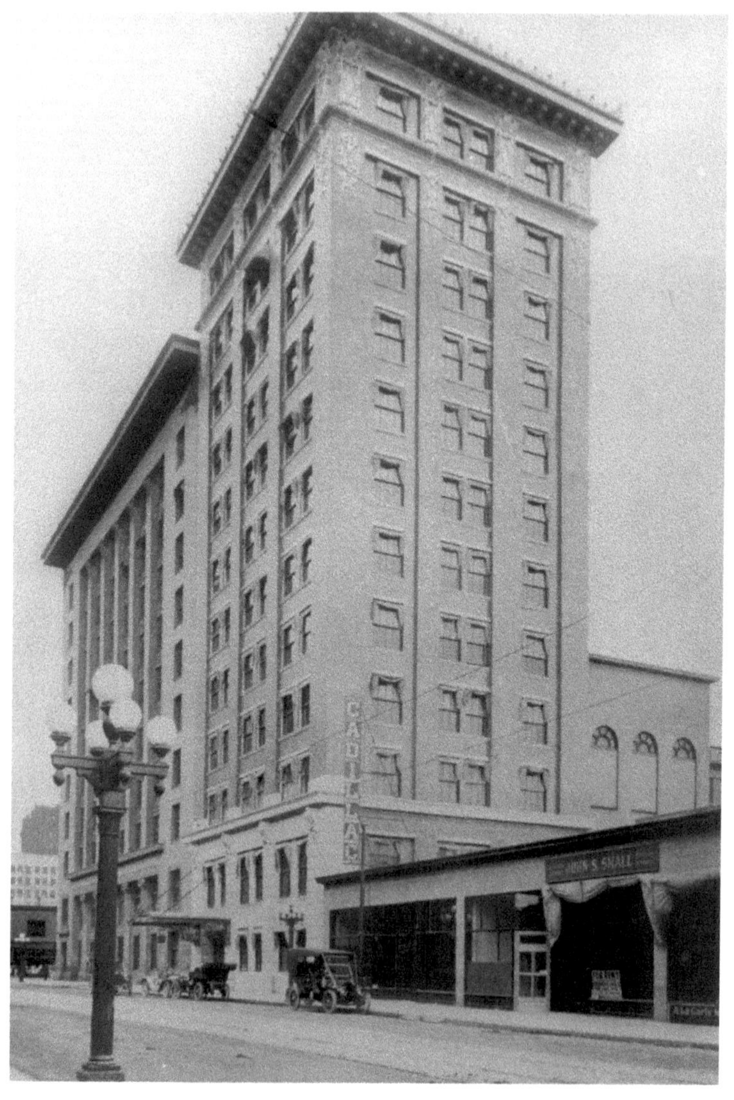

In 1907 a new ten-story Minneapolis Grain Exchange opened at the corner of Fourth Street South and Fourth Avenue South. This building became the largest structure in the world devoted to the grain and flour business.

This photograph, taken around 1910 at the corner of Washington and Nicollet avenues, illustrates the wide variety of businesses that populated the thriving downtown shopping district.

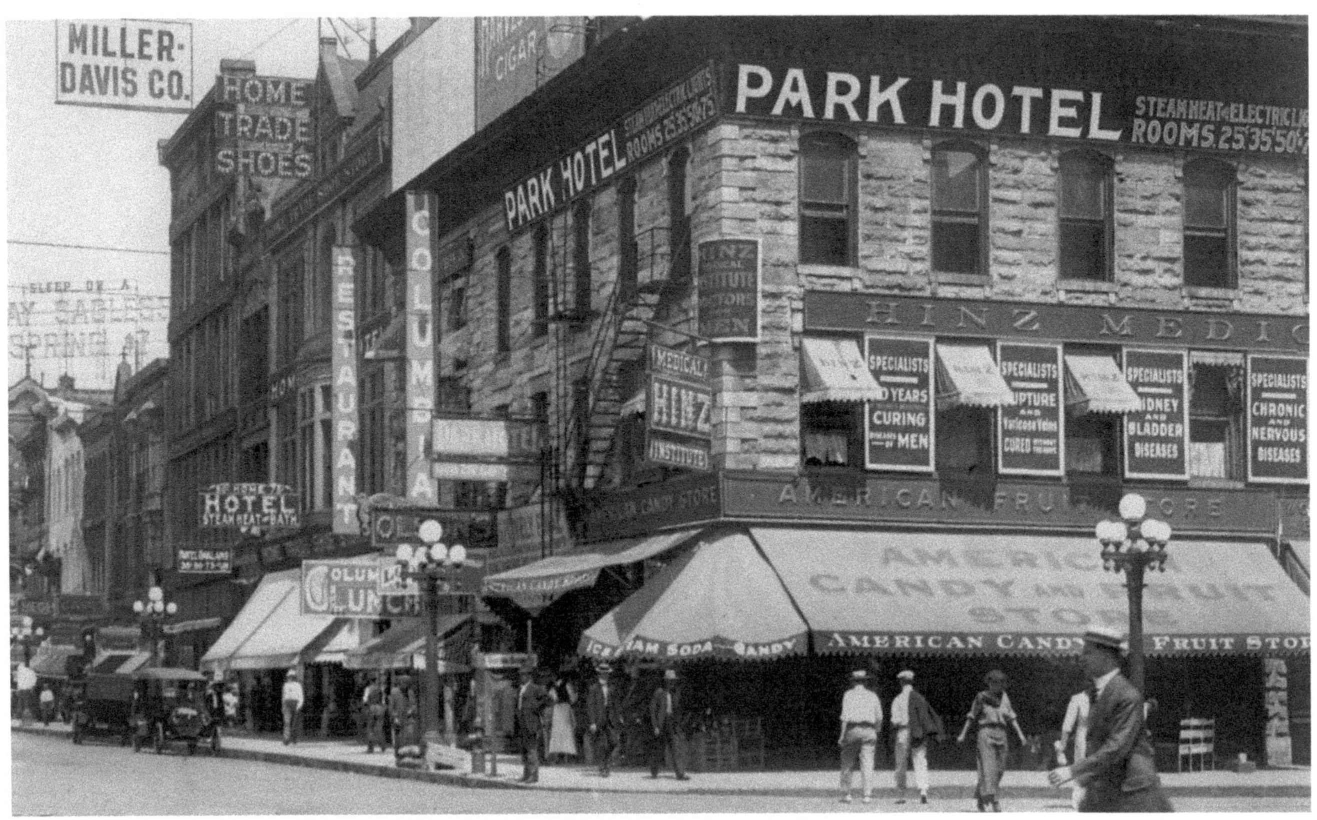

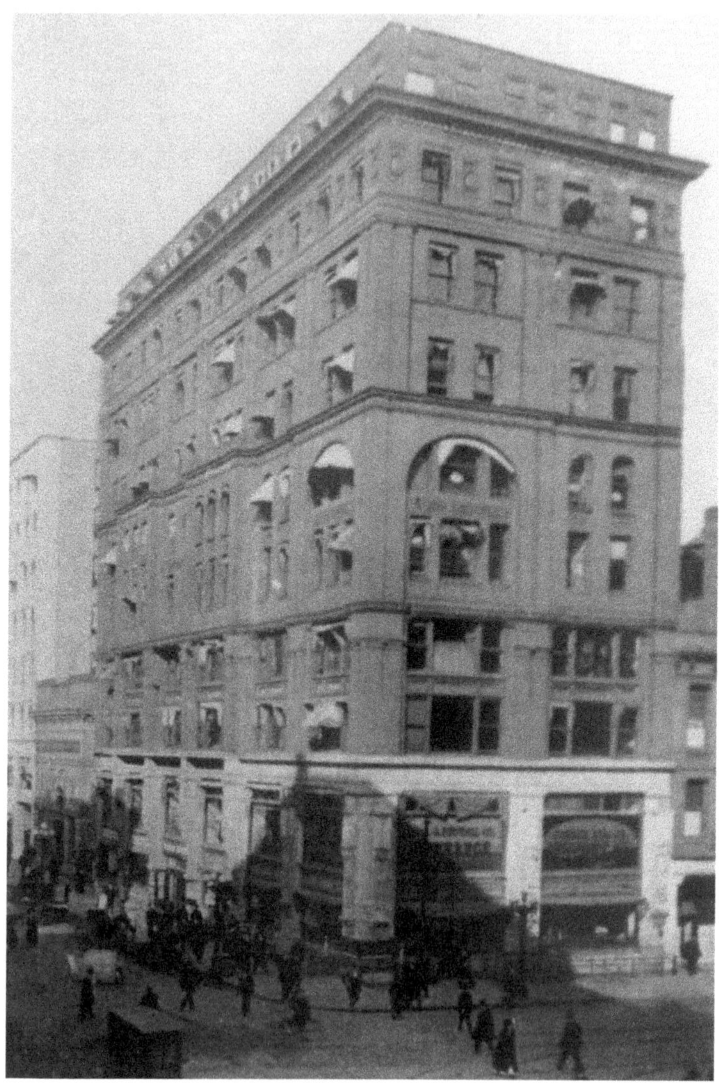

The Phoenix Building, seen here around 1909, occupied the corner of Fourth Street and Marquette Avenue. The edifice earned its moniker because it stood on the site where the Minneapolis Tribune's offices were headquartered before fire destroyed that building in 1889.

In 1908 the Park Board acquired a prime piece of downtown real estate near the Hennepin Avenue Bridge. By 1915, about the time this image was recorded, architects Hewett & Brown had transformed the area into Gateway Park. The park featured gardens, a fountain, and a curving colonnade.

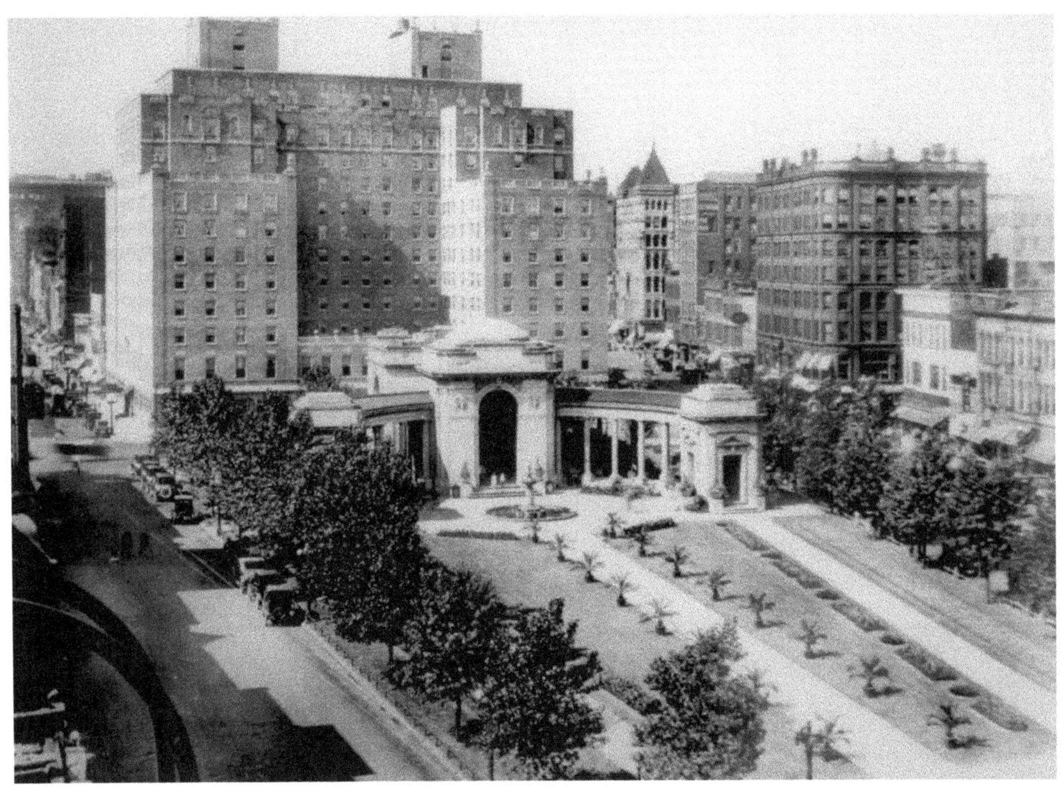

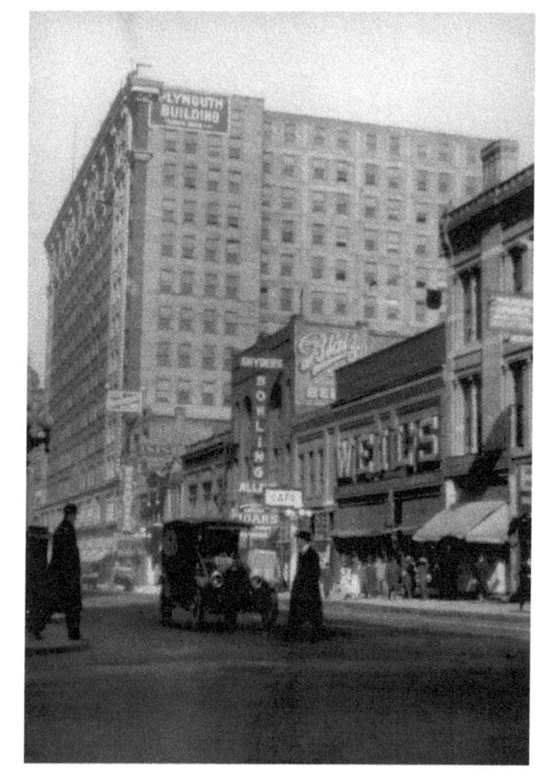

The Plymouth Building, a twelve-story brick and stone edifice at the corner of Sixth Street and Hennepin Avenue, was erected in 1910 and is pictured here around 1915. The ground floor of the building housed shops while offices occupied the upper floors.

Lake Nokomis, originally called Lake Amelia, is pictured here in 1915. The lake's name was changed in 1910 to honor Nokomis, the grandmother of the legendary Native American hero Hiawatha immortalized in Longfellow's poem.

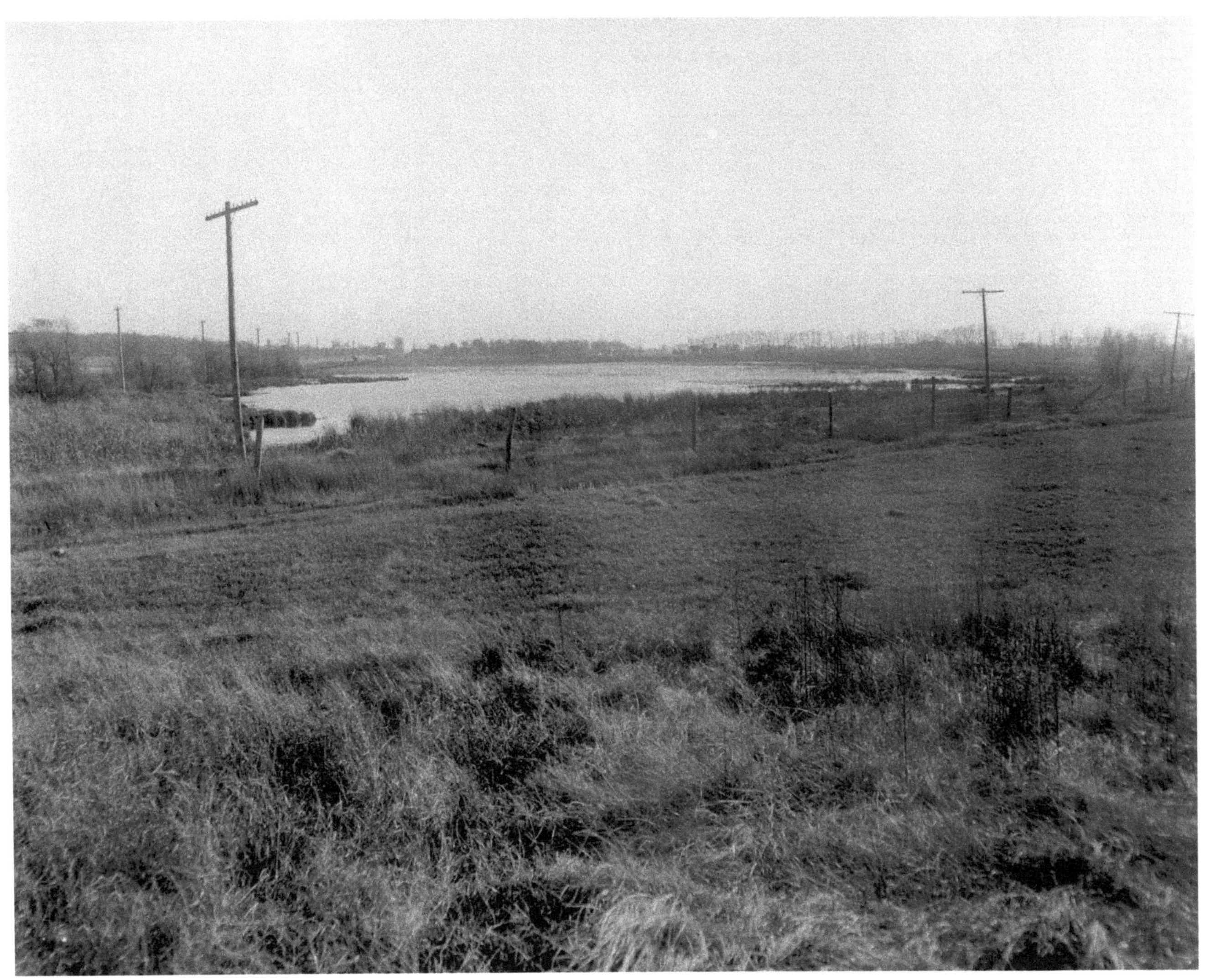

The four-story Loeb Arcade building, erected in 1914 at the corner of Fifth Street and Hennepin Avenue, provided an indoor shopping venue for the city's residents. The building housed clothing stores, jewelry stores, a cafeteria, and a selection of other small businesses.

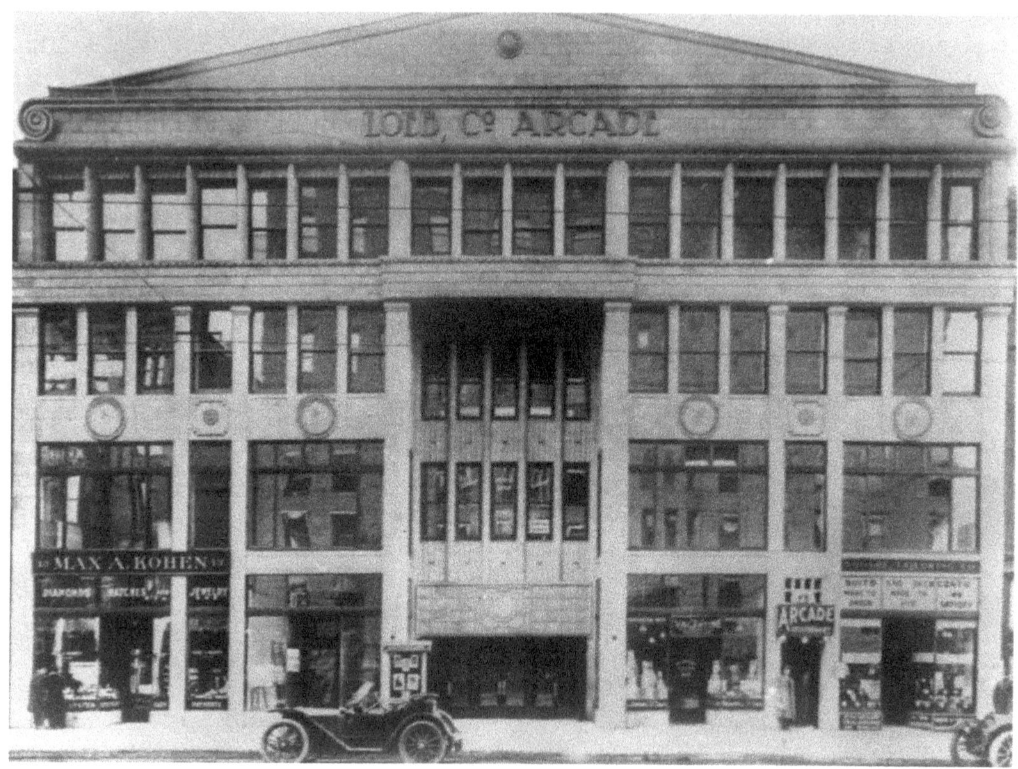

Serving as typesetters here in 1909, women work side-by-side at the Albert A. Dalin Print Shop on Washington Avenue in north Minneapolis.

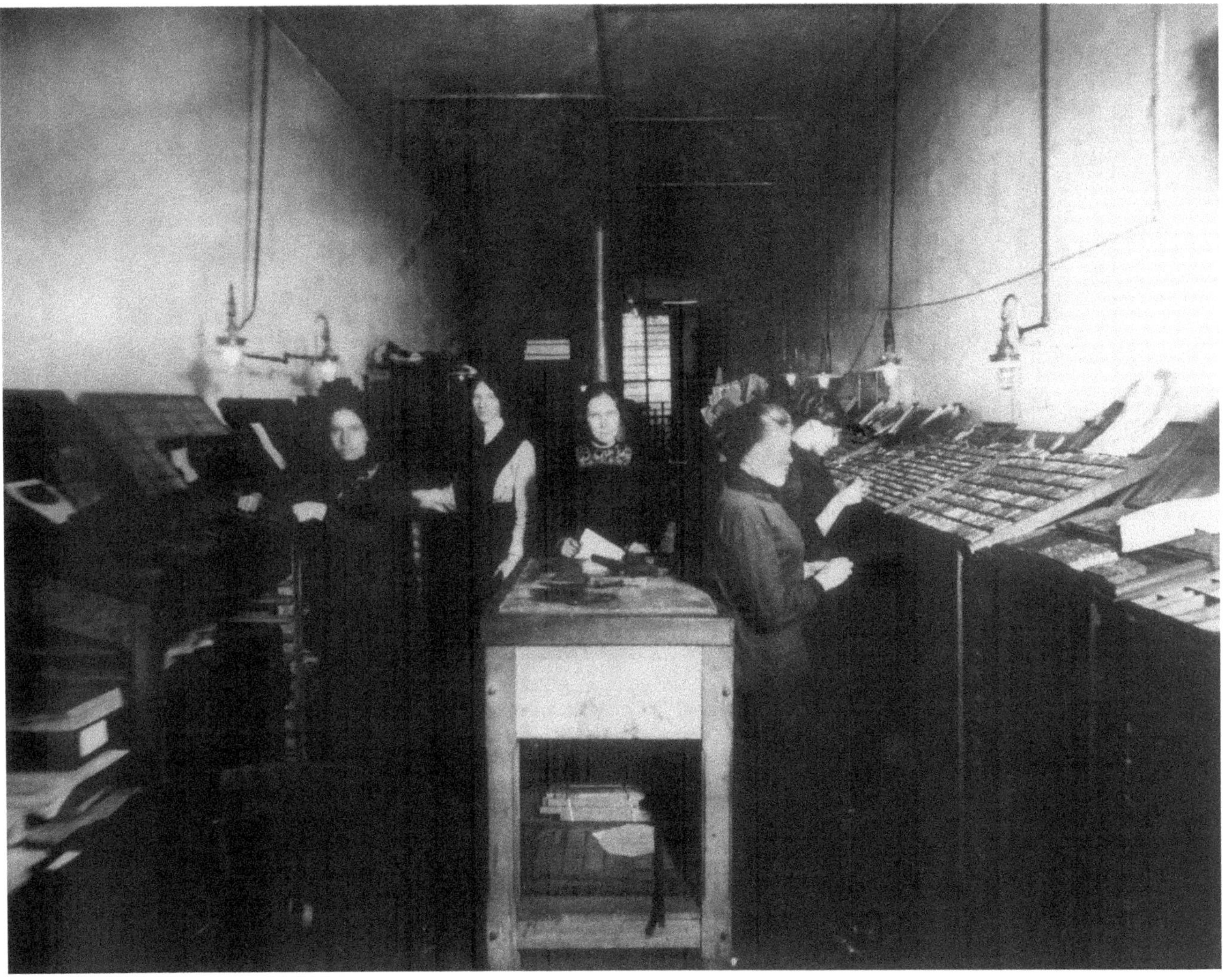

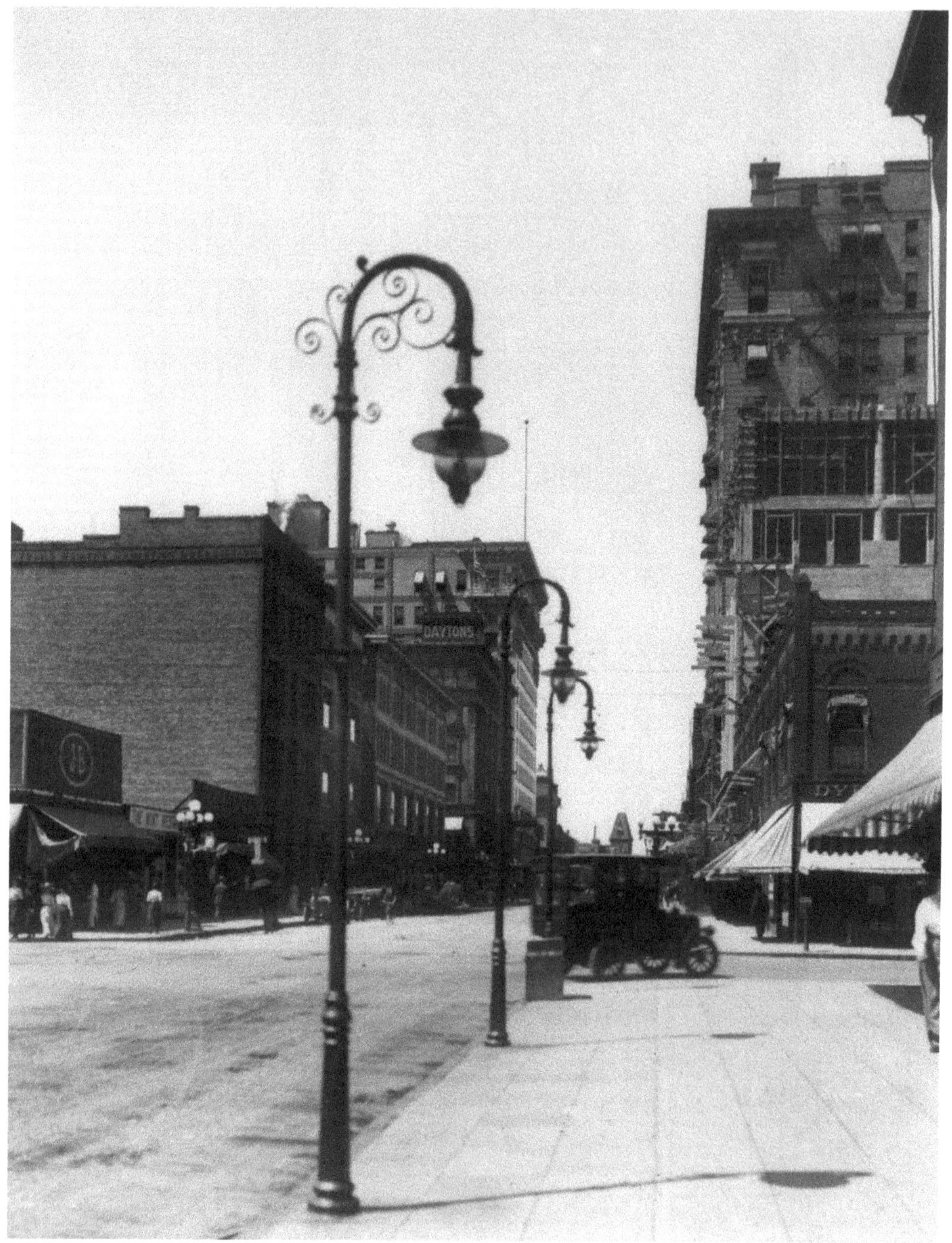

This 1910 photograph records an image of Seventh Street facing west from Marquette Avenue. Identifiable businesses include the Mint Restaurant, the YWCA, Dayton's Department Store, the Radisson Hotel, and Donaldson's Department Store.

An American Railway Express wagon parks in front of the Red Cross building on Fifth Street and Fourth Avenue South in Minneapolis around 1920. The American Railway Express Company formed in 1918 as the result of a merger between Wells Fargo and American Express.

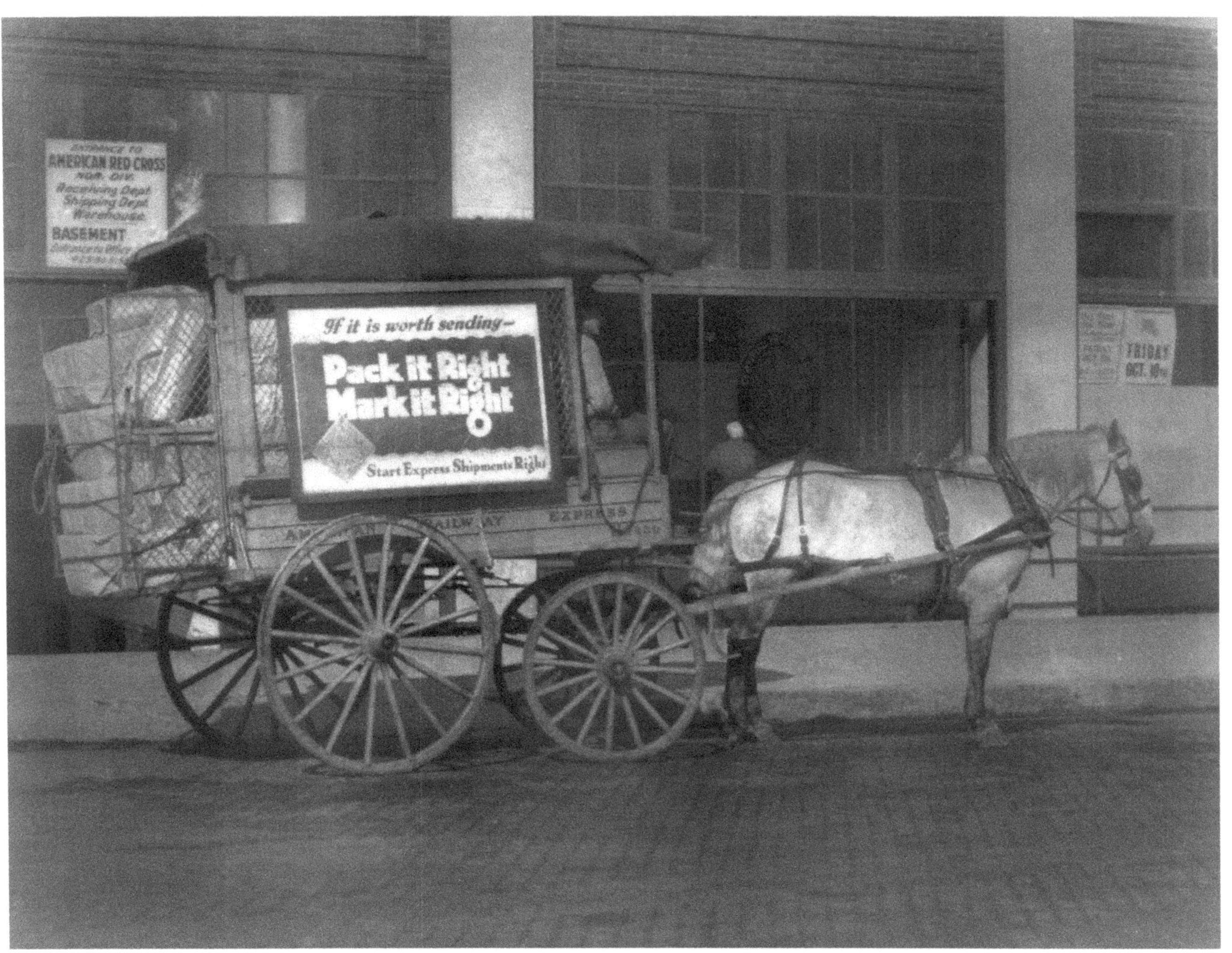

A parade, probably political in nature, proceeds down Nicollet Avenue from Fourth Street around 1910.

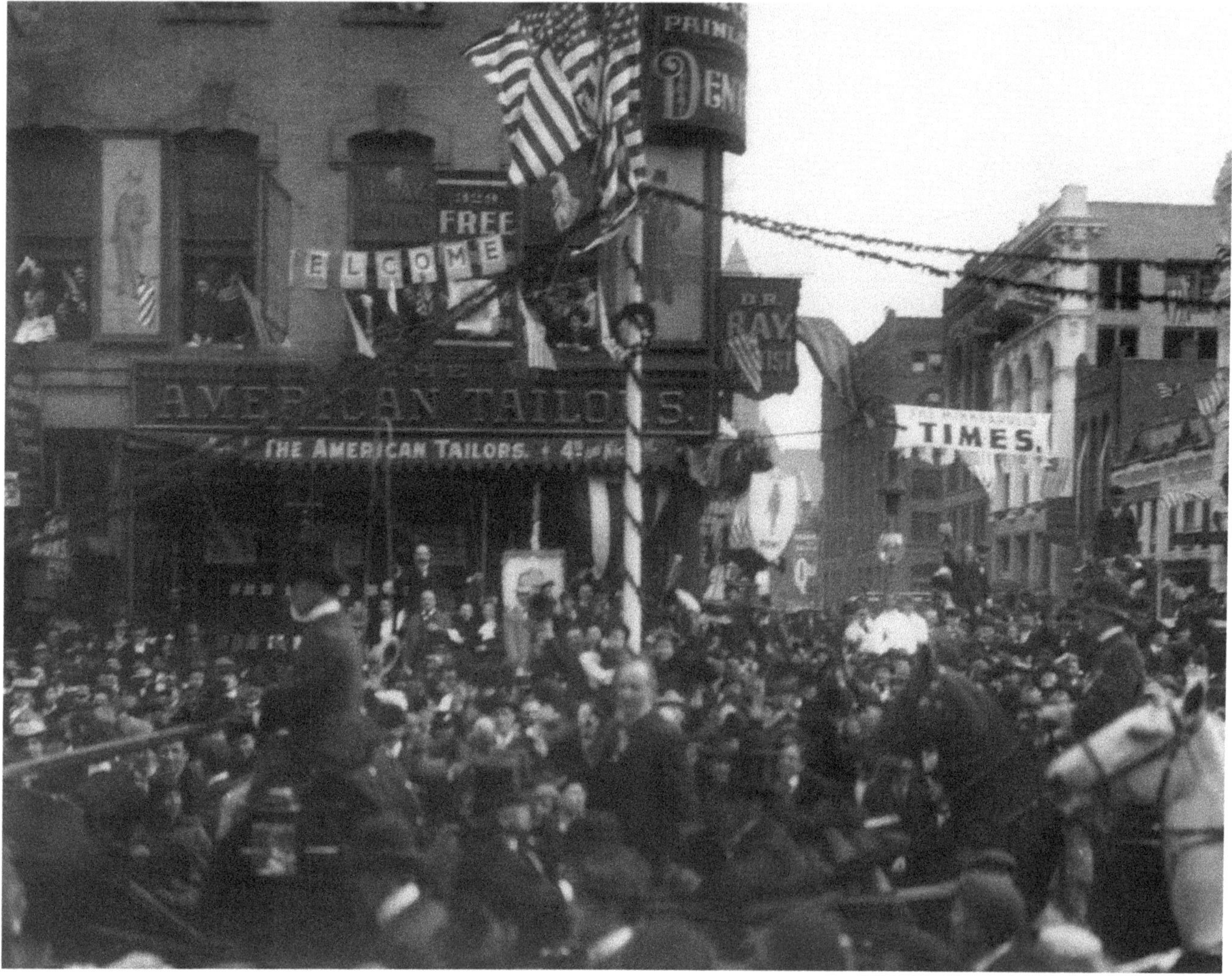

A little girl watches an organ grinder and his monkey around 1910.

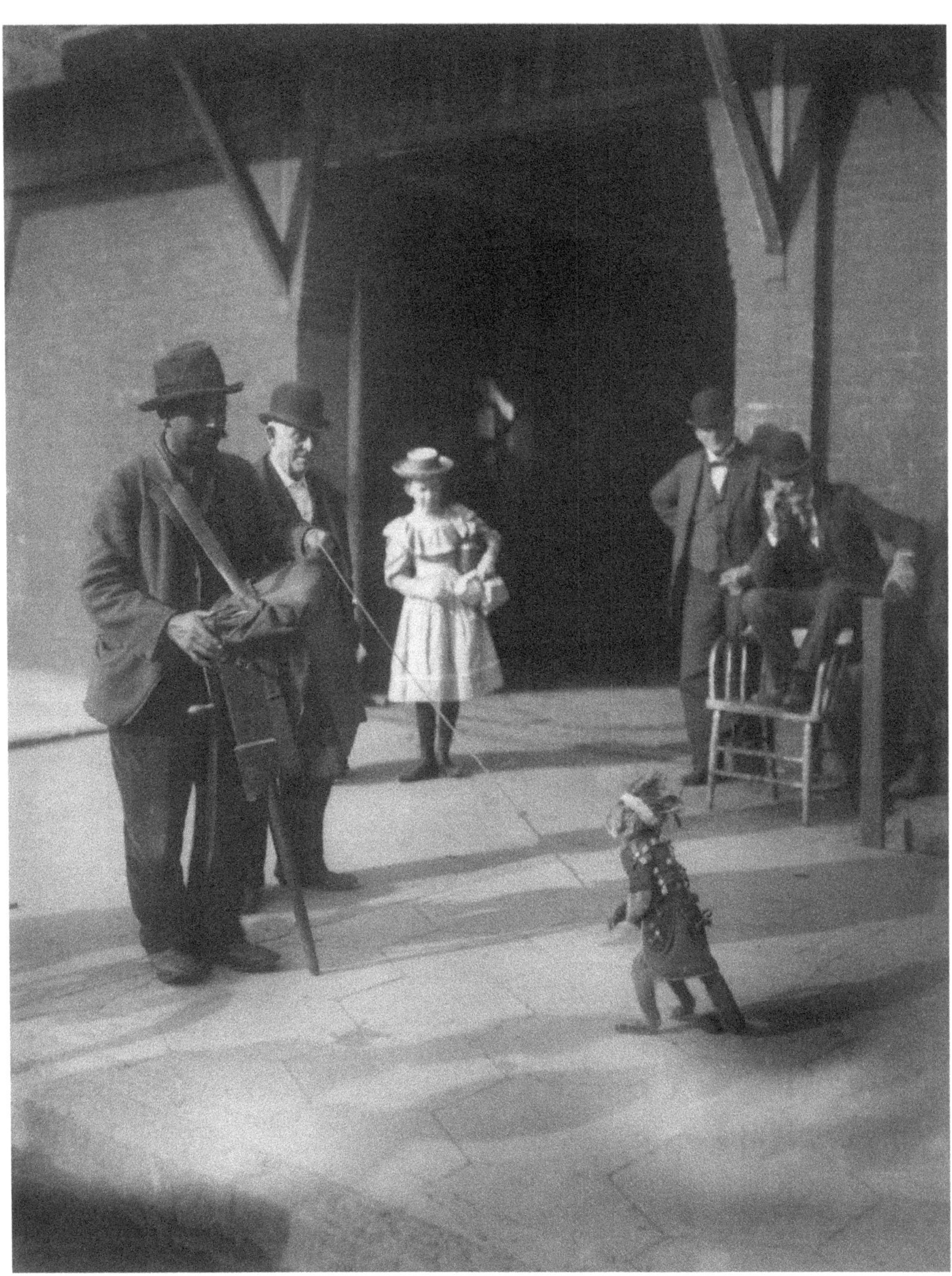

Streetcars and pedestrians traverse slushy Hennepin Avenue near its intersection with Sixth Street around 1910. The large stone building in the center of the photograph is the Masonic Temple.

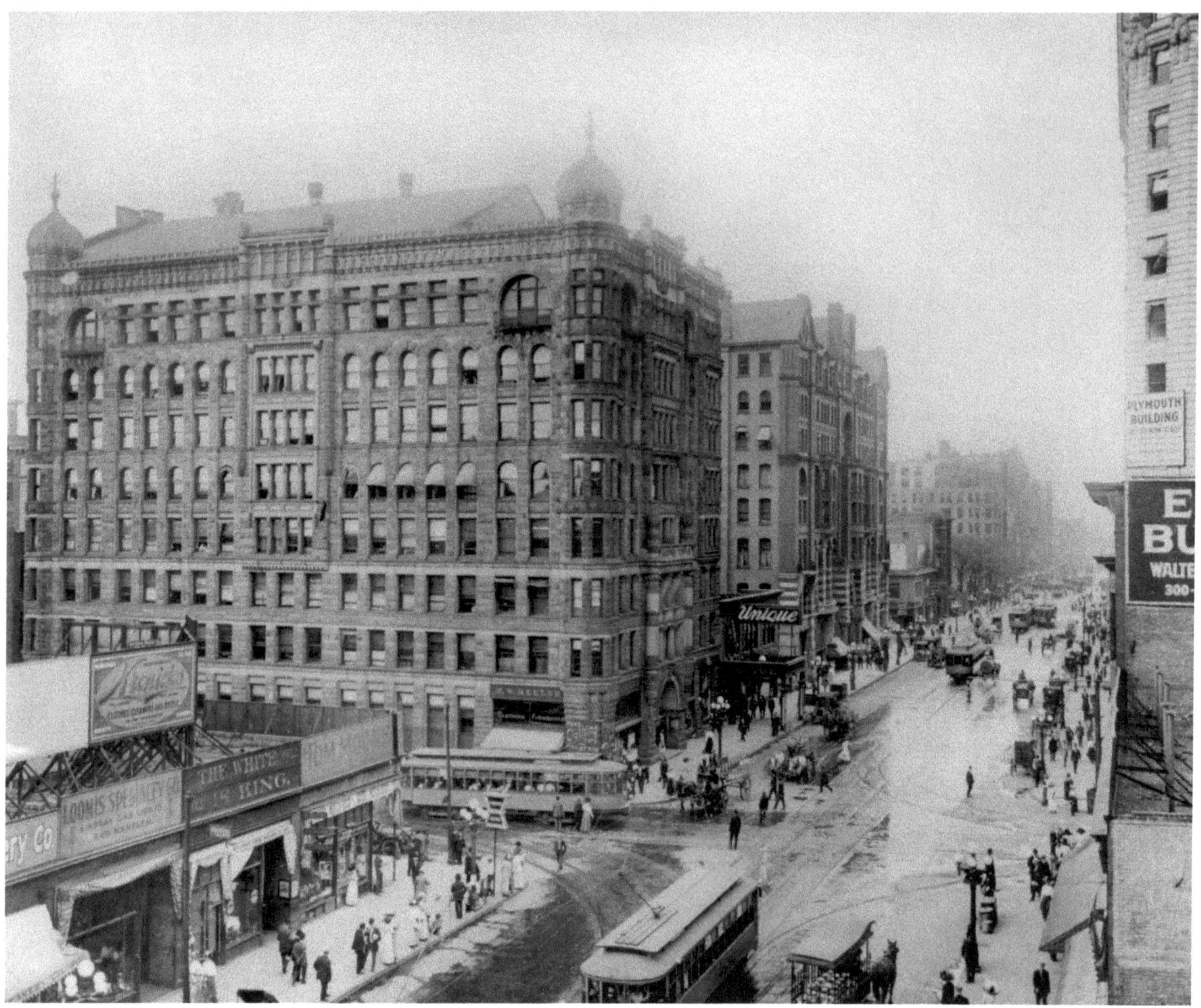

In 1911 the Parks Department completed a waterway connecting Lake of the Isles and Lake Calhoun in south Minneapolis. The city marked the joining of the lakes with a week-long civic celebration that included a parade of ships, fireworks, and band concerts.

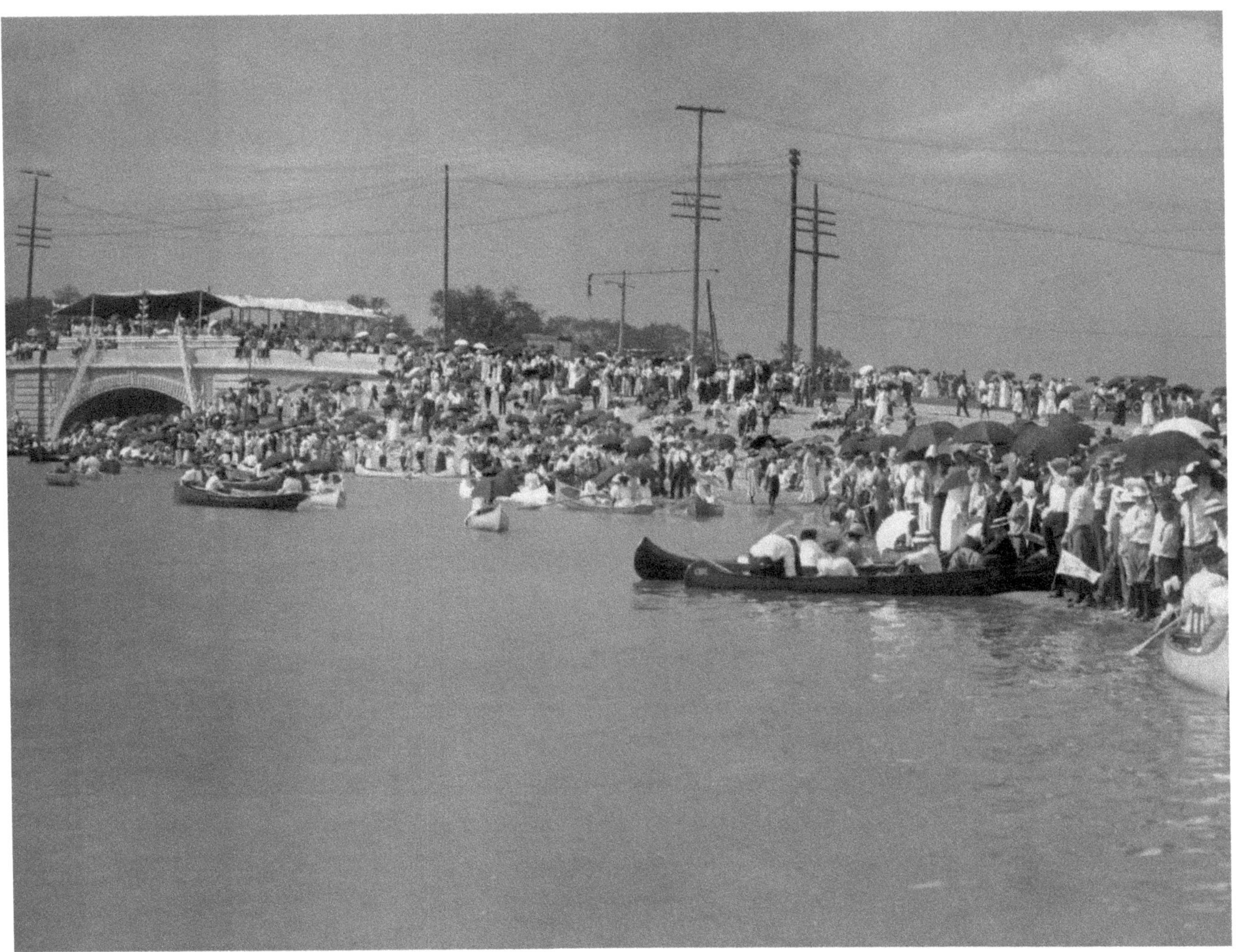

This panorama captures downtown Minneapolis as it appeared in 1911.

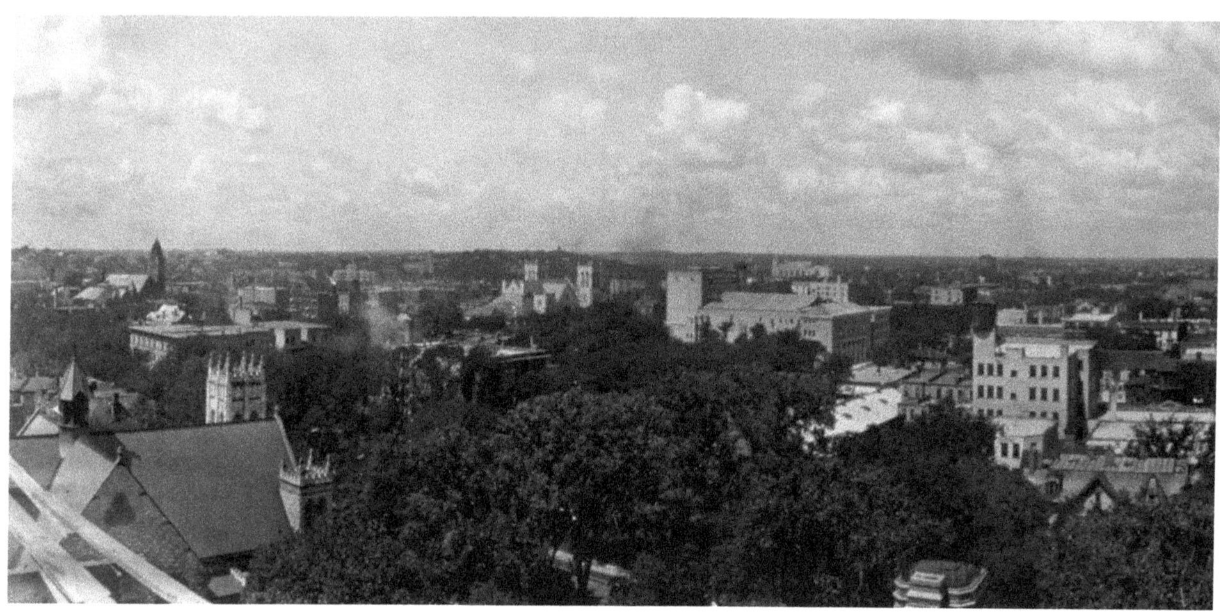

The gardens in the forefront of this 1913 image rest on the grounds of the Minneapolis Armory. The background reveals St. Mark's Episcopal Church, built in 1910 by parishioner and architect Edwin Hawley Hewitt. In 1941 the church was designated a cathedral.

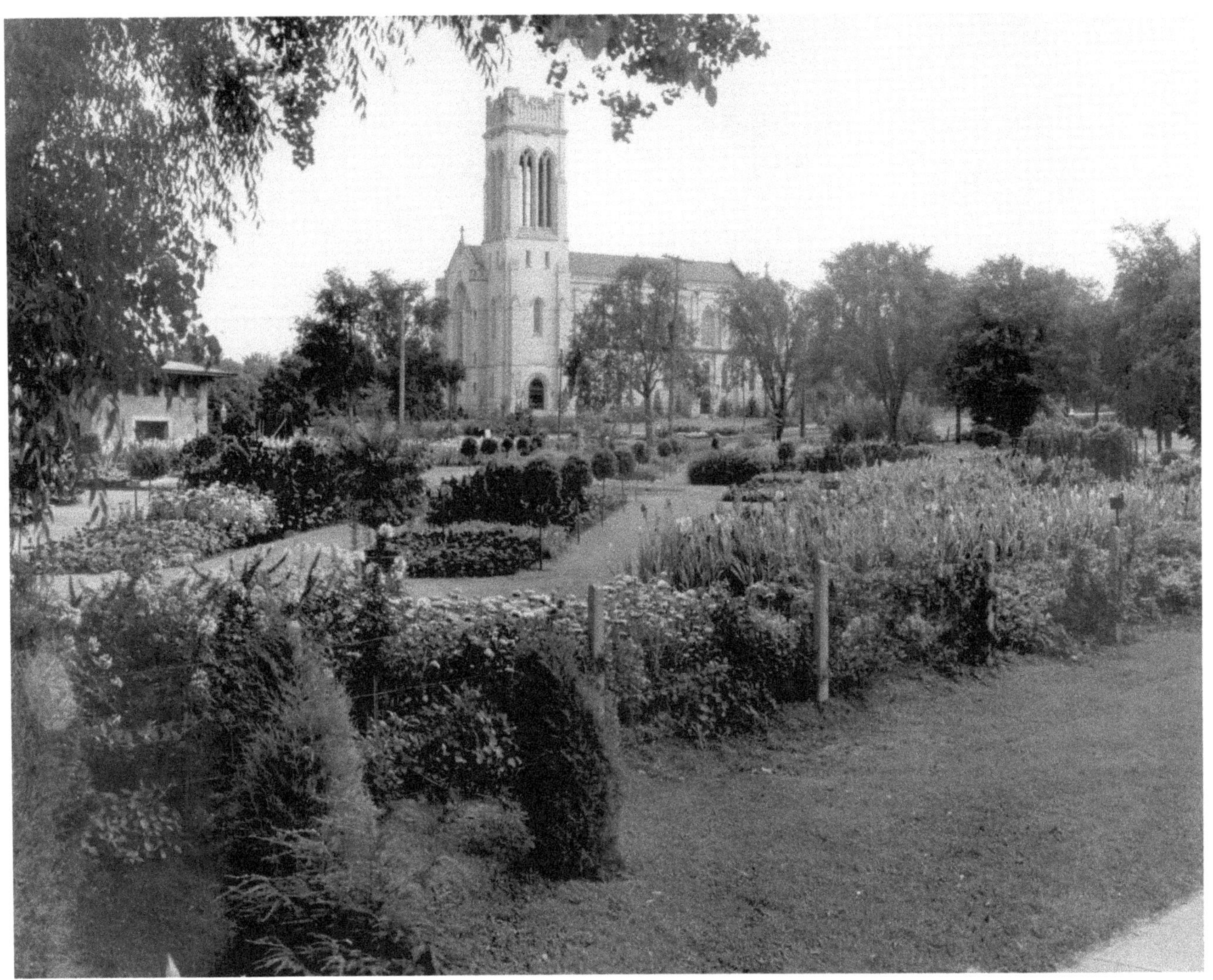

A snowy Nicollet Avenue around 1913. Dayton's Department Store is visible at left. Another department store, the Pearce Cloak Company, is seen here directly across the street from Dayton's.

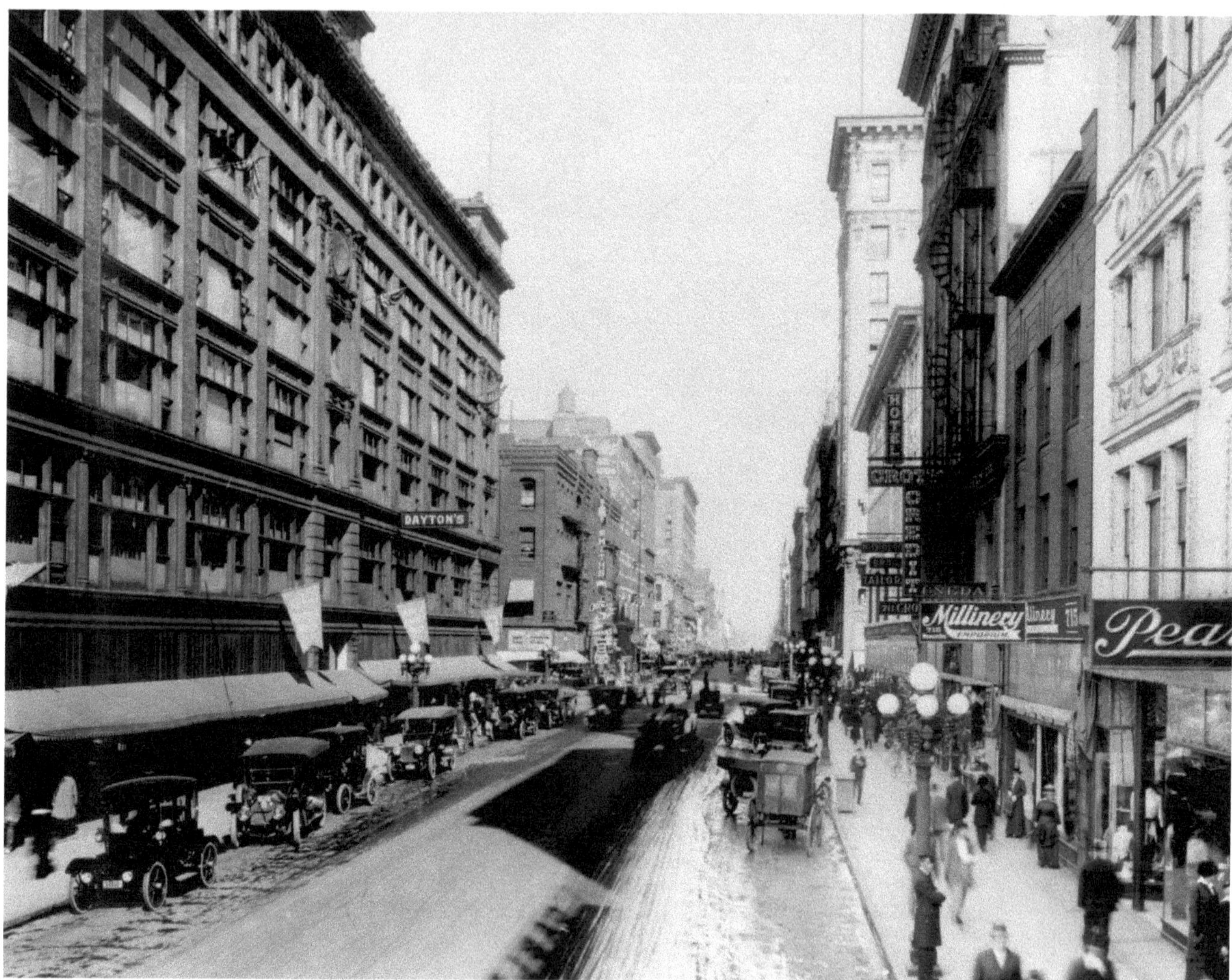

During the summer of 1915 Minneapolitans flocked to Calhoun Beach on the north shore of Lake Calhoun. The 1918 Hudson's *Dictionary of Minneapolis* notes that Lake Calhoun could be reached from downtown via streetcar in just thirty minutes.

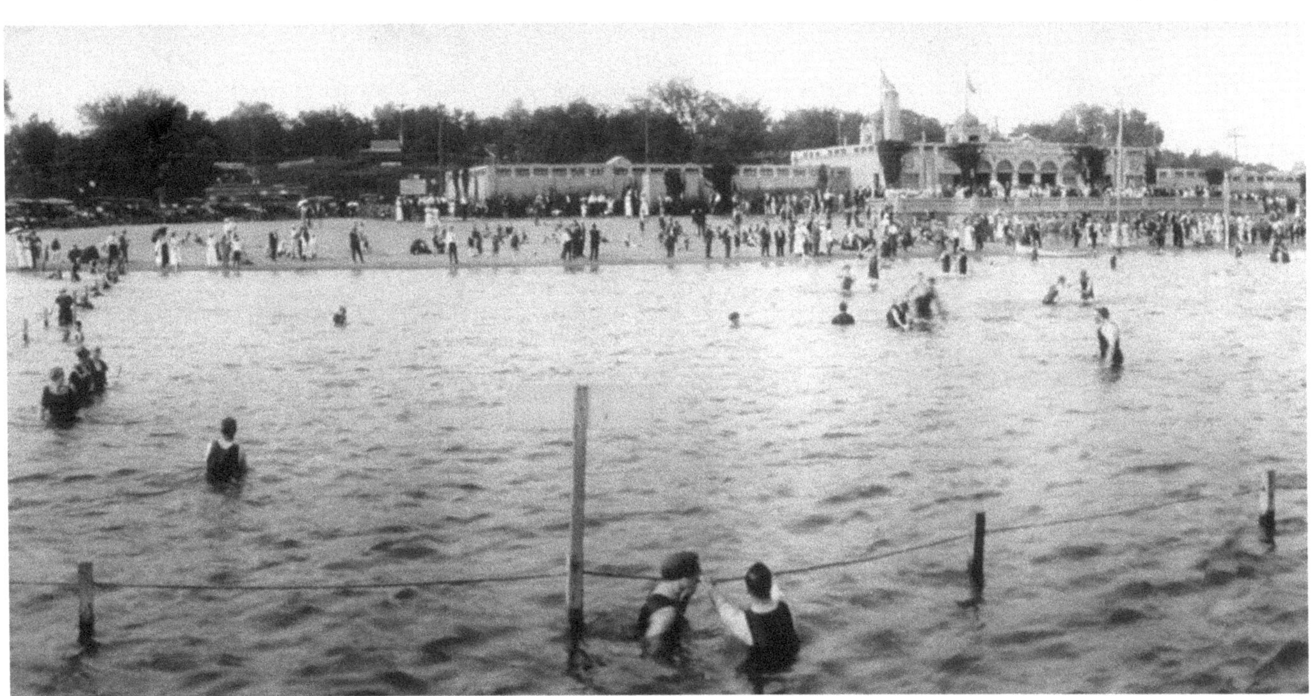

Railroad tycoon James J. Hill financed the construction of the Great Northern Railway Station in 1914. This station, located at the point where Hennepin Avenue meets the Mississippi River, served the city until a dearth of railway traffic led to its closure in 1978.

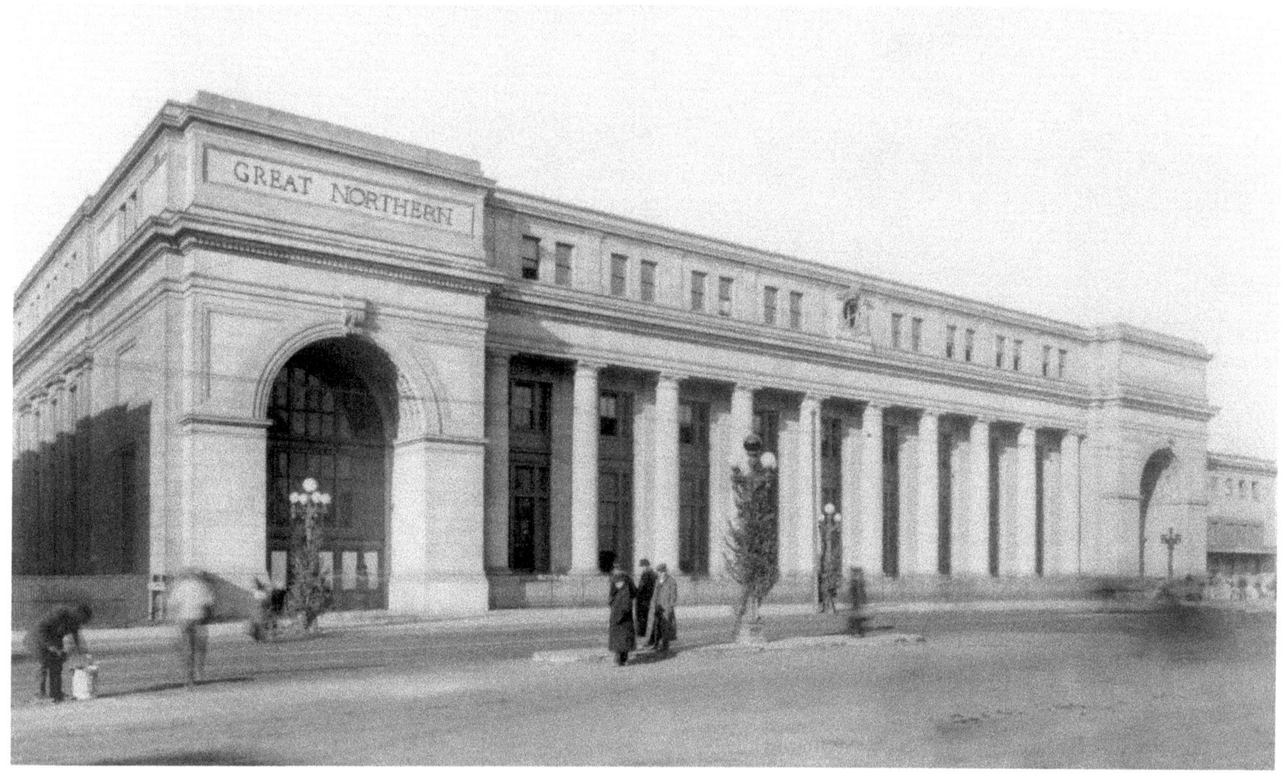

In 1868 James Pauly opened a hotel at the corner of High Street and Nicollet Avenue, seen here about 1920. The three-story building held fifty guest rooms, a small lobby, and a dining room.

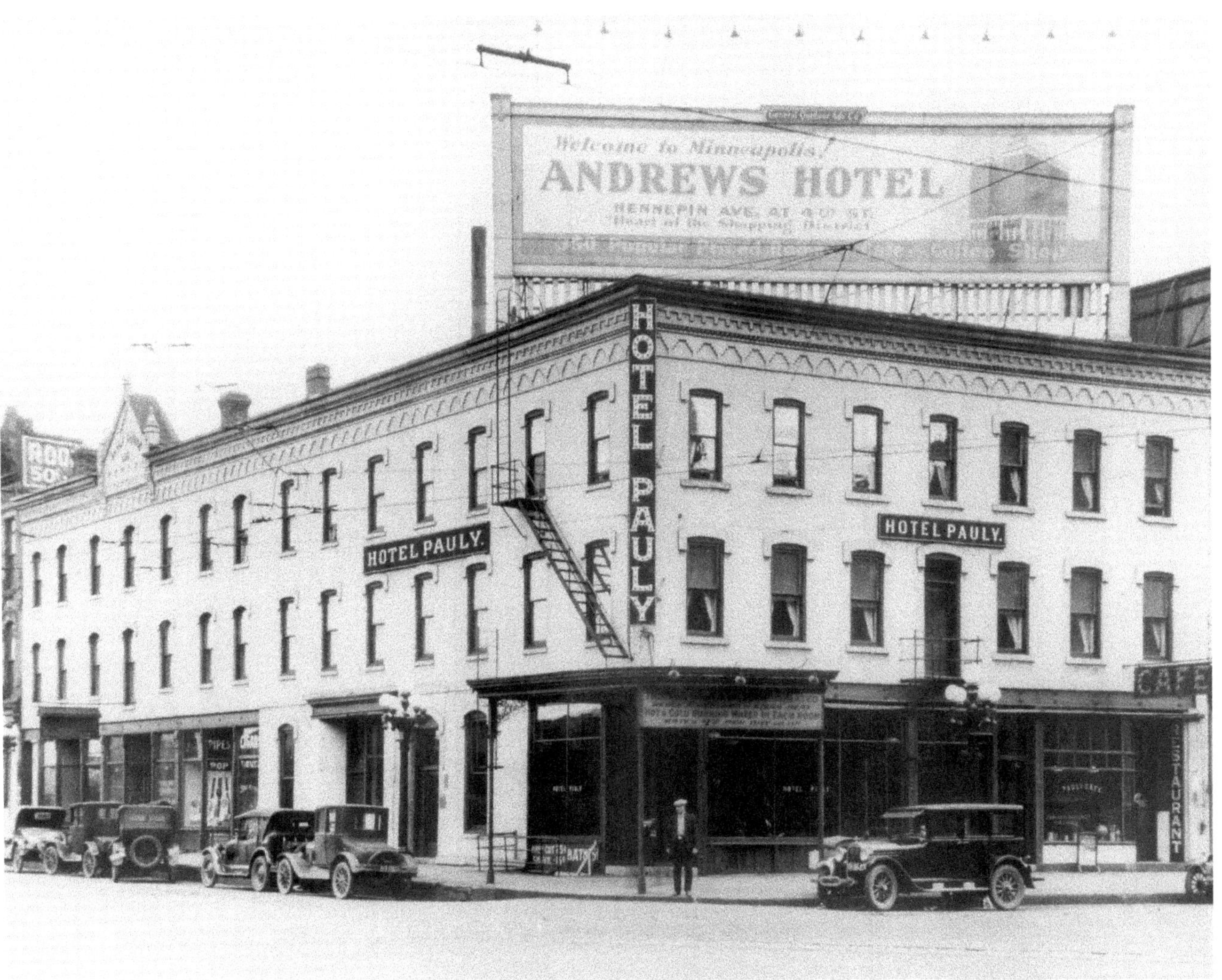

Crowds at the Lake Harriet pavilion watch canoers in the water below. This photograph was taken about 1916, when the popularity of boating at Minneapolis parks reached its zenith. During that year the Parks Department registered 1,825 watercraft on city lakes.

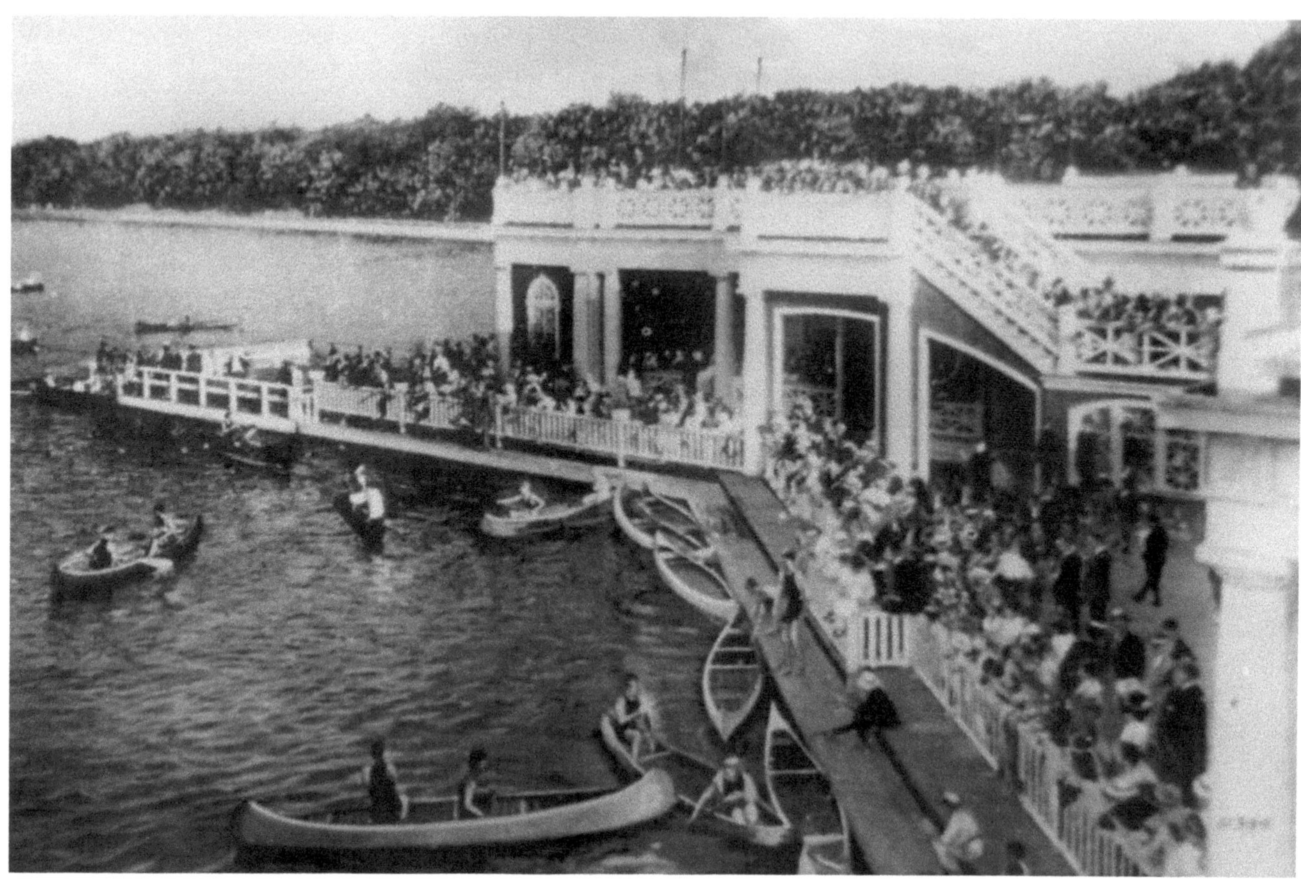

This panorama, recorded in 1912, captures a moment in the heyday of the flour milling industry. Between 1909 and 1920, the city exported an average of sixteen million barrels of flour each year.

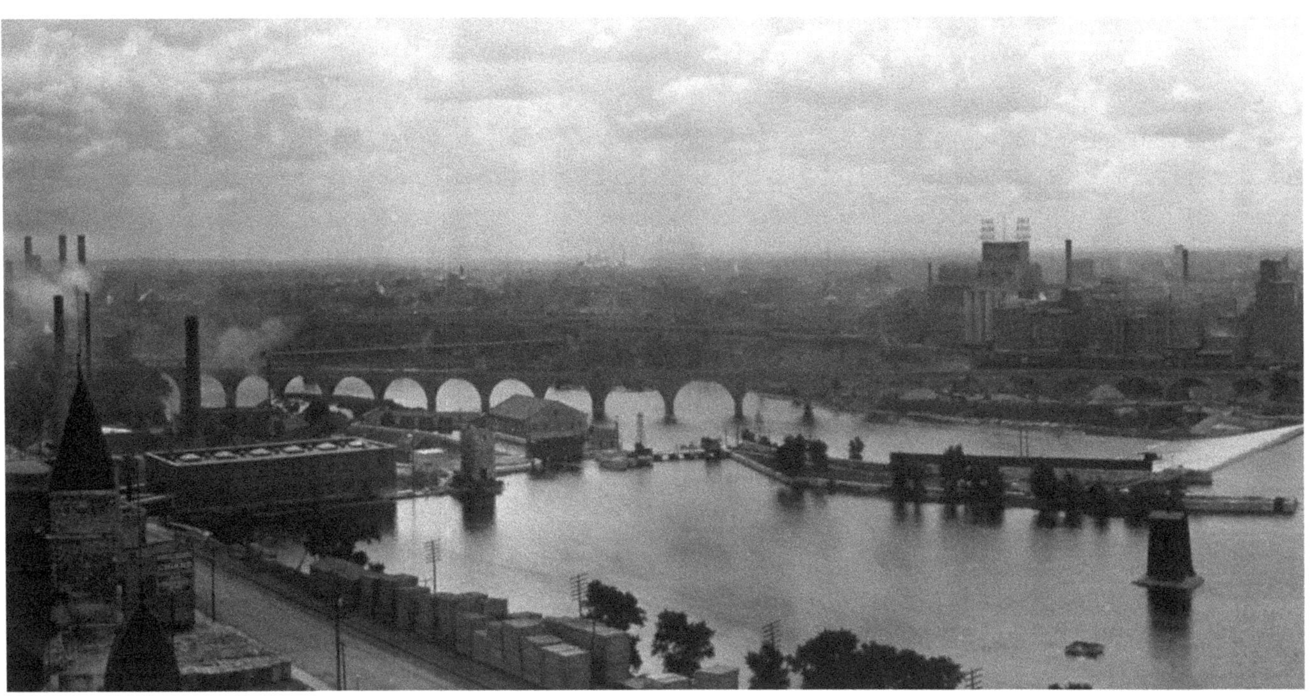

Almost 12,000 men from Minneapolis served overseas during World War I. Of this total a startling 4,844 died while fighting and another 1,090 were wounded. Here members of the Company K Citizen's Auxiliary Volunteers stand at attention in front of the Andrus Building in 1917.

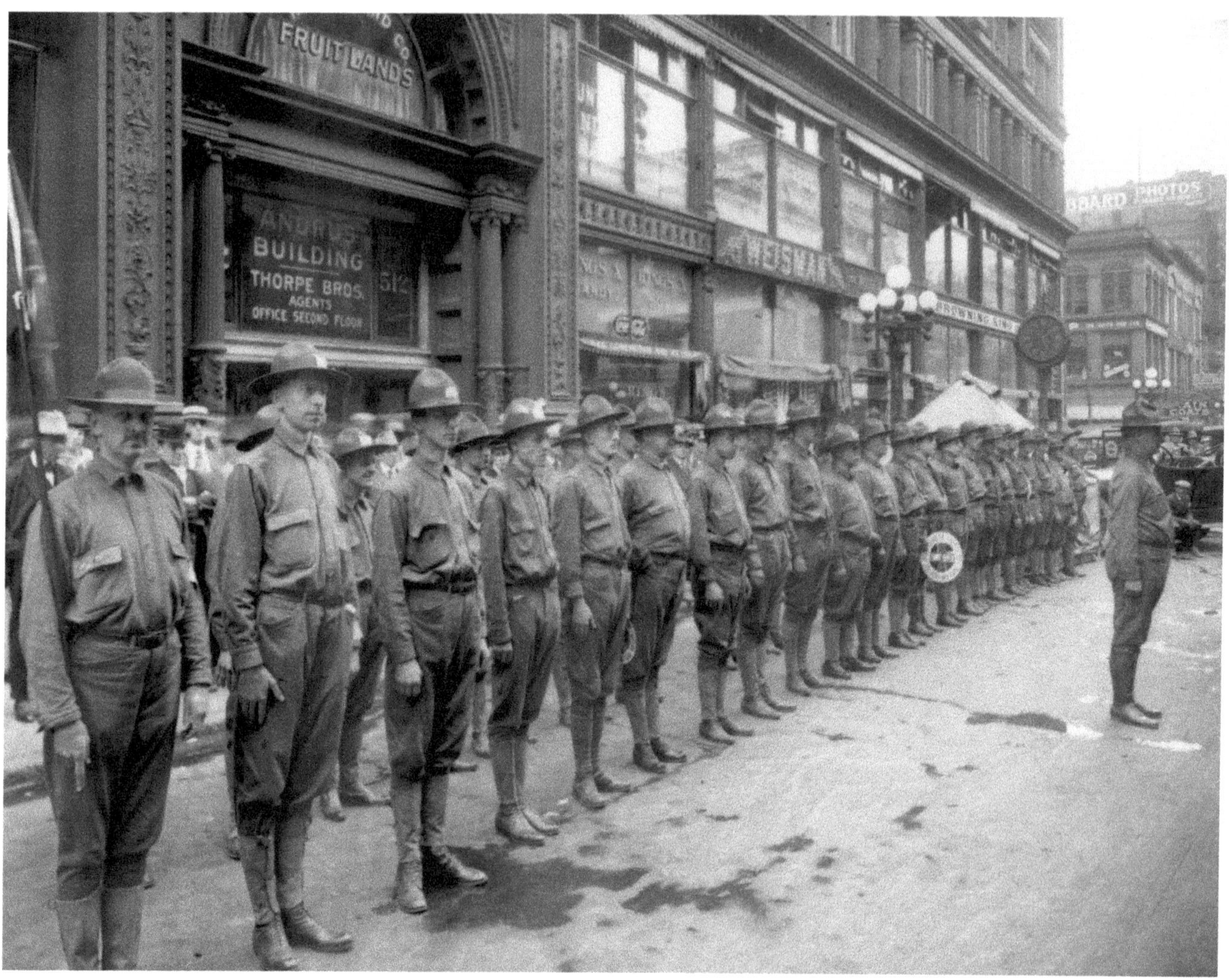

In 1918 Minneapolitans organized a citywide drive to garner funds for local benevolent organizations involved with the war effort including the Red Cross, the Salvation Army, the Knights of Columbus, and the Jewish Relief Board. The amount of money raised was charted on this mammoth obelisk that stood in the middle of Seventh Street near Nicollet Avenue. The other side of the shaft listed the names of Minneapolis's fallen soldiers.

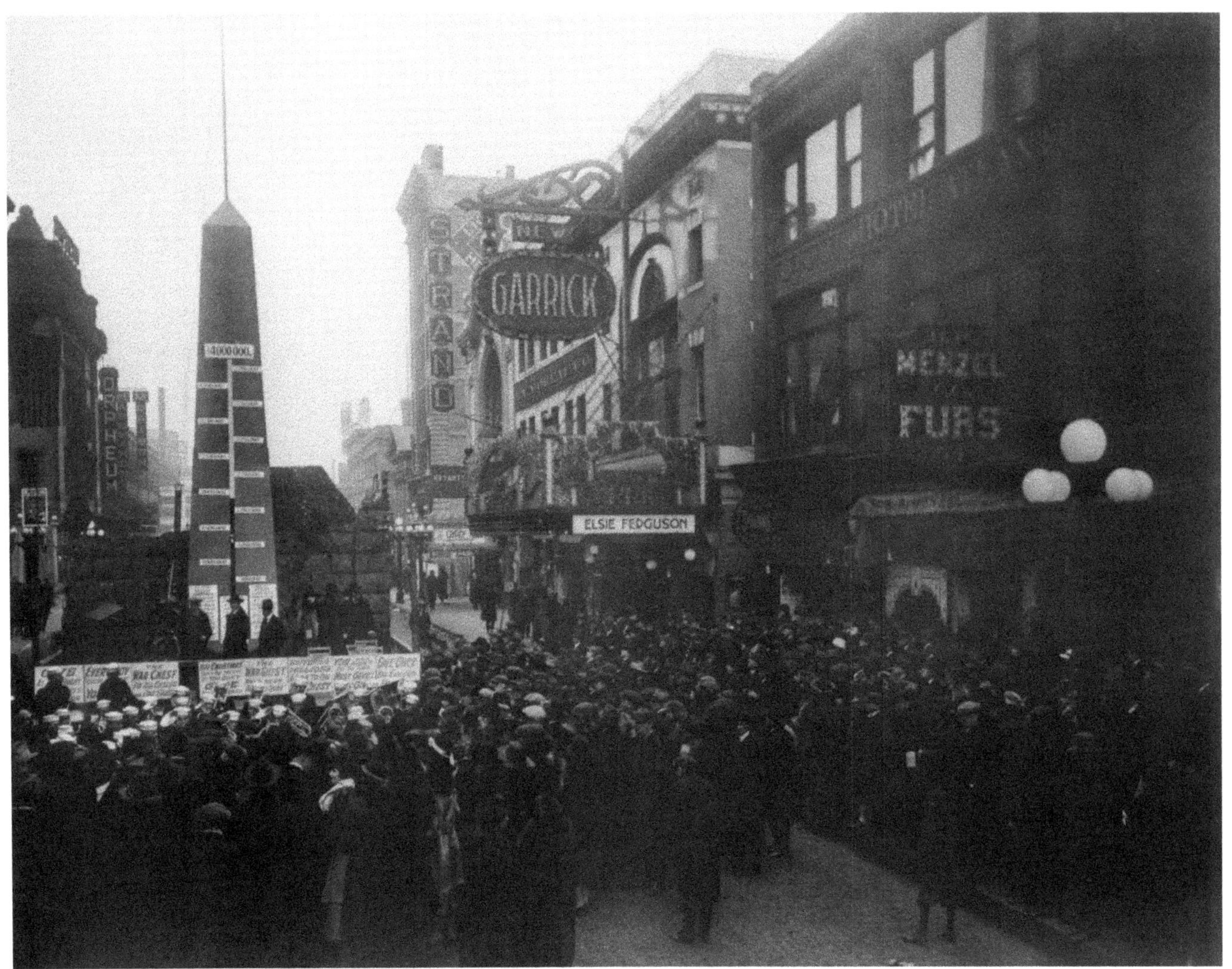

The Gibbs Hotel, a nondescript four-story building, sat at the corner of Twelfth Street and Hennepin Avenue. The hotel caught fire in February 1917 and is seen here in the aftermath of the blaze. Twelve people died before the flames could be extinguished.

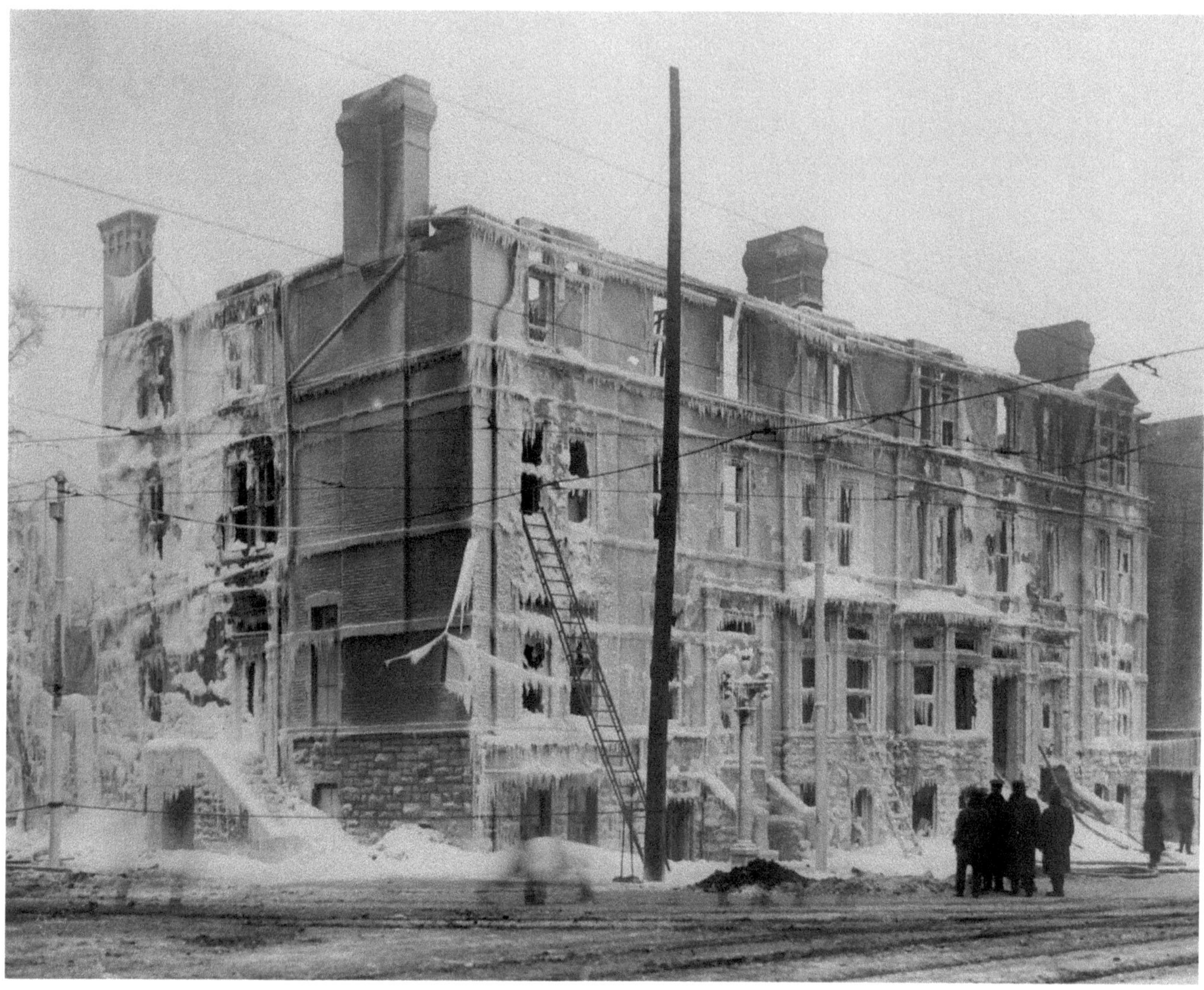

Early movie star Annette Kellerman is pictured here in 1920, probably at the premiere of her new motion picture *What Women Love,* which opened at Minneapolis's Garrick Theater on August 29.

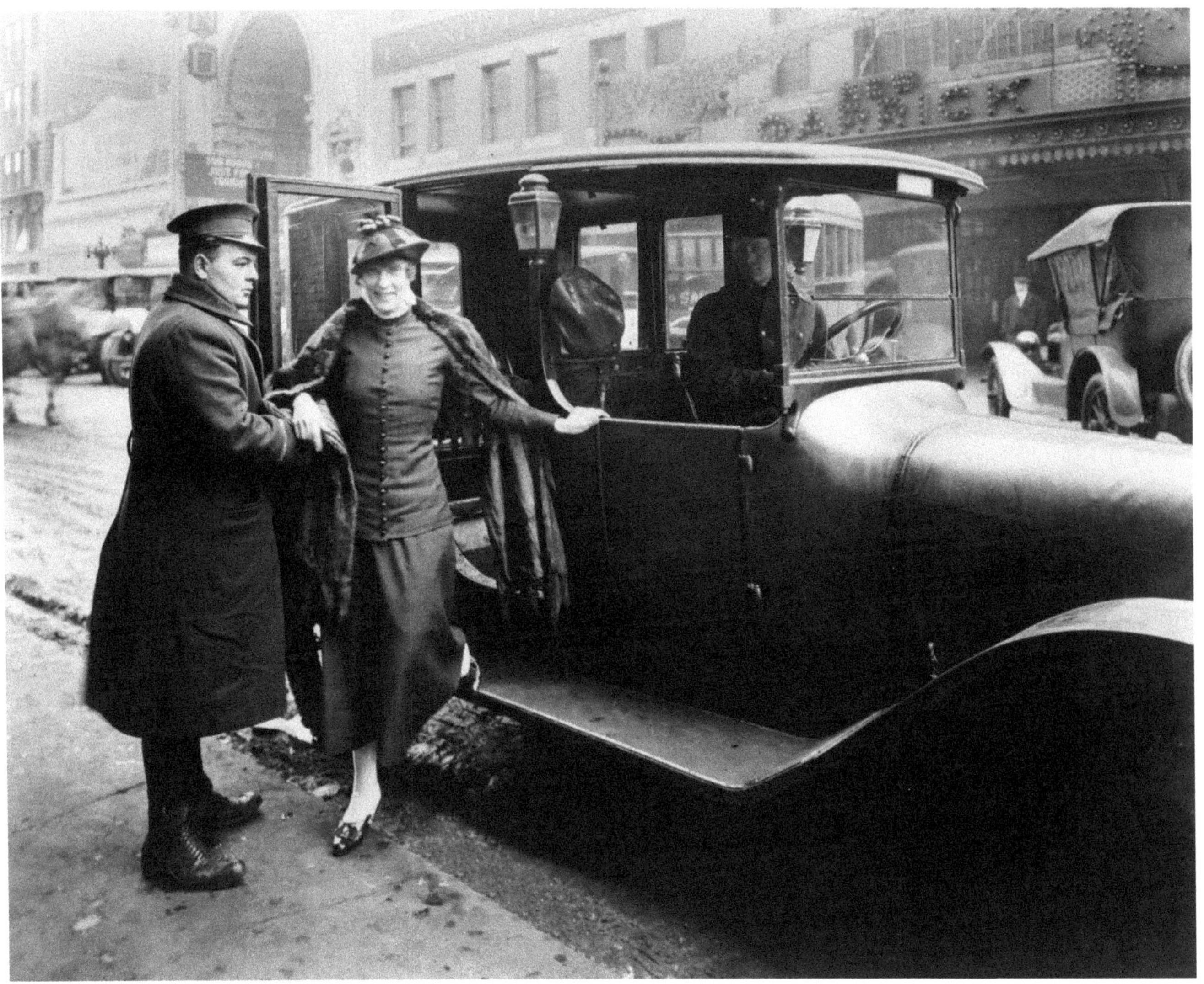

Downtown Minneapolis in 1918. This view north along Nicollet Avenue near Seventh Street reveals the dramatically increasing popularity of automobiles.

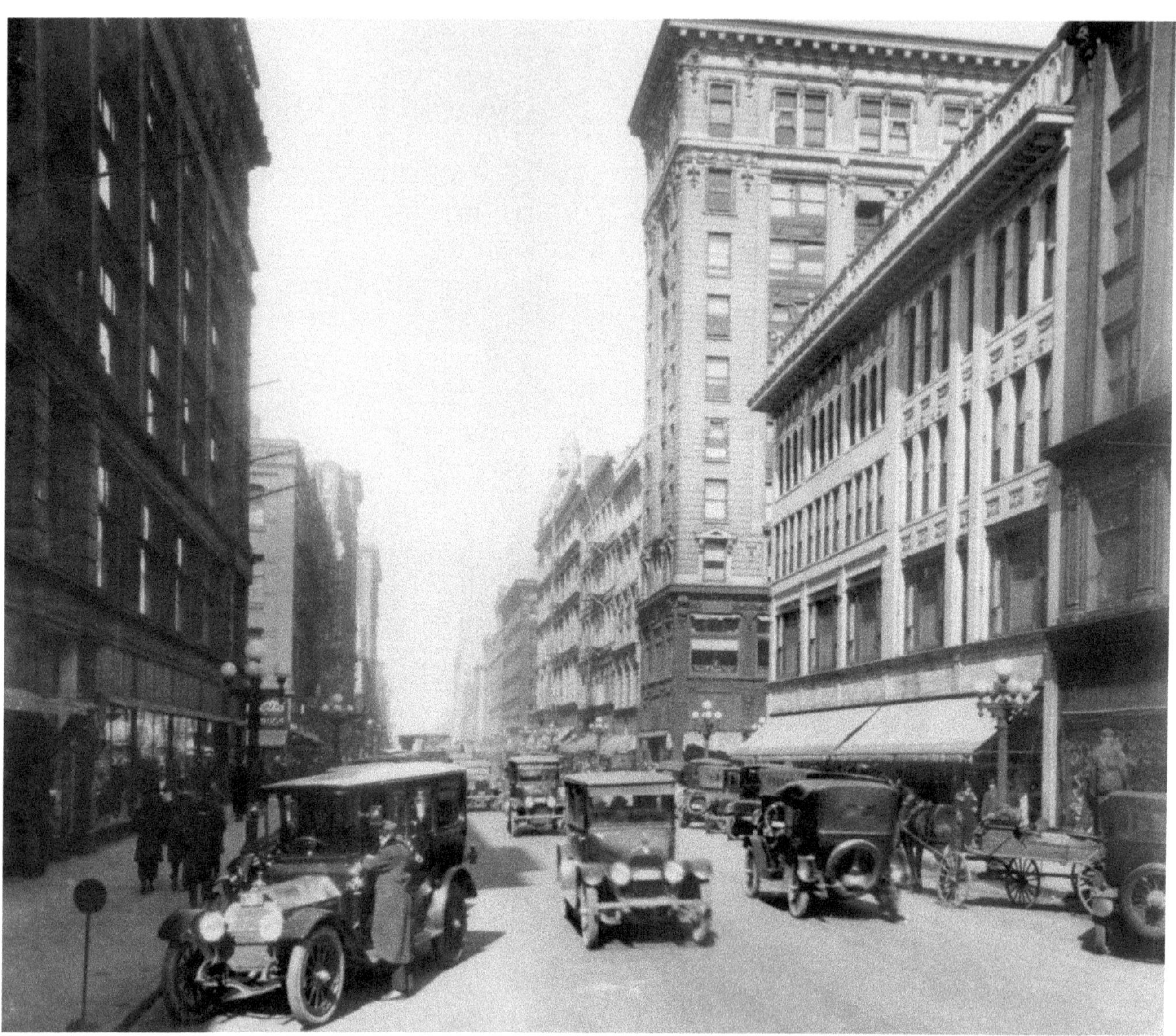

A hunter and member of the Minneapolis Gun Club brings down a duck at Lake of the Isles in south Minneapolis around 1910.

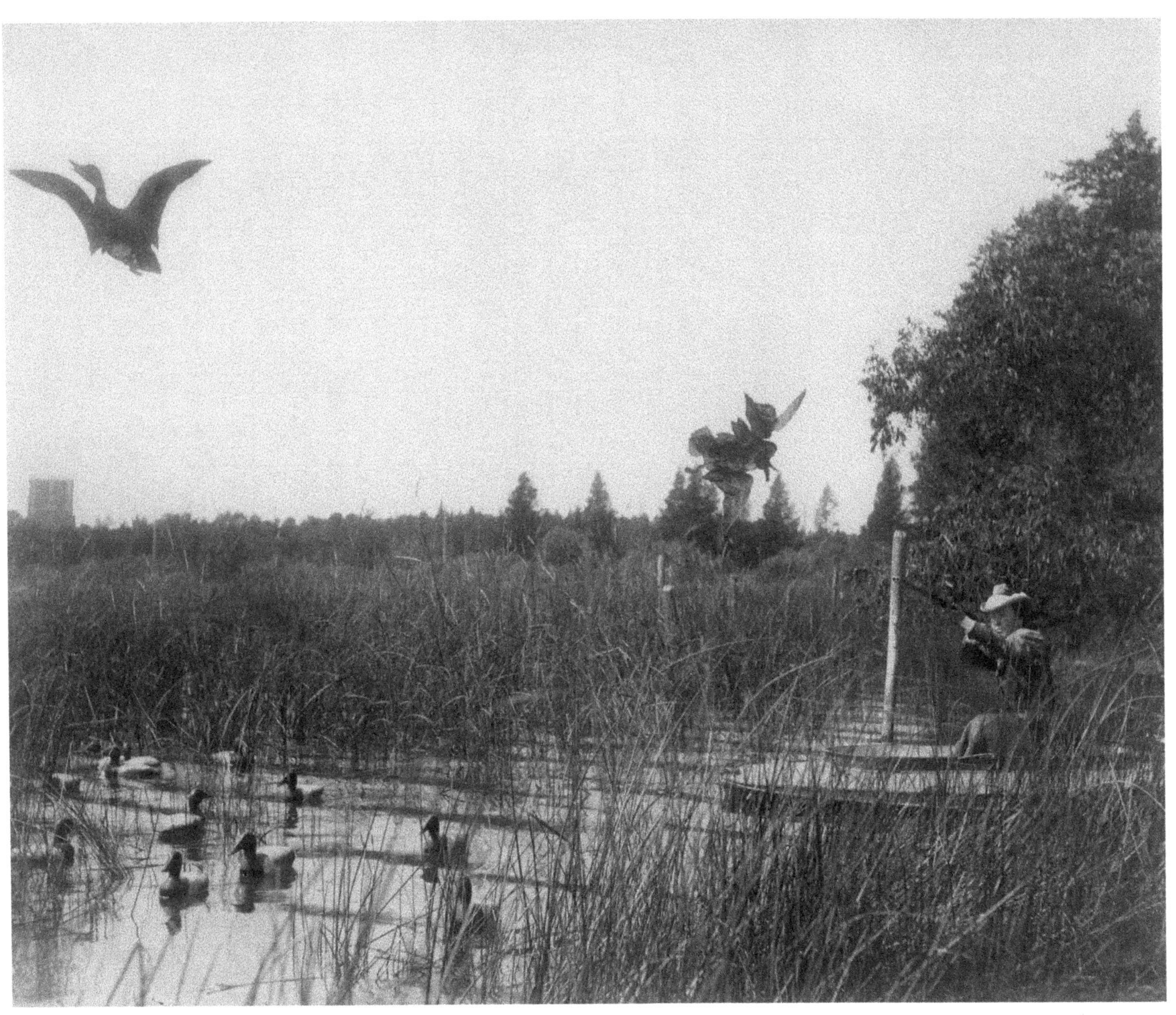

Students of the Society of Fine Arts School practice drawing classical figures around the turn of the century. The Fine Arts School met on the top floor of the Minneapolis Public Library between1889 and 1915, when the school moved to the newly opened Minneapolis Institute of Arts building.

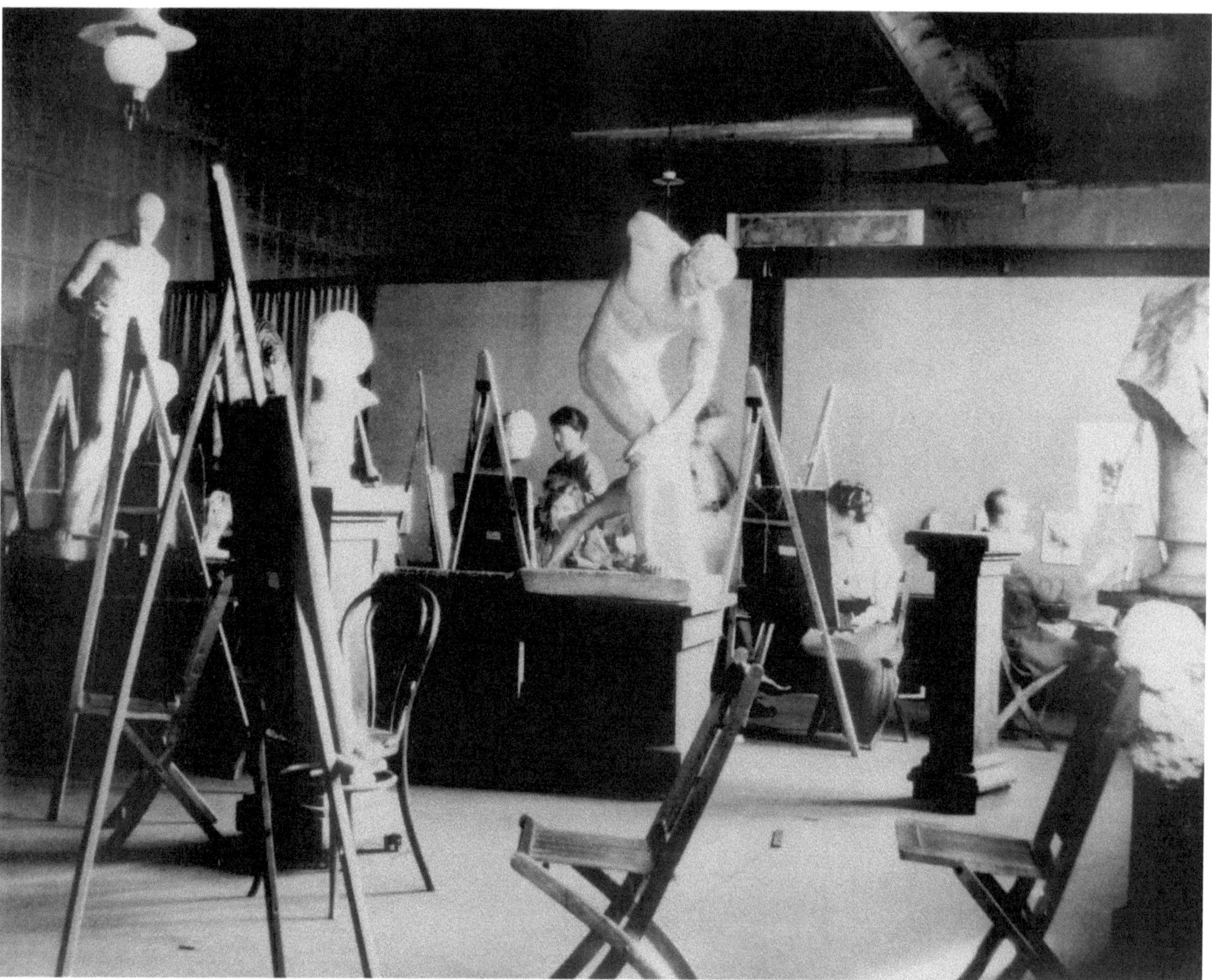

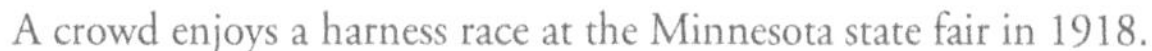

A crowd enjoys a harness race at the Minnesota state fair in 1918.

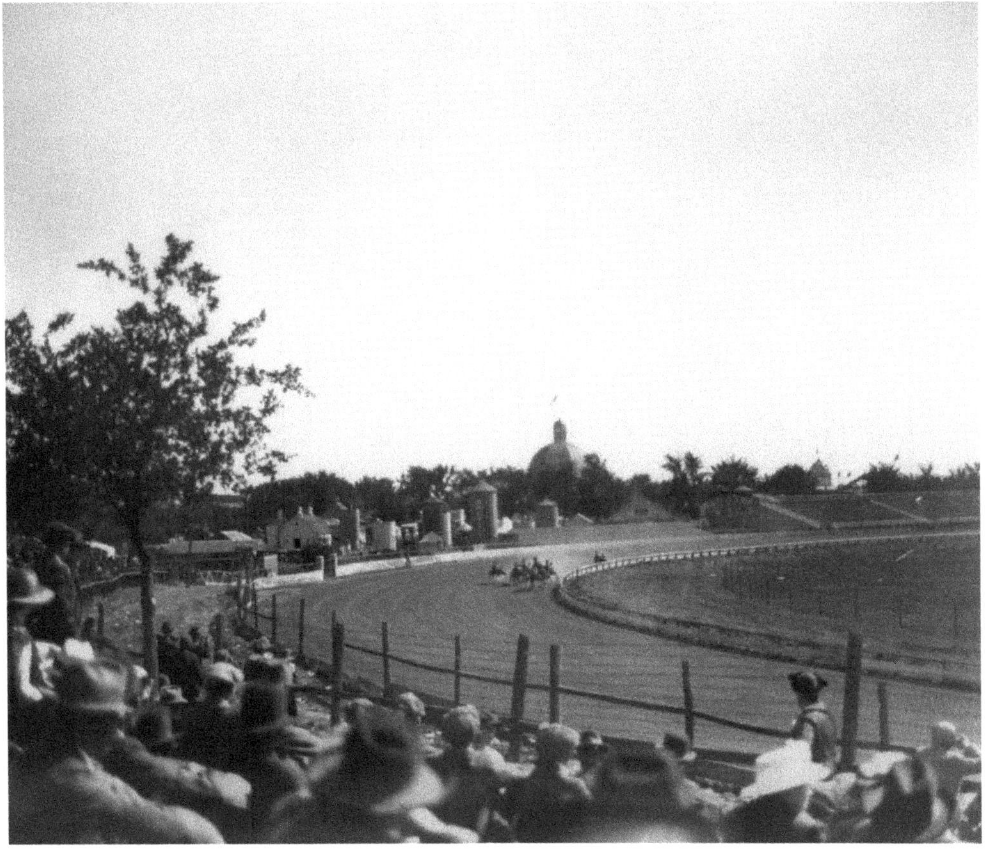

Former Governor John Lind (in the first row wearing a bow tie) and three-time presidential candidate William Jennings Bryan (to Lind's immediate left) stand outside Lind's residence at 1775 Colfax Avenue South during a 1908 meeting. Bryan and Lind shared populist political views, and the two men met and corresponded frequently.

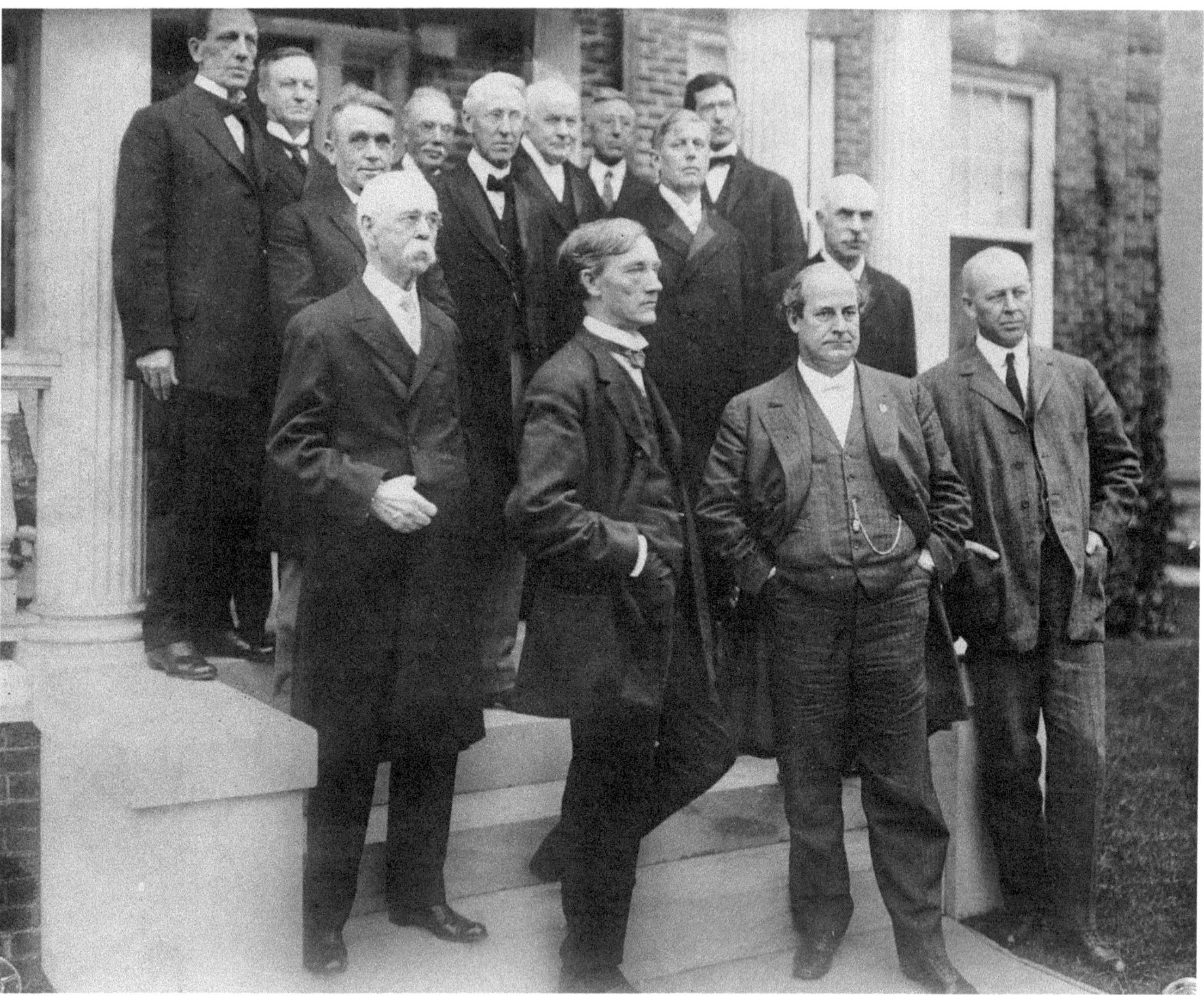

Members of the Red Cross Women's Auxiliary in the summer of 1917 pose with signs that read "Stand Behind the Fighting Man: Red Cross War Fund: I Have Given."

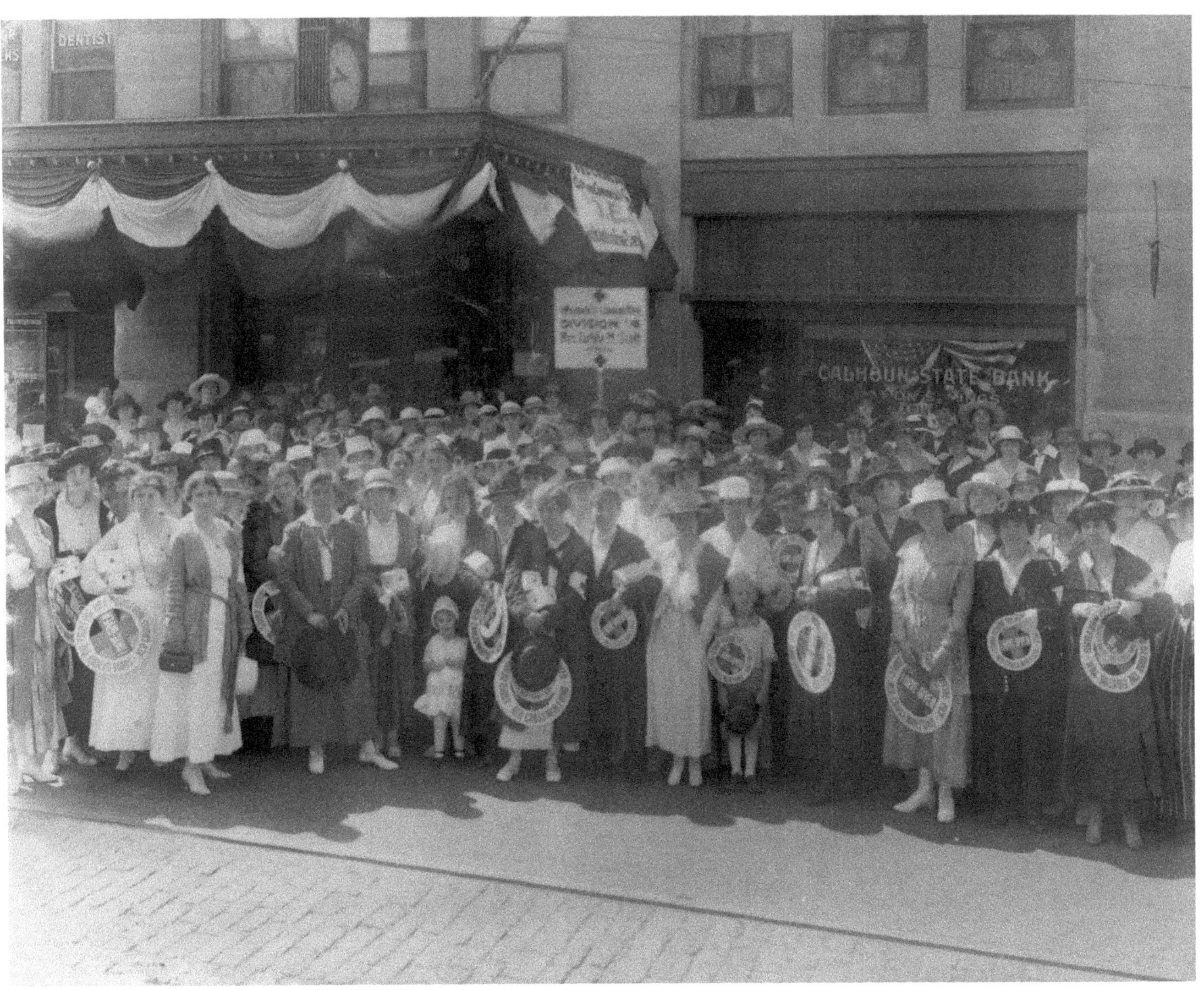

Children at the Clara Barton School in southwest Minneapolis knit on behalf of the 1918 war effort of the Red Cross.

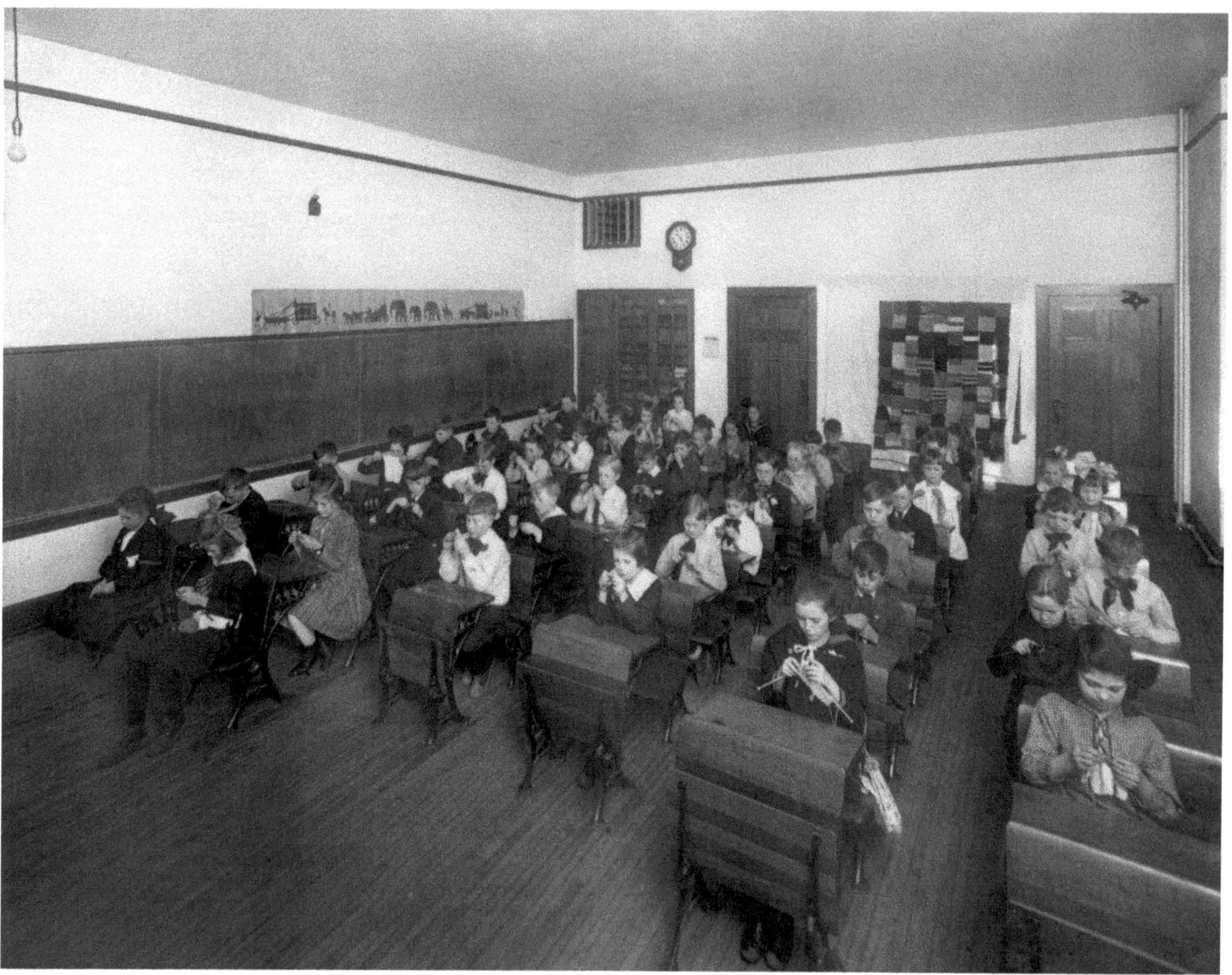

A City of Contrasts

(1921–1946)

Minneapolis entered a period of optimism in the first years after the Great War. The city continued to erect buildings at breakneck speed and the downtown skyline underwent dramatic change. Foshay Tower, a 447-foot skyscraper modeled after the Washington Monument, became an instant landmark following its completion in 1929. It reigned as the city's tallest building for the next forty-three years. That same year the sleek, twenty-six-story Rand Tower appeared just three blocks away. With the erection of these formidable structures Minneapolis proclaimed itself a metropolis.

The Minneapolis Public School District added thirty new schools between 1916 and 1930. The number of churches also skyrocketed. In 1910 two hundred and twenty-five houses of worship maintained a presence within city limits; by 1935 the number had reached 350. The colossal Minnesota Theater, the fifth-largest theater in the nation, opened its doors in 1928. Other local organizations, such as Abbott Hospital and the Minneapolis Women's Club, also improved and expanded their buildings during this time.

As always, some citizens languished even as others prospered. The city's Gateway District with its centerpiece park, designed to be downtown's crown jewel, attracted destitute men even before the Great Depression, and their numbers only swelled in the wake of the stock market crash. One contemporary observer who visited the area noted that "along Washington Avenue and lower Hennepin and neighboring streets the unmistakable evidences of deterioration are to be seen—the rescue mission, the smelly 'hash house,' the dingy beer parlor, the pawn shop, the second-hand store . . . and the employment agency."* Inspired by the social gospel movement, Minneapolis's churches had established settlement houses and rescue missions around the city in the early years of the twentieth century, and many expanded their services as the depression wore on. These benevolent organizations focused on bettering the lives of the city's neediest residents: the sick, the jobless, recent immigrants, and ethnic minorities.

The depression lifted as the Second World War commenced, and Minneapolis factories operated around the clock to supply the troops with everything from generators to snowplows. Minneapolitans, like their counterparts in every American city, personally committed themselves to securing victory for the Allied forces. To that end they bought war bonds and put in long hours on assembly lines.

*Calvin F. Schmid, *Social Saga of Two Cities: An Ecological and Statistical Study of Social Trends in Minneapolis and St. Paul* (Minneapolis: Minneapolis Council of Social Agencies, 1937), p. 51.

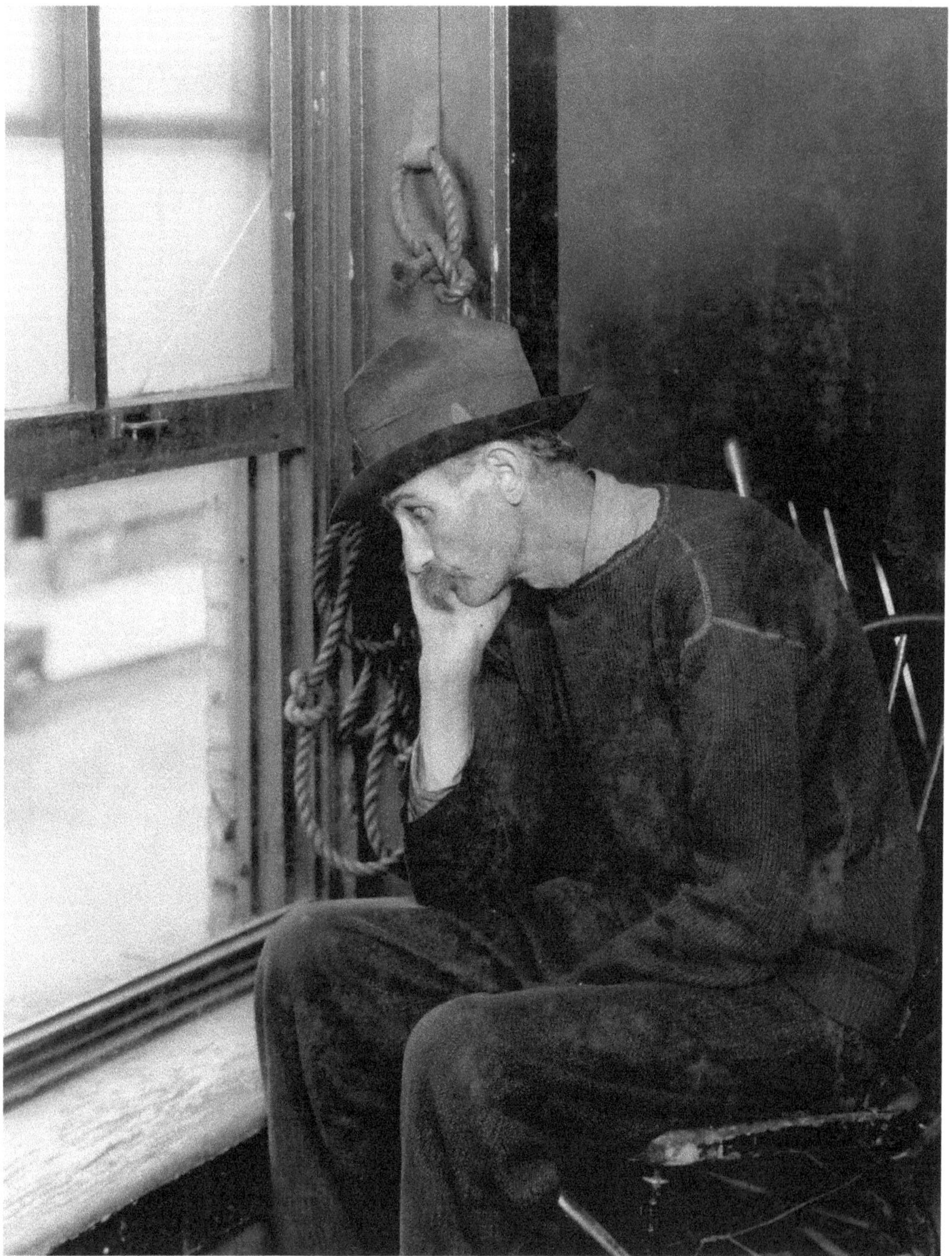

The nondenominational Union City Mission, located in the Gateway District, provided food, lodging, and religious instruction to the throngs of homeless men who occupied Minneapolis's "skid row." This image was captured in 1925.

The Phyllis Wheatley House opened in 1924 to provide accommodations for visitors who could not find lodging in the city's white-only hotels. It soon began operating as a multi-racial community center, as illustrated by this 1925 Christmas photograph.

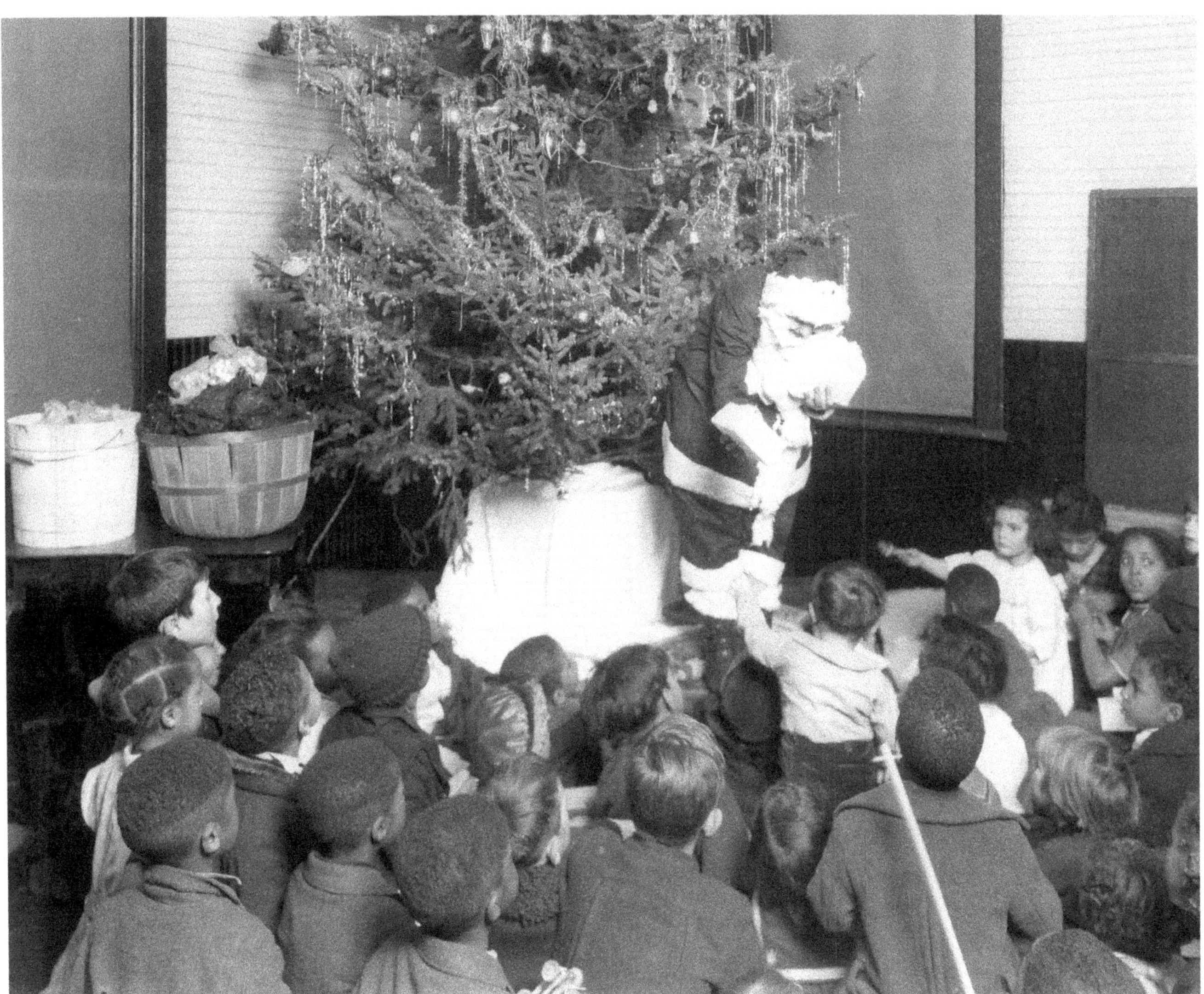

By the early twentieth century, the Twin Cities led the nation in grain storage capacity. Concrete grain elevators, such as the Midway Elevator at 917 Thirteenth Avenue Southeast, became popular around 1910. The Midway Elevator is pictured here in 1925.

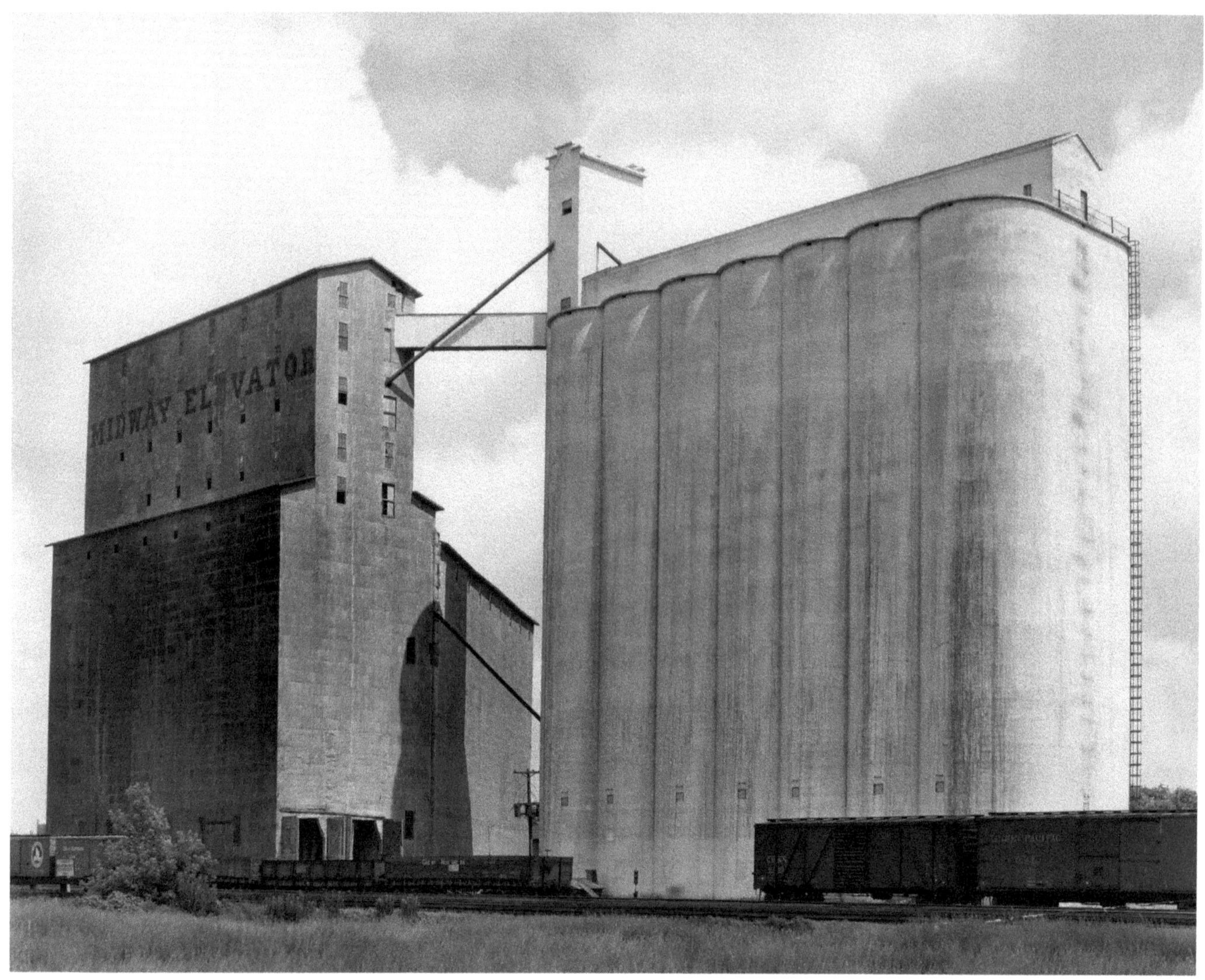

Marshall High School students and their teacher delve into a lesson in 1925. The school, located at 1313 Southeast Fifth Street, opened its doors just one year earlier.

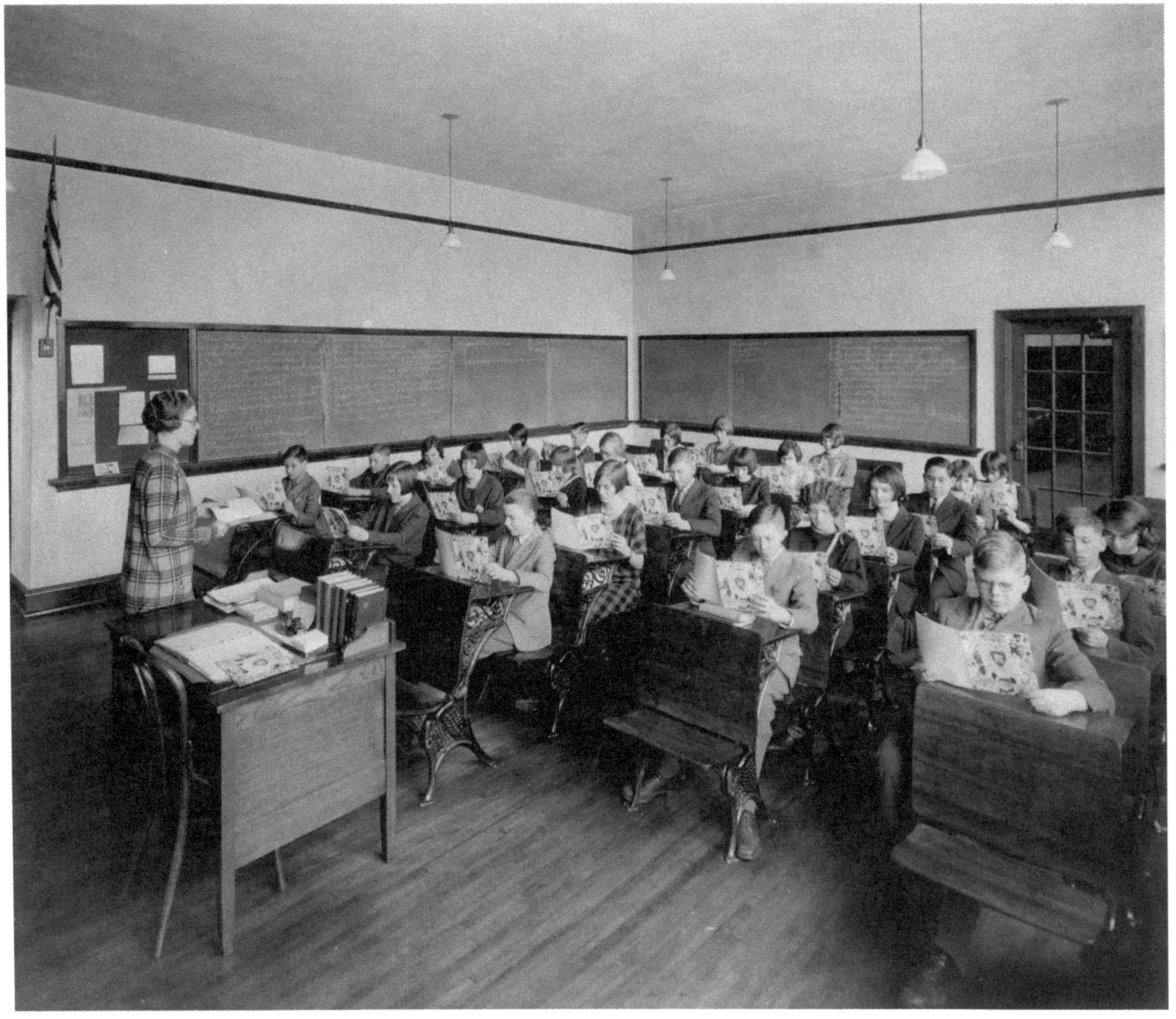

The Pillsbury Settlement House began in 1879 as a mission project sponsored by the Plymouth Church. The organization quickly established kindergarten classes and a daycare program to serve the underprivileged, as this 1925 photograph illustrates.

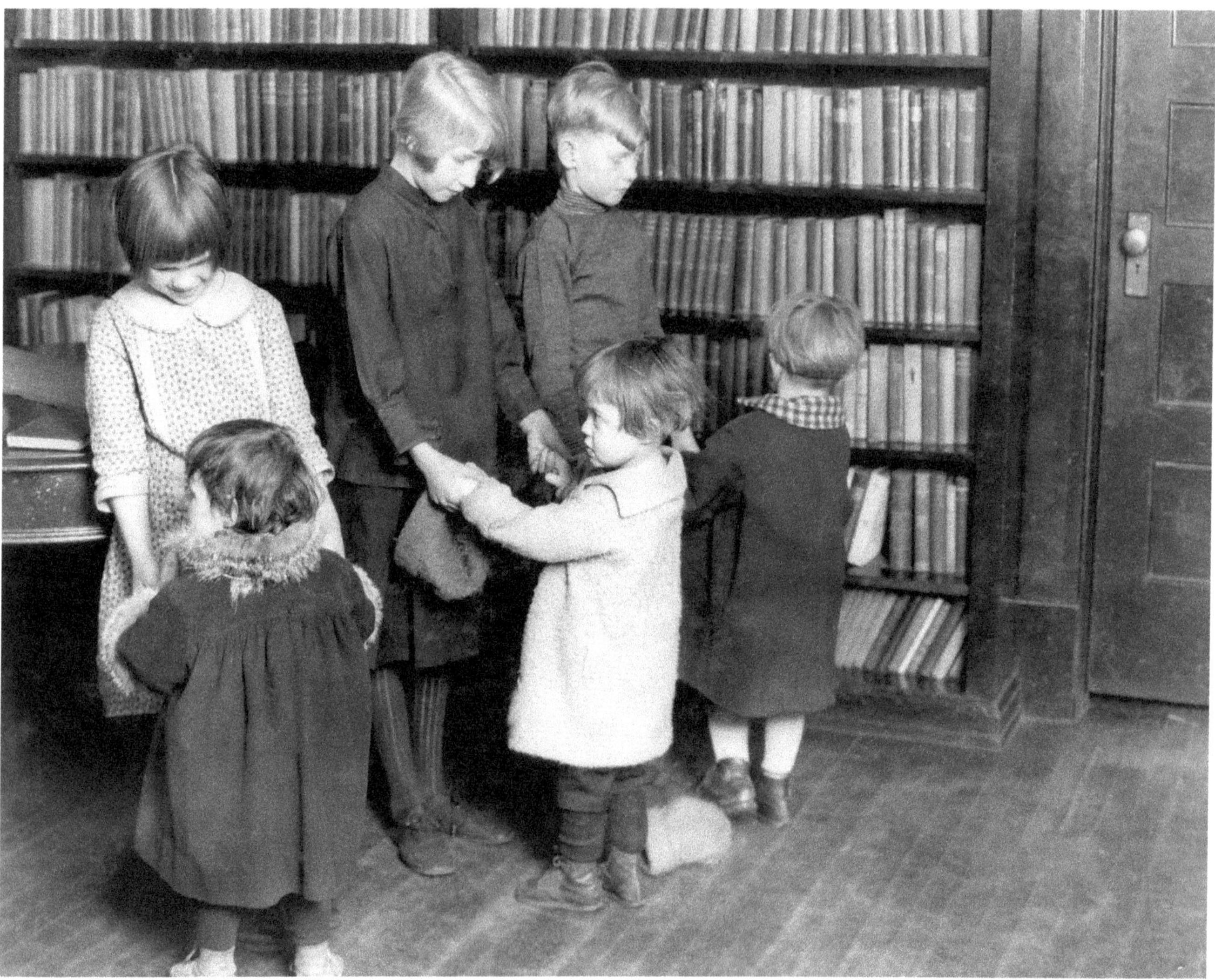

The Pillsbury Settlement House also strove to provide children, many of whom were recent immigrants, with opportunities to learn new skills and to build "resourcefulness, responsibility, and a sense of values." In this 1926 photograph a staff member leads a baking demonstration for an attentive group of young girls.

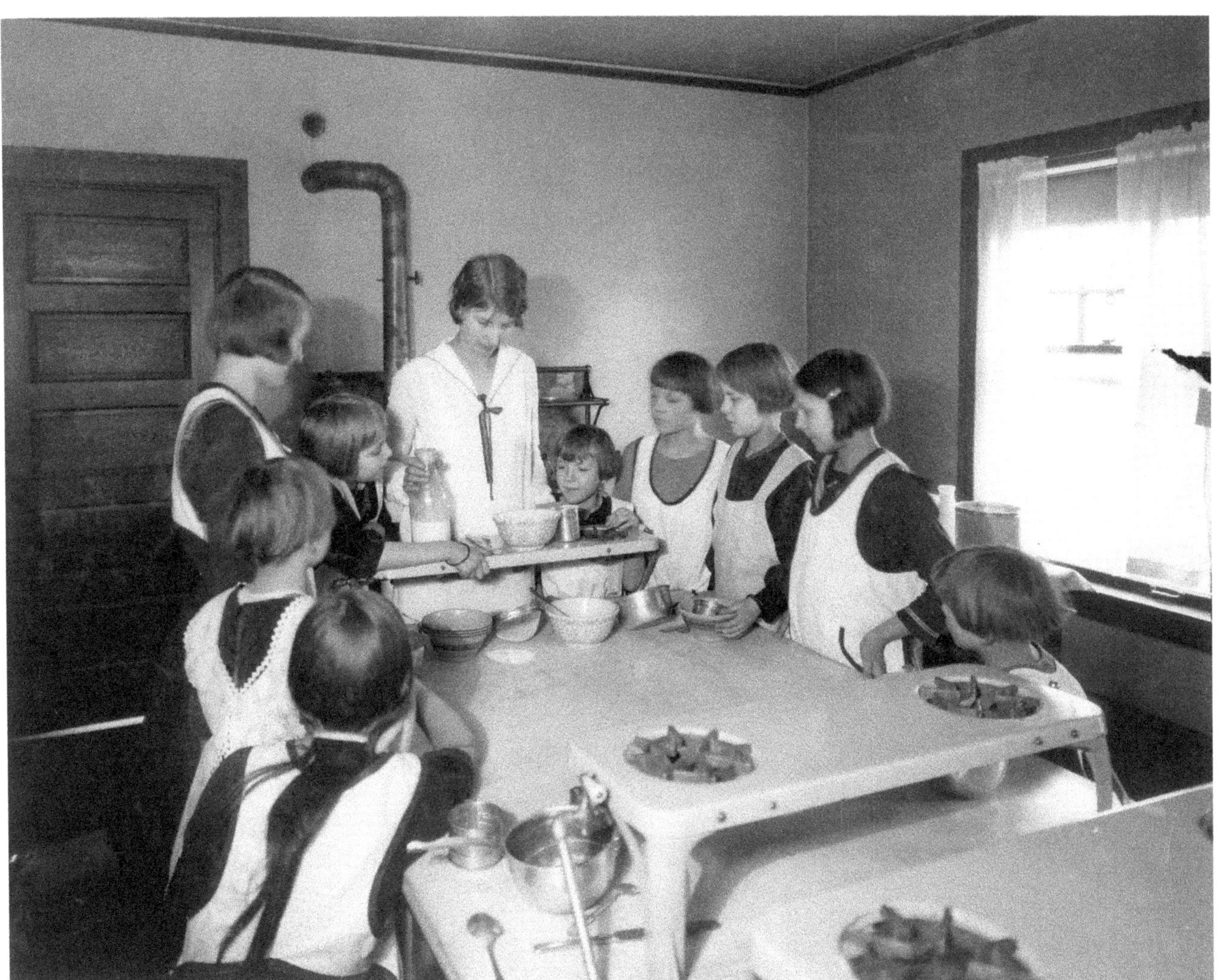

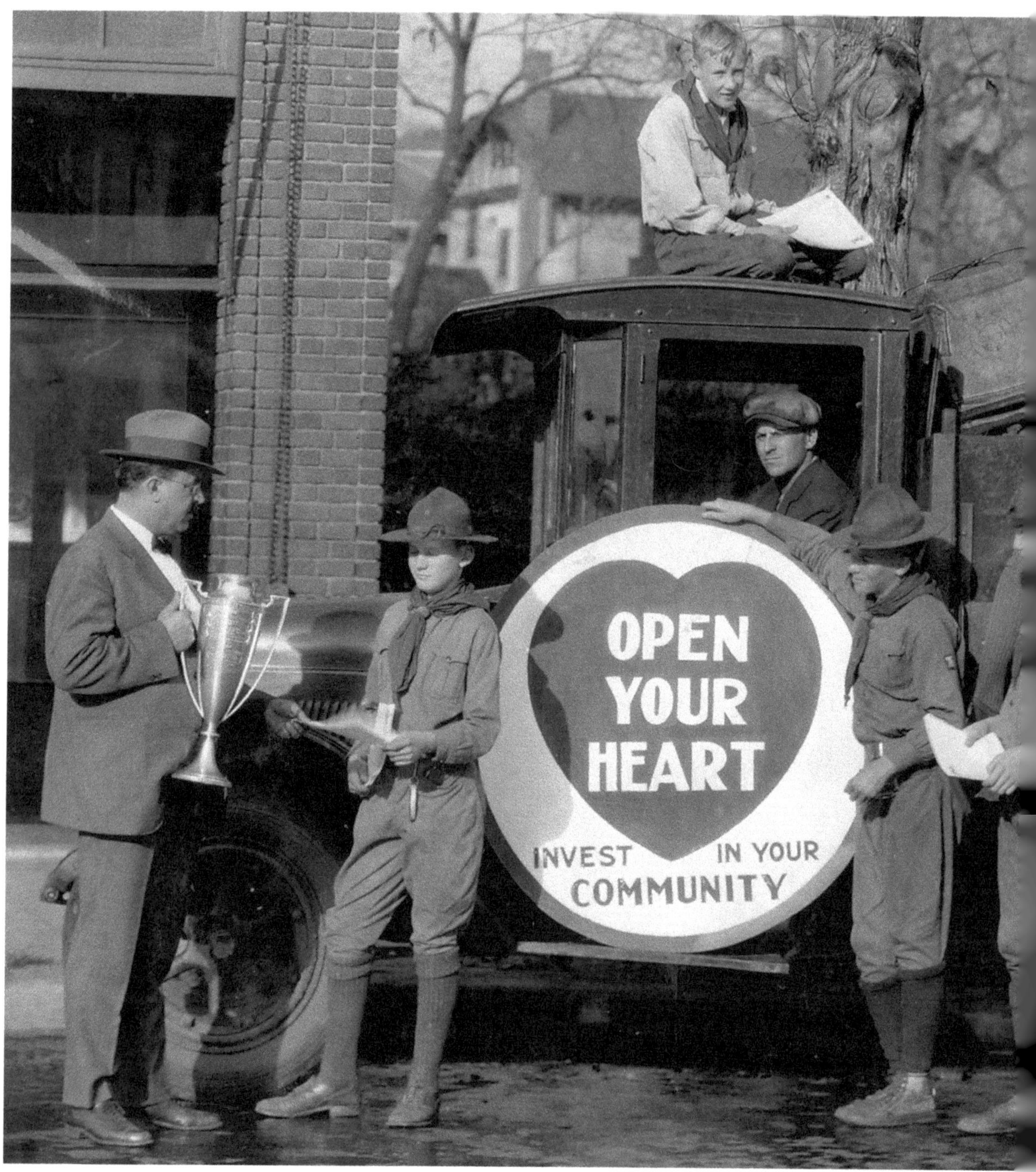
OPEN
YOUR
HEART
INVEST IN YOUR
COMMUNITY

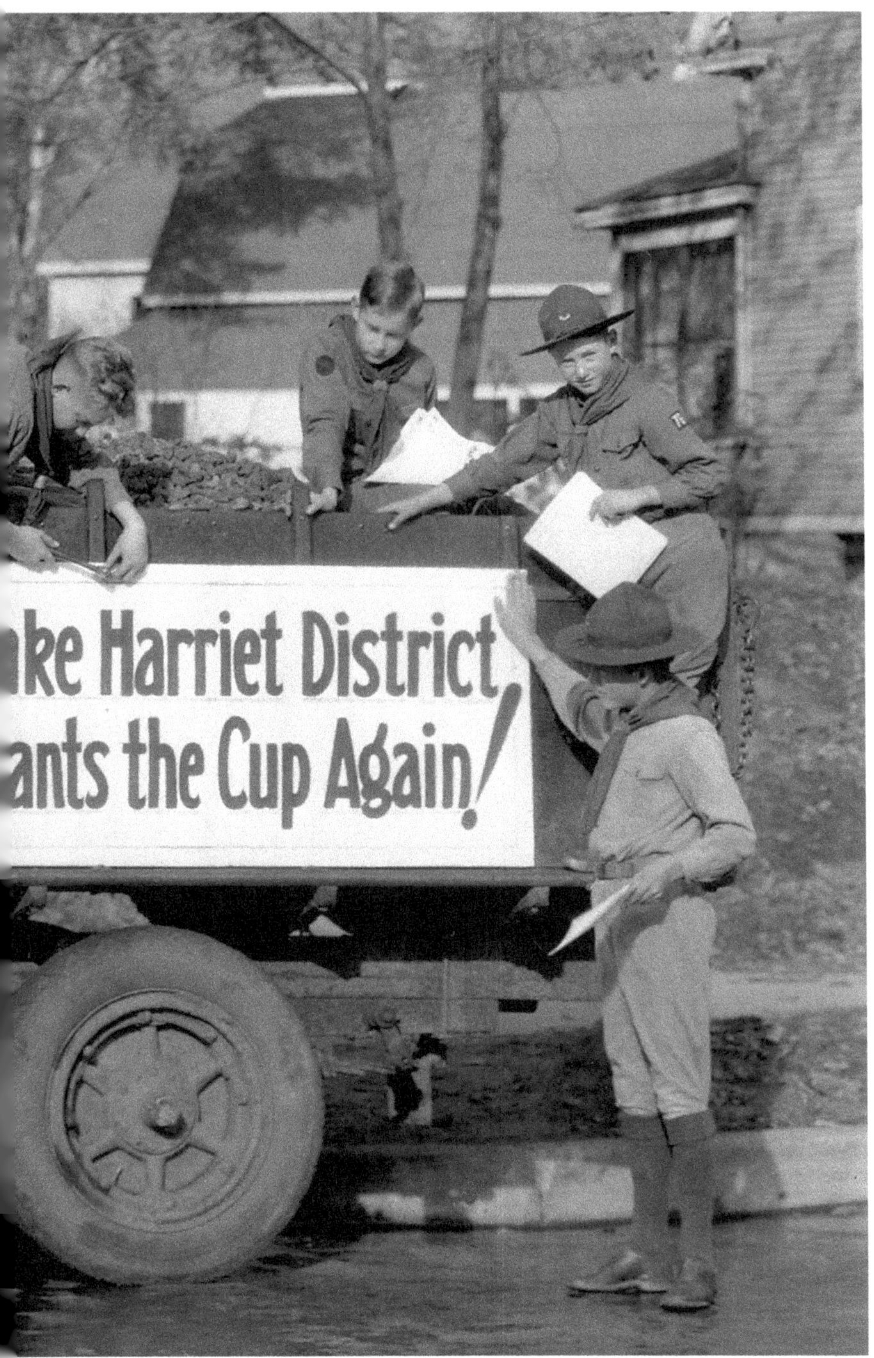

By 1927, when this photograph was taken, the Boy Scouts claimed more than 785,000 members nationwide. This south Minneapolis troop proudly receives a community fund drive trophy.

Foshay Tower is pictured here during its construction in 1928. Utilities trader Wilbur Foshay lost ownership of the building to creditors in the 1929 stock market crash, just months after the tower's opening.

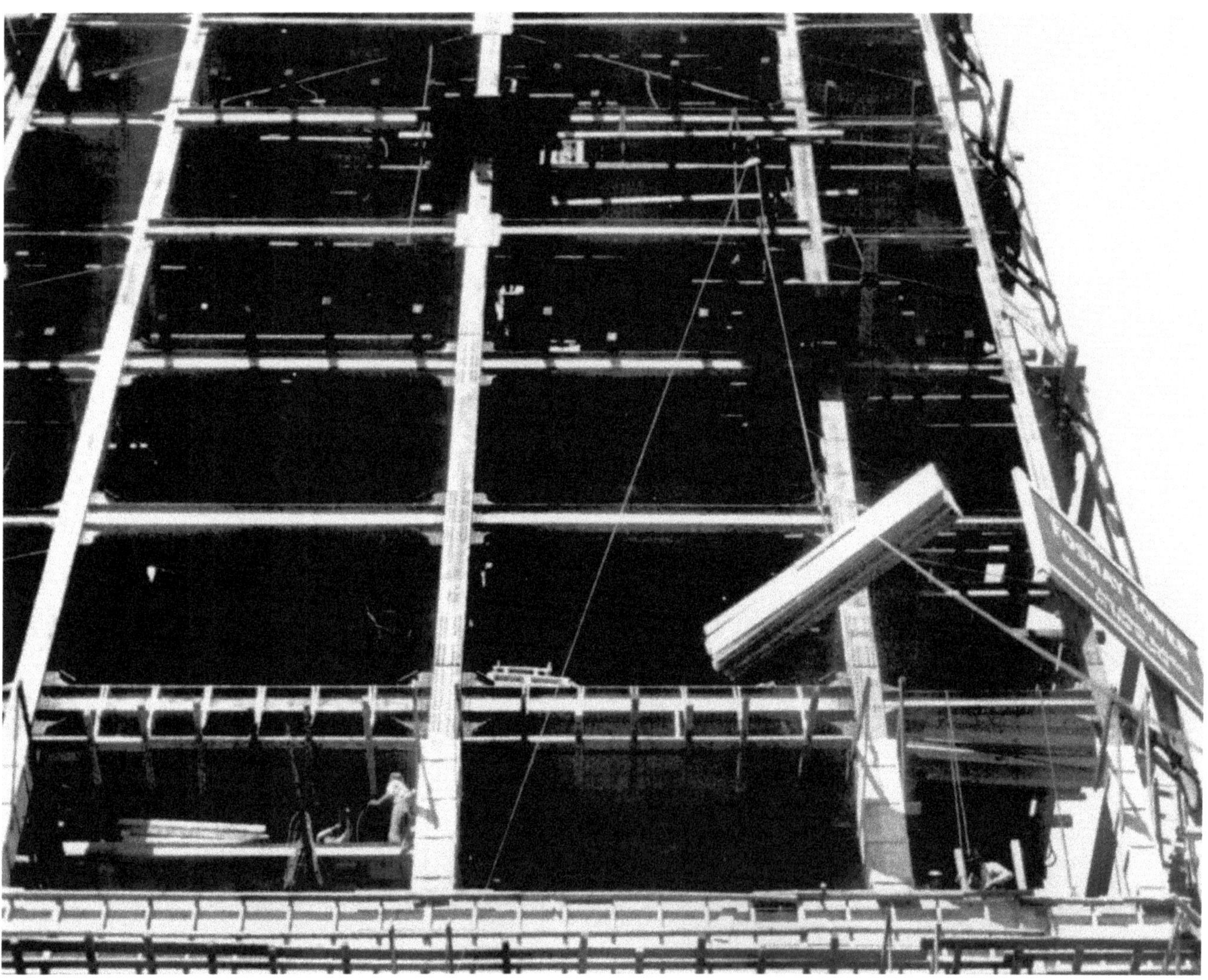

When it opened in 1928, the Minnesota Theatre held the distinction of being the largest theater in the region. Situated at the corner of Ninth Street and LaSalle Avenue, the theater struggled financially and ultimately closed in 1938.

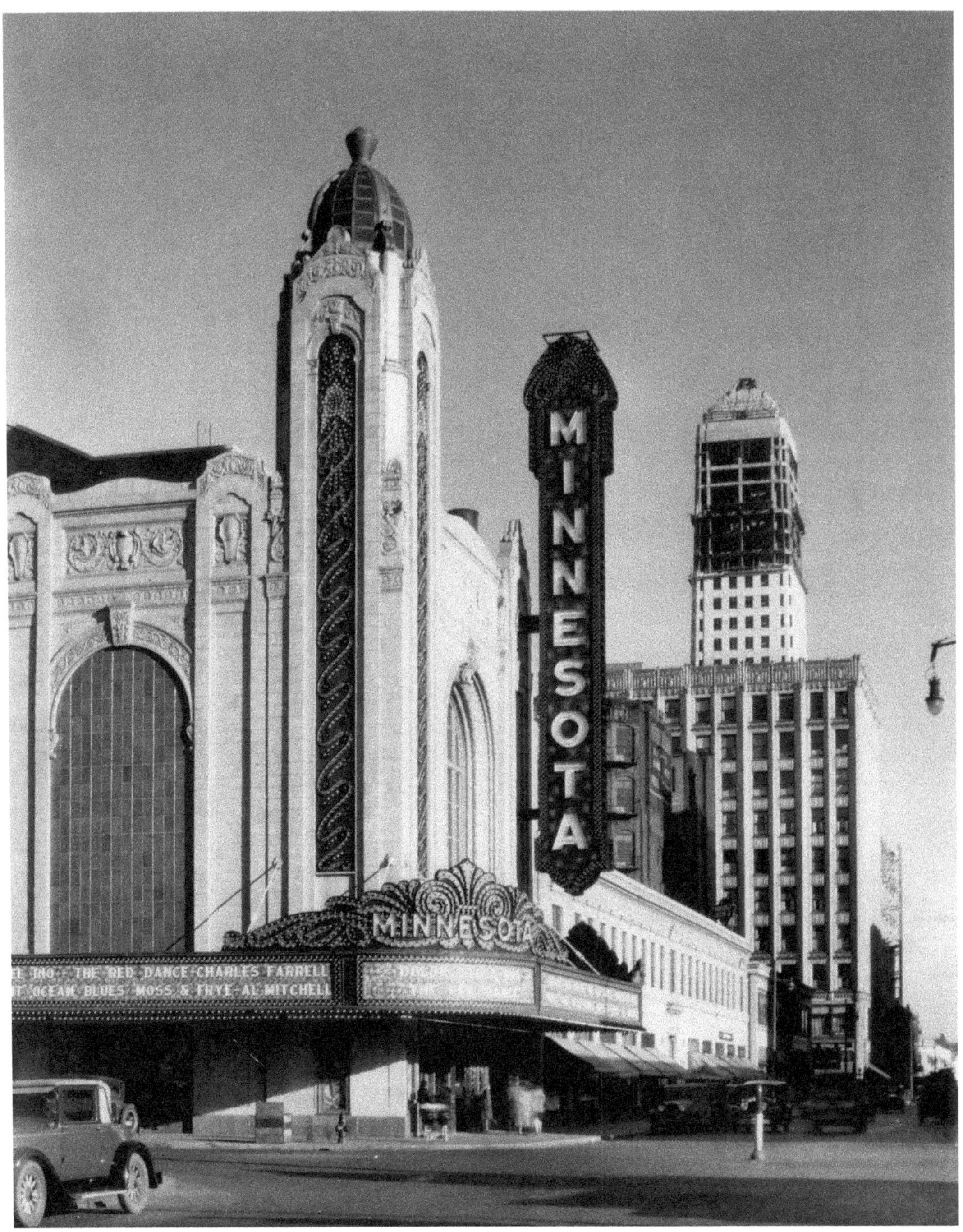

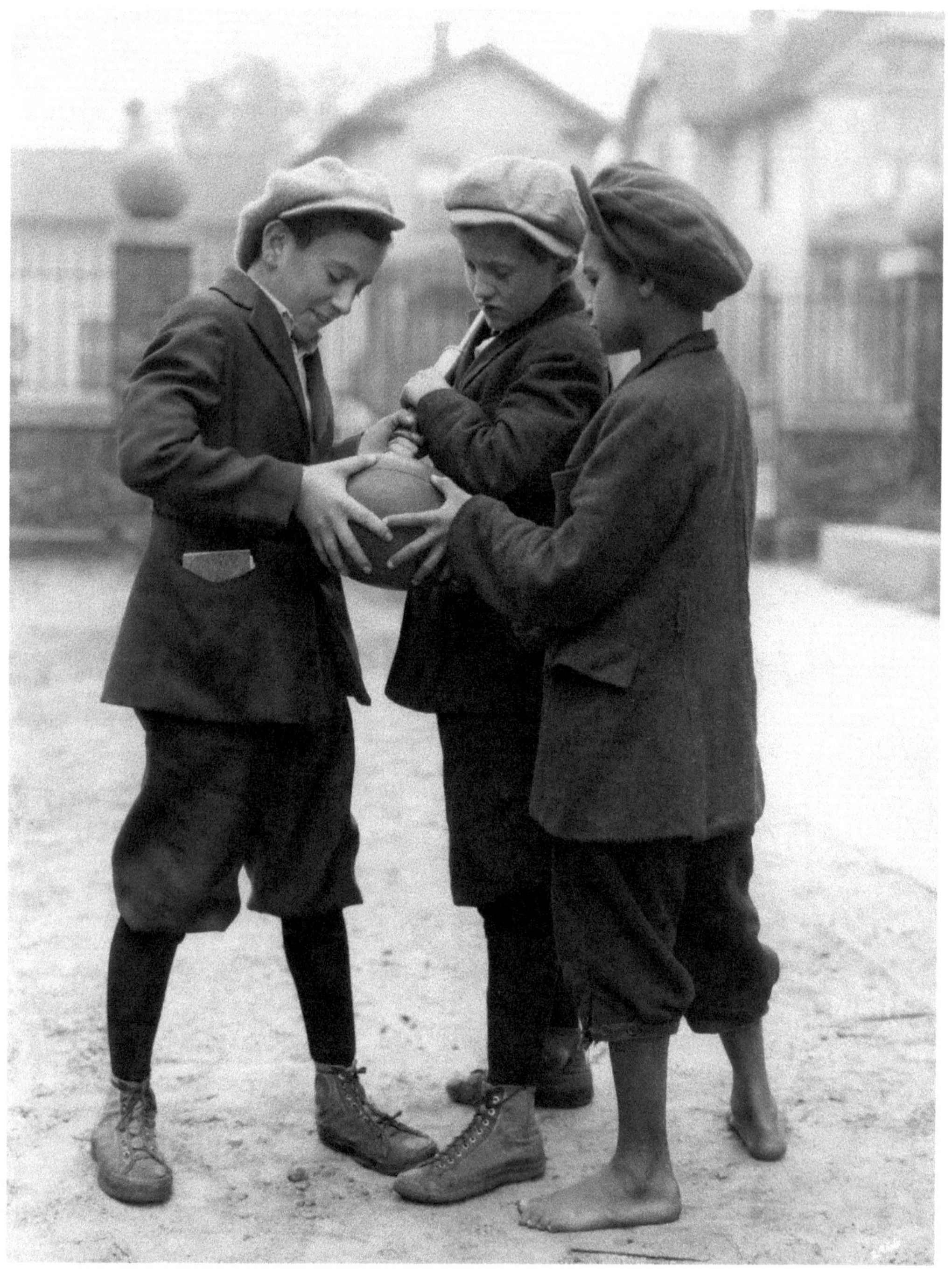

Three boys attempt to inflate a football around 1925. Football fever seized Minneapolis in the 1920s, and residents routinely packed the stands at the University of Minnesota's new Memorial Stadium, which opened in 1924.

The Minneapolis skyline is depicted here in 1929. Foshay Tower looms large on the right. St. Mary's Basilica, the first basilica in the United States, is visible in the foreground. The Municipal Building's clock tower appears at center.

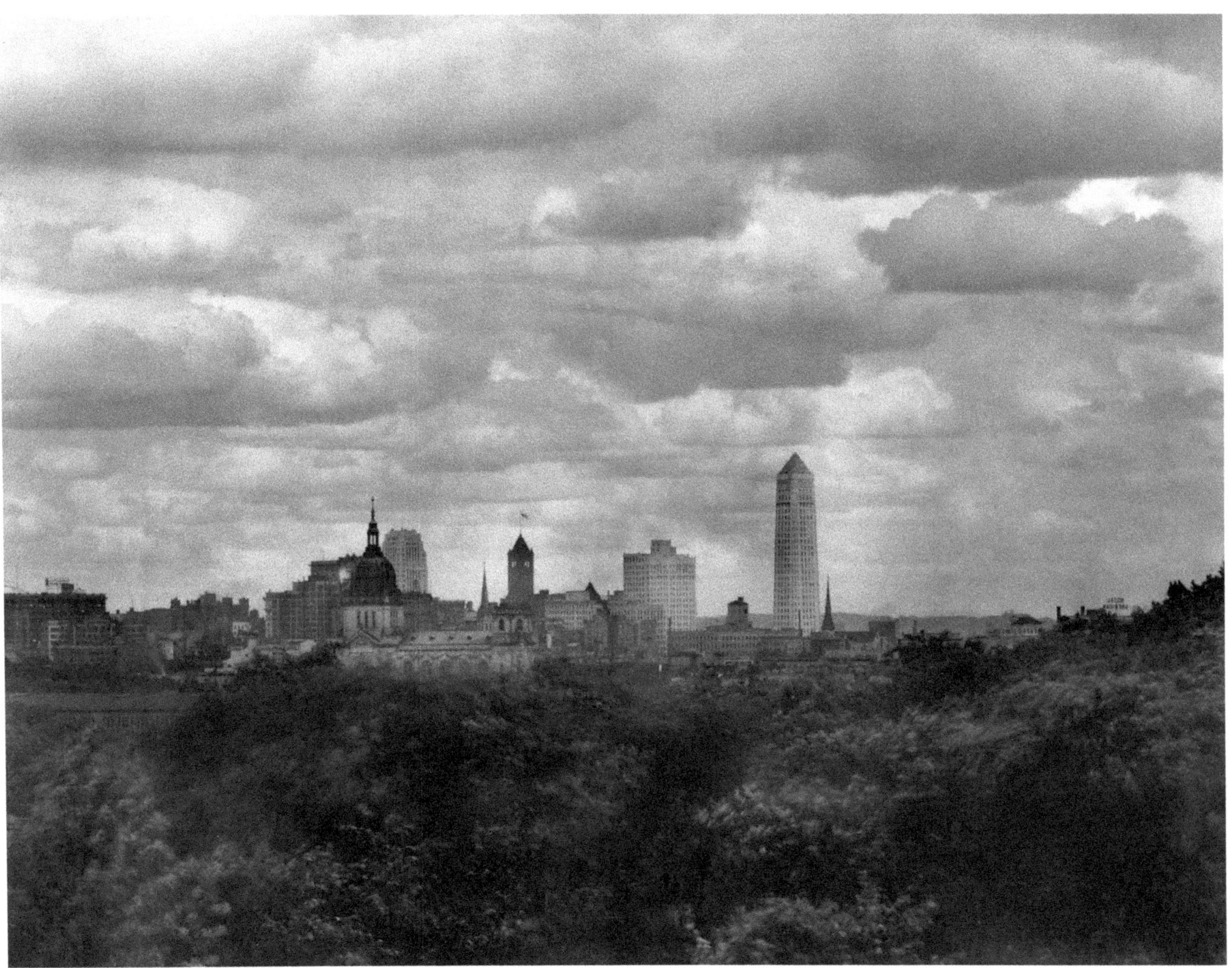

A brash entrepreneur named Elizabeth Quinlan, who was for many years the only woman clothing buyer in the nation, moved her company to this building at Ninth Street and Nicollet Avenue in 1926. Her success selling ready-to-wear clothing soon silenced her critics.

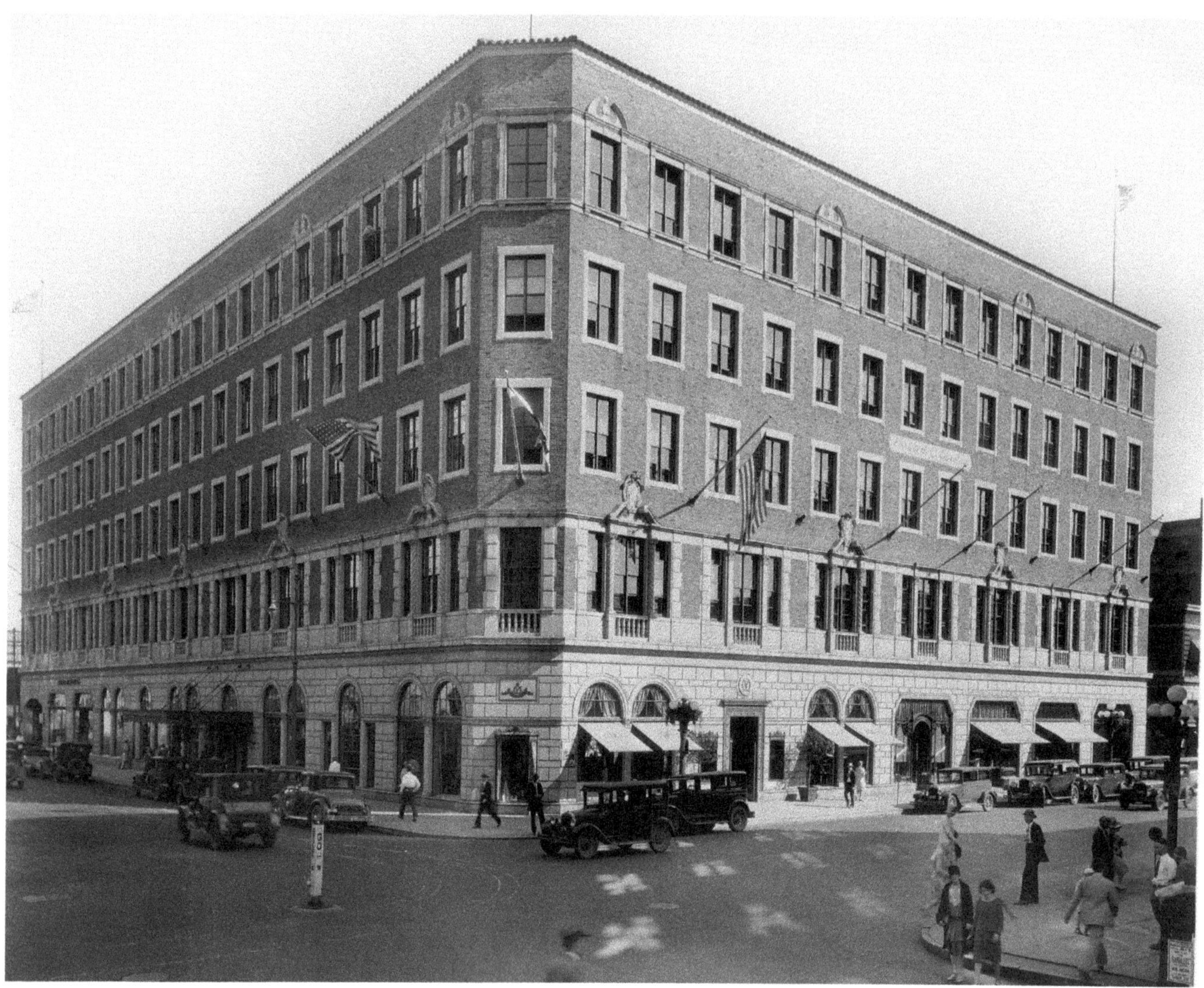

Strikes occurred frequently in all industries throughout the early years of the twentieth century as workers protested low wages and substandard working conditions. Here two women picket in front of D. B. Rosenblatt, an overcoat manufacturer, in 1929.

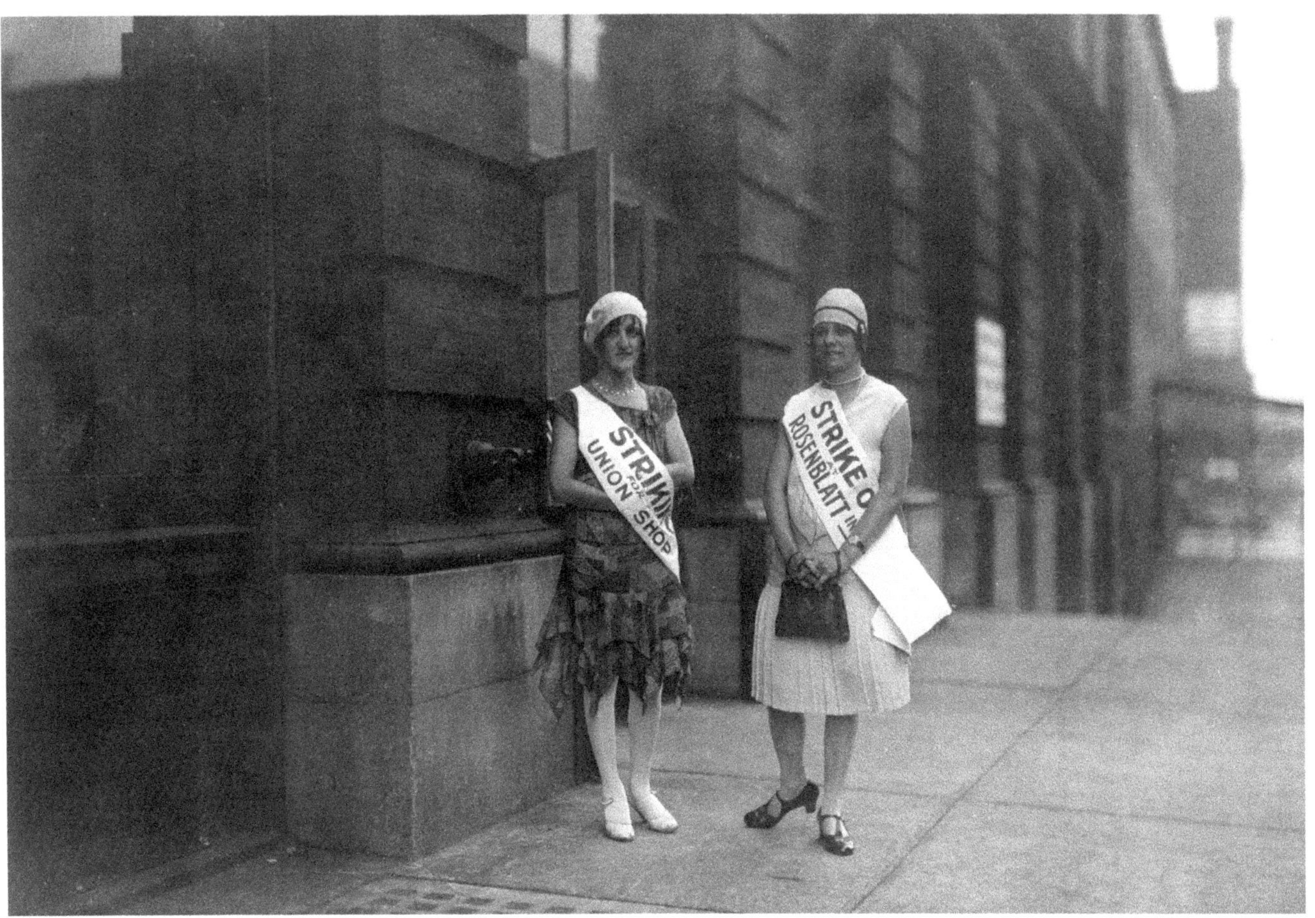

As automobiles became the dominant form of transportation, gasoline stations seemed to sprout on every corner. In 1929, the year this Shell station was photographed, the City Directory listed almost two hundred gas stations in Minneapolis.

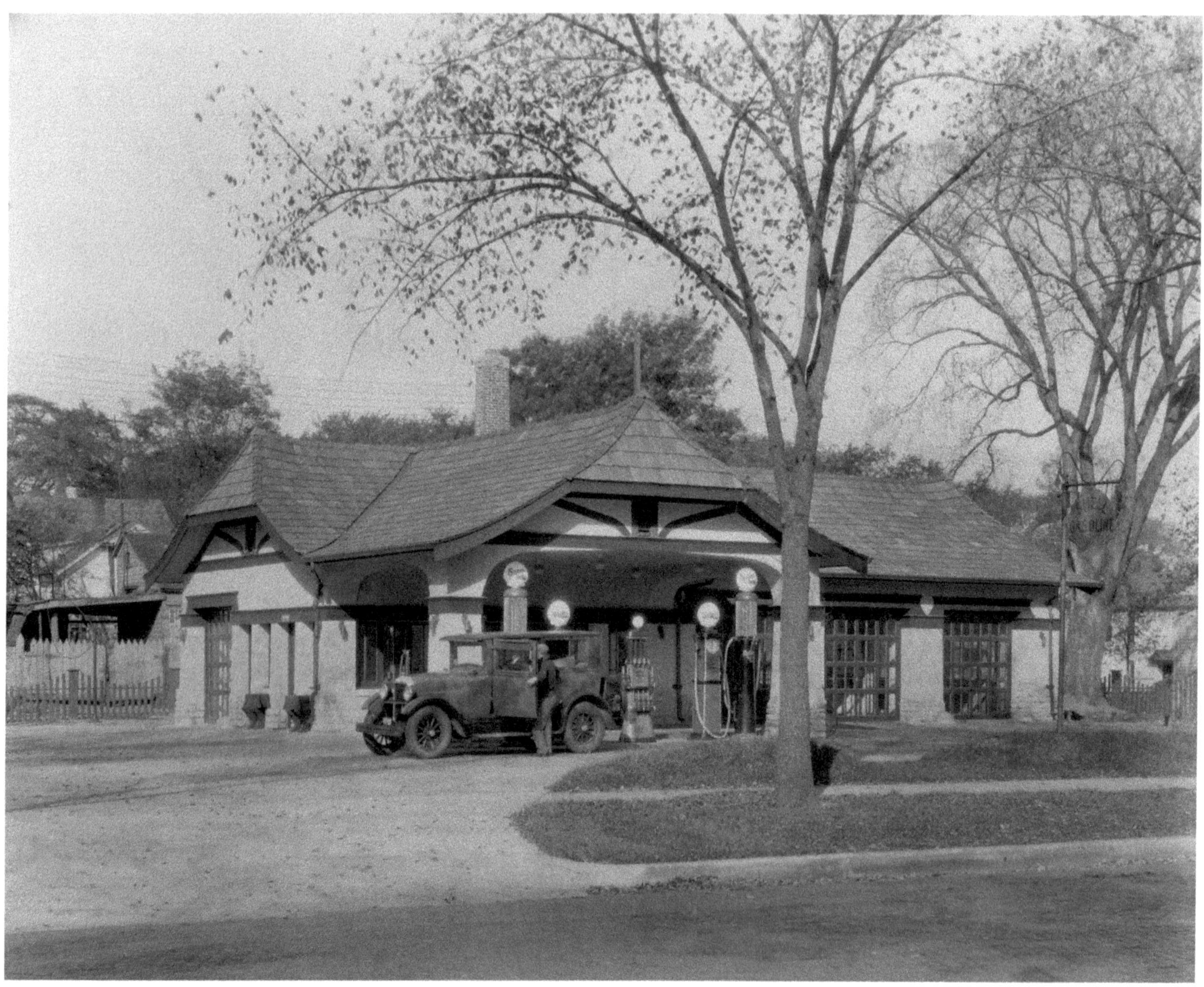

The Shubert Theatre, seen here in 1929, first opened in 1910. It struggled financially and by 1934 the theater, renamed the Alvin, survived by hosting burlesque shows. In 1999 the 2,900-ton building was moved a quarter mile down Hennepin Avenue and is currently undergoing renovation.

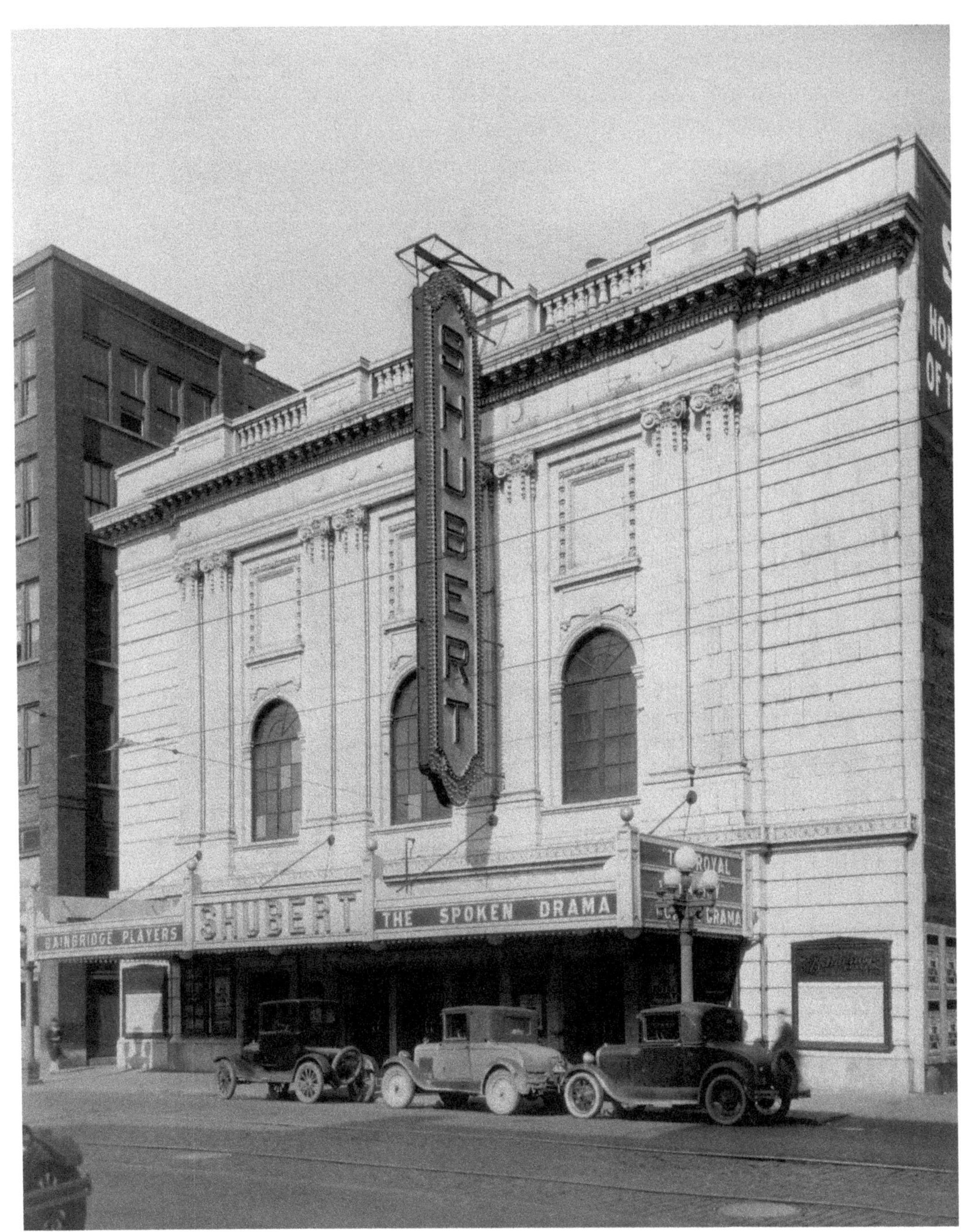

At the time of its dedication in 1928, Central Lutheran Church was believed to be the largest Lutheran cathedral-style structure in North America. The building, located in downtown Minneapolis, boasts a seating capacity of 3,000. The church's choir is seen here in 1929.

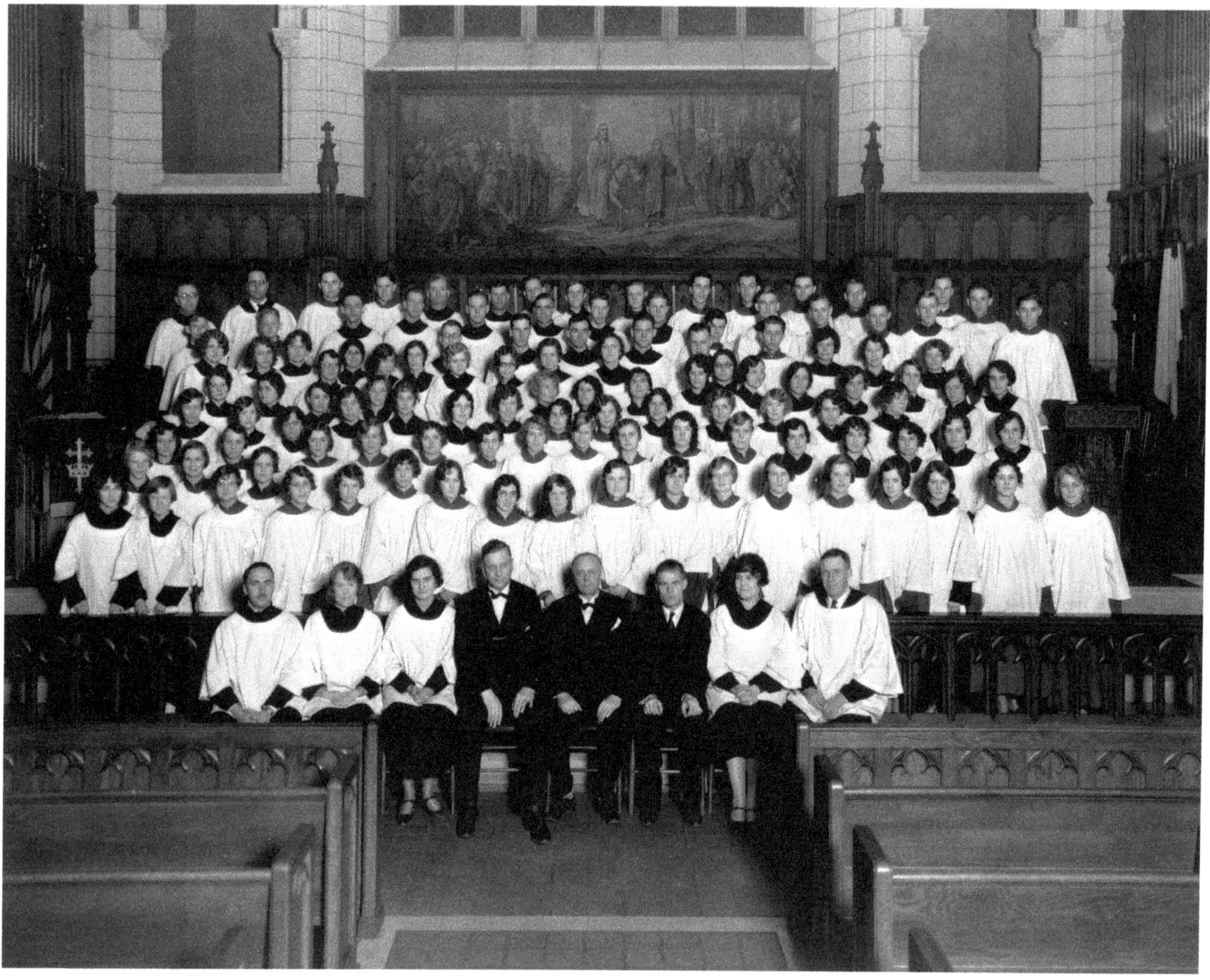

Twenty-five of the city's most prominent women joined together to found the Minneapolis Woman's Club in 1907. In 1928 the growing organization moved to this elegant clubhouse at 410 Oak Grove. The building's amenities included a theater, a ballroom, and a library.

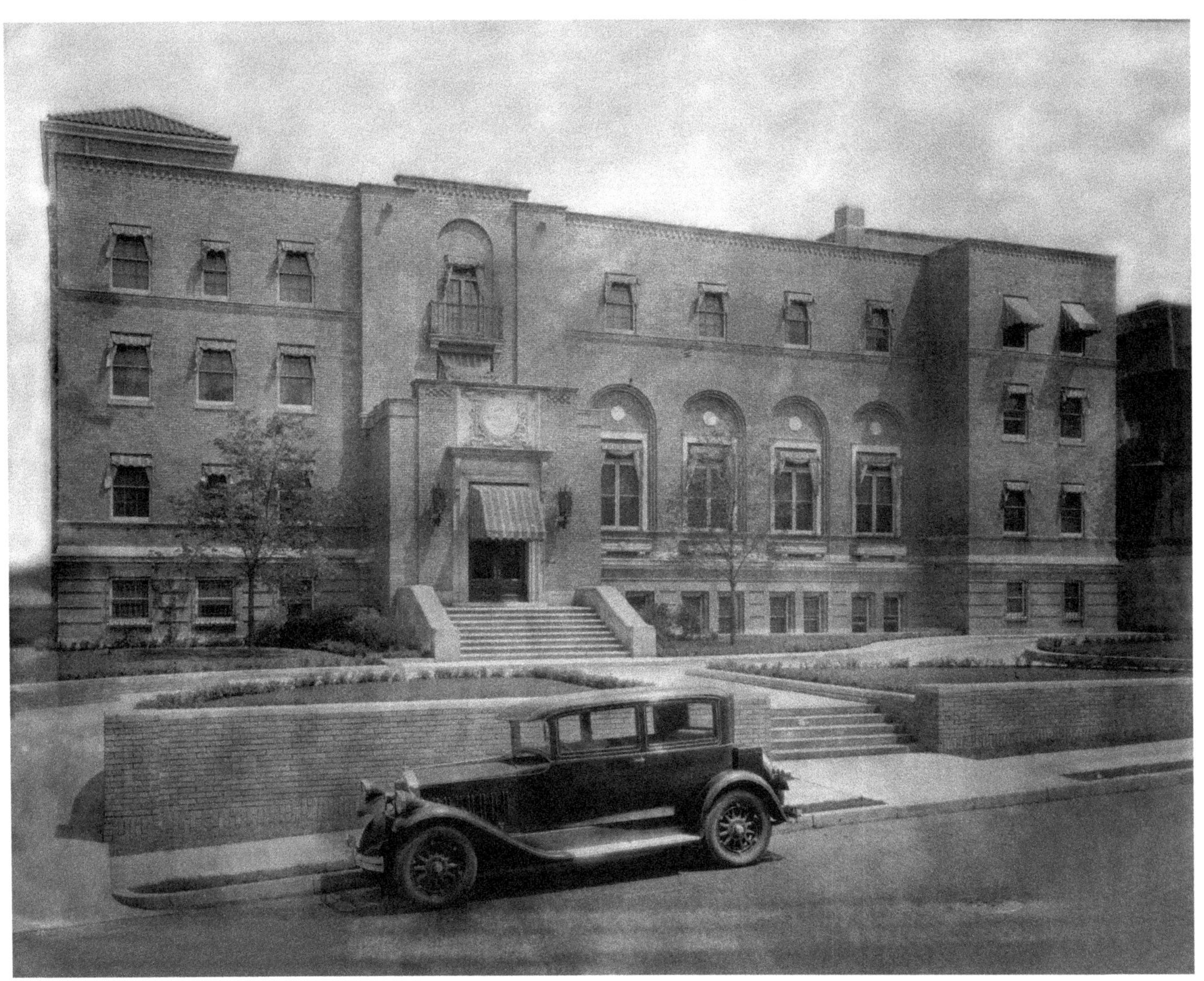

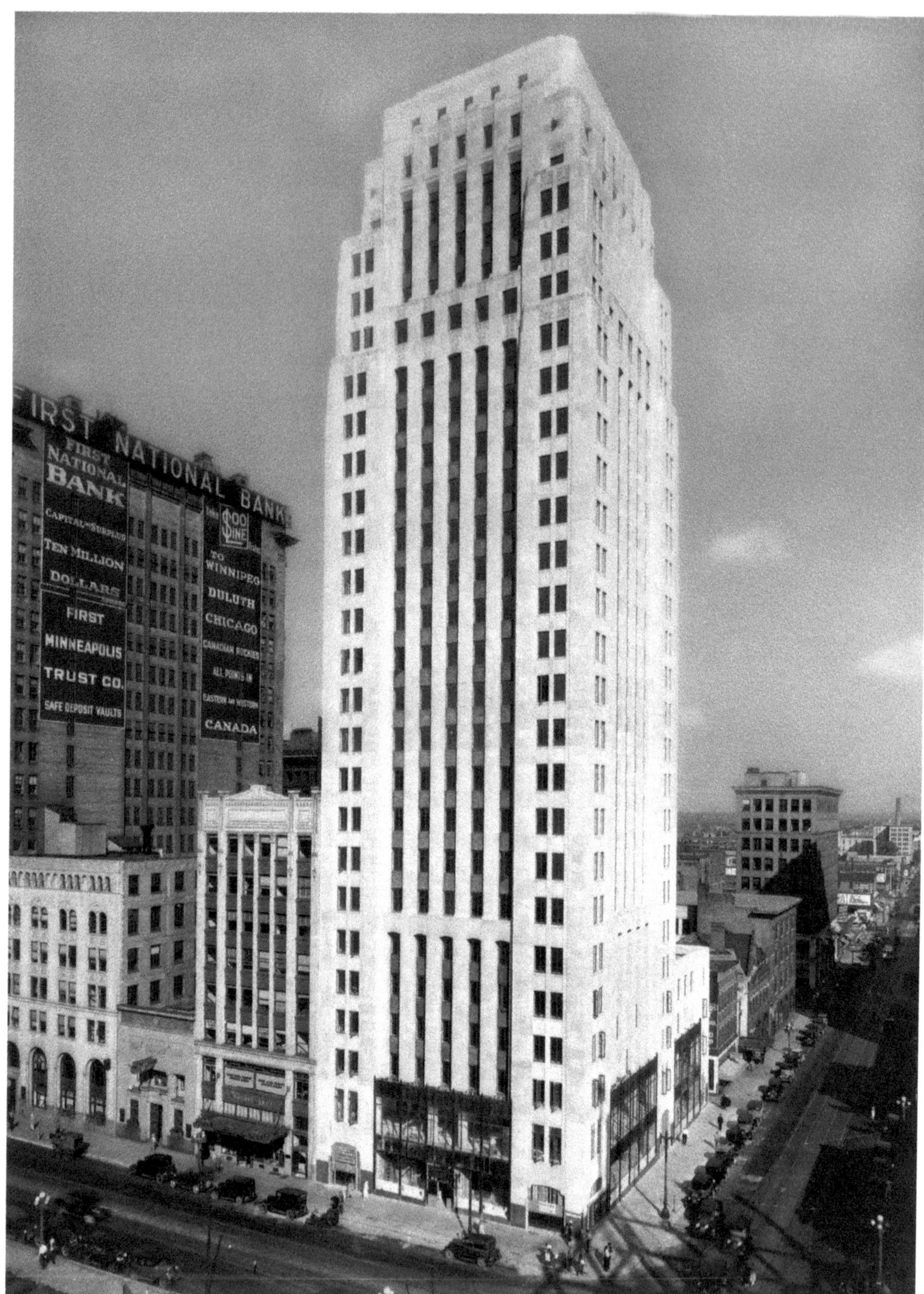

In 1929 Rufus R. Rand, Jr., a member of the family that owned the Minneapolis Gas Company, opened the twenty-six-story Rand Tower. This art deco–style skyscraper, pictured here around the time of its opening, occupies 527-529 Marquette Avenue.

Abbott Hospital moved from a small brick house to a true hospital building, located between Seventeenth and Eighteenth streets on First Avenue South, in 1911. In 1920 the growing hospital added a children's pavilion. Here young patients and a nurse pose around 1930.

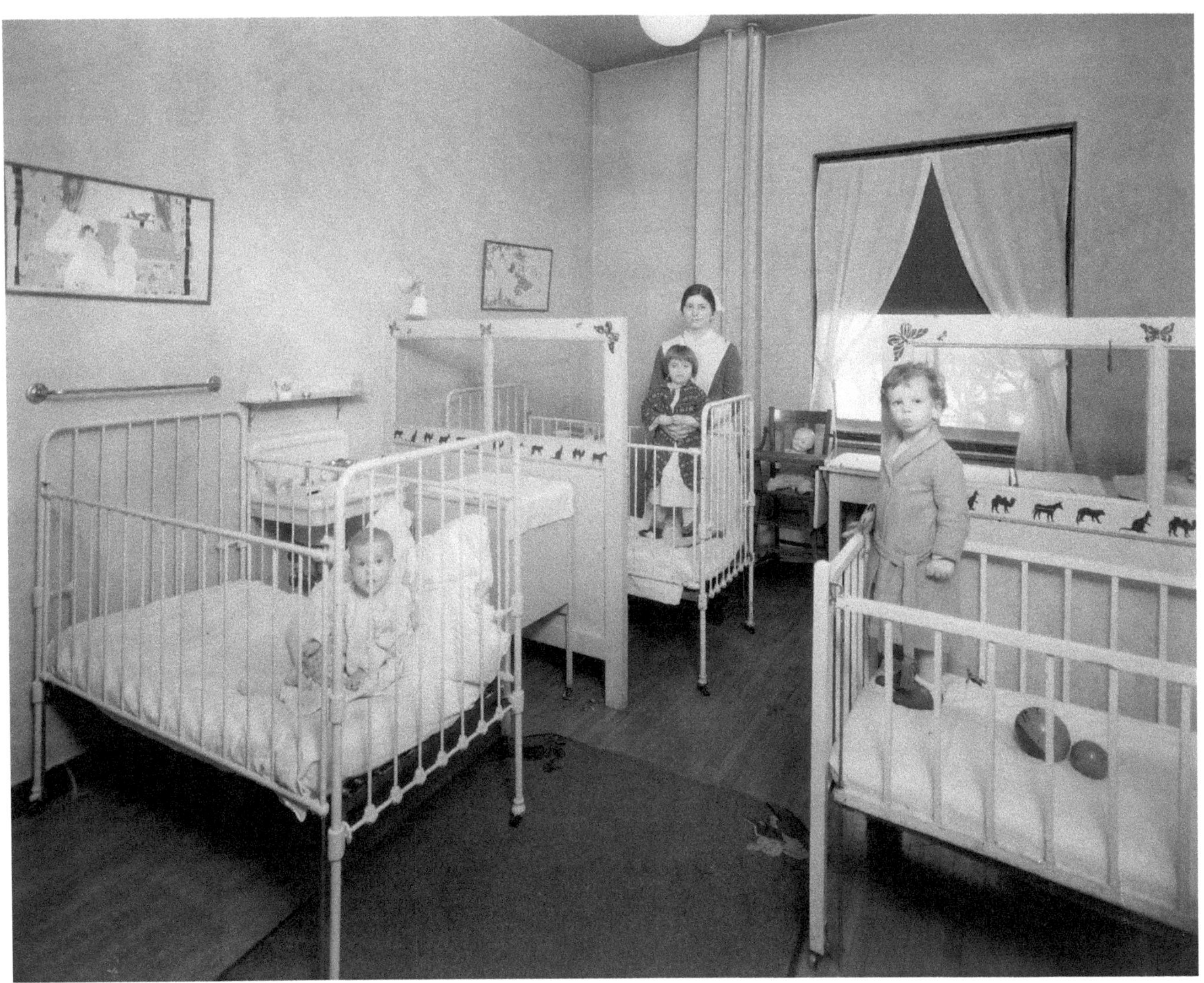

The Minneapolis Institute of Arts, established in 1883, moved to this building located at 2400 Third Avenue South in 1915. The architectural firm of McKim, Meed, and White designed the neoclassical structure.

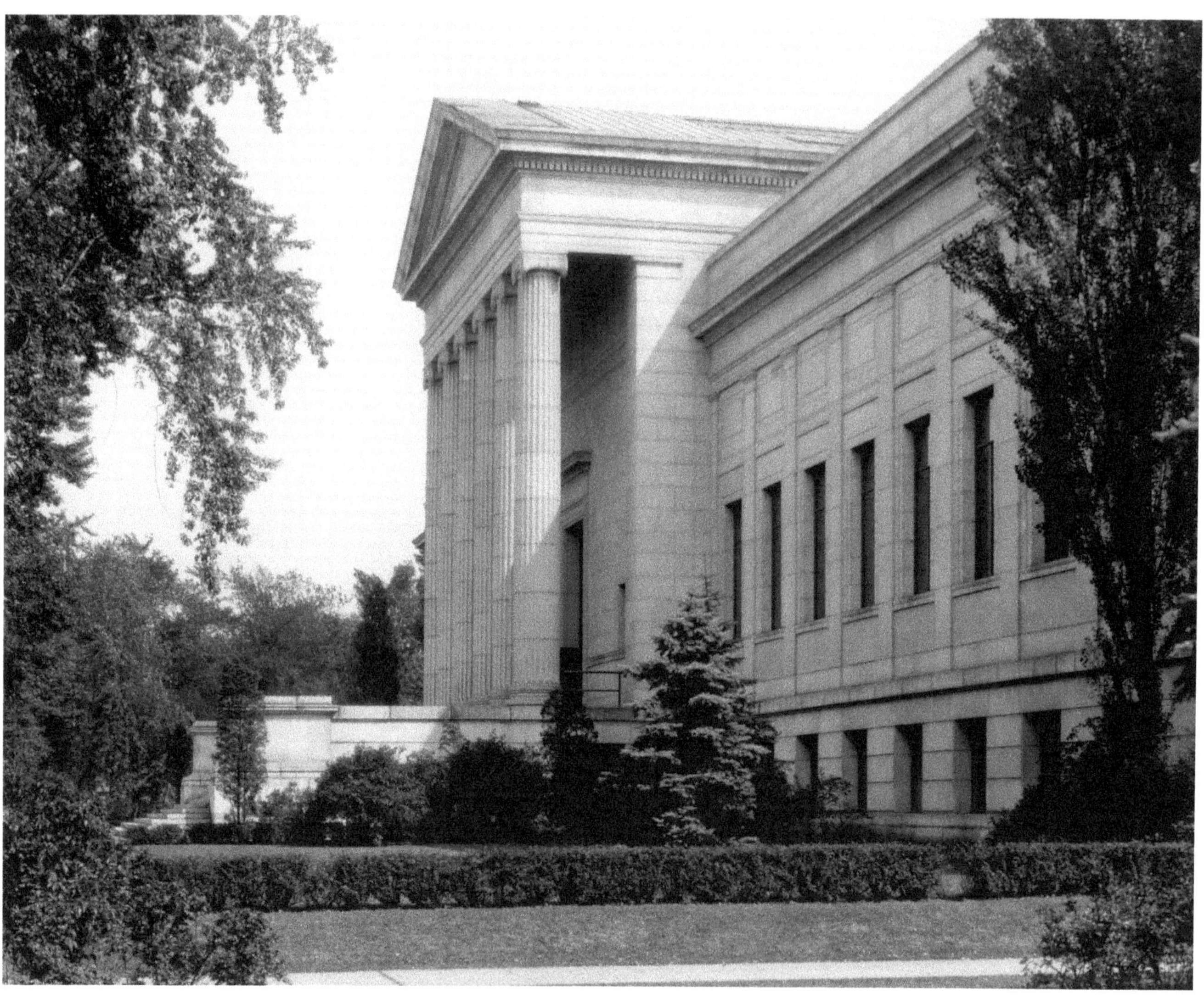

This image depicts the south side of Gold Medal Foods Elevator Number One in the Minneapolis milling district as it appeared in 1930. The Washburn Crosby Company christened its finest flour Gold Medal after the product won a gold medal for quality at an 1880 exposition.

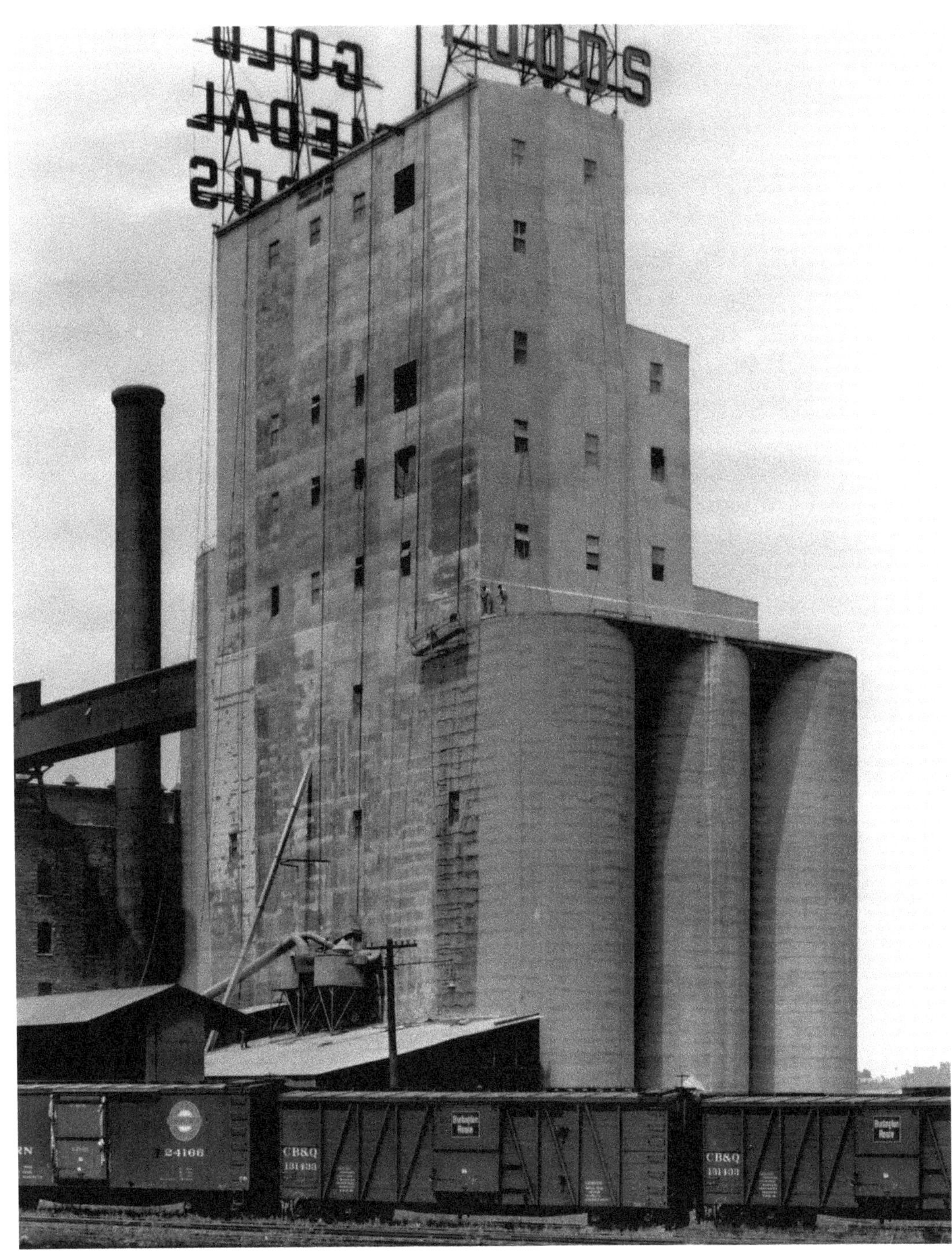

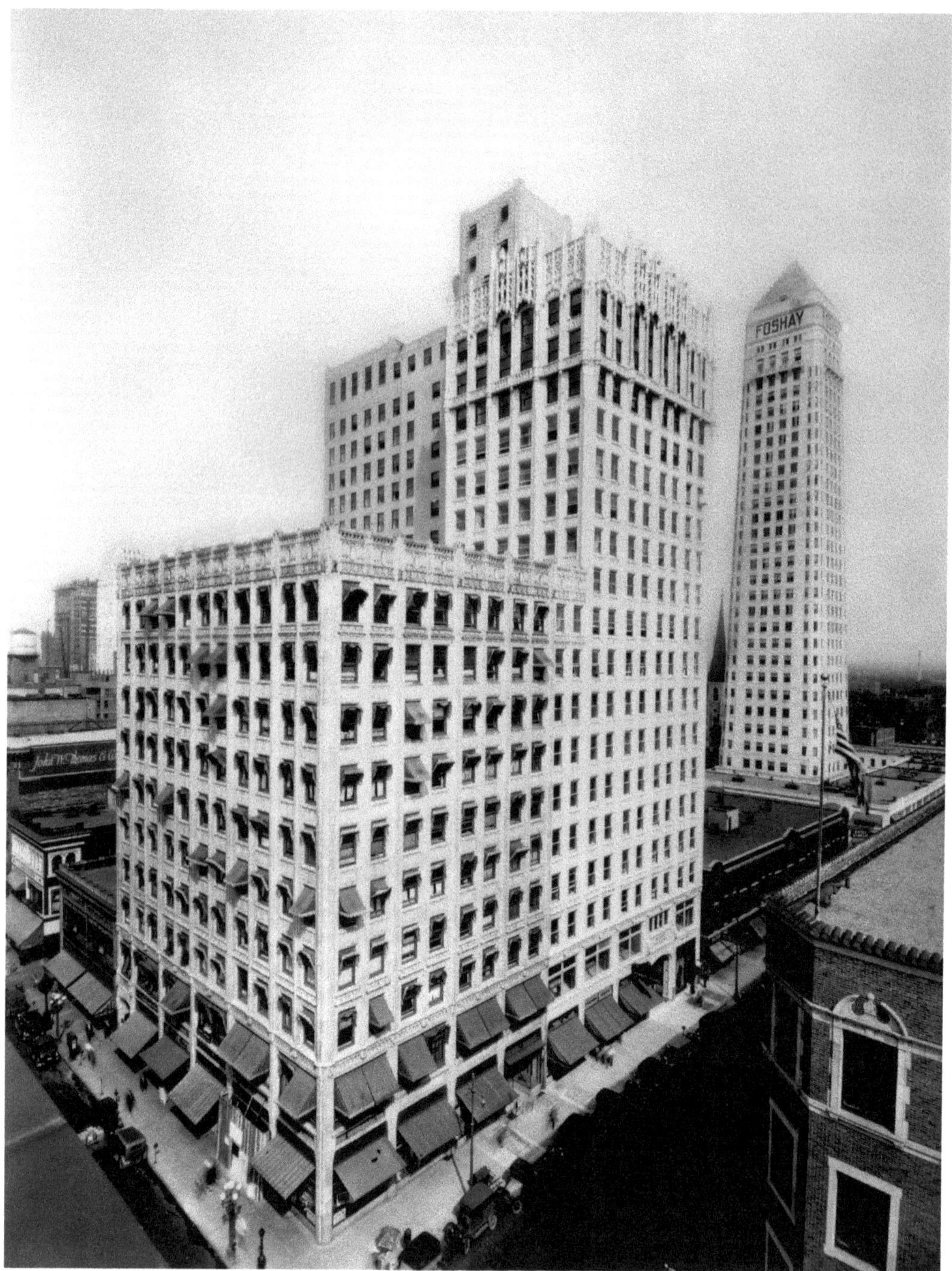

In 1923 a modest six-story structure known as the Yates Building was erected at the corner of Ninth Street and Nicollet Avenue. By the time this image was captured in 1930, a series of additions had transformed the edifice into the nineteen-story Medical Arts Building.

Jordan Jr. High School, located at 1616 Twenty-ninth Avenue North, welcomed its first class of students in 1922. By 1930, a year after this photograph was taken, the Minneapolis public school district was operating a total of one hundred and eleven schools.

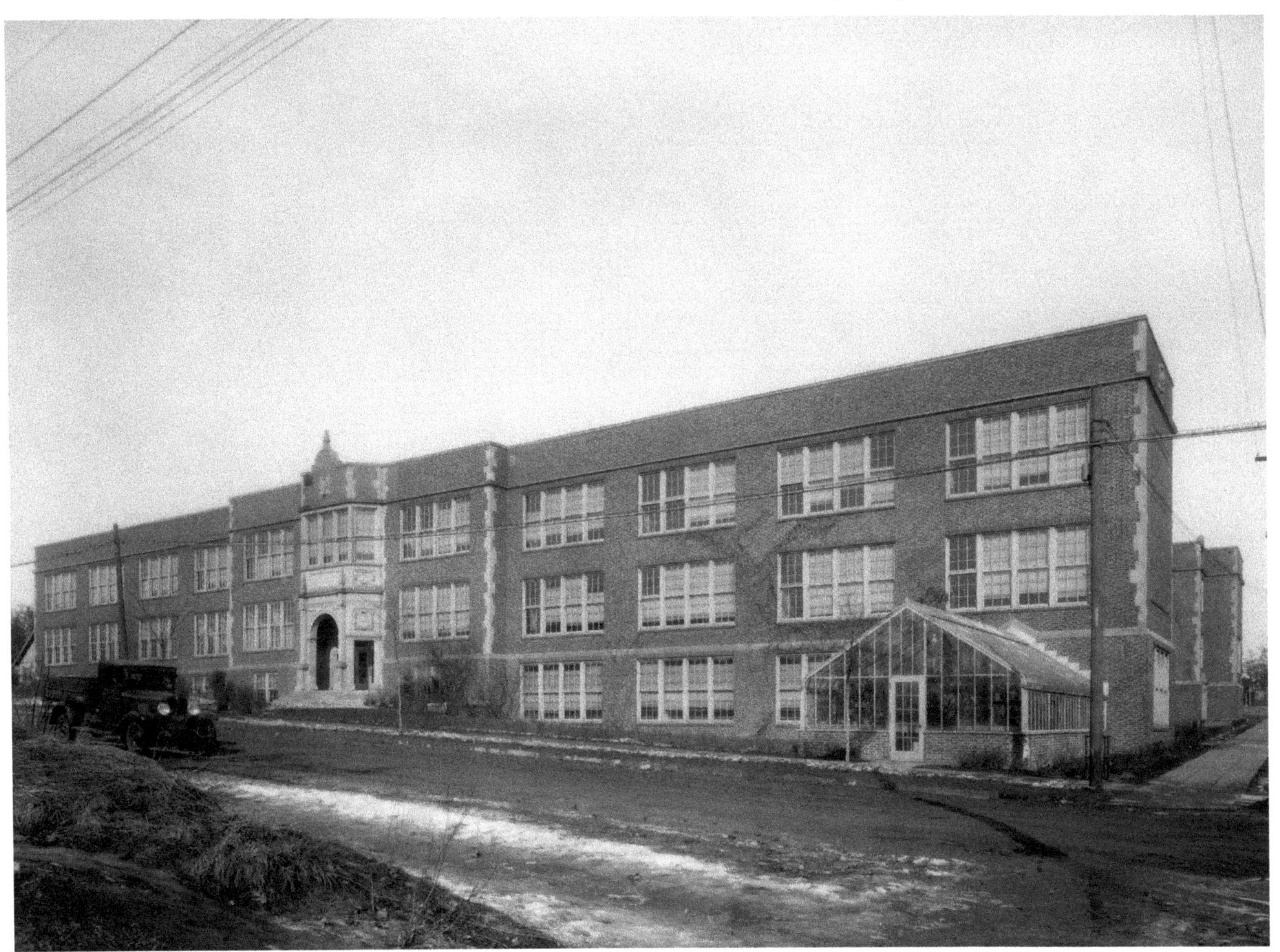

Members of the Minneapolis police department hone their skills at the department's shooting range in 1930.

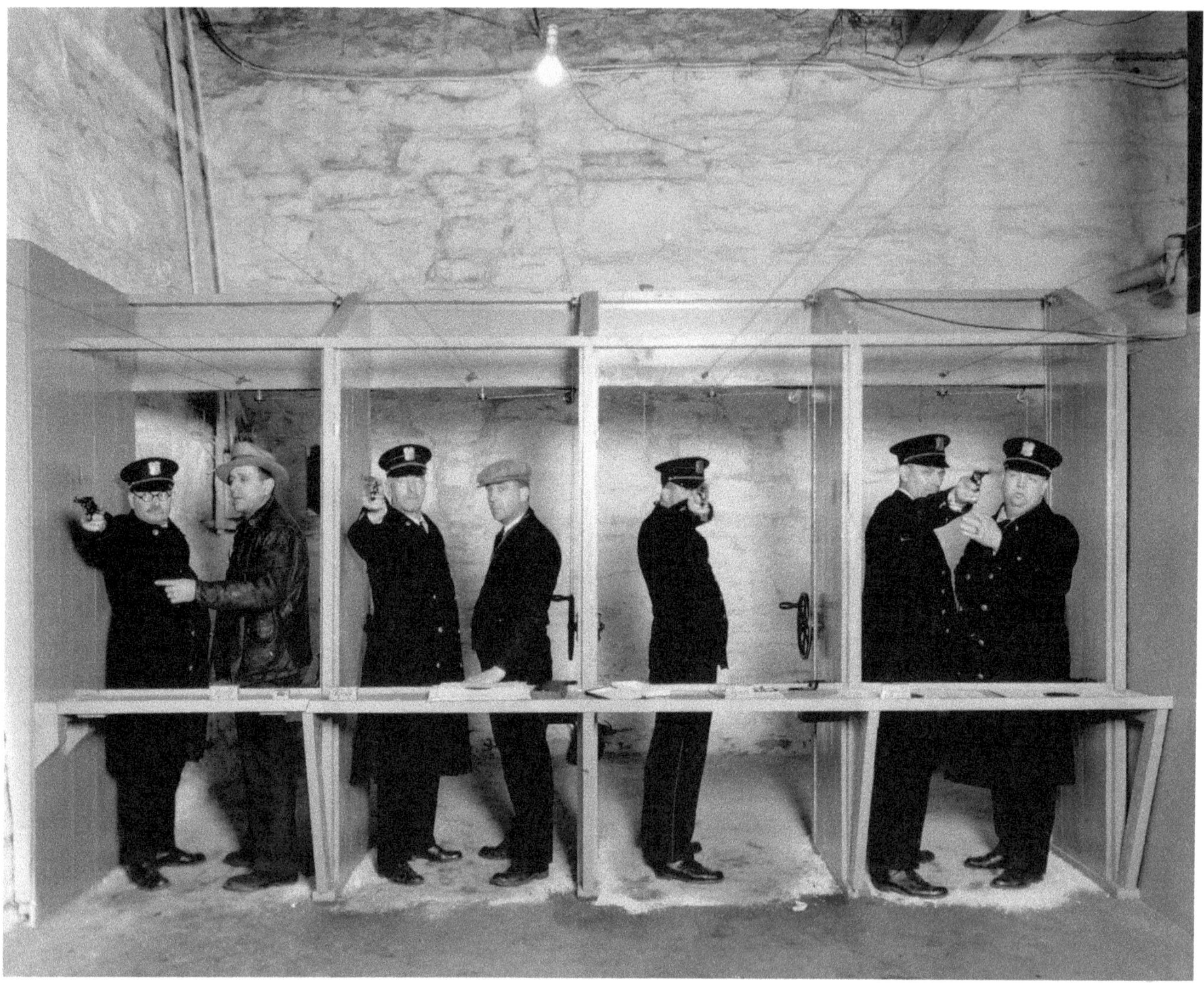

Unity House, a settlement house in north Minneapolis, is seen here in 1931. The young men and women who staffed Unity House offered free classes in English, sewing, drawing, and bookkeeping to neighborhood residents, many of whom were impoverished, recently arrived immigrants.

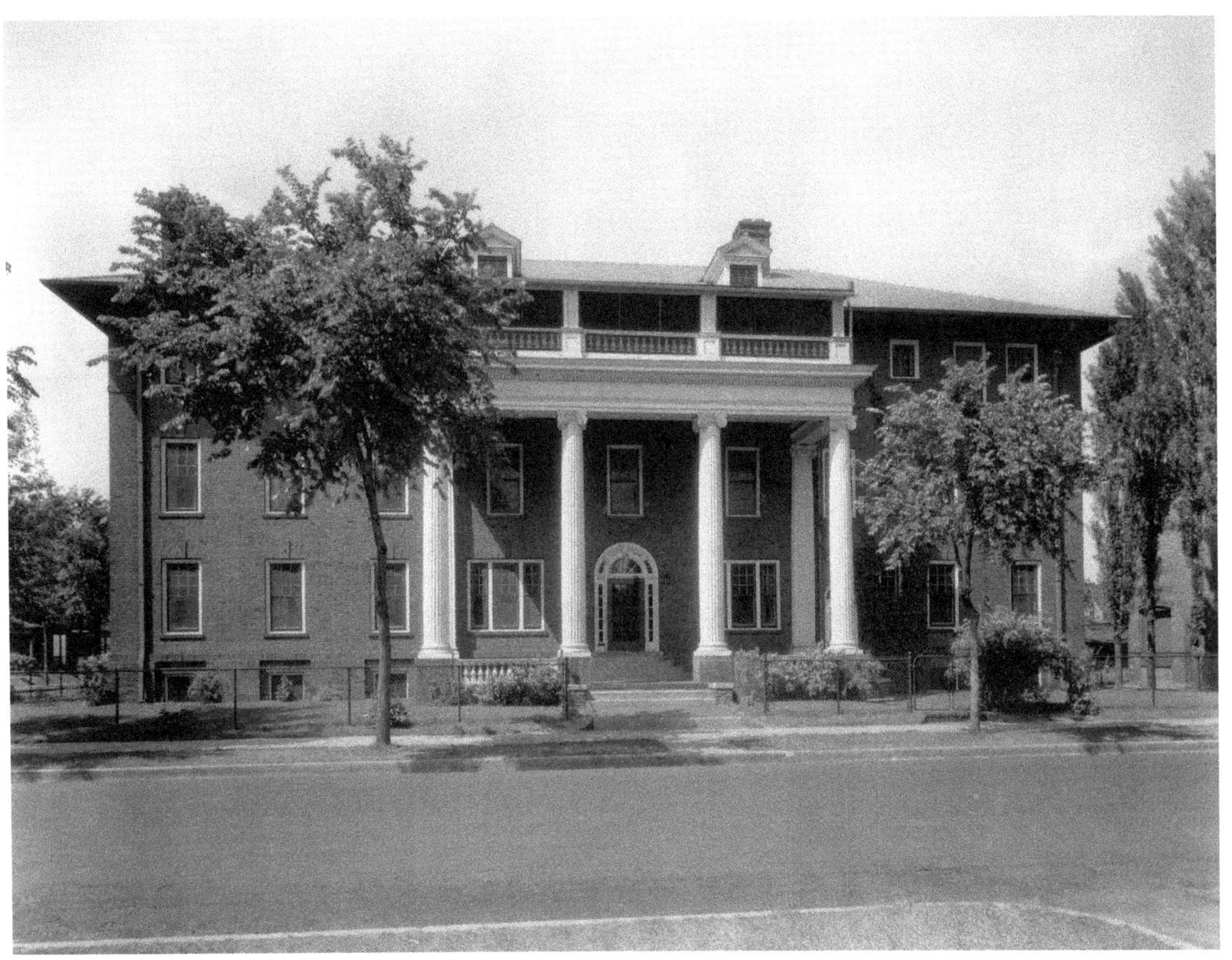

Patients at Shriners Hospital for Crippled Children, located on East River Road, enjoy a birthday party in 1936.

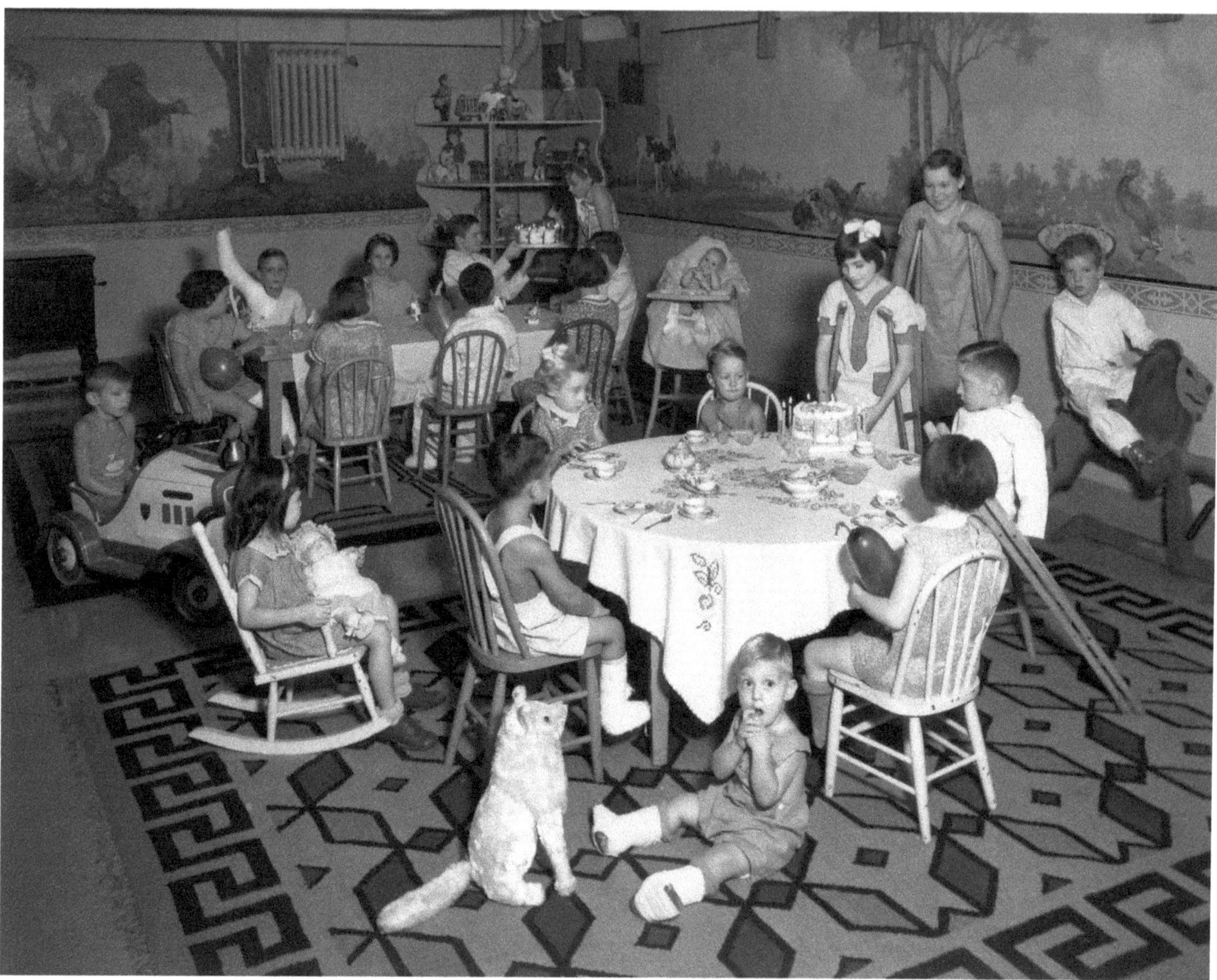

A woman admires the gardens at Loring Park, formerly known as Central Park, in 1939.

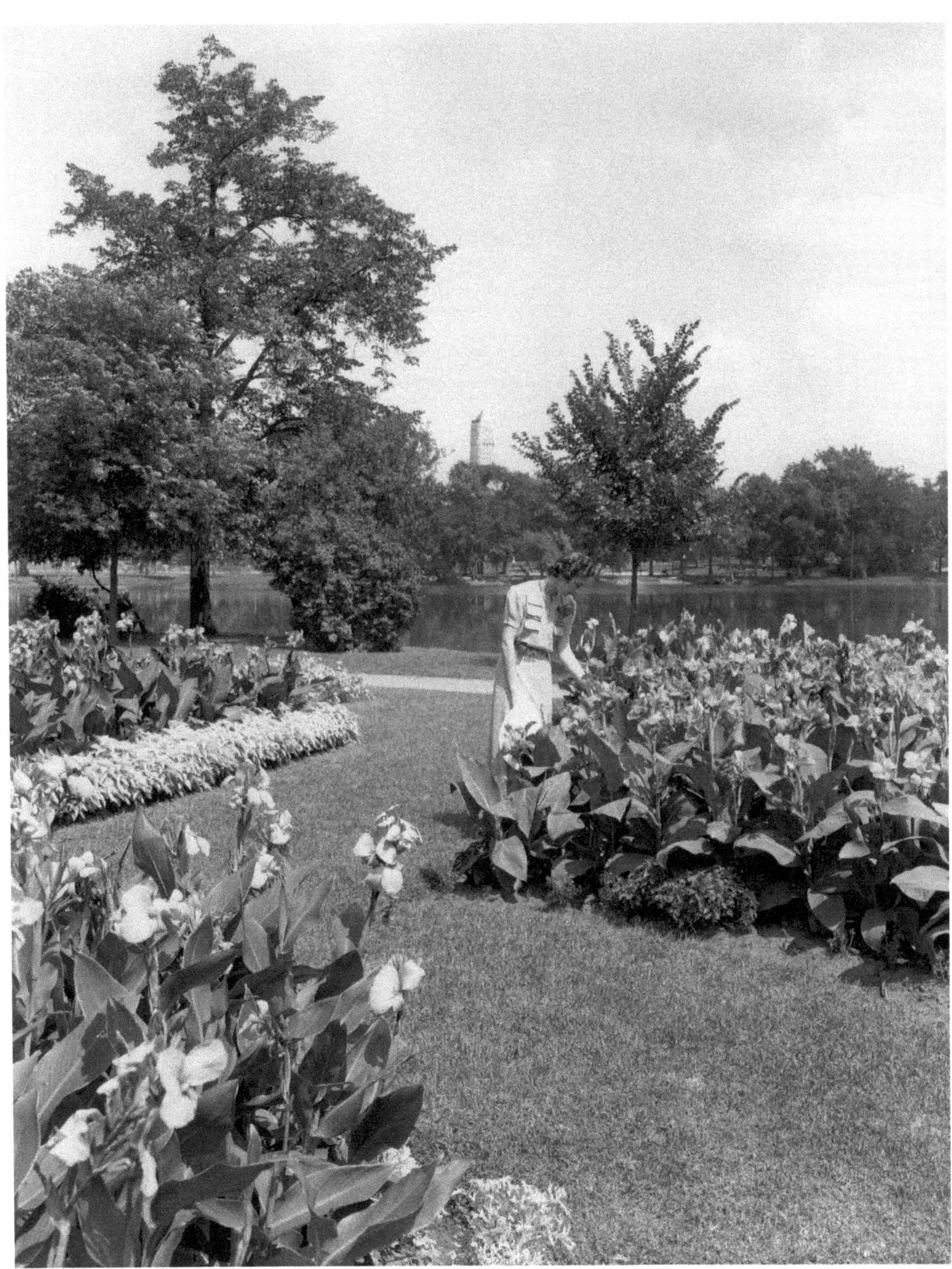

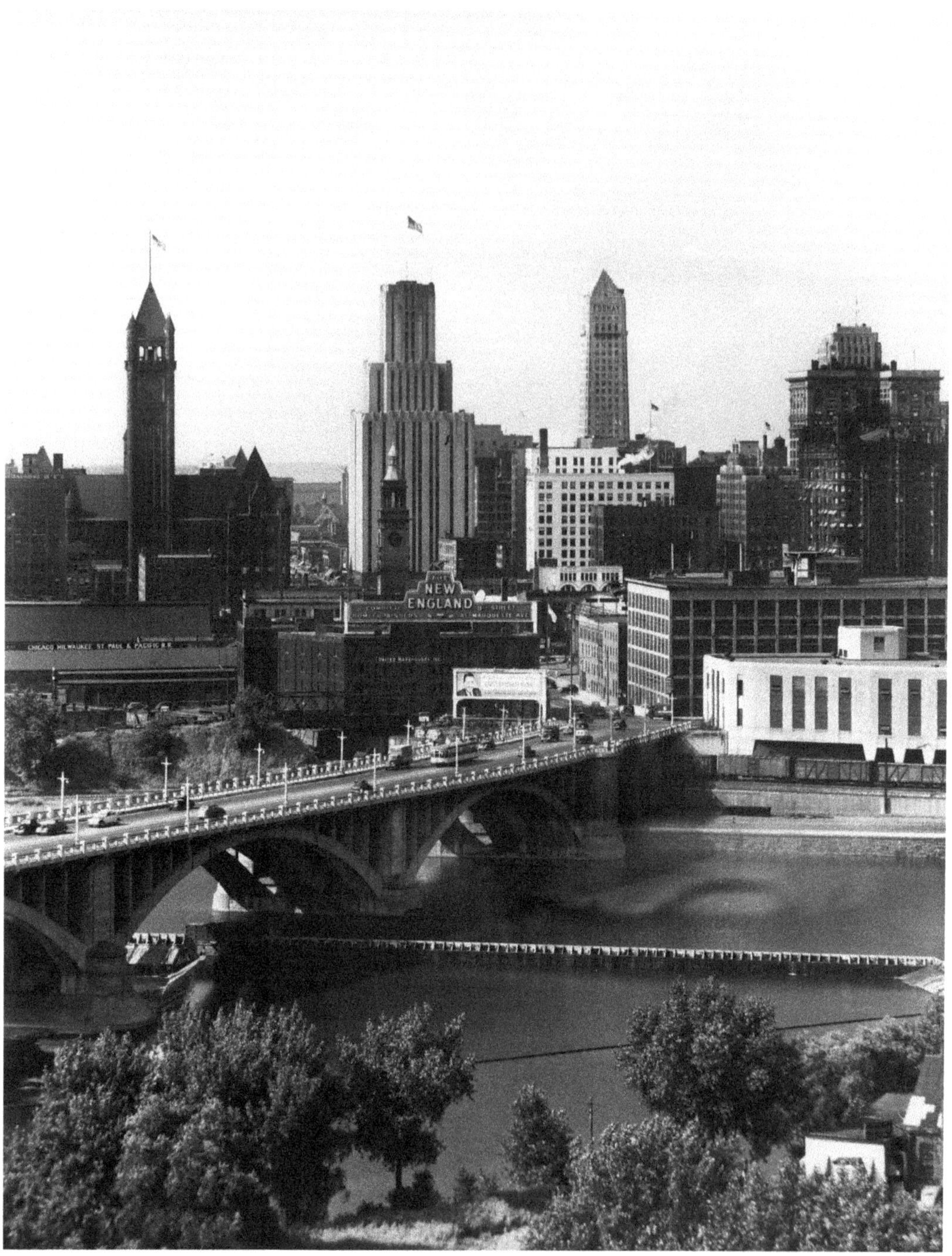

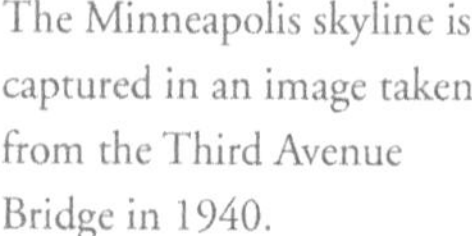

The Minneapolis skyline is captured in an image taken from the Third Avenue Bridge in 1940.

In 1914 a community of Swedish Lutherans in north Minneapolis founded the Gustavus Adolphus Lutheran Church. When the congregation outgrew their first building, they built a new church at 1509 Twenty-seventh Avenue Northeast, pictured here as it appeared in 1939.

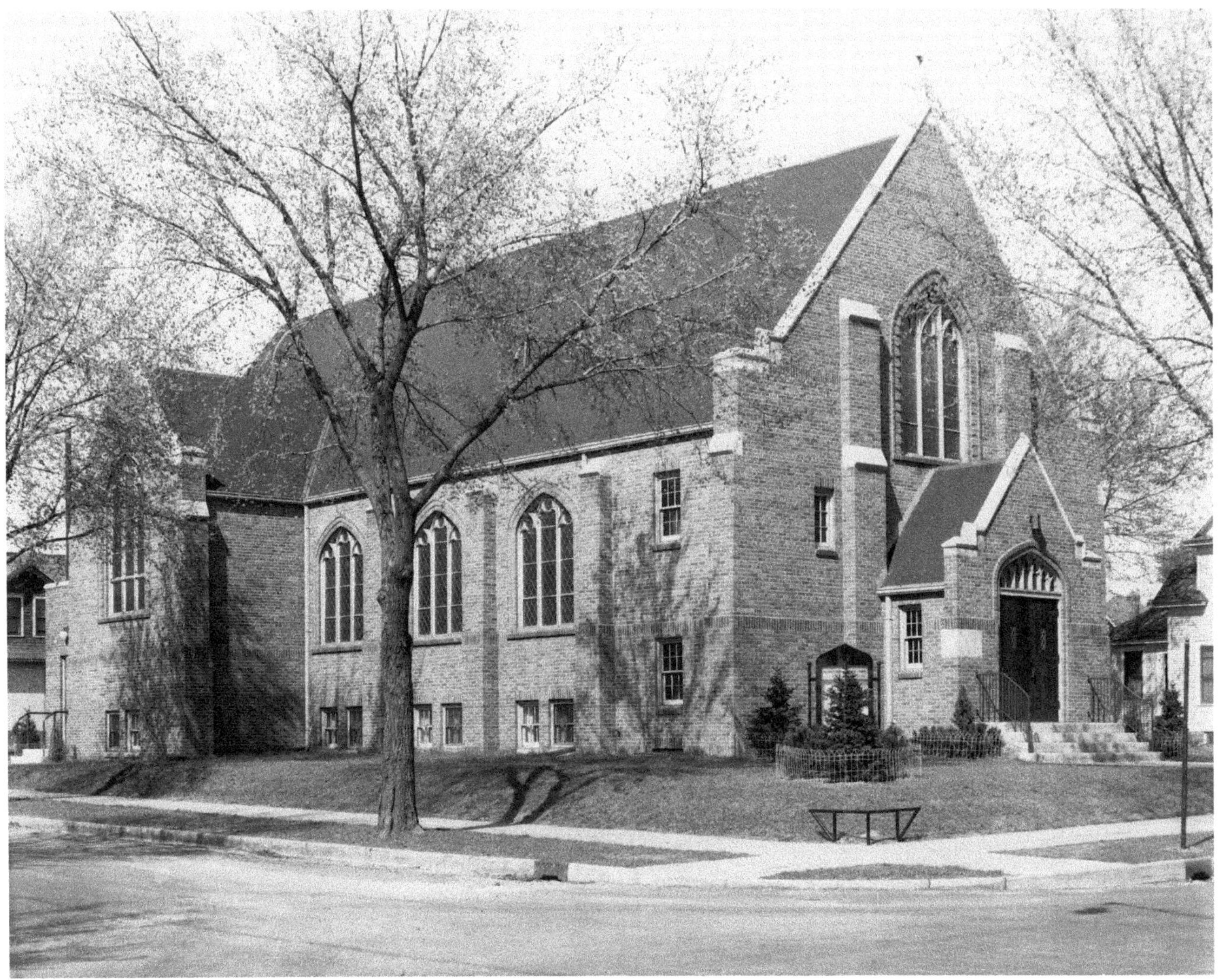

The National Biscuit Company, better known as NABISCO, operated a regional bakery at 256 Third Avenue North. The Minneapolis plant shipped twenty-five kinds of crackers and cookies to states throughout the Midwest.

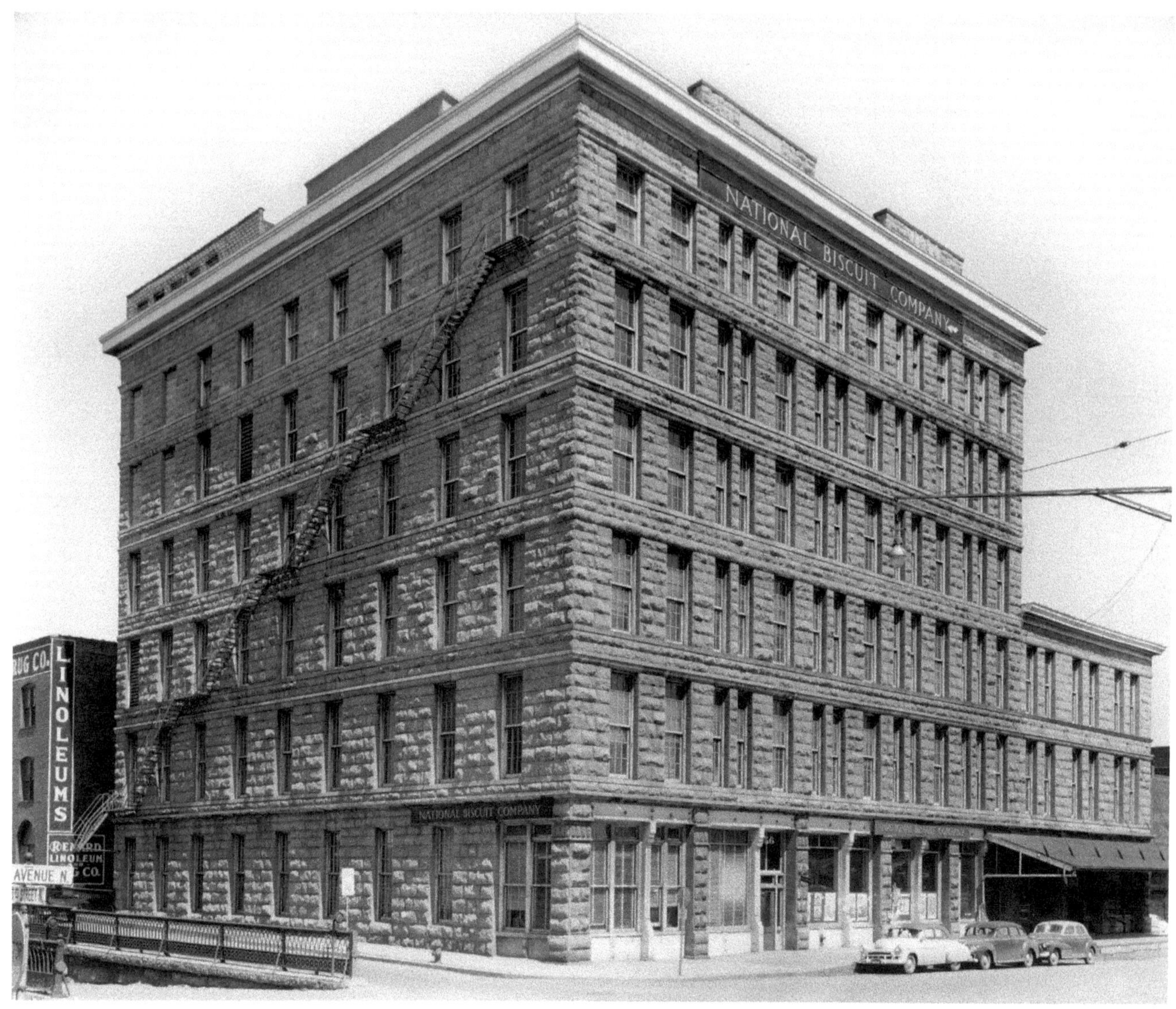

In 1930 the Knights of Columbus commissioned a statue to celebrate the 250th anniversary of Fr. Louis Hennepin's sighting of St. Anthony Falls. The statue, installed on the grounds of St. Mary's Basilica, is pictured here in 1940.

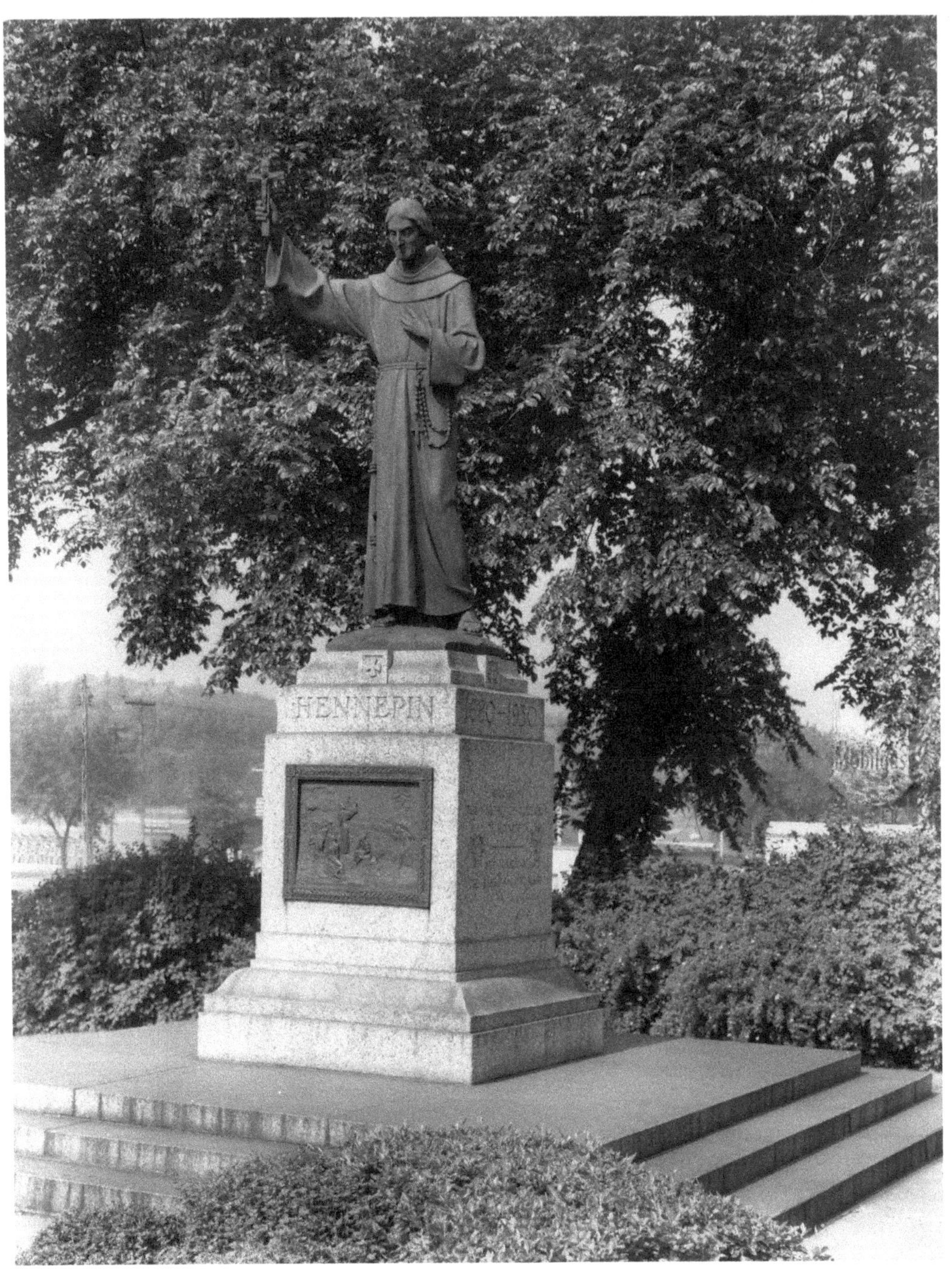

The Minneapolis Park Board acquired the property that formed the nucleus of Glenwood Park in 1890. In 1938, two years before this image was captured, the park was renamed Theodore Wirth Park in honor of longtime park board superintendent Theodore Wirth.

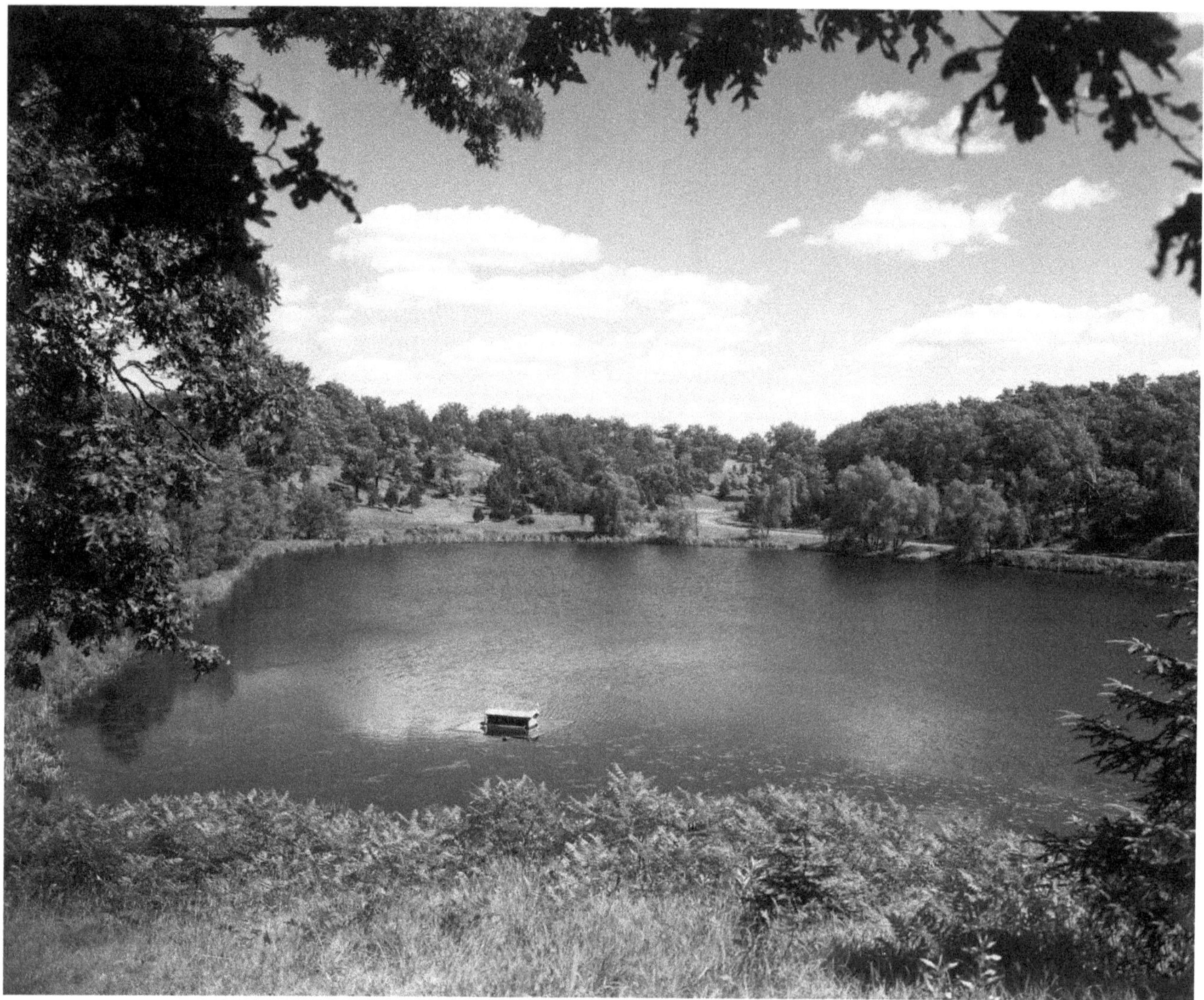

The Minneapolis Aquatennial, a ten-day summer celebration conceived by local businessmen to draw visitors to the city, began in 1940. Here a float sponsored by Dayton's Department Store participates in the inaugural Aquatennial Parade.

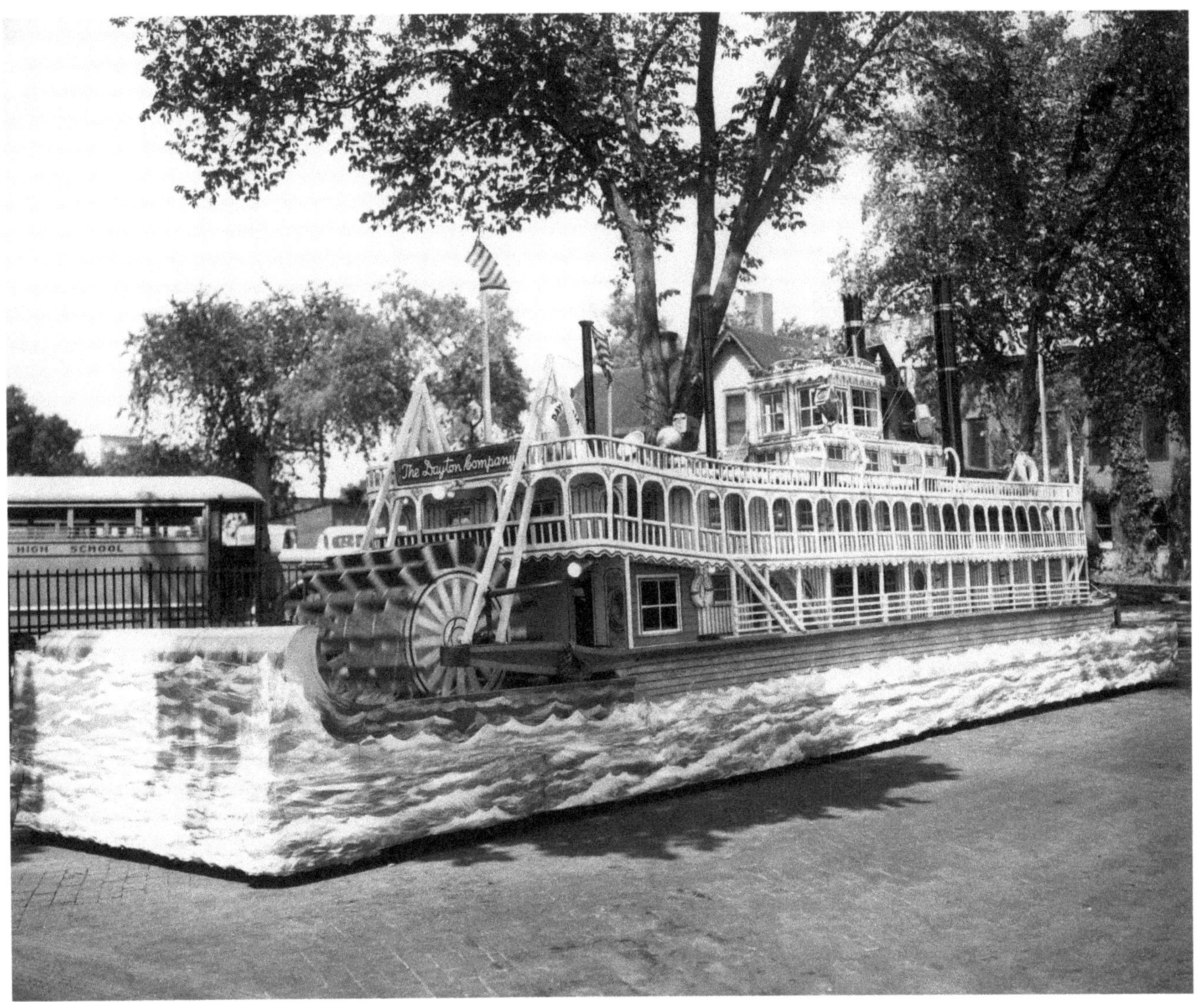

In 1902 George D. Dayton opened his namesake Dayton's Department Store at the corner of Seventh Street and Nicollet Avenue. The store became a venerable Minneapolis institution and eventually gave rise to the Target Corporation. Dayton's toyland department is pictured here in 1940.

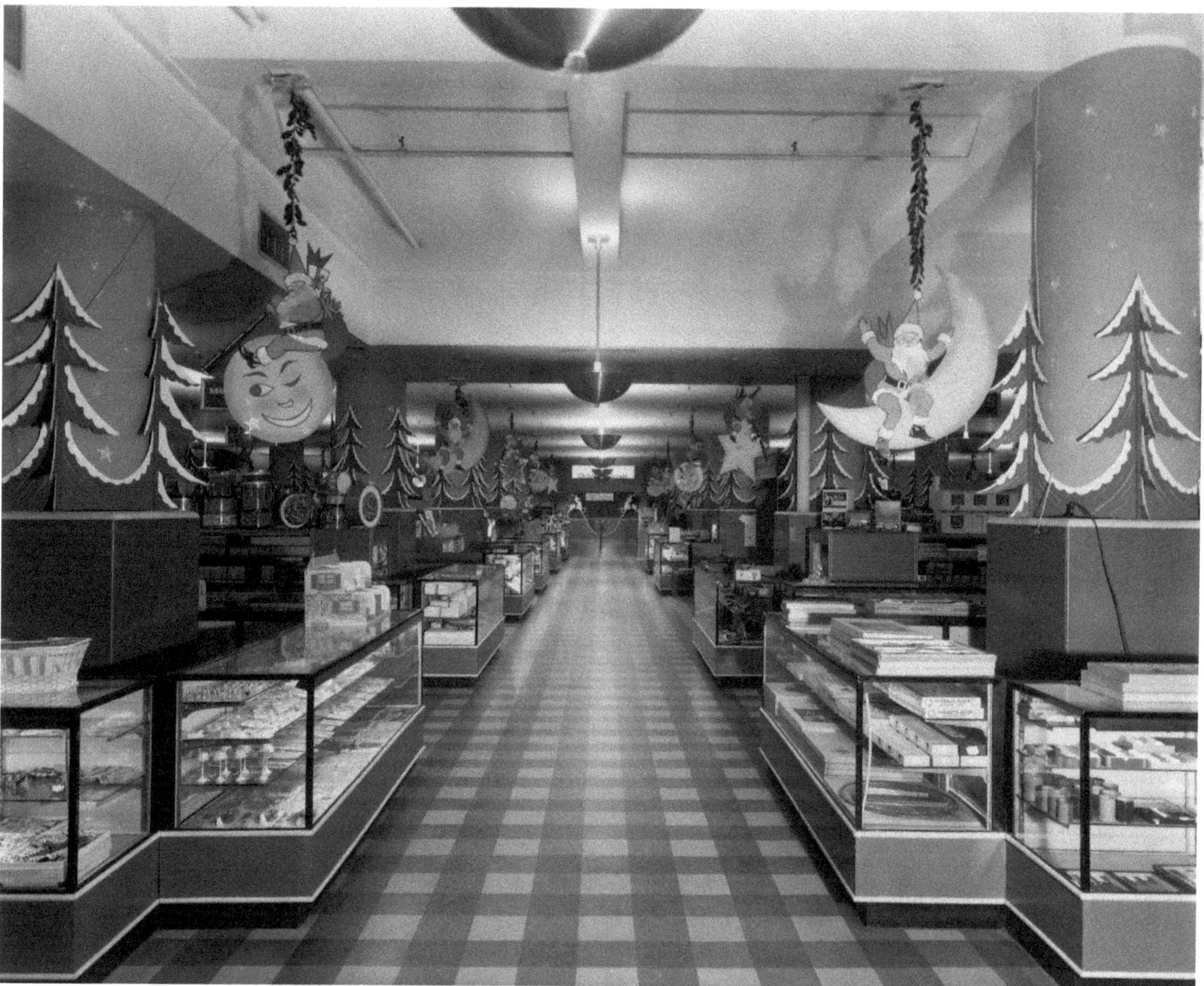

This mammoth Sears Store anchored a shopping district on East Lake Street from 1928 until 1992, when Sears shuttered the old building and moved to a new location at the Mall of America. The building now houses offices, condominiums, and restaurants.

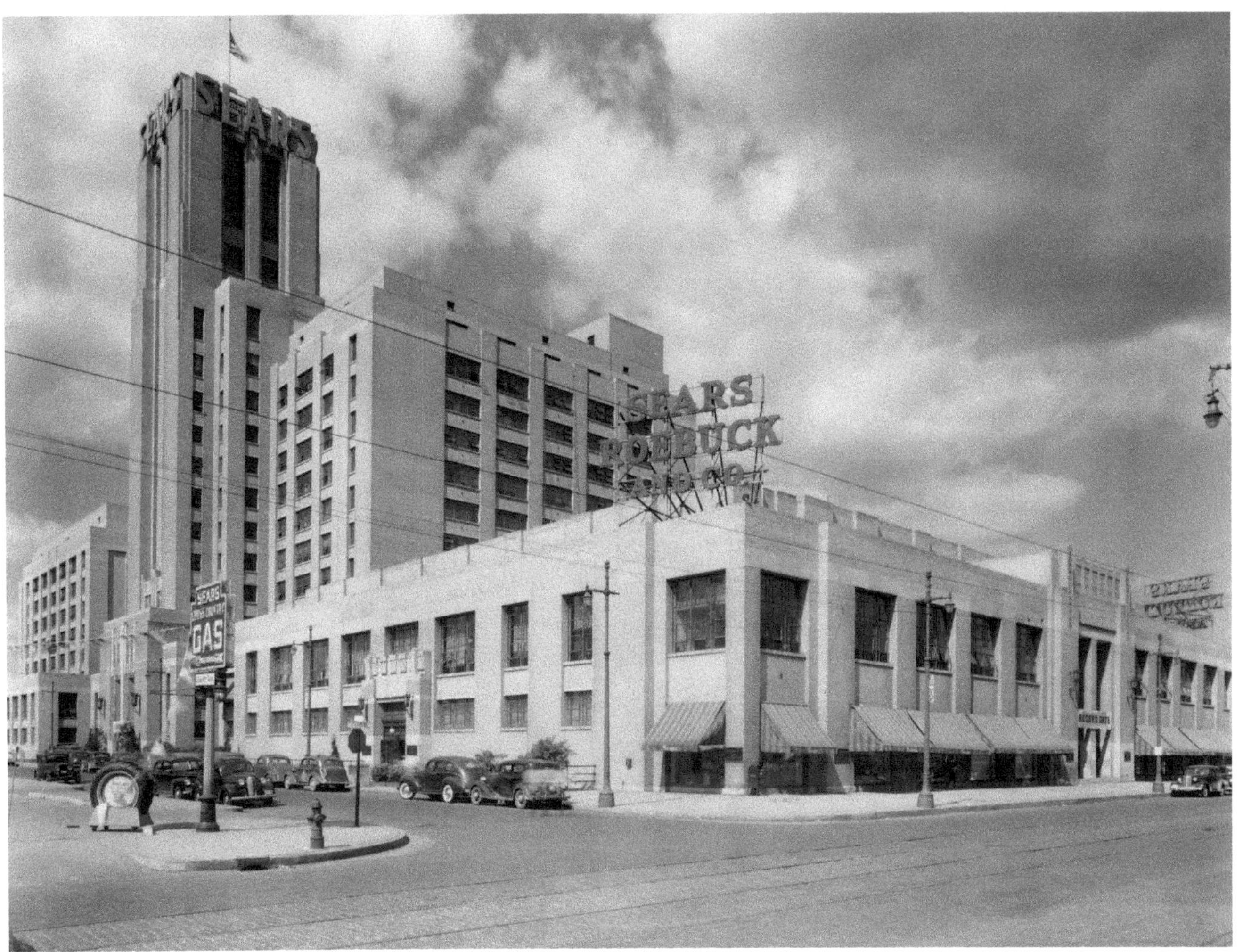

During World War II, employees at Powers Department Store on Fifth Street and Nicollet Avenue do their part to aid the war effort by selling bonds, as illustrated in this 1942 photograph.

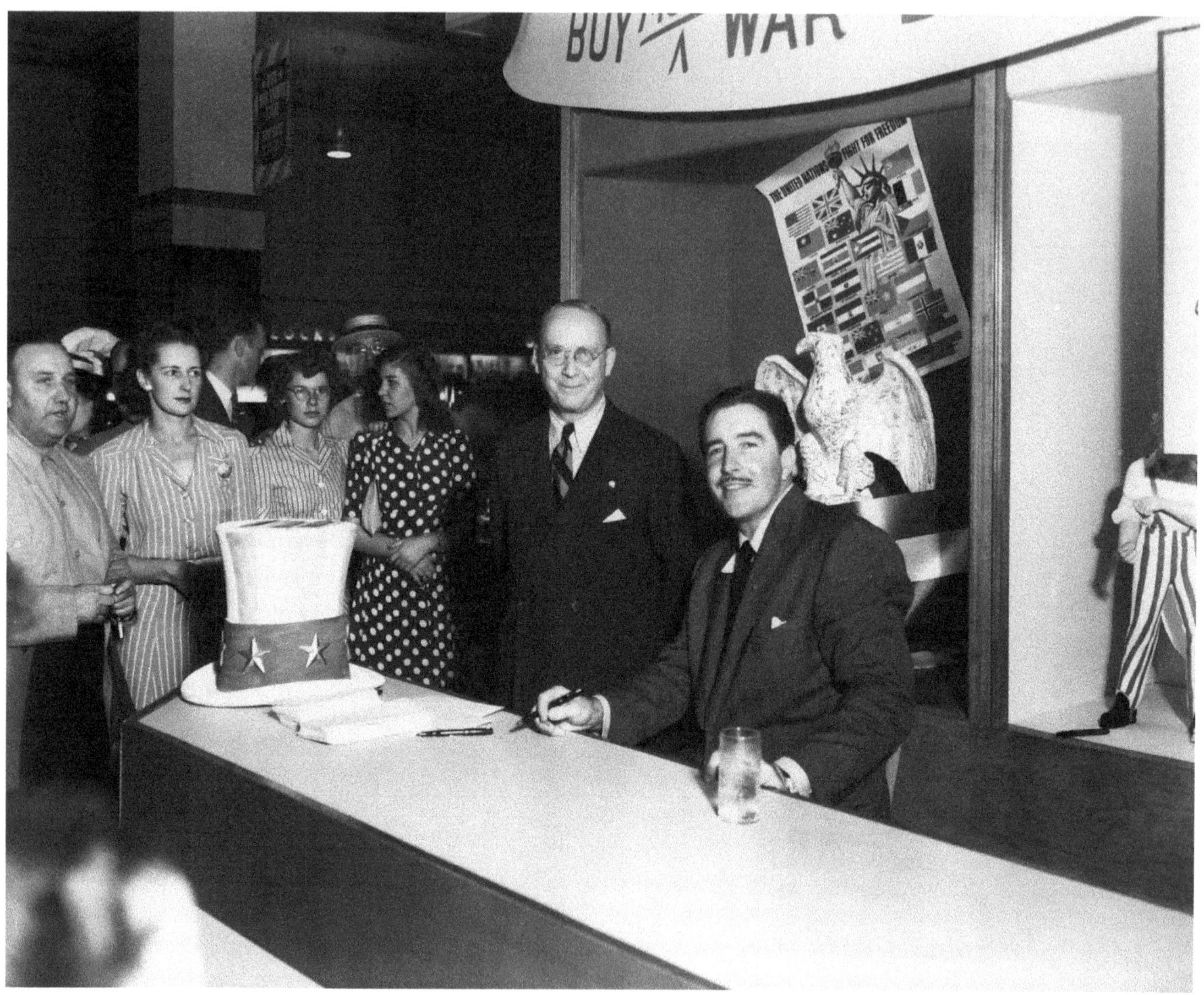

In 1942, women work the assembly line at the D. W. Onan and Sons manufacturing plant. The sprawling 250,000-square-foot University Plant churned out power-generating equipment and engines.

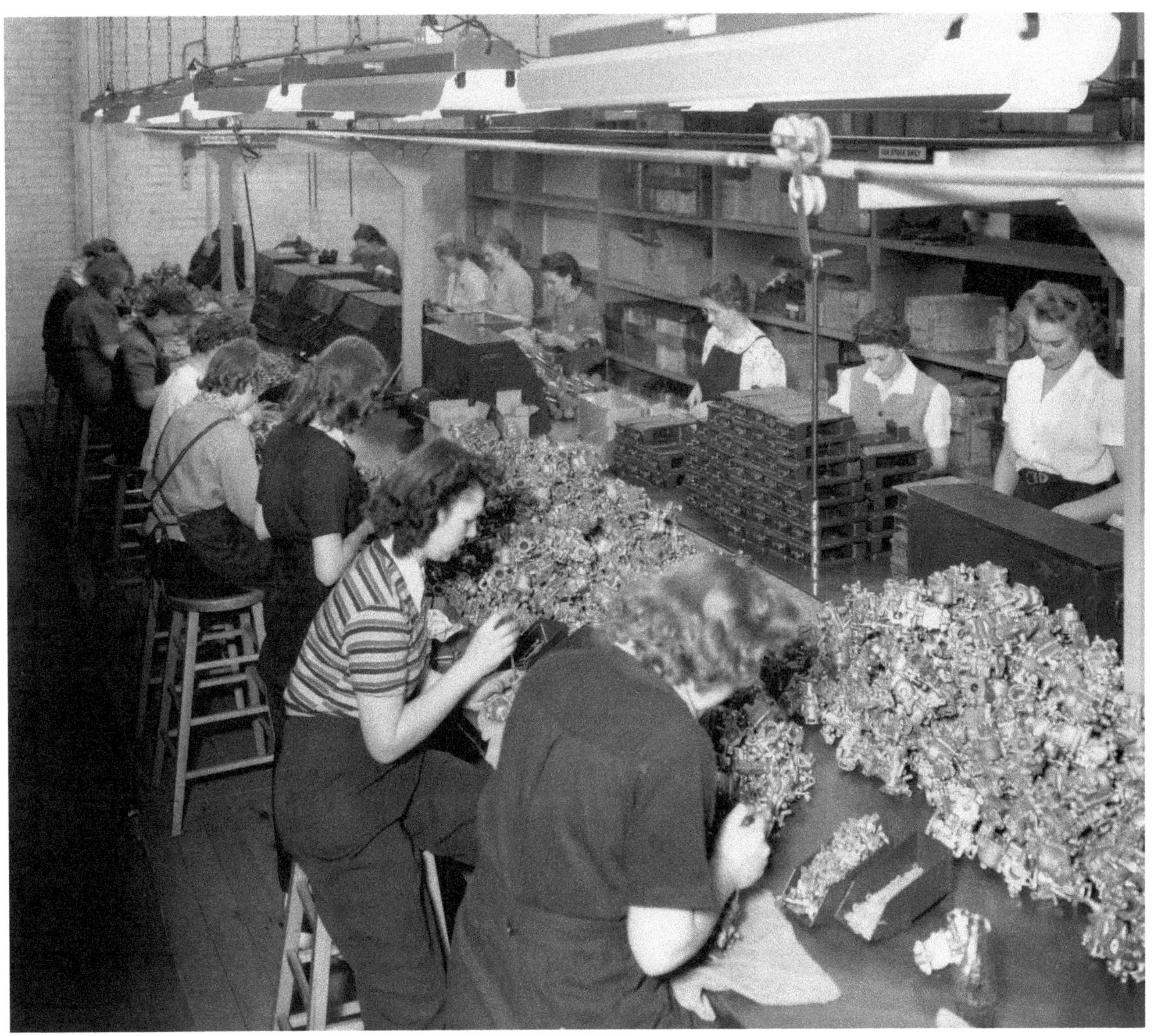

The William Brothers Boiler and Manufacturing Company specialized in steel fabrication. The Minneapolis firm produced tugboats for the Navy and snowplows for the Army during World War II.

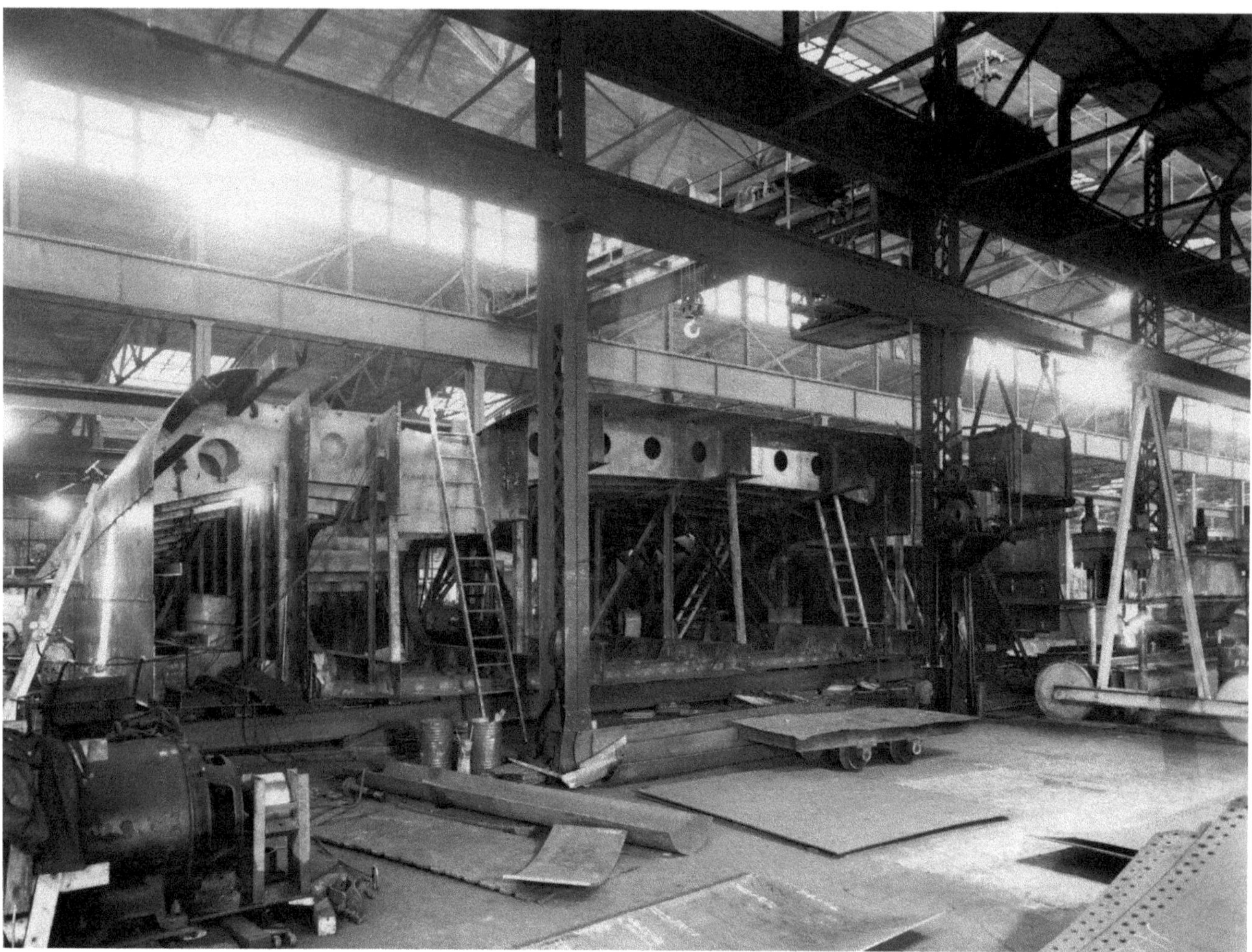

The Hospitality House for Service Men, located at 902 Hennepin Avenue South, is seen here in 1945. The Hospitality House offered returning soldiers a place to shower, have a drink, and do their laundry.

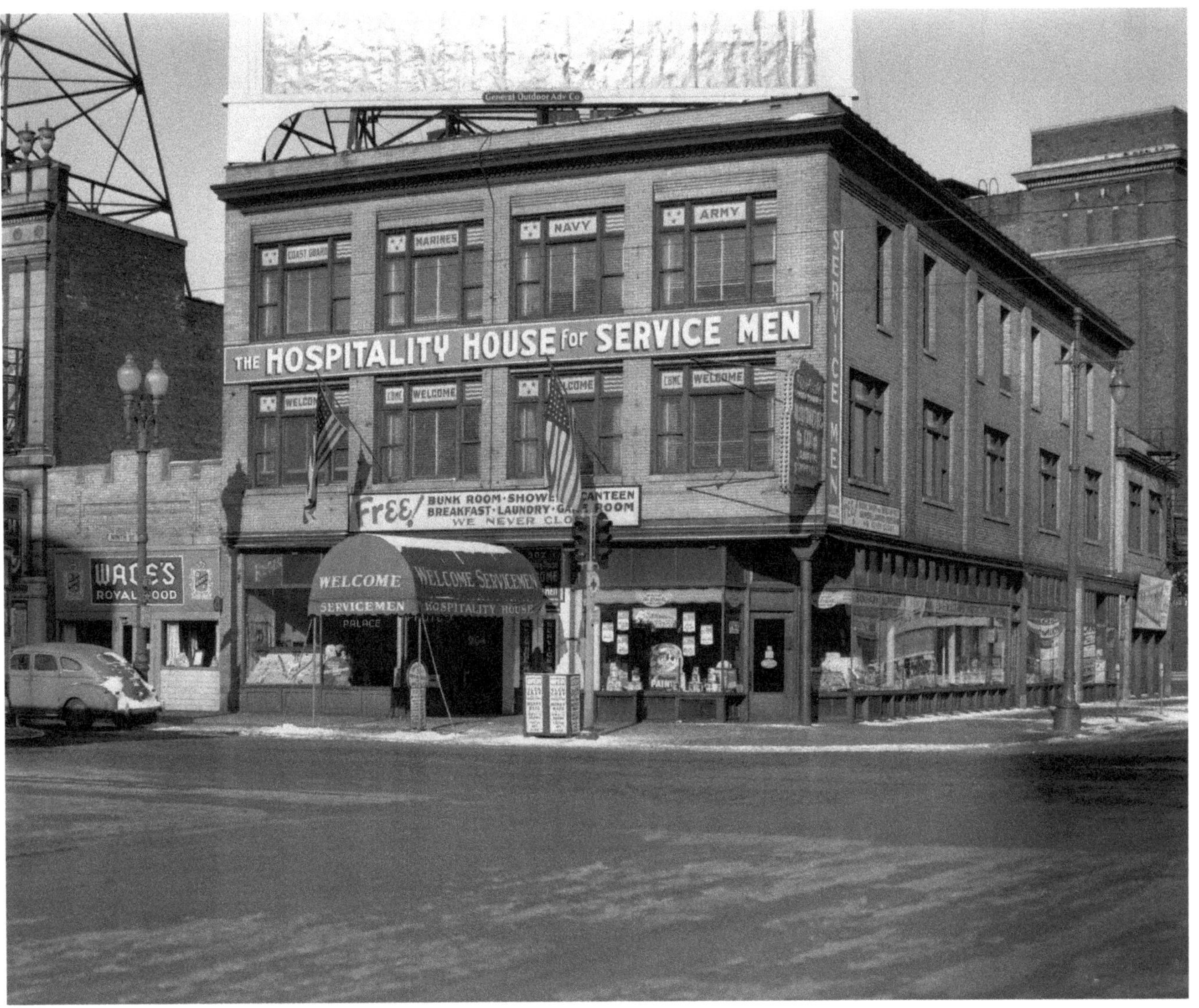

During its first sixty years in Minneapolis, Northrup, King, and Company's seed business expanded from a one-room house on Hennepin Avenue to a massive fifteen-acre complex between Fourteenth and Eighteenth avenues northeast. Here two workers at the plant fill bags with seeds in 1943.

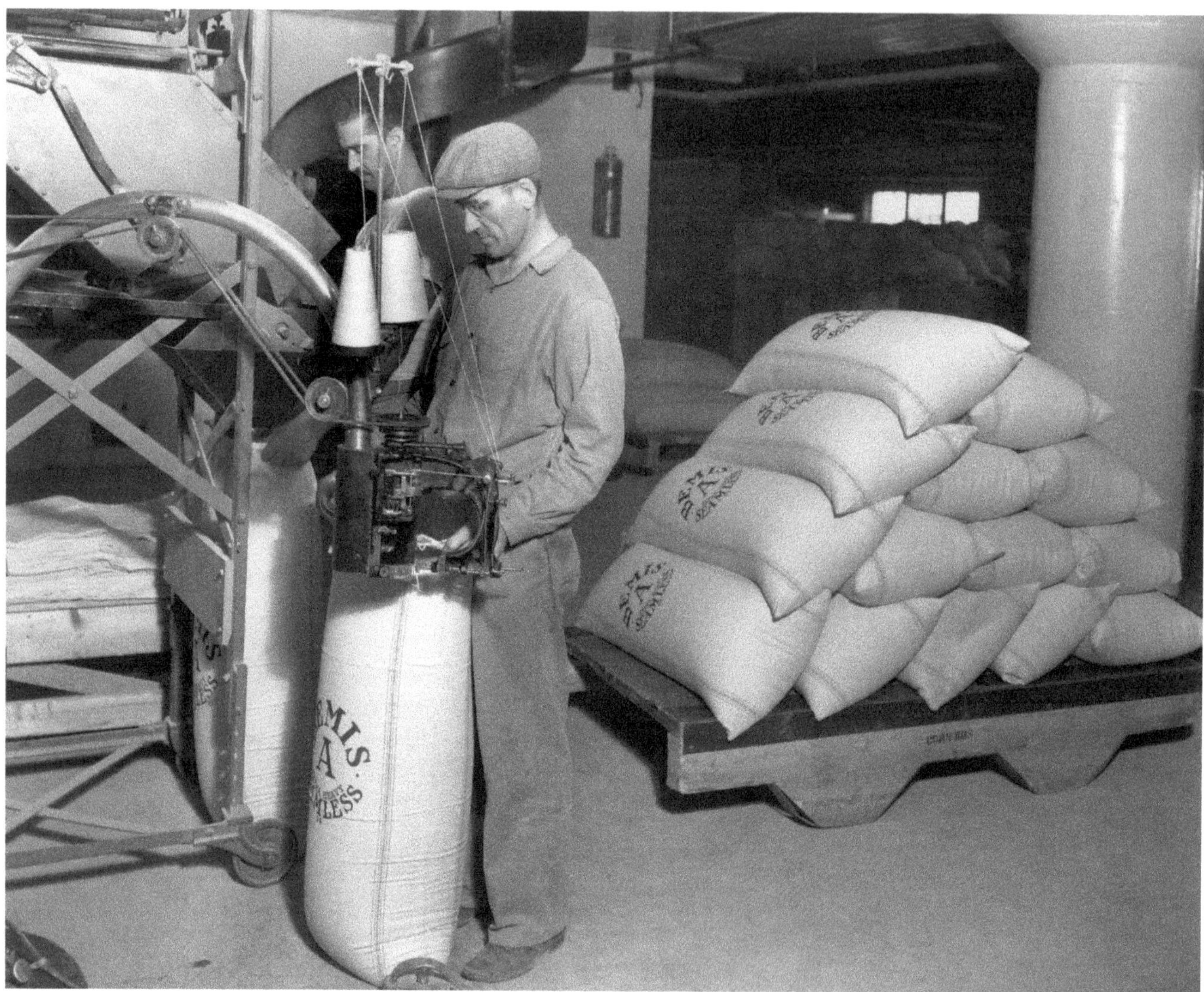

Fifty-three-foot Minnehaha Falls as it appeared on a spring morning in 1945.

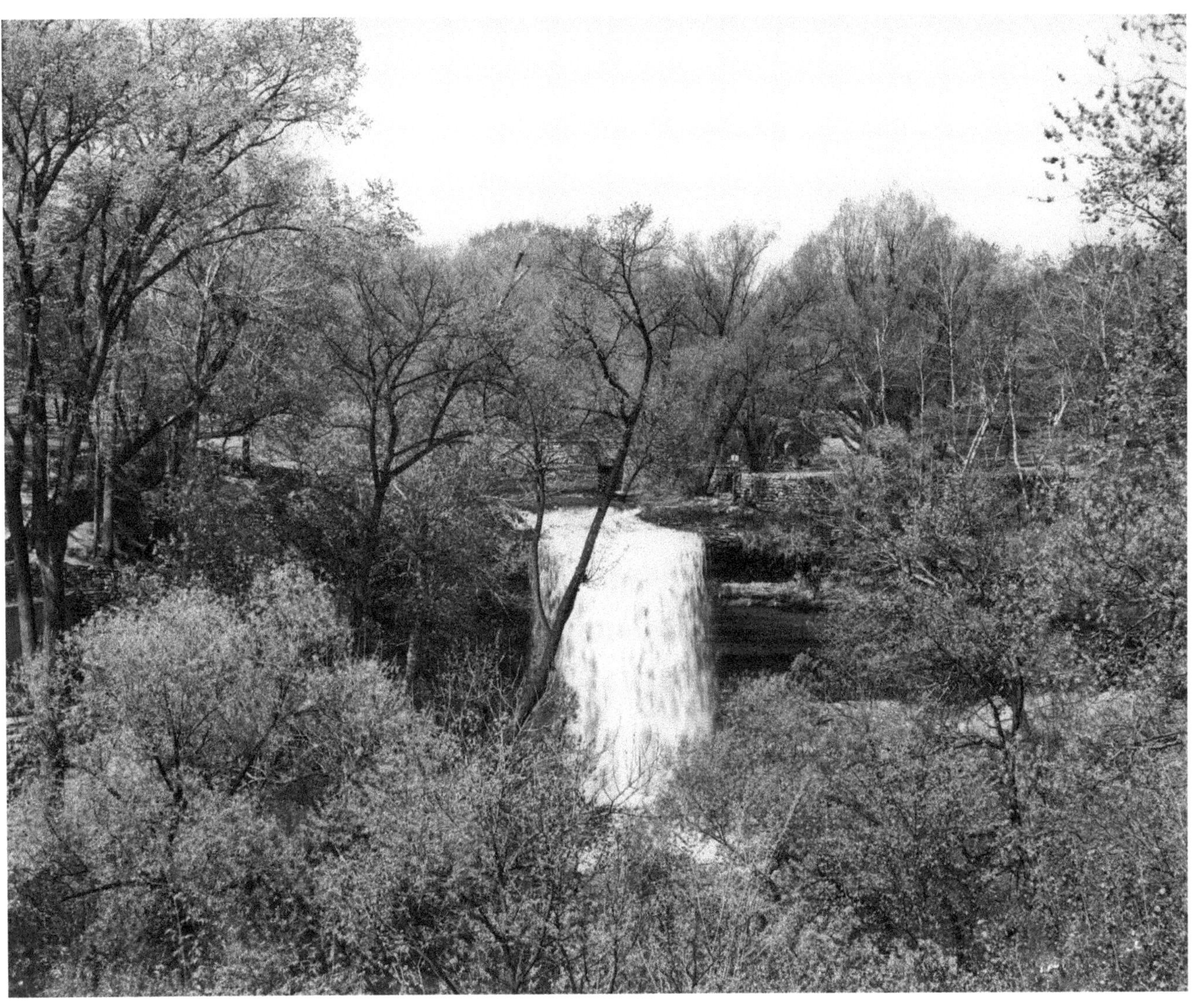

The Swedish Hospital School of Nursing graduated its first class, comprising three women, in 1901. The school had grown considerably by the time these pupils received their caps in the 1940s.

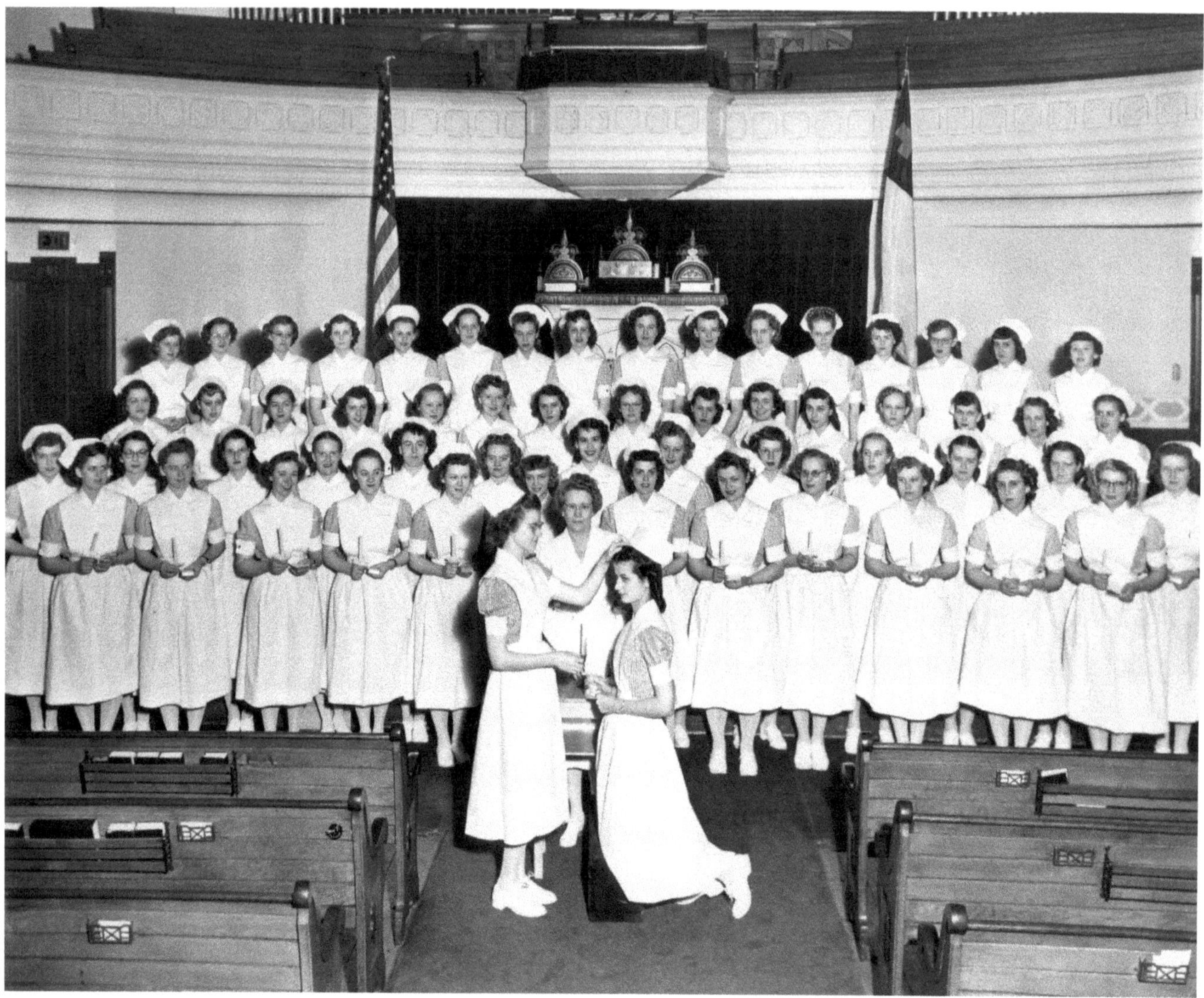

Modern Minneapolis

(1947–1970)

Many Minneapolitans remember the postwar years with great fondness. Shopping centers seemed to sprout on every corner in the 1950s. City parks offered young baby boomers innumerable recreational opportunities, and a proliferation of drive-in restaurants attracted the teenaged crowd. Those with more discerning tastes drove their new Chevrolets downtown to dine at Charlie's Café Exceptionale. In 1958 thousands gathered at the Minneapolis Auditorium to celebrate Minnesota's centennial year.

The decades following World War II ushered in an era of drastic change in the city's physical landscape. Prompted by the Federal-Aid Highway Act of 1956, the Twin Cities metro area added 708 new freeway lane miles between 1959 and 1969. Entire neighborhoods were razed and countless buildings fell before an army of bulldozers as the state constructed I-94, which connected St. Paul to Minneapolis, and I-35W, which linked downtown Minneapolis to the southern suburbs. At the same time the city of Minneapolis turned its attention to the Gateway District. The city decided that the impoverished and crime-ridden neighborhood could not be rehabilitated and chose to level the entire area, which constituted about one-third of downtown Minneapolis. Almost 200 buildings, many of architectural or historical significance, were destroyed in the name of urban renewal.

Less dramatic changes also shaped downtown during this time. The year 1962 marked the introduction of the skyway system. Skyways, enclosed pedestrian walkways that connected downtown buildings, allowed Minneapolitans to move among retail outlets and office buildings in complete comfort regardless of the weather. Later in the decade the city focused its efforts on revitalizing Nicollet Avenue, the city's historic shopping district. The city chose to ban automobile traffic on a twelve-block stretch of Nicollet Avenue that ran through the heart of downtown and worked with local business leaders to renovate many of the stores. The new Nicollet Mall opened to great fanfare in 1968. The mall gained national attention when it appeared in the opening sequence of the Mary Tyler Moore show in 1972.

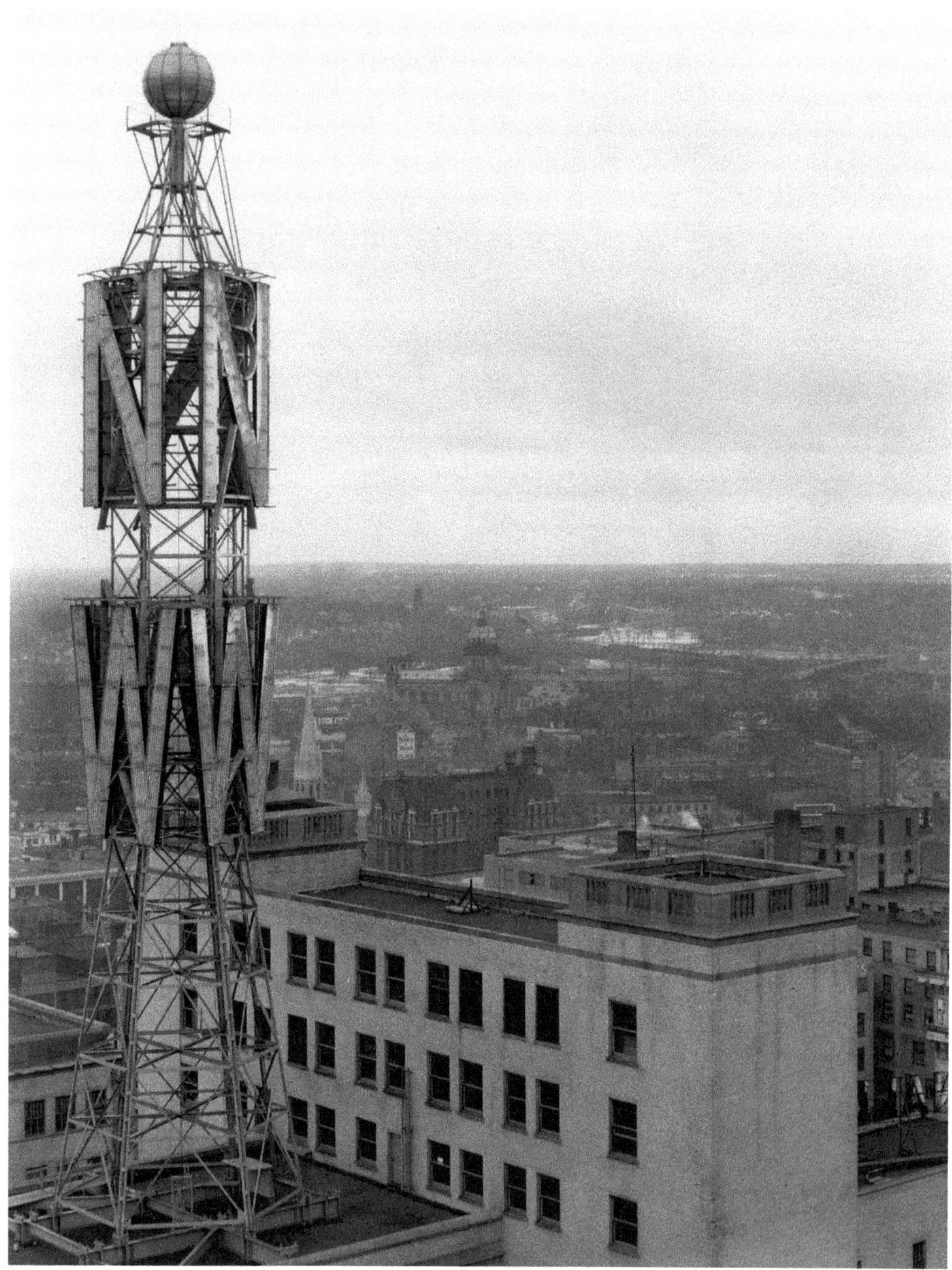

In 1949 the Northwest Bank Building installed a ten-foot sphere, the Weatherball, on its roof. Minneapolis residents learned that when the ball glowed red the weather would turn warm, that the color green indicated no change in the temperature, that white predicted a cold front, and that blinking lights signaled impending precipitation.

A Minneapolis fire crew dispatcher listens to a message over his two-way radio in 1950. Two-way radio consoles, first used by the Minneapolis fire department in 1946, enabled firefighters to respond to alarms more quickly and to call for backup without delay.

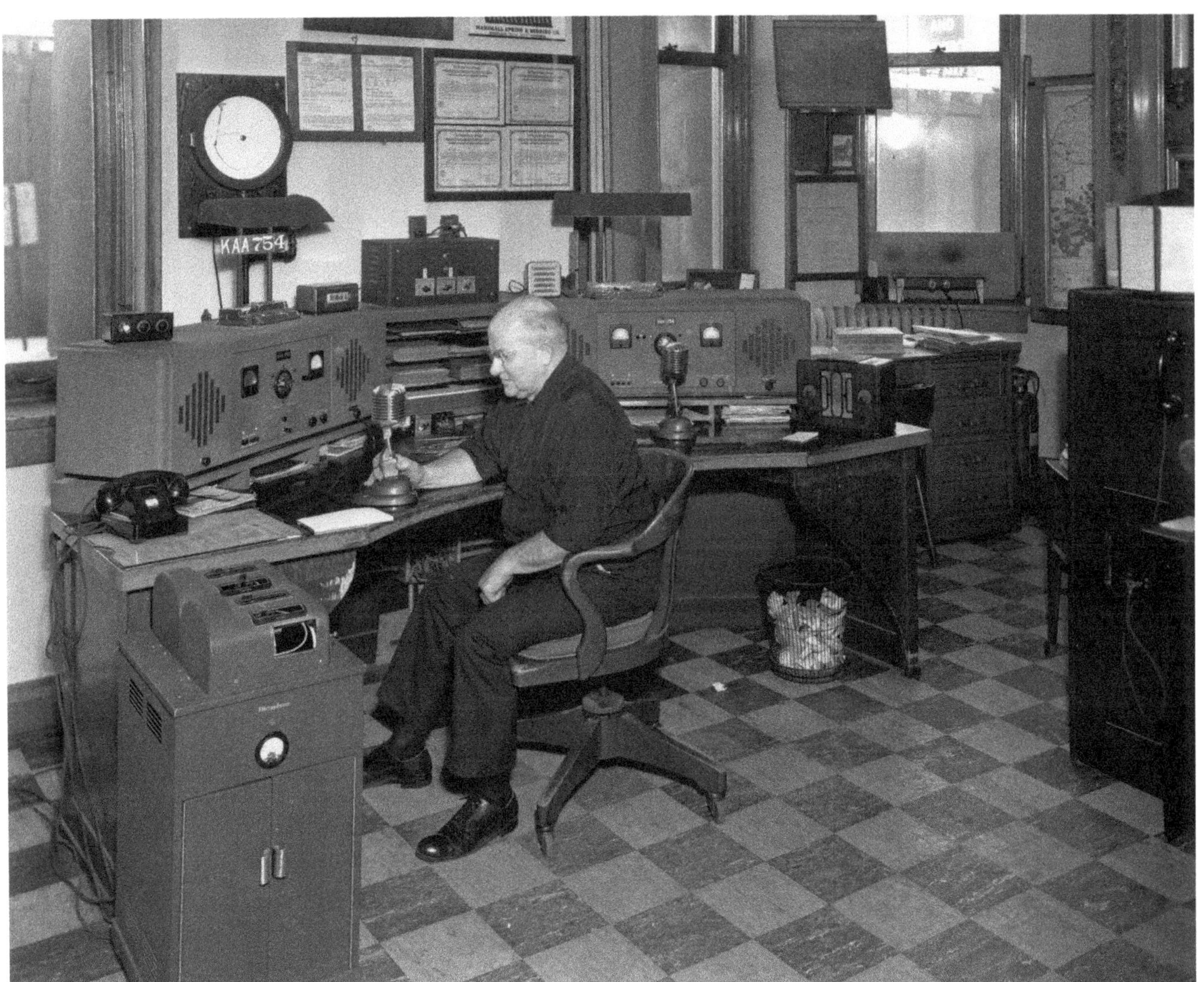

On March 7, 1950, a Northwest Airlines Martin 202 crashed into a house on Minnehaha Parkway when it lost control while trying to land in a blizzard. Two people in the house and thirteen airline passengers died in the incident.

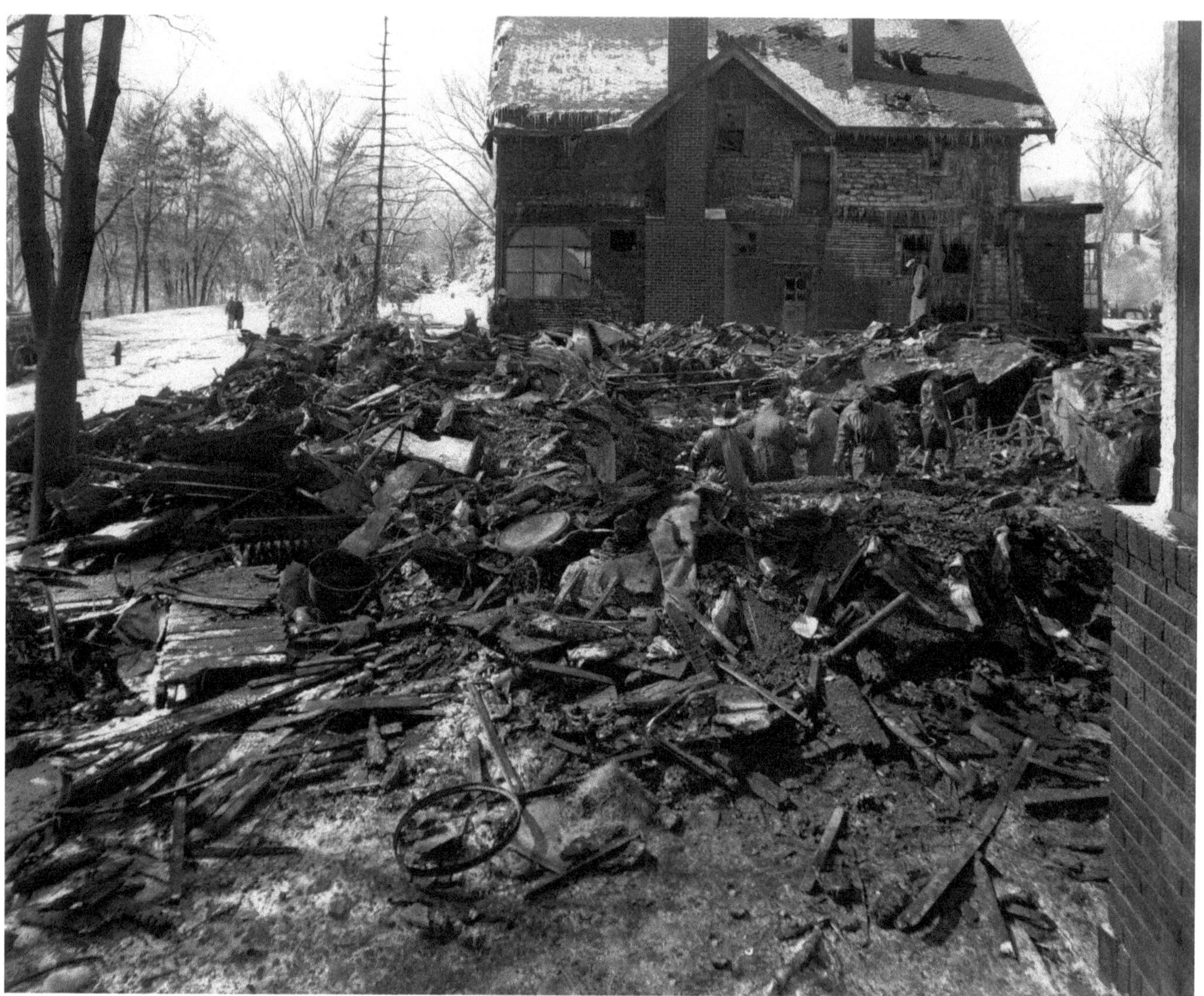

The Minneapolis Public Library opened its first branch at 1834 Emerson Avenue North in 1890. The North Branch Library, seen here in 1950, served north Minneapolis until the high cost of needed renovations led to the building's closure in 1977.

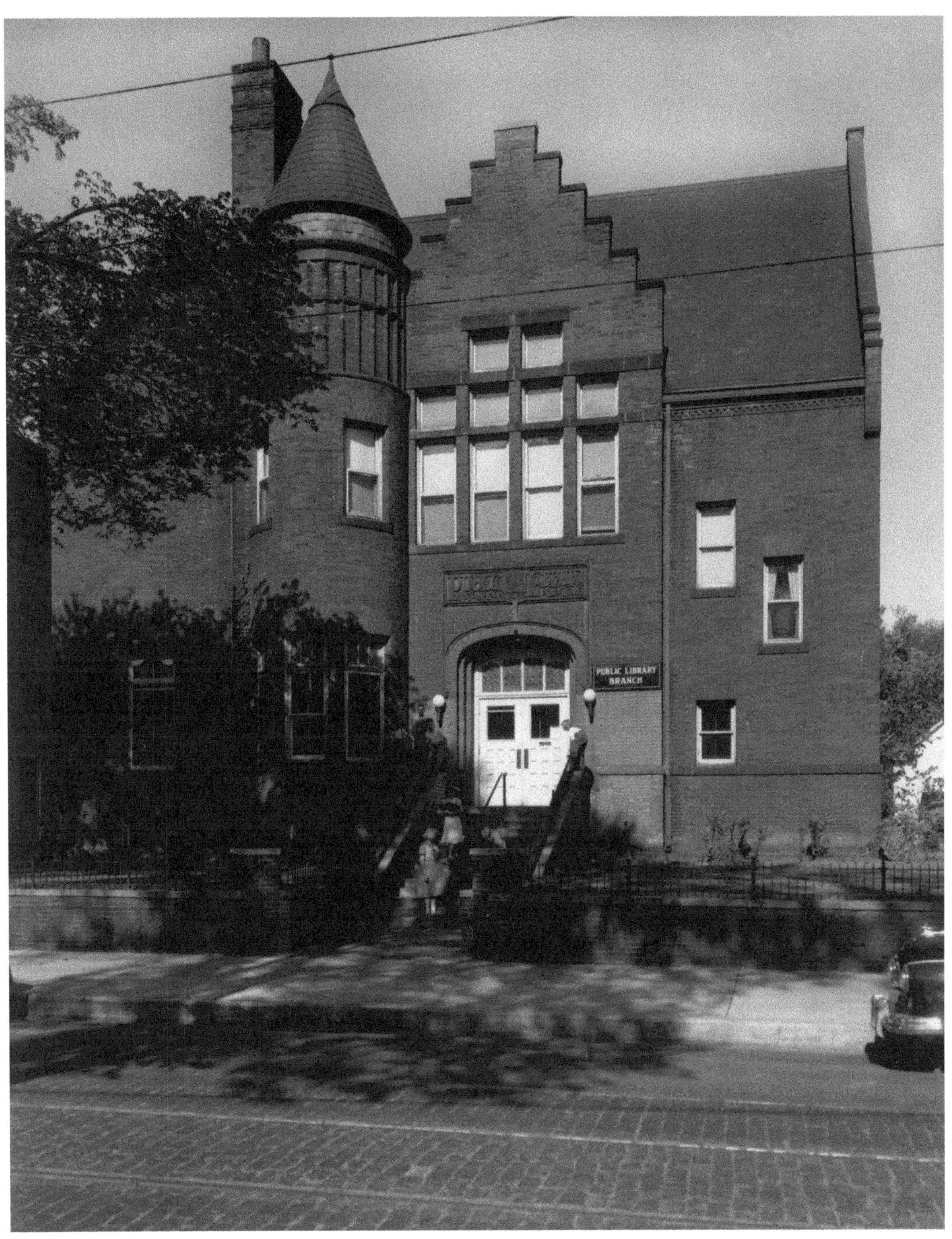

New cars adorn the showroom of Anderson Chevrolet Company, 4208 East Lake Street, in 1950.

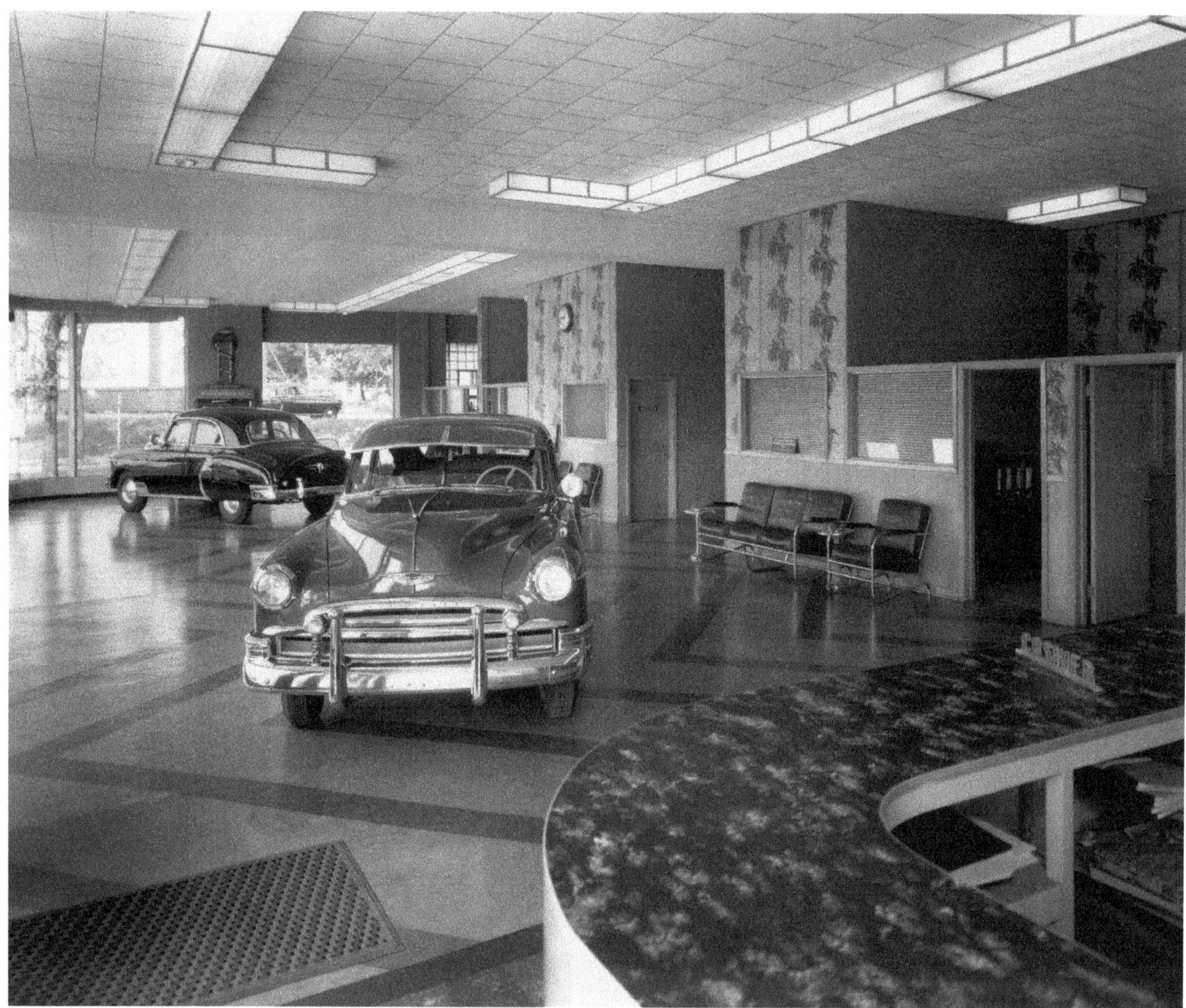

Football players pose at North Commons Park, the largest park on the city's north side, in 1950. By the 1950s the park boasted two football fields, eight baseball and softball fields, five tennis courts, a hockey rink, and a figure skating area.

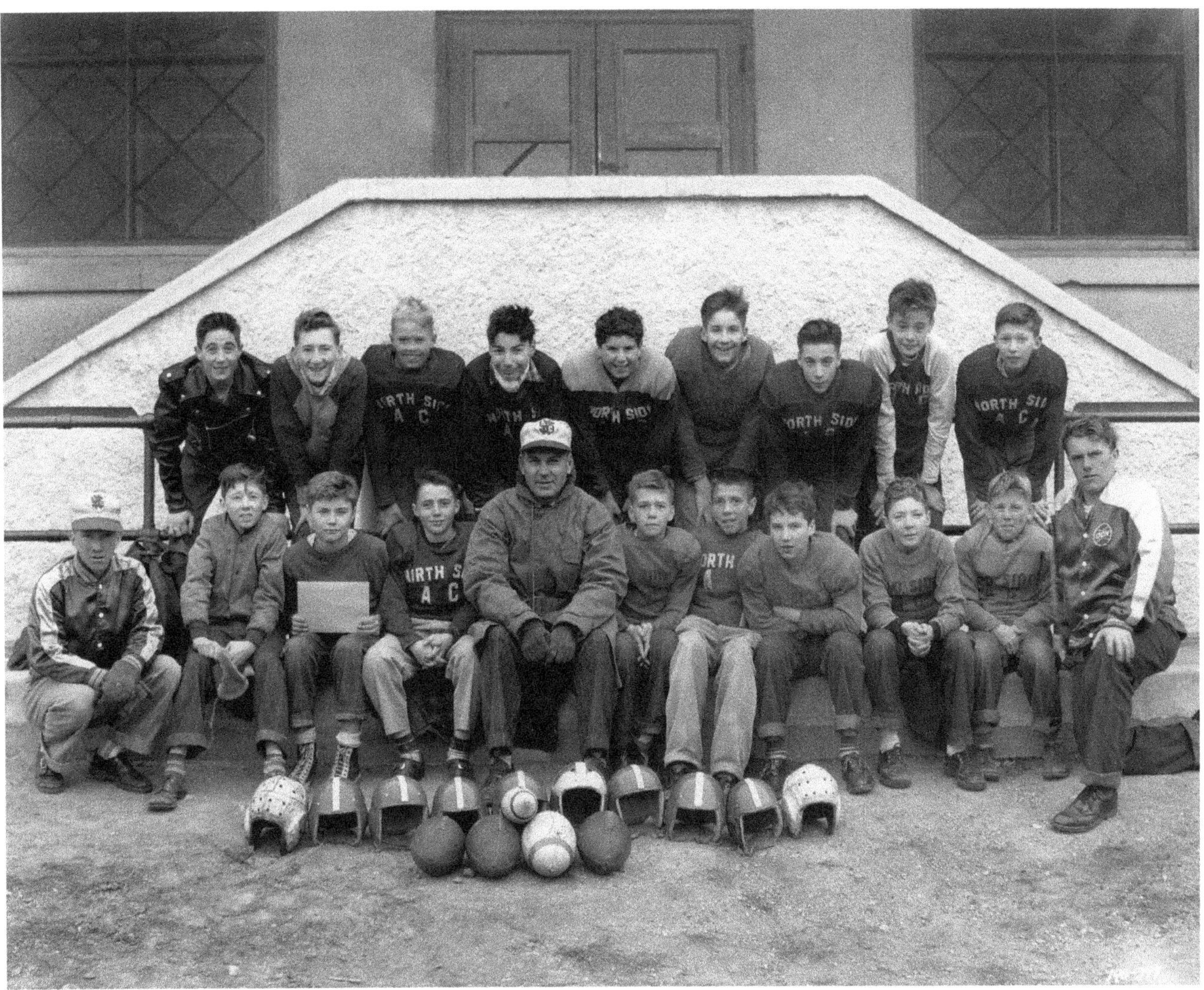

The Greek Orthodox Church has maintained a continual presence in Minneapolis since 1900. St. Mary's Greek Orthodox Church, located at 2947 Tenth Avenue South, is pictured here in 1951. The growing community moved to a new building near Lake Calhoun six years later.

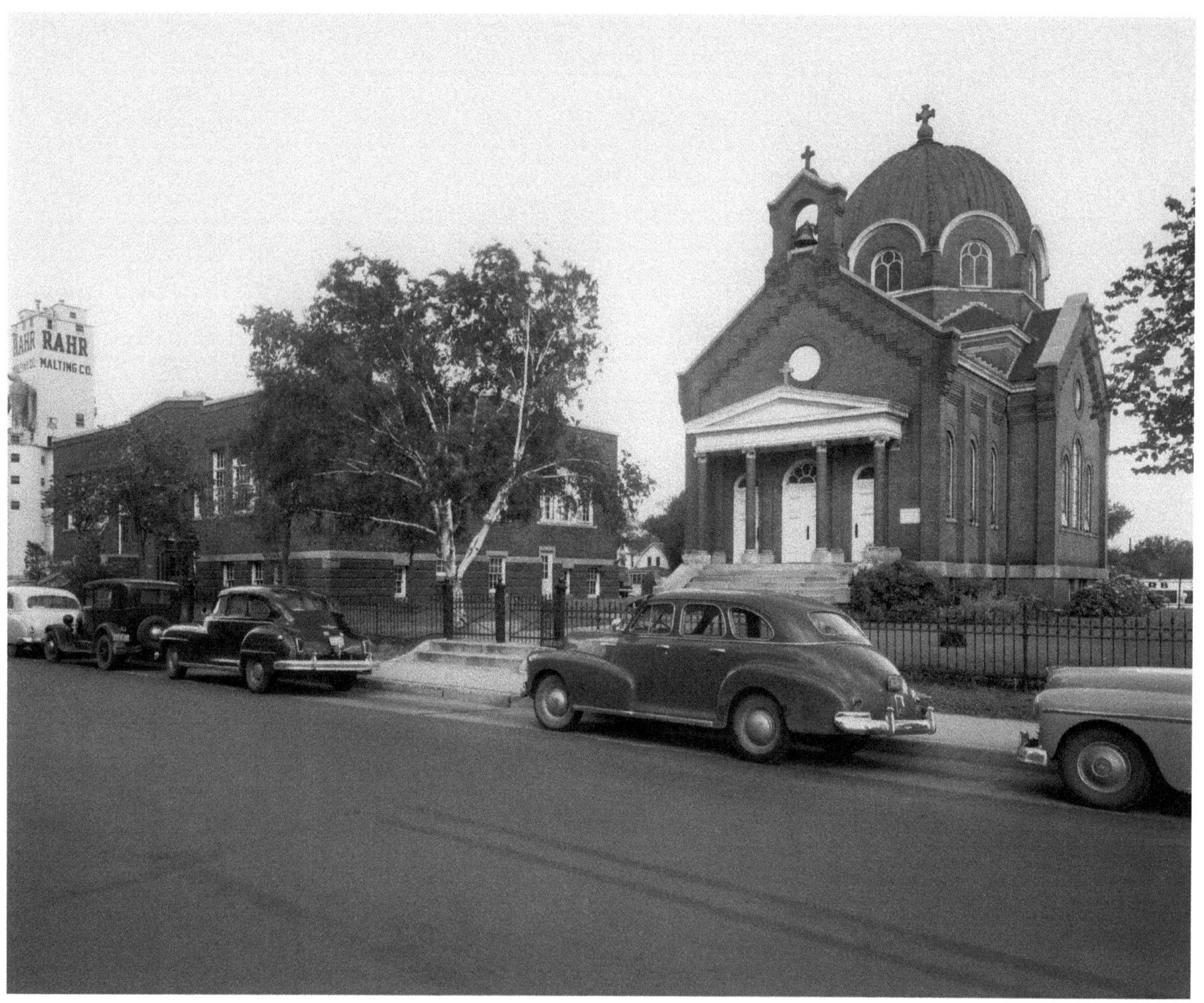

In a scene very familiar to Minneapolitans, snow drifts cover sidewalks and blanket streets during a late spring storm in 1951.

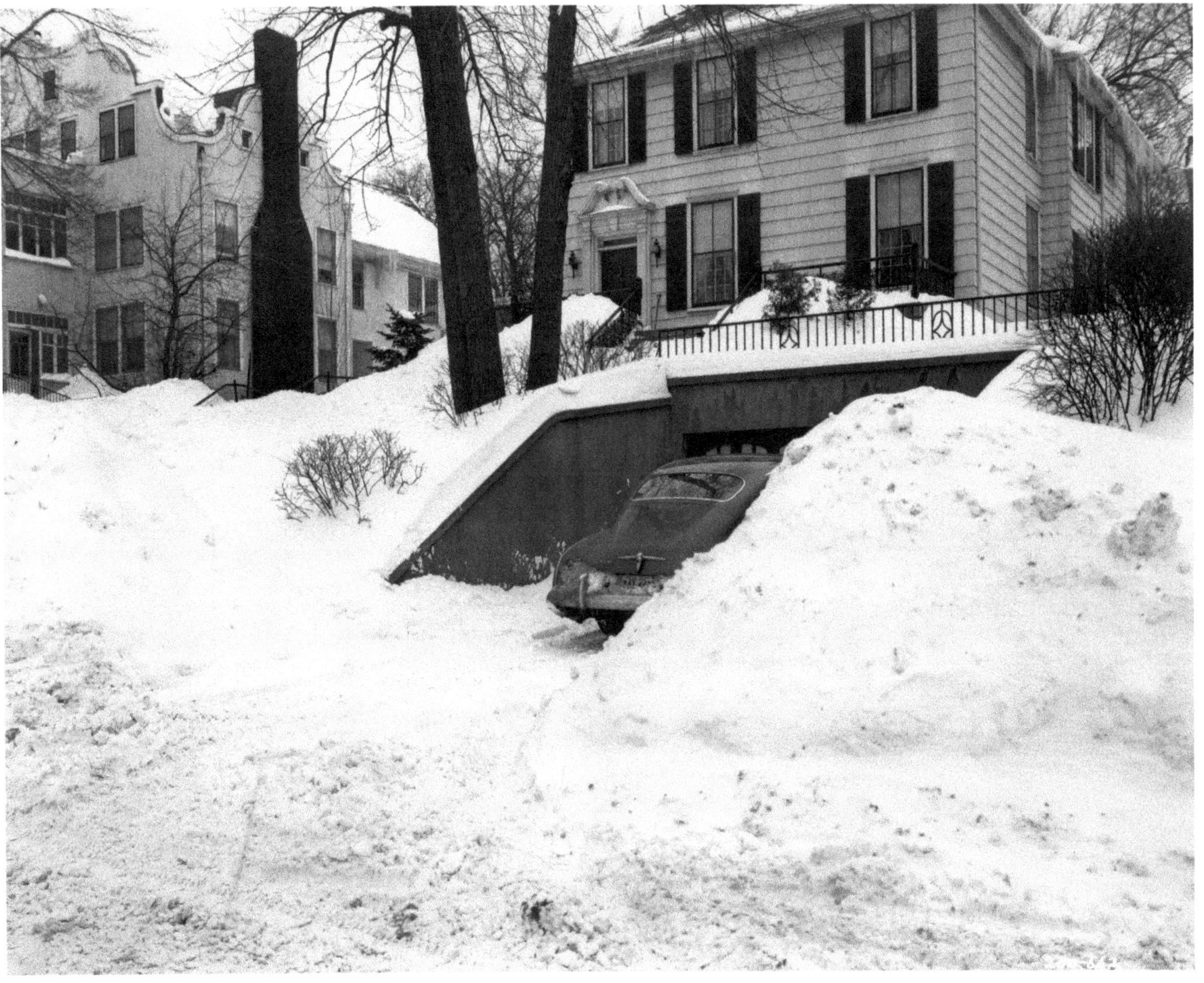

This image of downtown Minneapolis, as seen from Loring Park, was captured in 1951.

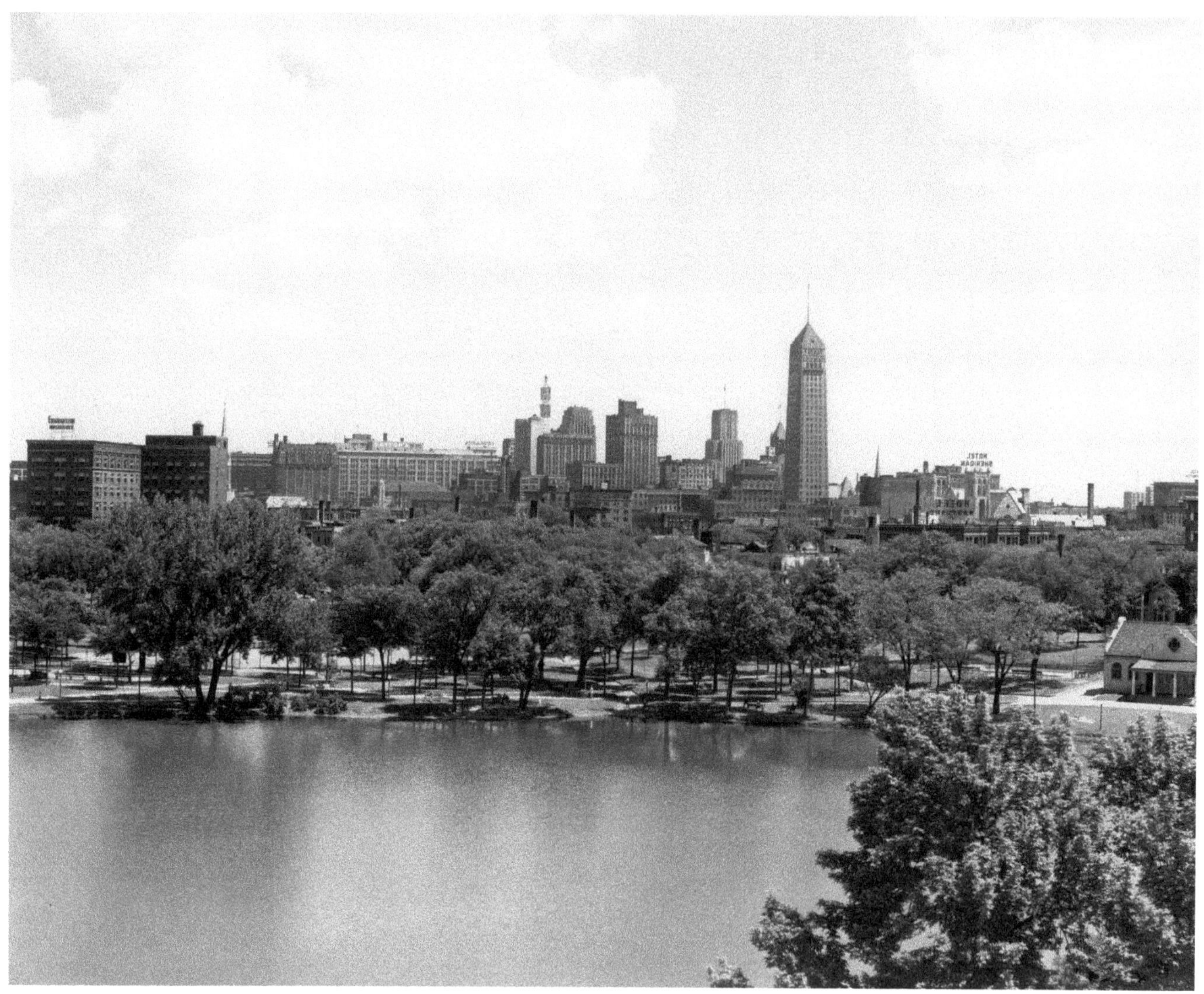

Since 1872 Lakewood Cemetery has served as the final resting place for the city's most prominent businessmen, politicians, and entertainers. The cemetery features an exquisite domed chapel, seen here in 1953, designed by prominent Minneapolis architect Harry Wild Jones.

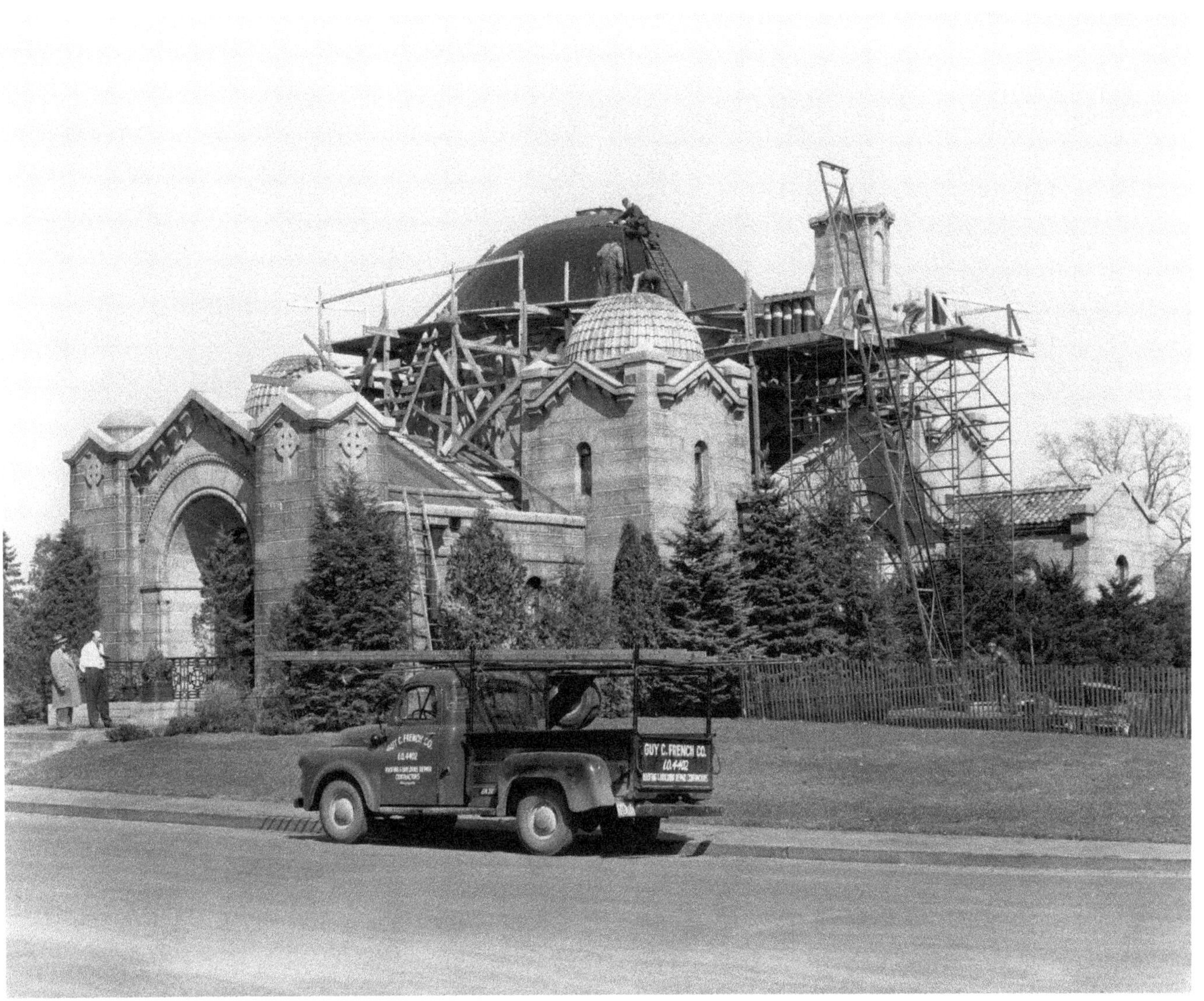

Peeling carrots at the William Howe Smith residence, 3140 West Calhoun Boulevard, on February 5, 1952.

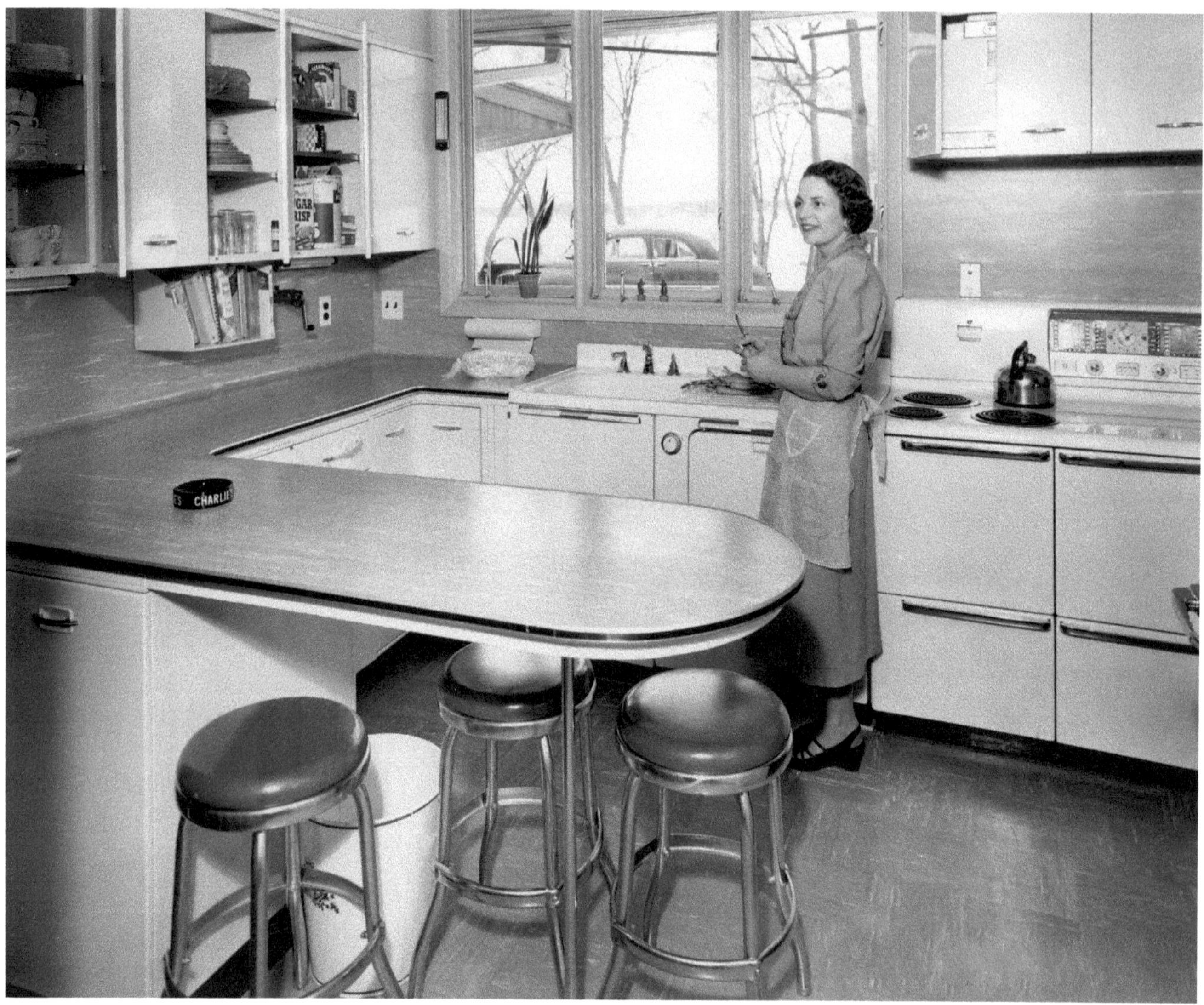

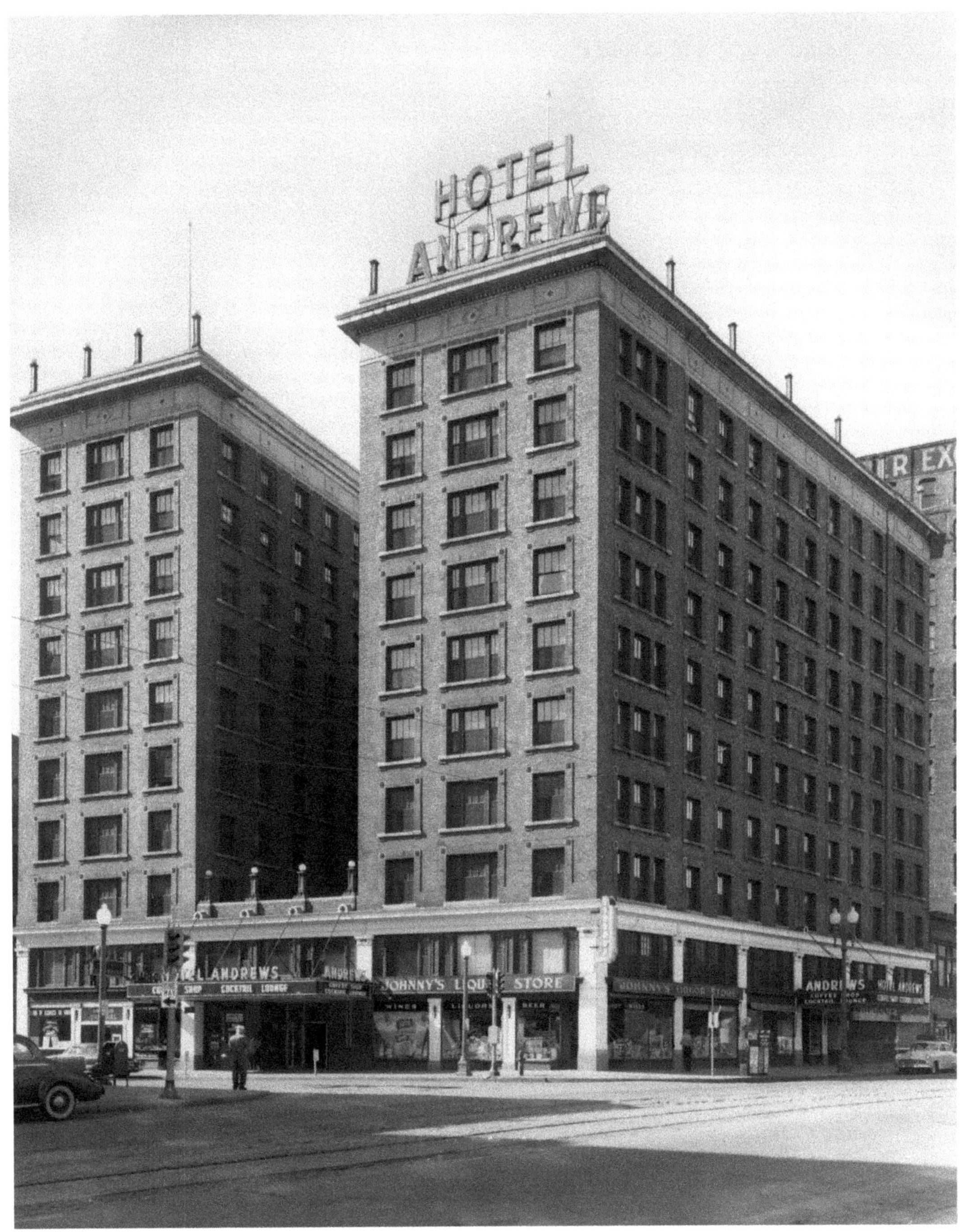

The Andrews Hotel, located at Fourth Street and Hennepin Avenue and seen here in 1953, catered to business travelers. The hotel first established a presence in Minneapolis in 1912. In 1986 this building succumbed to the wrecking ball as part of the city's efforts to revitalize downtown.

The intersection of Hennepin Avenue and Oak Grove Street is captured on a December day in 1954. The Walker Art Center is the building on the right.

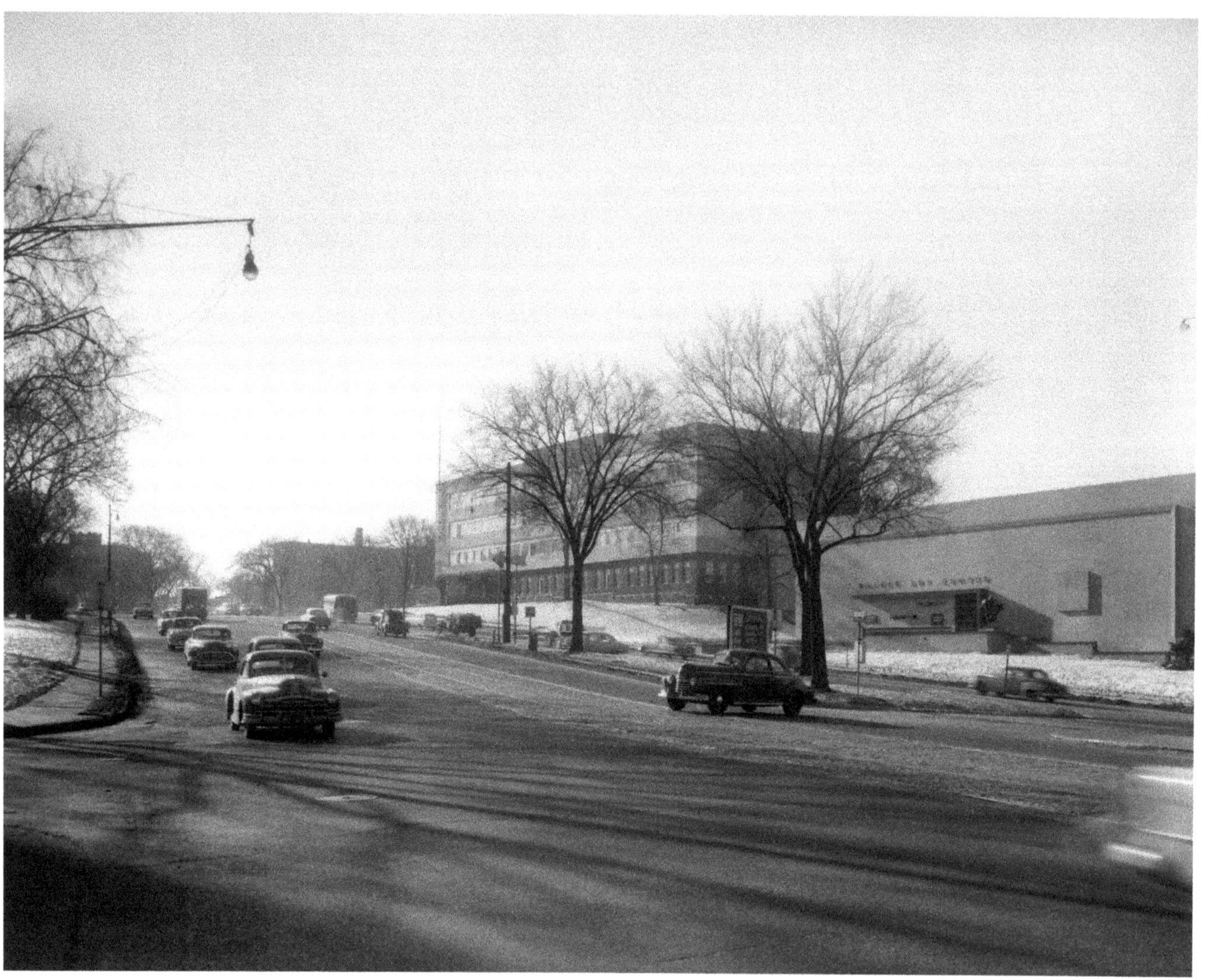

Workers oversee the assembly line at the Ry-Krisp cracker factory in southeast Minneapolis in 1956, six years before the company was bought out by Ralston-Purina.

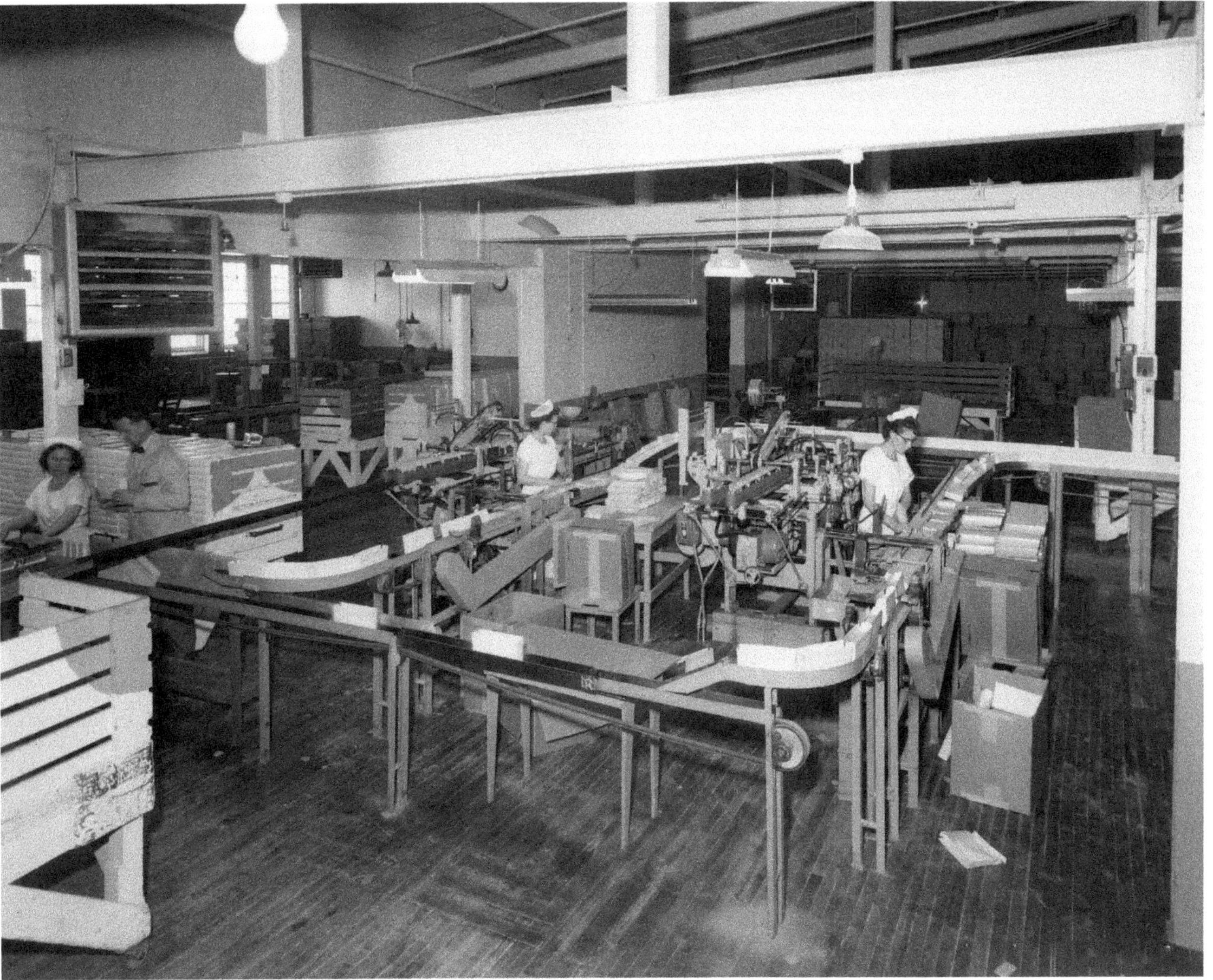

Cedar Lake, named for the eastern red cedars that lined its shores, is shown here in 1955. A relatively small lake located north of Lake Calhoun and west of Lake of the Isles, it has served as a popular picnic and swimming destination since the early 1900s.

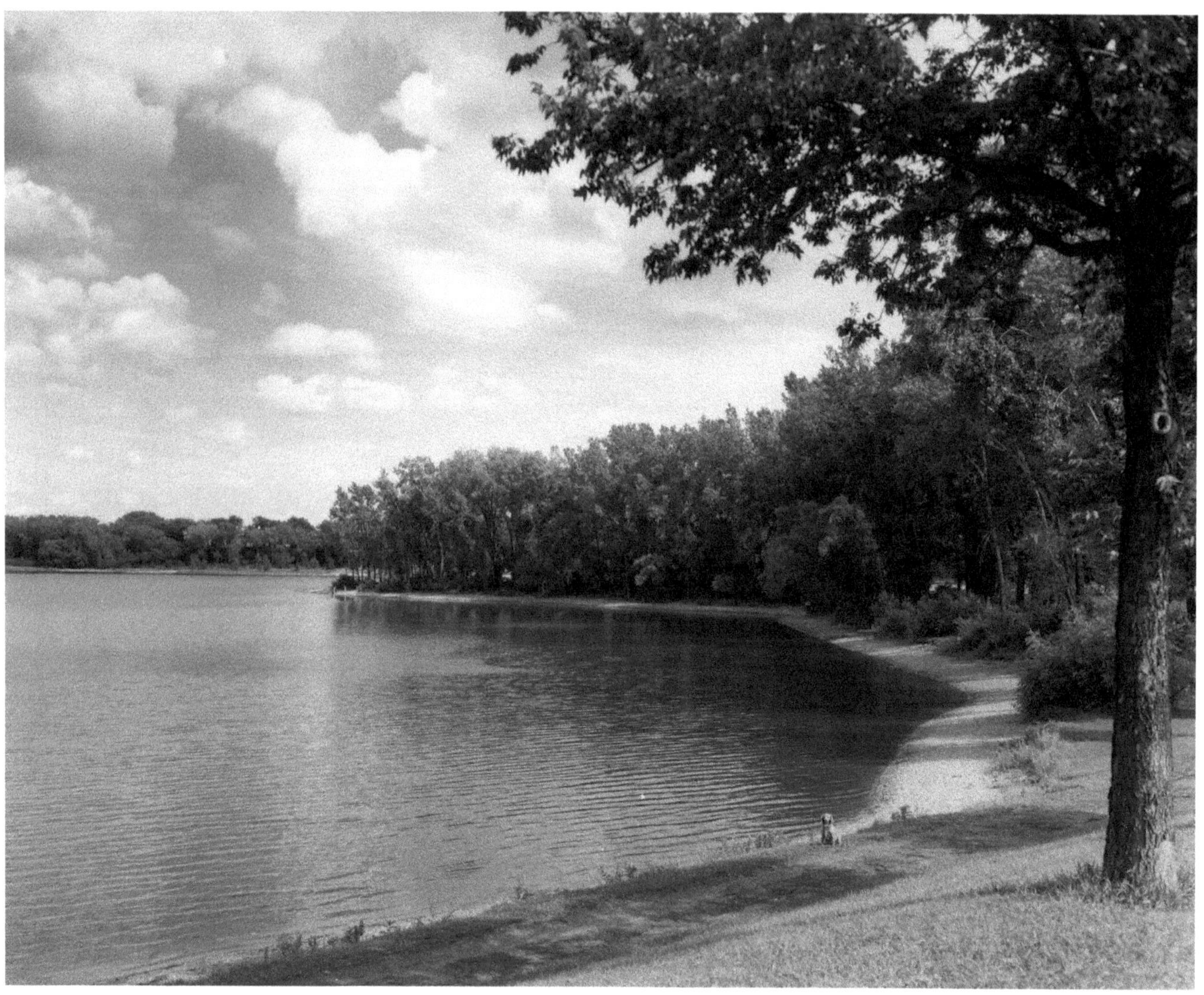

The Dunwoody Institute opened in 1915 with the stated purpose of providing "instruction in the industrial and mechanical arts . . . without distinction on account of race, color, or religious prejudice." Here a Dunwoody Institute baking class meets in 1955.

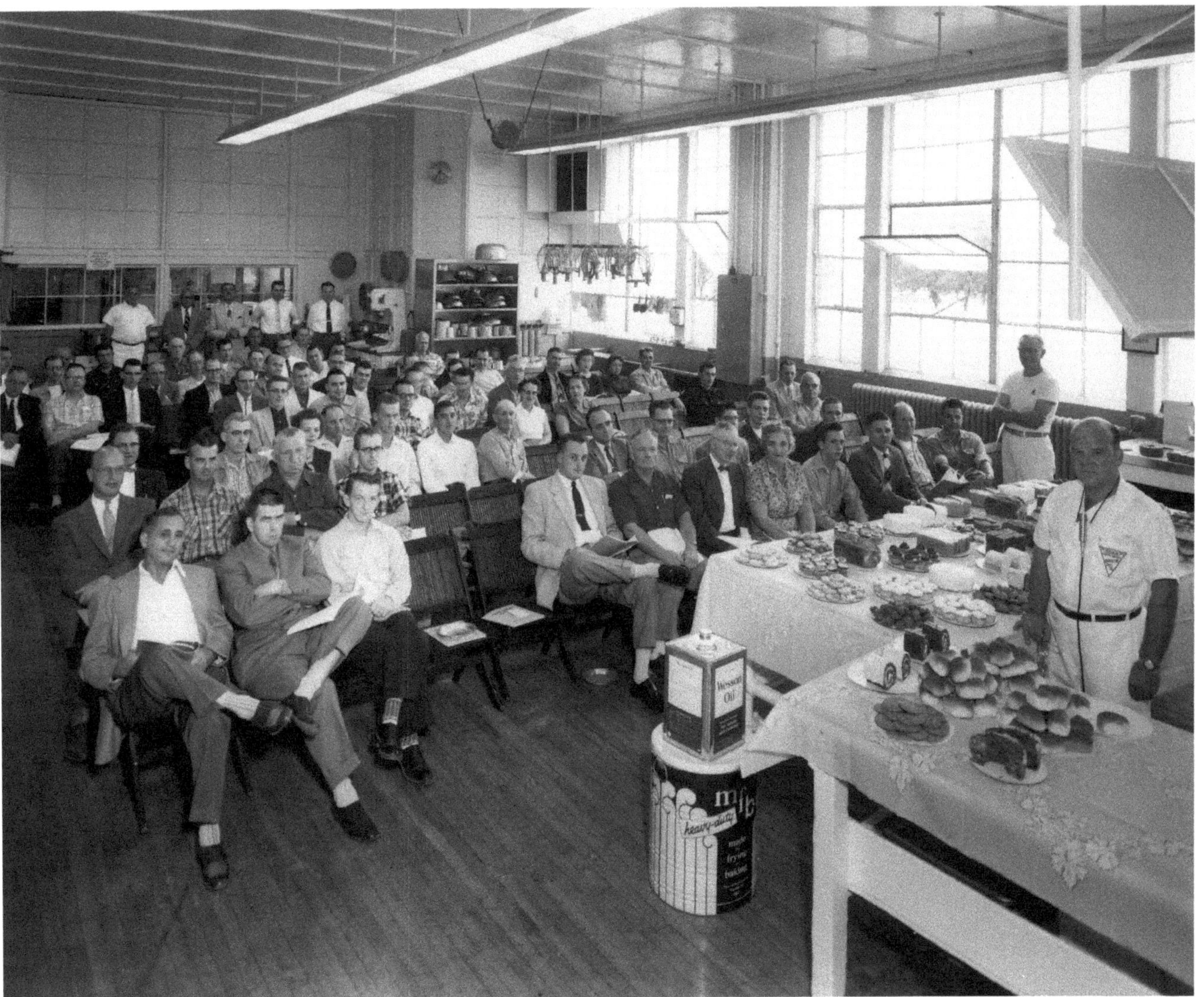

The Eastgate Shopping Center, located at the corner of Central Avenue and University Avenue Southeast, is seen as it appeared on May 28, 1956. In 2005 developers razed the shopping center and replaced it with condominiums and a high-end grocery store.

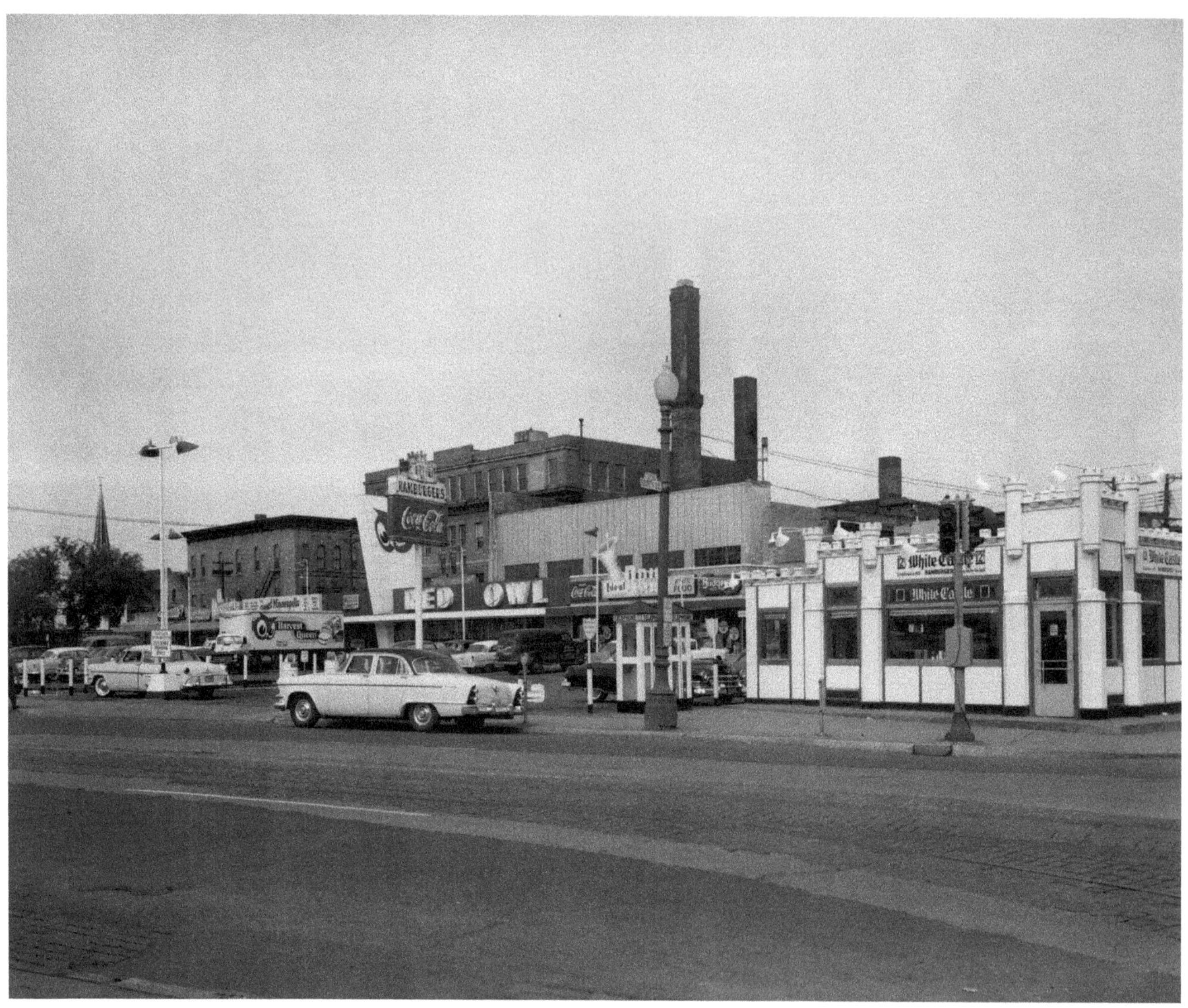

Delivery men and a waitress pose in front of the Ford Bridge Drive-In, located at 4556 Forty-sixth Avenue South, in the summer of 1956.

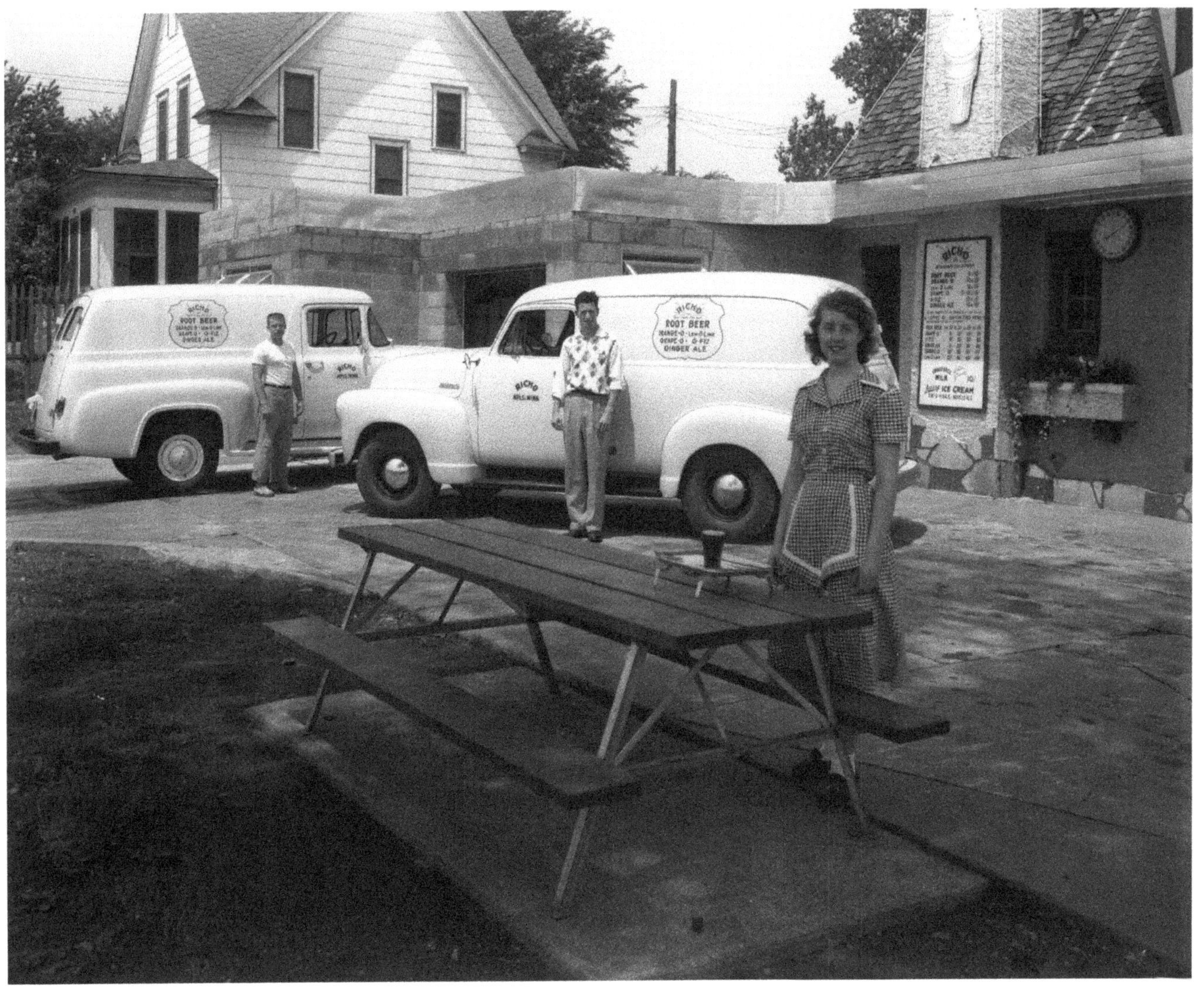

Archbishop John Ireland established St. Bridget's Catholic Church in 1915 and seven years later the Sisters of St. Benedict opened the parish's school. In 1930 the sisters moved to this convent, located at 3840 Emerson Avenue North and seen here in 1957.

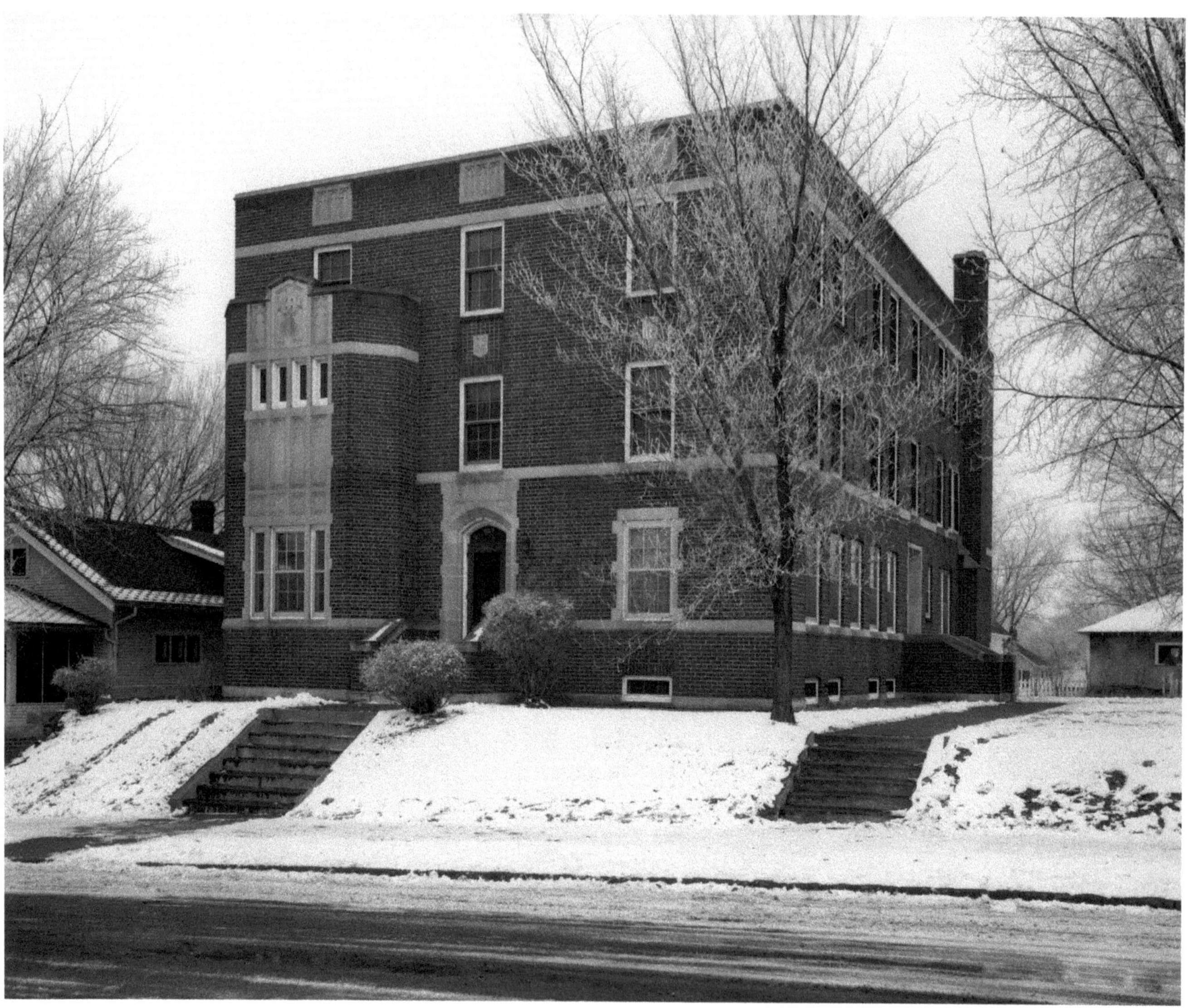

Visitors explore an exhibit at the Minneapolis Auditorium during the Minnesota state centennial celebration in 1958.

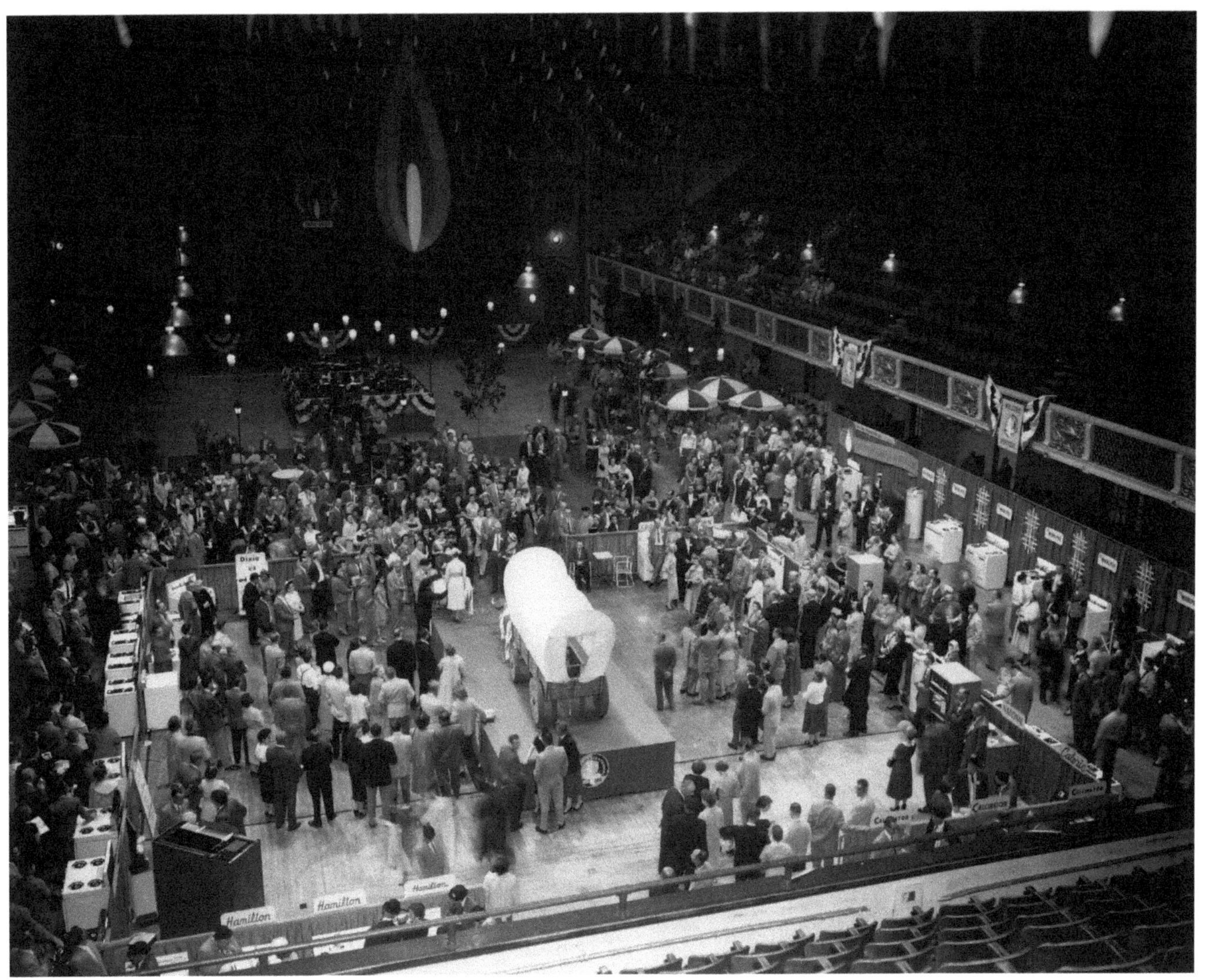

After fire destroyed the Minneapolis General Electric Company's power plant near St. Anthony Falls in 1911, the company decided to rebuild farther from the milling district. The result was the Riverside Generating Plant, which opened in 1912 and is depicted here in 1959.

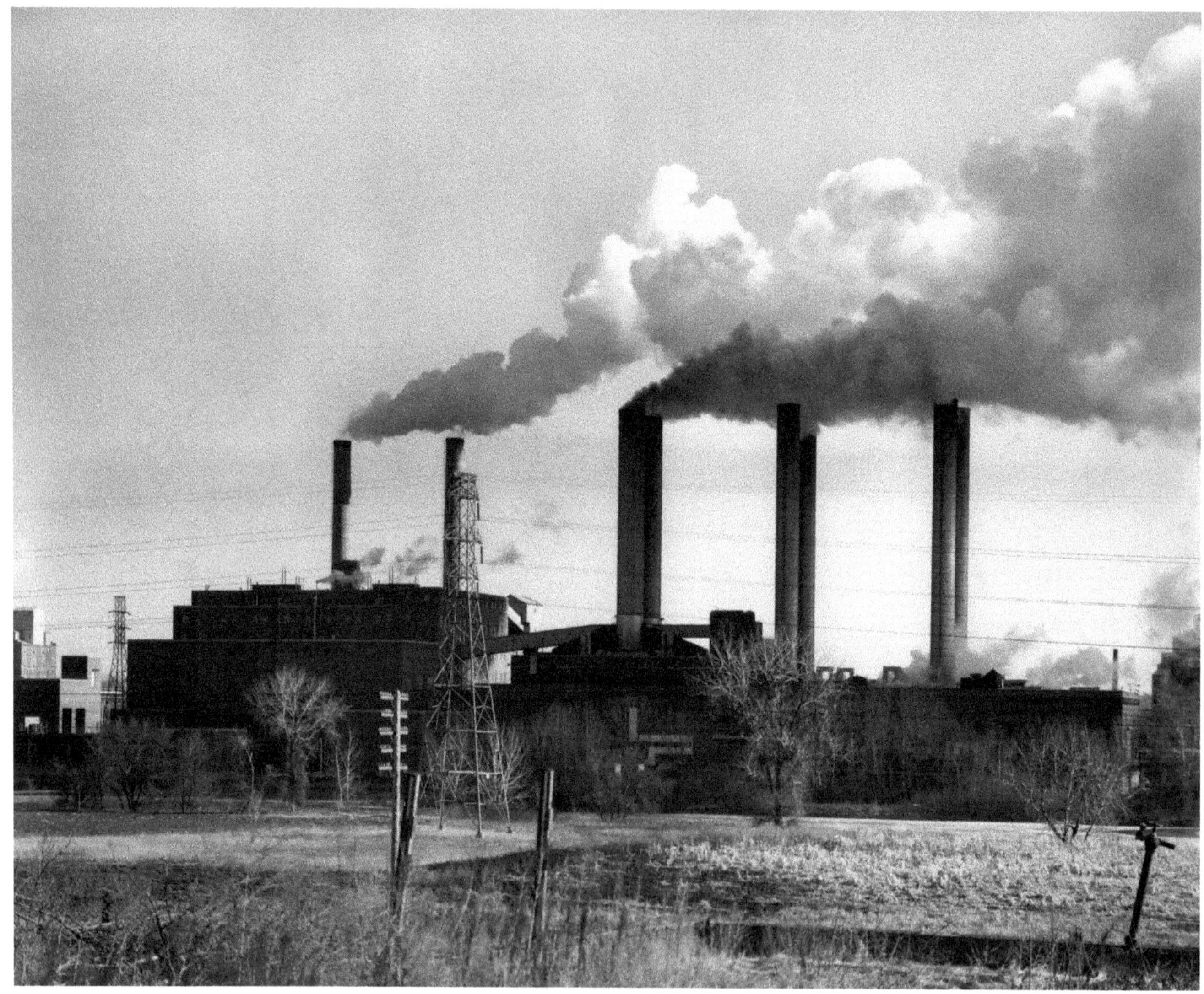

Charlie's Café Exceptionale, seen here in 1961, first opened its doors in 1933. In 1958 the restaurant moved to a new location at 701 Fourth Avenue South. Diners ate in one of four dining rooms, all decorated in oak but each with a distinct personality.

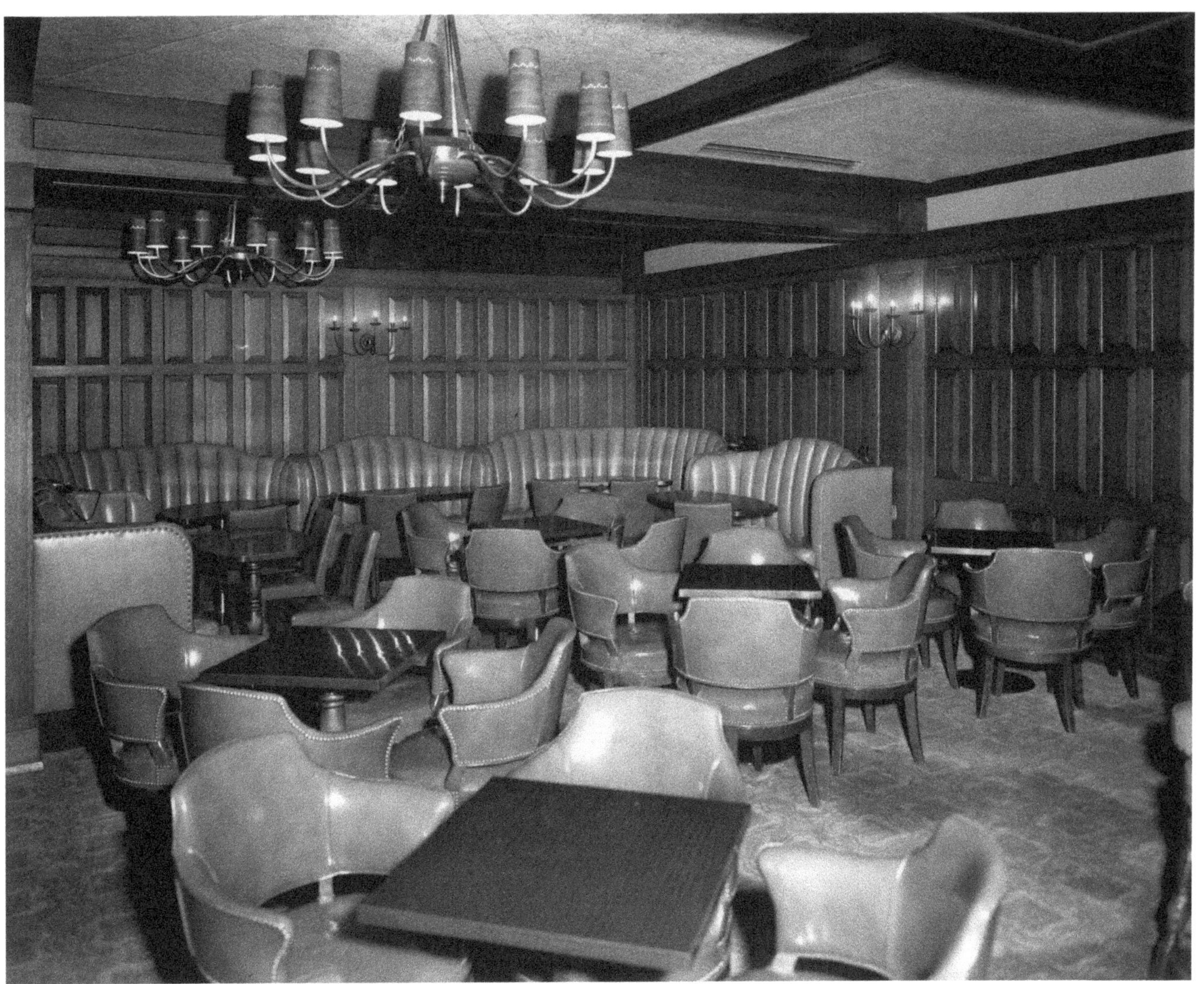

In 1967 the city converted Nicollet Avenue into a twelve-block pedestrian mall, one of the first in the nation. This shot captures the new Nicollet Mall at Tenth Street looking north.

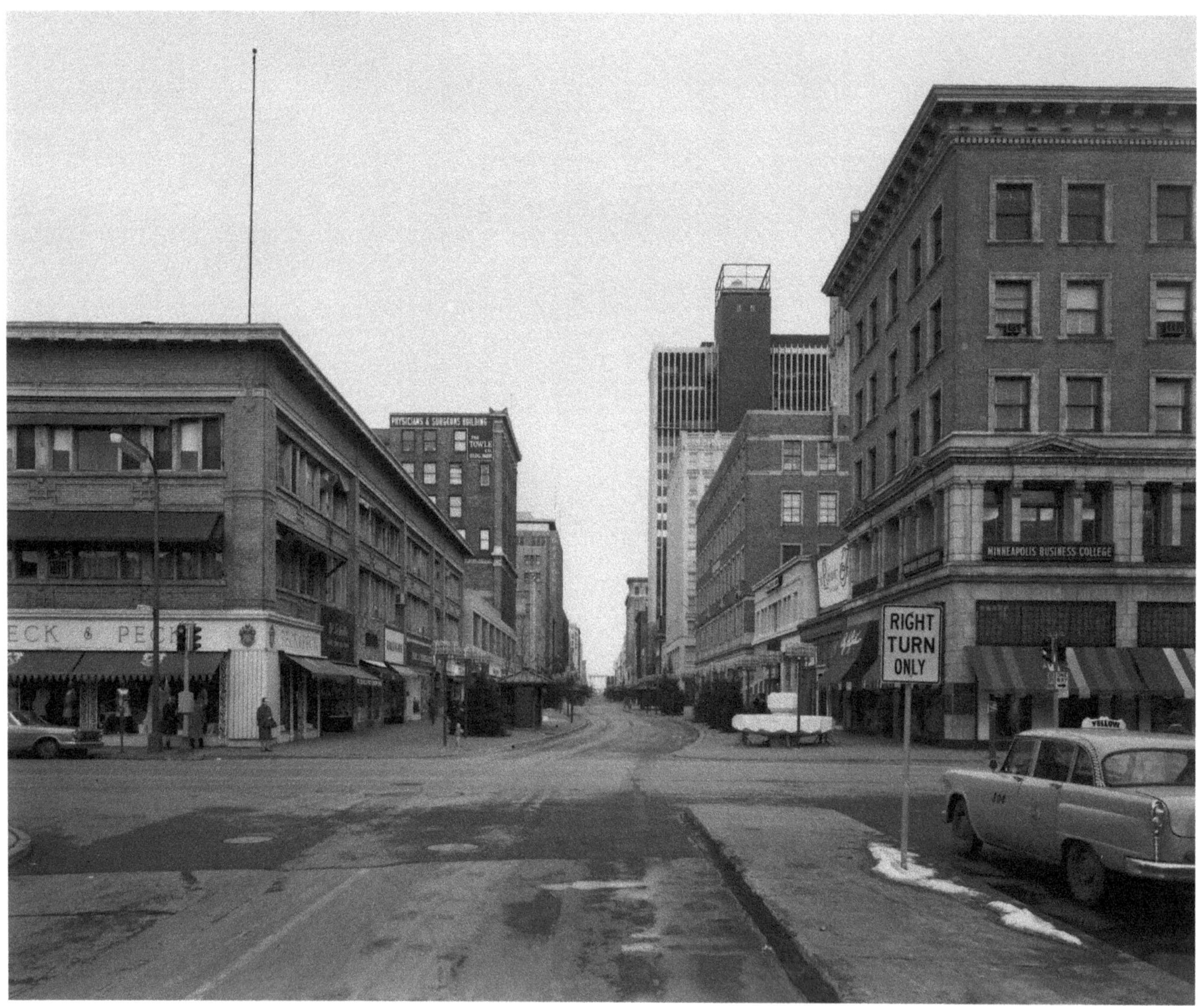

The construction of the Twin Cities interstate system commenced in 1962 and utterly changed the landscape of both Minneapolis and St. Paul. This photograph captures the construction of Interstate 94, which now links the two cities, near Blaisdell Avenue in Minneapolis in 1966.

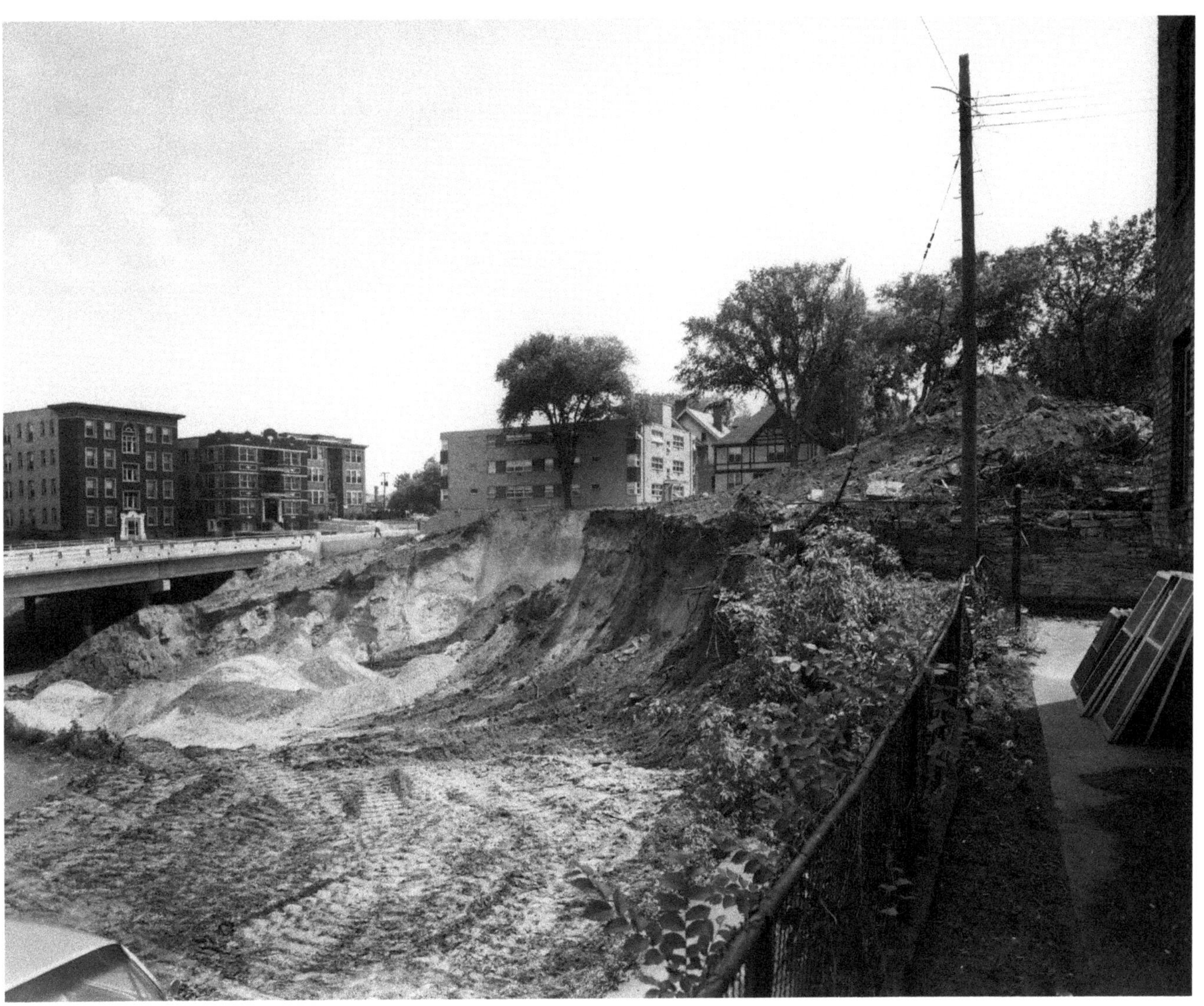

Notes on the Photographs

These notes, listed by page number, attempt to include all aspects known of the photographs. Each of the photographs is identified by the page number, photograph's title or description, photographer and collection, archive, and call or box number when applicable. Although every attempt was made to collect all available data, in some cases complete data was unavailable due to the age and condition of some of the photographs and records.

ii Stone Arch Bridge
Library of Congress, Prints & Photographs Division
LC-DIG-det-4a18465

vi Hotel Leamington
Minnesota Historical Society
Norton & Peel Collection
281065, Negative NP281065

x Hennepin Avenue
Minneapolis Public Library
Minneapolis Collection
m4864

2 First National Bank
Minneapolis Public Library
Minneapolis Collection
m0872

3 Courthouse
Minneapolis Public Library
Minneapolis Collection
m0430

4 Early Streetcars
Minneapolis Public Library
Minneapolis Collection
m0135

5 Academy of Music
Minneapolis Public Library
Minneapolis Collection
m0091

6 Hot-air Balloon
Minneapolis Public Library
Minneapolis Collection
m0569

7 Exposition Building
Minneapolis Public Library
Minneapolis Collection
m5139

8 Donaldson's Store
Minneapolis Public Library
Minneapolis Collection
m3901

9 Milling District
Minneapolis Public Library
Minneapolis Collection
m5628

10 Riverside Mission
Minneapolis Public Library
Minneapolis Collection
m5615

11 Lake Harriet Pavilion
Minneapolis Public Library
Minneapolis Collection
m0903

12 City Market
Minneapolis Public Library
Minneapolis Collection
m1222

13 City Hall
Minneapolis Public Library
Minneapolis Collection
m0074

14 Lake Harriet
Minneapolis Public Library
Minneapolis Collection
m0902

15 Vine Place
Minneapolis Public Library
Minneapolis Collection
m0101

16 Nicollet Avenue
Minneapolis Public Library
Minneapolis Collection
m0606

17 Hennepin Methodist
Minneapolis Public Library
Minneapolis Collection
m0942

18 Savings Bank
Minneapolis Public Library
Minneapolis Collection
m0587

19 Horsedrawn Streetcar
Minneapolis Public Library
Minneapolis Collection
m0808

20 Edina Mills
Minneapolis Public Library
Minneapolis Collection
m5620

21 Light Mast
Minneapolis Public Library
Minneapolis Collection
m3836

22 Brackett Block
Minneapolis Public Library
Minneapolis Collection
m0084

23 Circus Parade
Minneapolis Public Library
Minneapolis Collection
m0099

24 Academy of Music Fire
Minneapolis Public Library
Minneapolis Collection
m4928

25 Milling District
Minneapolis Public Library
Minneapolis Collection
m0465

26 Steamer
Minneapolis Public Library
Minneapolis Collection
m5639

27 INDUSTRIAL MINNEAPOLIS
Minneapolis Public Library
Minneapolis Collection
m5626

28 LIFE INSURANCE BLDG.
Minneapolis Public Library
Minneapolis Collection
m5632

29 SUTHERLAND'S DENTAL OFFICE
Minneapolis Public Library
Minneapolis Collection
m0104

30 FIRST PUBLIC LIBRARY
Minneapolis Public Library
Minneapolis Collection
m0717

31 POWDERHORN PARK
Minneapolis Public Library
Minneapolis Collection
m5613

32 FIFTH STREET
Minneapolis Public Library
Minneapolis Collection
m1172

33 BATHHOUSE
Minneapolis Public Library
Minneapolis Collection
m1769b

34 LOWRY'S BLUFF
Minneapolis Public Library
Minneapolis Collection
m0644

36 FAIR OAKS
Minneapolis Public Library
Minneapolis Collection
m0023

37 BOUTELL BROTHERS
Minneapolis Public Library
Minneapolis Collection
m0552

38 ADMIRAL SCHLEY
Minneapolis Public Library
Minneapolis Collection
m3700

39 ELKS PARADING
Library of Congress, Prints & Photographs Division
LC-USZ6-144

40 MUNICIPAL BUILDING
Minneapolis Public Library
Minneapolis Collection
m0515

41 GRAND OPERA HOUSE
Minneapolis Public Library
Minneapolis Collection
m4104

42 POLICE CAPTAIN QUALEY
Minneapolis Public Library
Minneapolis Collection
m3812

43 NEWSPAPER ROW
Minneapolis Public Library
Minneapolis Collection
m5720

44 HARVEST FESTIVAL
Minneapolis Public Library
Minneapolis Collection
m0348

45 BOHEMIAN FLATS
Minneapolis Public Library
Minneapolis Collection
m1829

46 FIRST STREET RAILS
Minneapolis Public Library
Minneapolis Collection
m0674

47 CHRISTMAS LAKE
Minneapolis Public Library
Minneapolis Collection
m0714

48 BANK OF MINNEAPOLIS
Minneapolis Public Library
Minneapolis Collection
m0518

49 SPANISH-AMERICAN WAR VETERANS
Minneapolis Public Library
Minneapolis Collection
m0124

50 ANDRUS BUILDING
Minneapolis Public Library
Minneapolis Collection
m0814

51 DOWNTOWN
Minneapolis Public Library
Minneapolis Collection
m4485

52 CHILDREN AT VETERANS HOME
Minneapolis Public Library
Minneapolis Collection
br1108

54 BAND AT FOOTBALL GAME
Minneapolis Public Library
Minneapolis Collection
br0124

55 PARADE FLOAT
Minneapolis Public Library
Minneapolis Collection
br0087

56 OPERA HOUSE
Minneapolis Public Library
Minneapolis Collection
br0109

57 STREETCAR COMPLETION
Minneapolis Public Library
Minneapolis Collection
br0218

58 HOME INTERIOR
Minneapolis Public Library
Minneapolis Collection
w276

59 RESIDENTIAL STREET
Minneapolis Public Library
Minneapolis Collection
br0201

60 HORSE-DRAWN BOAT TRAILER
Minneapolis Public Library
Minneapolis Collection
w011

62 CAMEL PARADE
Minneapolis Public Library
Minneapolis Collection
br0983

63 ST. MARK'S CATHEDRAL
Minneapolis Public Library
Minneapolis Collection
m0192

64 BOHEMIAN FLATS
Minneapolis Public Library
Minneapolis Collection
m0526

65 SIXTH STREET
Minneapolis Public Library
Minneapolis Collection
m0095

66 STATE FAIR
Minneapolis Public Library
Minneapolis Collection
m1214

67 Nicollet House
Minneapolis Public Library
Minneapolis Collection
m5315

68 Bismarck Bar
Minneapolis Public Library
Minneapolis Collection
m4830

69 Post Office
Library of Congress, Prints & Photographs Division
LC-D4-70646 B

70 Powderhorn Park
Minneapolis Public Library
Minneapolis Collection
m5612

71 Second Avenue
Minneapolis Public Library
Minneapolis Collection
m0609

72 Donaldson's Department Store
Minneapolis Public Library
Minneapolis Collection
m3835

73 Milk Delivery Wagons
Minneapolis Public Library
Minneapolis Collection
m5045

74 Tonka Bay
Minneapolis Public Library
Minneapolis Collection
m0420

75 Benson Bottling
Minneapolis Public Library
Minneapolis Collection
m4997

76 Bicycle Craze
Minneapolis Public Library
Minneapolis Collection
m1568

77 Cream of Wheat Building
Minneapolis Public Library
Minneapolis Collection
m0121

78 The Armory
Library of Congress, Prints & Photographs Division
LC-D4-18159

80 Lake of the Isles
Library of Congress, Prints & Photographs Division
LC-D4-36327

82 Carriage Ride
Minneapolis Public Library
Minneapolis Collection
m1849

83 West Hotel
Library of Congress, Prints & Photographs Division
LC-D4-18154

84 Wonderland Amusement Park
Minneapolis Public Library
Minneapolis Collection
m0731

85 Father of Waters
Minneapolis Public Library
Minneapolis Collection
m0476

86 First National Bank
Minneapolis Public Library
Minneapolis Collection
m0588

87 Watering Trough
Minneapolis Public Library
Minneapolis Collection
m0108

88 Flour Exchange Building
Minneapolis Public Library
Minneapolis Collection
m0428

89 Horse-drawn Fire Engine
Minneapolis Public Library
Minneapolis Collection
m0328

90 St. Anthony Falls
Library of Congress, Prints & Photographs Division
LC-D4-70647

92 Eddy Hall
Library of Congress, Prints & Photographs Division
LC-D4-70595

93 Nicollet Park
Minneapolis Public Library
Minneapolis Collection
m1721

94 Hennepin Avenue
Library of Congress, Prints & Photographs Division
LC-D4-70637

95 Central Provision Employee
Minneapolis Public Library
Minneapolis Collection
m1749

96 Milwaukee Road Depot
Library of Congress, Prints & Photographs Division
LC-D4-70635

97 United Cigar Shop
Minneapolis Public Library
Minneapolis Collection
m5629

98 Grain Exchange
Minneapolis Public Library
Minneapolis Collection
m5052

99 Washington Avenue
Minneapolis Public Library
Minneapolis Collection
m0110

100 Phoenix Building
Minneapolis Public Library
Minneapolis Collection
m0280

101 Gateway Park
Minneapolis Public Library
Minneapolis Collection
m3837

102 Plymouth Building
Minneapolis Public Library
Minneapolis Collection
m5631

103 Lake Nokomis
Minneapolis Public Library
Minneapolis Collection
m4118

104 Loeb Arcade
Minneapolis Public Library
Minneapolis Collection
m5234

105 Typesetters
Minneapolis Public Library
Minneapolis Collection
m0064

106 Seventh Street
Minneapolis Public Library
Minneapolis Collection
m0017

107 American Railway Express
Minneapolis Public Library
Minneapolis Collection
m1011

108 Parade on Nicollet
Minneapolis Public Library
Minneapolis Collection
m0001

109 Organ Grinder
Minneapolis Public Library
Minneapolis Collection
m0002

110 Hennepin Avenue
Minneapolis Public Library
Minneapolis Collection
m0505

111 Linking of the Lakes
Minneapolis Public Library
Minneapolis Collection
m1766

112 Downtown Panorama
Library of Congress, Prints & Photographs Division
pan 6a13581

113 Minneapolis Armory
Minneapolis Public Library
Minneapolis Collection
m0197

114 Dayton's
Minneapolis Public Library
Minneapolis Collection
m0094

115 Calhoun Beach
Library of Congress, Prints & Photographs Division
pan 6a06831

116 Great Northern
Minneapolis Public Library
Minneapolis Collection
m1836

117 Hotel Pauly
Minneapolis Public Library
Minneapolis Collection
m0625

118 Lake Harriet Pavilion
Minneapolis Public Library
Minneapolis Collection
m1850

119 Mill Heyday
Library of Congress, Prints & Photographs Division
pan 6a13591

120 Company K
Minneapolis Public Library
Minneapolis Collection
m1210

121 War Fundraiser
Minneapolis Public Library
Minneapolis Collection
m0379

122 Gibbs Hotel Fire
Minneapolis Public Library
Minneapolis Collection
m0693

123 Annette Kellerman
Library of Congress, Prints & Photographs Division
LC-USZ62-106392

124 North on Nicollet
Minneapolis Public Library
Minneapolis Collection
m0606

125 Minneapolis Gun Club
Minneapolis Public Library
Minneapolis Collection
br1102

126 School of Arts
Minneapolis Public Library
Minneapolis Collection
m0563

127 Horse Race
Minneapolis Public Library
Minneapolis Collection
w182

128 Governor Lind
Library of Congress, Prints & Photographs Division
LC-DIG-ggbain-03089

129 Red Cross Women's Auxiliary
Minneapolis Public Library
Minneapolis Collection
m1209

130 Clara Barton School
Minneapolis Public Library
Minneapolis Collection
m1208

132 Union City Mission
Minnesota Historical Society
Norton & Peel Collection
HV1.43 p12

133 Phyllis Wheatley House
Minnesota Historical Society
Norton & Peel Collection
GT4.82 p12, Negative 97773

134 Midway Elevator
Minnesota Historical Society
Norton & Peel Collection
MH5.9 MP3.1M p42, Negative 96463

135 Marshall High School
Minnesota Historical Society
Norton & Peel Collection
L3.2 p38, Negative 79626

136 Pillsbury Settlement
Minnesota Historical Society
Norton & Peel Collection
L3.1 p48

137 Cooking Lessons
Minnesota Historical Society
Norton & Peel Collection
HV1.41 p51, Negative 65774

138 Boy Scouts
Minnesota Historical Society
Norton & Peel Collection
HV1.12 p46, Negative 89835

140 Foshay Tower
Minneapolis Public Library
Minneapolis Collection
M5158

141 Minnesota Theatre
Minnesota Historical Society
Norton & Peel Collection
MH5.9 MP3.1M p119, Negative 6915-B

142 Football Fever
Minnesota Historical Society
Norton & Peel Collection
GV3.13 p65, Negative no. 15160

143 Minneapolis Skyline
Minnesota Historical Society
Norton & Peel Collection
MH5.9 MP1i p20, Negative 10997

144 Quinlan Department Store
Minnesota Historical Society
Norton & Peel Collection
MH5.9 MP3.1Y p5, Negative 48997

145 Women Picketing
Minnesota Historical Society
Norton & Peel Collection
HG3.17 r2, Negative 32567

146 Gas Station
Minnesota Historical Society
Norton & Peel Collection
MH5.9 MP3.1S p105,
Negative no. 53293

147 Shubert Theatre
Minnesota Historical Society
Norton & Peel Collection
MH5.9 MP3.1S p103,
Negative 53299

148 Central Lutheran
Minnesota Historical Society
Norton & Peel Collection
B1.32 p39; Negative 3753-B

149 Woman's Club
Minnesota Historical Society
Norton & Peel Collection
75204, Negative NP75204

150 Rand Tower
Minnesota Historical Society
Norton & Peel Collection
76265, Negative NP76265

151 Abbott Hospital
Minnesota Historical Society
Norton & Peel Collection
R3.2 p40, Negative 42747

152 Institute of Arts
Minnesota Historical Society
Norton & Peel Collection
77229, Negative NP77229

153 Elevator Number One
Minnesota Historical Society
Norton & Peel Collection
84126, Negative 5620-B

154 Yates Building
Minnesota Historical Society
Norton & Peel Collection
81331, Negative NP81331

155 Jordan Jr. High School
Minnesota Historical Society
Norton & Peel Collection
81061, Negative NP81061

156 Shooting Range
Minnesota Historical Society
Norton & Peel Collection
81835, Negative NP81835

157 Unity House
Minnesota Historical Society
Norton & Peel Collection
91144, Negative NP91144

158 Shriners Hospital
Minnesota Historical Society
Norton & Peel Collection
NP 116716,
Negative NP116716

159 Loring Park
Minnesota Historical Society
Norton & Peel Collection
131036, Negative NP131036

160 Third Avenue Bridge
Minnesota Historical Society
Norton & Peel Collection
135212, Negative NP135212

161 Gustavus Adolphus Lutheran Church
Minnesota Historical Society
Norton & Peel Collection
130029, Negative NP130029

162 NABISCO
Minnesota Historical Society
Norton & Peel Collection
MH5.9 MP3.1N p21,
Negative 53944

163 Fr. Hennepin
Minnesota Historical Society
Norton & Peel Collection
134534, Negative NP134534

164 Theodore Wirth Park
Minnesota Historical Society
Norton & Peel Collection
134666, Negative NP134666

165 Aquatennial
Minnesota Historical Society
Norton & Peel Collection
134877, Negative NP134877

166 Dayton's Department Store
Minnesota Historical Society
Norton & Peel Collection
136163, Negative NP136163

167 Sears Store
Minnesota Historical Society
Norton & Peel Collection
138163, Negative NP138163

168 Powers Department Store
Minnesota Historical Society
Norton & Peel Collection
142490, Negative NP142490

169 Assembly Line
Minnesota Historical Society
Norton & Peel Collection
143858, Negative NP143858

170 William Brothers
Minnesota Historical Society
Norton & Peel Collection
145602, Negative NP145602

171 Hospitality House
Minnesota Historical Society
Norton & Peel Collection
155053, Negative NP155053

172 Factory Workers
Minnesota Historical Society
Norton & Peel Collection
147162, Negative NP147162

173 Minnehaha Falls
Minnesota Historical Society
Norton & Peel Collection
156310, Negative NP156310

174 Nursing School
Minnesota Historical Society
Norton & Peel Collection
R2.2 p56, Negative 31822

176 Weatherball
Minnesota Historical Society
Norton & Peel Collection
QC3.1 p4, Negative 6739-B

177 Fire Crew Dispatcher
Minnesota Historical Society
Norton & Peel Collection
192784, Negative NP192784

178 Martin 202 Crash
Minnesota Historical Society
Norton & Peel Collection
193658, Negative NP193658

179 Minneapolis Public Library
Minnesota Historical Society
Norton & Peel Collection
195433, Negative NP195433

180 Chevrolet Showroom
Minnesota Historical Society
Norton & Peel Collection
195990, Negative NP195990

181 Football Players
Minnesota Historical Society
Norton & Peel Collection
198399, Negative NP198399

182 Greek Orthodox Church
Minnesota Historical Society
Norton & Peel Collection
204339, Negative NP204339

183 Snow Drifts
Minnesota Historical Society
Norton & Peel Collection
200662, Negative NP200662

184 Downtown
Minnesota Historical Society
Norton & Peel Collection
202498, Negative NP202498

185 Lakewood Cemetery
Minnesota Historical Society
Norton & Peel Collection
215356, Negative NP215356

186 Smith Residence
Minnesota Historical Society
Norton & Peel Collection
GT2.23 p12 , Negative 43643

187 Andrews Hotel
Minnesota Historical Society
Norton & Peel Collection
217536, Negative NP217536

188 Walker Art Center
Minnesota Historical Society
Norton & Peel Collection
227695, Negative NP227695

189 Ry-Krisp Assembly Line
Minnesota Historical Society
Norton & Peel Collection
229207, Negative NP229207

190 Cedar Lake
Minnesota Historical Society
Norton & Peel Collection
232404, Negative NP232404

191 Dunwoody Institute
Minnesota Historical Society
Norton & Peel Collection
233231, Negative NP233231

192 Eastgate Shopping Center
Minnesota Historical Society
Norton & Peel Collection
238024, Negative NP238024

193 Drive-In
Minnesota Historical Society
Norton & Peel Collection
238394, Negative NP238394

194 St. Bridget's Parish Convent
Minnesota Historical Society
Norton & Peel Collection
249673, Negative NP249673

195 Centennial Exhibit
Minnesota Historical Society
Norton & Peel Collection
251871, Negative NP251871

196 Riverside Generating Plant
Minnesota Historical Society
Norton & Peel Collection
256774, Negative NP256774

197 Charlie's Café Exceptionale
Minnesota Historical Society
Norton & Peel Collection
274613, Negative NP274613

198 Nicollet Avenue
Minnesota Historical Society
Norton & Peel Collection
304832, Negative NP304832

199 Interstate Construction
Minnesota Historical Society
Norton & Peel Collection
298160, Negative NP298160

206 First Skyway
Minnesota Historical Society
Norton & Peel Collection
MH5.9 MP9 p37, Negative
97548

The first skyway, which led from the Northstar Center to Northwestern National Bank, was dedicated in 1962.

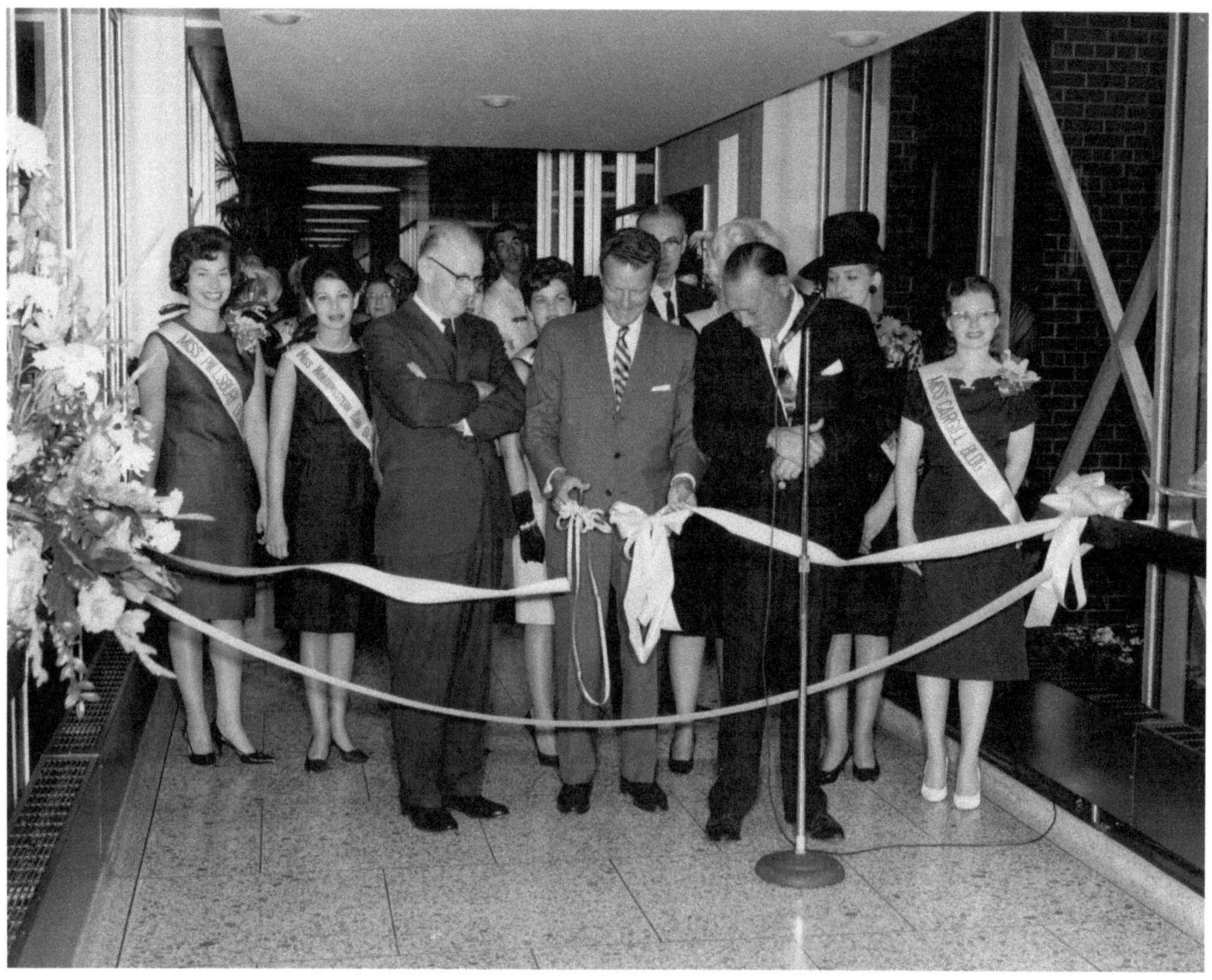

HISTORIC PHOTOS OF MINNEAPOLIS

Minneapolis is an American city quintessentially founded upon change. From its birth to the present, Minneapolis has consistently built and reshaped its appearance, ideals, and industry. Through changing fortunes, Minneapolis has continued to grow and prosper by overcoming adversity and maintaining the strong, independent culture of its citizens.

Historic Photos of Minneapolis captures this journey through still photography selected from the finest archives. From Minneapolis as leader of the nation's flour production to the revitalization of the Gateway District, *Historic Photos of Minneapolis* follows life, government, education, and events throughout the city's history.

This volume captures unique and rare scenes through the lens of hundreds of historic photographs. Published in striking black and white, these images communicate historic events and everyday life of two centuries of people building a unique and prosperous city.

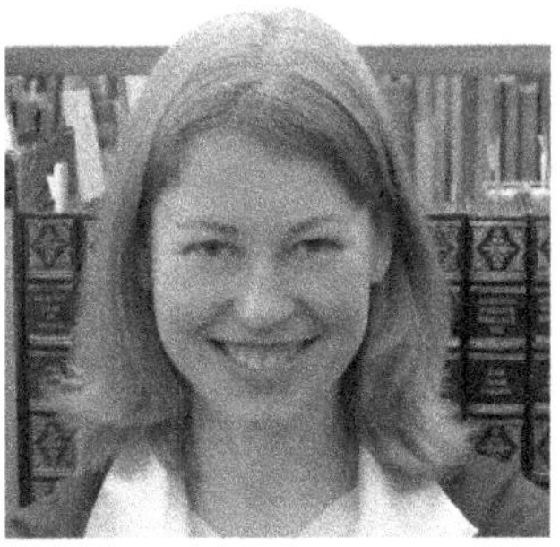

Heather Block Lawton manages the James K. Hosmer Special Collections Library at the Minneapolis Public Library. She holds a masters of arts degree in history, and a masters of science degree in library and information science and archives management. Although she originally hails from Denver she now considers Minneapolis home and currently resides in the Uptown neighborhood.

WWW.TURNERPUBLISHING.COM

www.ingramcontent.com/pod-product-compliance
Lightning Source LLC
LaVergne TN
LVHW060611110826
845154LV00003B/69

* 9 7 8 1 6 8 3 3 6 9 4 2 4 *